I0902108

MUSIC VIDEO MISCHIEF

Ozzy to Britney, Oasis to Gn'R, McCartney to Cher
A Lifetime of Rock and Chaos

A MEMOIR BY
NIGEL DICK

TROUSER PRESS
BOOKS

Music Video Mischief is © 2026 by Nigel Dick

All rights reserved. No part of this book may be reproduced or stored in a retrieval system or transmitted in any form or by any means — electronic, mechanical, photocopying, recording or otherwise — without the express written permission of the publisher.

Cover and interior pages designed by Kristina Juzaitis

Publisher's note: The author's use of British English (BE) spellings has been preserved.

All uncredited photos are from the author's personal collection.

ISBN 979-8-9990487-8-3

Library of Congress Control Number: 2026934209

Published by Trouser Press Books
Brooklyn, New York

First printing July 2026
BMB262
Distributed by Publishers Group West/Ingram

www.trouserpressbooks.com
books@trouserpress.com

To Kastle

(who has patiently let me tell her these stories over and over again!)

...and, in alphabetical order, to every
AD
Art Dog
Artist / Band Member
Camera Assistant
Casting Person
Client
Colorist
DP
Editor
Electric
Grip
Make-up & Hair
Manager
PA
Producer
Production Manager
Rep
Rigger
Roadie
Runner
Sound Person
Stylist
Transpo
Wardrobe...

...I have ever worked with.
Without you none of this would have been possible.

(See the glossary at the end of the book for details of these titles and more.)

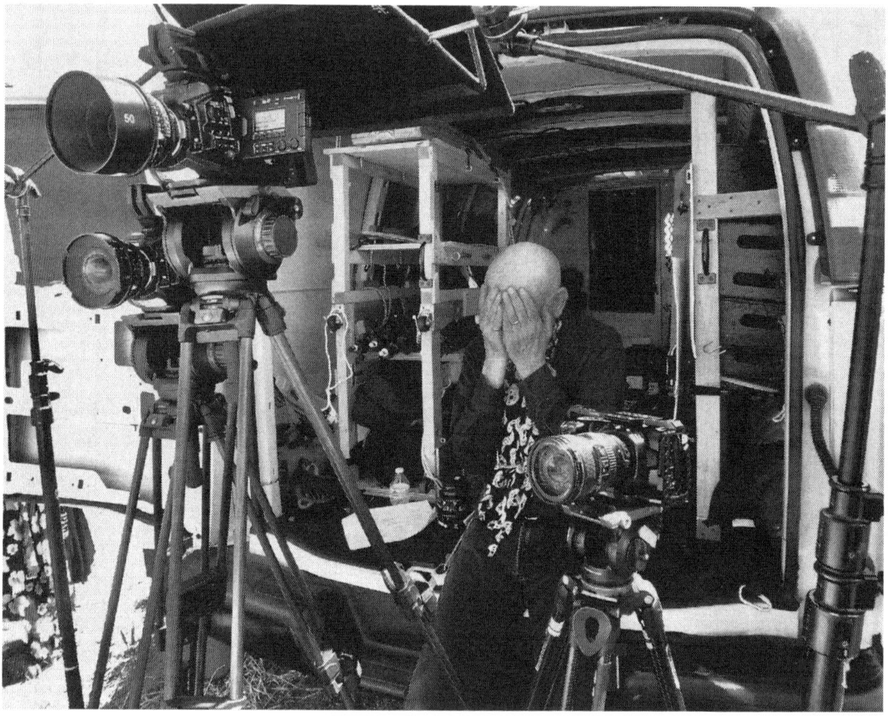

Photo by E.J. Carr

Table of Contents

Foreword

"The remembrance of things past is not necessarily the remembrance of things as they were."
—Marcel Proust

WHAT I'M ABOUT TO TELL YOU isn't necessarily the whole truth — but I'd like to think that it is.

A while back I travelled to Hanna, Alberta. Hanna sits in the midst of the featureless Canadian prairies and, as I approached from the south, a large sign beside the road announced, "Hanna welcomes you. Proud to be the home of Nickelback." It was because of Nickelback that I was driving into town on a sunny, windy afternoon. I'll explain why later, but one story that sticks in my mind seems pertinent to mention here.

After checking in to the Super 8 hotel, I spent a couple of days driving around town, looking at locations and taking photographs. Pretty soon, everyone in town knew what I was up to. One kind soul approached me and explained how the band started. The two Kroeger brothers, Chad and Mike, who remain in the band to this day, had lived just down the road from him. He said Chad was the driving force of the band and was responsible for getting their career underway. As an example, he said, Chad once called a pub 200 miles away to ask if the owner would give them a gig. He told Chad that he'd consider it if he could hear a cassette. Chad put the phone down, climbed in his van and drove across the prairie with the cassette. Impressed by the tape as well as Chad's determination, the landlord agreed to let them play in his pub. I loved this story and proceeded to share it many times.

Many years and many jobs for Nickelback later, I was back in Canada shooting another video for the band when I was interviewed by a British film crew making a documentary about them. I felt it appropriate to share the story of the cassette, the pub landlord and Chad's 200-mile cross-country drive as an example of the way the band functioned and their no nonsense, can-do attitude.

A while later, Chad walked up to me. "I heard what you had to say about our early days. Great story, dude." Then he beamed one of his million-dollar smiles, leaned closer and put his hand on my shoulder, "Unfortunately, none of it is true!" He laughed, and I blushed.*

I bring this up not because I'm worried about setting the story straight but because part of me is concerned that perhaps every story I have in my quiver may be tainted, like whiskey maturing in a barrel, by the undeniable effects of embellishment and retelling. A lot of what I'm about to tell you happened long ago. Over the years, I've shared these stories many times and it's possible that some of the details may have become, shall we say, unconsciously enhanced. I walked away from that conversation with Chad wondering if the kind soul in Hanna had told me a fib or if I had subconsciously polished the story to make it better. Even worse, I wondered if I hadn't made the whole thing up!

While most of us who've met Chad can agree that he's an ambitious, driven, charming and handsome man, it is entirely possible that he never drove 200 miles across the prairie just to get his unknown band a gig. But I swear that is the story that I heard. Even if it has not

*Chad says, "Mike [Kroeger] was the one stocking music stores with CDs. [Ryan] Peake was trying to get us gigs. I was the one calling radio stations to try to get adds. Hahaha."

a shred of truth, it is true to the essence of the man that I know and the experiences I've had working with him. If what follows is not always the truth, it's what I remember.

I've discovered a number of reasons for writing a book like this. Most importantly, I wanted to write it all down because I got lucky. I was (and remain) a huge music fan, and just to meet and work with some of my idols was an impossible dream that came true. To then also find myself present at some historic pop music moments was even more of a blessing. This life experience I happened upon has been a gift. I can't tell you how often I've thought to myself, *Wow! How the fuck did this happen?* To have been given this gift and not share it seems like the most awful selfishness.

I have no complaints. I've travelled all over the world and seen sights that many can only dream about. I've worked with lords, ladies, princesses, Oscar-winners, Grammy-winners, world champions, addicts, drinkers, jailbirds, dreamers and others who are simply among the most famous people on Earth. I've shovelled pigshit and cowshit and delivered drugs off the back of a motorcycle in the pouring rain. I've been hired by crooks and millionaires and fired twice by *Playboy* Playmates. I've shot film on every continent except Antarctica (there's still time). I've slept in fabulous hotels and flea-ridden dives, hung out of helicopters and off the sides of buildings, been paid to dress up as a snowman and Uncle Sam, worked with glamorous models and James Bond beauties and swept floors in the Sewage Division of the Anglian Water Authority. This journey has been many things, but it has not been boring. And all of it happened because what I *really* wanted to do was play guitar in a rock and roll band, make records and appear on *Top of the Pops*.

The life of a video director is not what it might appear to be. The most memorable moments I've had are at dawn in a snow-blown field as the crew is wrapping and I'm chugging a final hot coffee, or sitting in the shade on a dusty road on the third day of a location scout as my producer tries to find a cell phone signal, wondering if

I'll ever find that post-apocalyptic wasteland that seemed like such a good idea when I described it in my treatment.

There's a saying that "Film is war." And, just like battle, there are certainly intense moments of victory and frightening moments of defeat. There are times when you get to meet generals and heroes, but mostly it's about trudging through the mud and counting down the hours till the next meal. For every superstar moment there are hundreds of miserable hours and sleepless nights in shitty hotel rooms far from home, wondering if the Wi-Fi is working better down in the lobby. But these are the moments I cherish the most — battling indifference, impossible schedules, ridiculous budgetary constraints and bad catering to deliver memorable pieces of film.

Many of these stories are about things that went wrong. But a tale that starts with, "They asked me to do this job, it turned out great, we finished on time, everyone was happy with the first cut, and I won an award for it" would make for dull reading. No one goes to see a film where Tom Cruise knocks out the bad guy with one punch.

So, OK then. Are we ready? "Roll camera ... ACTION!"

CHAPTER 1

Twist and Shout

IT WAS A GREY SEPTEMBER AFTERNOON when everything turned to shit. I was 11 years old. My mum and dad were dropping me off at a boarding school. As my dad's battered Vauxhall scrunched away up the gravel drive, I noticed that the other dads were driving Jags and Mercs. An instant feeling of not belonging overwhelmed me.

My dad was in the Royal Air Force; he left for his new posting in Cyprus, an island in the Mediterranean, three days later. I wouldn't see him again for almost a year, by which time my parents' marriage was in tatters. As I dragged my trunk into the schoolhouse, someone called me Dick. I didn't get my first name back until the 1970s.

I'd made it to this prestigious school by luck and the good graces of the RAF. I'd won a scholarship from the local education authority and, because my dad was posted overseas, the RAF paid the rest. As my dad was posted every few years around half of Europe and Britain, I'd already been to 11 schools, but this would be my toughest assignment. At my other schools, kids' dads worked in bakeries and banks. At this one, they *owned* the bakeries and banks. It seemed that every boy in the school was bigger, taller, harder and looking for fresh meat. I went into survival mode and kept my head down, but I was low on the pecking order and it didn't take long for the bullying to start.

British psychoanalyst Joy Schaverien has coined the term "Boarding School Syndrome" to describe the lasting psychological effects in adults who have endured the British boarding school system. I don't need to read her books to know how those emotional scars manifest themselves in some way or another every day of my adult life. That first night, I collapsed into a bed that was old and creaky and allowed myself a brief weep under the sheets.

Boarding school was a different country — they did things differently there and I was quickly forced to hide my homesickness in order to acquaint myself with a collision of new traditions, language and routines. The mathematics class had something called algebra in it. And then there was Latin.

Andrew Loog Oldham, onetime manager of the Rolling Stones, described his own trip to boarding school in his book *Stoned*: "I was leaving (home) for a life ... that has tortured British (children) from time immemorial... Interesting how the British idea of an aristocratic education resembles a poor and rather dirty imitation of Sparta."

The following summer, my mother and I travelled to Cyprus to stay in the house my father had found in the quiet mountain village of Platres. Once she discovered that my dad had been having an affair there, my parents started a shouting and crockery-throwing competition that lasted all summer until they drove me to Nicosia Airport and sent me back to school. By the Christmas holidays, the shouting had given way to resentment that never left their relationship.

Things got worse for me when my school report arrived. My mother, a retired school mistress, made me stand to attention as she scanned the latest overview, wagged her finger and gave me her final damning opinion, one that would be repeated constantly over the years: "The problem with you, Nigel Dick, is that you'll never amount to anything!" The night before my return to England my father found me crying. I shared with him how much I hated school and the bul lying. The next day at the airport they waved goodbye, told me to be brave and said, “Don’t worry, we’ll see you in six months.”

I buried the feeling of dread and loss. As the plane took off for Athens, then Rome, then London, I knew that my life had changed irrevocably: I was 12 years old and on my own. That mixture of anger and loneliness has never left me, but I was lucky: I had one vital, life-saving tool in my armoury that protected me, one that no one could take away: the Beatles.

One particular Sunday I was excited, as I’d been given permission to stay up late to watch *Sunday Night at the London Palladium* on TV, and the guest stars were the Beatles.

I can remember a lot about those few minutes of TV. John was playing his Rickenbacker, the black and white one; Paul and George sang together on the other side of the stage, Paul with his Hofner bass and George playing his guitar high up on his chest as he always did. Ringo was perched on his drum kit at the back, swinging his head back and forth with a big smile on his face as his hair shook. They played “She Loves You” and nothing in my world was ever the same again.

From that day forward my sketchbook was no longer filled with mighty Lancasters and burning Messerschmitts — from then on, all the drawings were of John, Paul, George and Ringo onstage. Like any decent artist, I was determined to record all of the crucial details. John and George were right-handed, but Paul wasn’t. Ringo had a big T in the middle of “Beatles” on his drum kit, and John, Paul and George all had wires that stretched from their guitars to boxes that had Vox written on them. John and George’s guitars had six strings, while Paul’s only had four.

In no time at all I was obsessed by the Beatles and guitars. In the garage at home there were pieces of wood and saws and hammers and nails and paint. My dad had taught me some simple carpentry skills, so I started building guitars. My guitars were special: painted, with nails for tuning pegs and cotton for guitar strings. Each pickup was actually another bridge with more nails on it so that the cotton strings had something to wind around on their way towards the neck. Guitar straps were made out of string but, due to a shortage of building materials, there was never a wire that went towards a box with Vox written on it.

In the hearts of all music fans across the country, you were expected to plant your flag in support of one particular group. Another band on the horizon at this point, who were felt to be the antithesis of the Fab Four, were the Rolling Stones. Though I liked "Mother's Little Helper" and would later get quite excited by "Satisfaction," there was no doubt about it: I was a Beatles kind of person and that was that.

While my mother listened to opera, Dad was a Glenn Miller fan and collected comedy records, which he kept in a special singles box in which he now let me keep my 45s. Within a few months, the space at the back of Dad's singles box started to fill up. As well as "She Loves You," I had managed to obtain copies of two earlier releases, "Love Me Do" and "Please Please Me." I played the records incessantly; I turned them over and spun the B-sides as well.

But the Beatles weren't the only artists whose records were filling up my part of Dad's record box — I had "Bits and Pieces" and "Glad All Over," the big hits by the Dave Clark Five, two instrumental hits by Jet Harris and Tony Meehan (ex-members of Cliff Richard's backing band, the Shadows) and the biggest, baddest instrumental of them all: "Telstar" by the Tornadoes. "Telstar" was named after a recently launched communications satellite and, even though it was recorded in Joe Meek's flat in North London, it really did sound like it had been beamed in from outer space. I had no idea how records were made, but they had an effect on me, and I felt happy while I pushed my ears closer to the radio.

CHAPTER 2

Court and Spark

DEPENDING ON HOW YOU DEFINE the term "rock star," John Phillips from the Mamas & the Papas was the first rock star I ever met.

I had been imprisoned with 400 other boys for eight years; though I'd failed to become fluent in Latin, I'd learned the name of every drummer, singer, guitar and bass player in every band mentioned in *Melody Maker*. I toyed with the idea of somehow getting into the music business. But how? My only showbiz contact was somebody I'd once met who said his brother was a friend of Jimmy Page's cousin. The pressure to focus on getting a real career was insurmountable. I enjoyed making things and building models, so I figured I'd go to Bath in Britain's West Country and spend the next six years studying architecture.

One summer, with another long university holiday at hand, I got myself a job as a waiter at a restaurant in the heart of town. The name of the establishment was Parsenn Sally, and the management team were a number of rich young things who lived in a commune, an old Jacobean manse called Surrendell Farm, a few miles outside of town.

Within a week, I'd met every member of the collective. It seemed there were about seven or eight of them. They spoke with posh accents and carried themselves with the relaxed assuredness that family wealth and refined bloodlines brings. It was whispered in the kitchen that one of them, a smiling young man called Roddy, was more than close to H.R.H. Princess Margaret — the Queen's sister.

What set Parsenn Sally apart from every other establishment on this sloping street in England's most beautiful city was the soundtrack. As I and my fellow waitpersons hurried up and down the long corridor-like building to the kitchen at the back we listened to the coolest albums of the era. That's where I started my long, languid, love affair with the music of Joni Mitchell. Everything about Joni and her *Court and Spark* album was the opposite of the brash, pelvic, male, lusty, driving, unpoetic music that I would listen to back at my flat.

Another favourite on the Parsenn Sally playlist was Randy Newman's *Good Old Boys*. He didn't have a guitar, his voice sounded like the noise of a miserable man with a bad cold who'd been locked in a dark room and made to sing against his will, and his songs were about a world that meant nothing to me. But I couldn't get his damn record out of my head. Its sound was timeless and, though newly released, somehow seemed 30 years old already.

The songs were catchy, too. As I toted plates of steaming pasta through the eatery, I gaily hummed, "Birmingham, Birmingham, the meanest city in Alabam" with no clear idea where on Earth I would find Alabam should I want to go there.

It was at Parsenn Sally that I had my first brushes with celebrity. I waited upon writer Jan Morris and her family. I had read *Conundrum*, the book about her transgender journey, and here she was in front of me, a pleasant middle-aged lady with grey hair ordering hamburgers with her children on a Saturday lunchtime.

In order to scare up a little publicity, the Parsenn managers invited some of their famous friends to come down to Bath for the day and be "guest waiters/waitresses." The first to show up was Helen Mirren, and I was asked to help her find her sea legs during the day she worked with us. How was I to know my afternoon spent sorting cutlery and folding napkins was with a future Oscar-winner? All I knew was that I was offering assistance to a stunning beauty I'd seen stark naked up on the big screen. I blushed uncontrollably every time she looked my way or asked what she should do with her tips.

The word in the papers was that Roddy was actually having an affair with Princess Margaret. The scandal grew with the rumour that pictures of Roddy and Margaret relaxing *à deux* on the island of Mustique would soon be published. If there was any truth to the gossip, you'd assume that they'd keep a low profile.

So much for common sense. We were told that her Highness would be coming for dinner with Roddy. Signs were posted outside that read CAFÉ CLOSED TONIGHT, PRIVATE PARTY.

I was chosen to be their waiter and asked to show up in what had become my signature waitperson's outfit. Glam rock was in full bloom and I, like every decent rock fan throughout the ages, dressed like my heroes. Not for me a white shirt, black pants, comfortable black shoes and a white apron that you might expect from a waiter in a popular bistro. No. My favoured and approved outfit was a white T-shirt with red stars spray-painted all over it, an orange pair of dungarees with the legs rolled up to the knees revealing red and white striped rugby socks which gave way to silver shoes — also spray-painted. I topped the look off with my new earring and a very bad perm to my still long hair.

Looking like Ronald McDonald's outrageous and badly coiffed cousin, I nervously stood in the kitchen and received orders on how the evening would progress. I only had to worry about one table, and I had to call Her Royal Highness "Ma'am" (pronounced "marm"). The normal menu of pastas and burgers had been ditched; a special menu of starters, mains and desserts especially tailored to the royal palate had been prepared. I was made aware that the couple would be joined by John Phillips, the man who had written "California Dreamin'," and his wife.

Her Royal Highness's security detail sat in each corner of the restaurant and ordered water. They looked at me suspiciously, probably wondering why any grown man would dress up in such an outfit and why this royal personage should surround herself with such unlikely courtiers. They imperceptibly shook their heads, as royals' henchmen must have done throughout the ages.

Roddy was his usual charming and witty self. Her Royal Highness seemed a little bit tipsy, but Phillips and his wife seemed to be in another world completely. I nervously ran through the menu and took their orders, but it quickly became clear that Roddy was really the only one with any appetite. The Princess played with her food; John and Genevieve didn't so much as take a bite. As I collected the plates the Princess looked up at me, gave me a wan smile and said, "Roddy tells me you're training to be an architect."

"Yes Ma'am."

"My husband's an architect."

I suppressed my desire to reply along the lines of "You think I don't read the friggin' newspapers?" and scurried back to the kitchen. The cook rushed over to see what the royal party had thought of her specially prepared meal. Before I could respond she looked down at the barely touched plates and her face fell.

Back at the royal table it was time for desserts. Roddy and HRH wanted more drinks. John Phillips and his wife wanted ice cream — and lots of it.

Years later, I purchased Phillips' autobiography, *Papa John*, and learned that he nursed a major heroin habit for many years; he was undoubtedly using at the time of his visit to Bath. While reading the book, I went to see Neil Jordan's newly released *Mona Lisa*, in which Bob Hoskins' character learns that all heroin addicts want to eat is ice cream — and lots of it. Suddenly my evening with Margaret, Roddy and Papa John all started to make sense. Looking back, the thing I remember clearly was the look of deep sadness on Princess Margaret's face during our brief conversation. The passionate affair she'd had with Group Captain Peter Townsend, which had been cruelly brought to an end because he was an older divorced man, and her subsequent miserable marriage to Lord Snowdon were all there in her eyes as she looked up at me. This wasn't even the look of a soul looking for help, it was the face of a depressed and defeated woman imprisoned in a life from which it seemed she was gaining little joy.

The day after the royal visit, the Parsenn's managers gave me a £10 tip. I went and bought Led Zeppelin's newly released *Presence* album with some of the loot. Soon after, I was back at university designing an airport building. A year later, I picked up my architecture degree. But what was I going to do next?

CHAPTER 3

Do What You Want, Be What You Are

ONE BALMY EVENING I accidentally let a couple of wan soul singers from Philadelphia alter the course of my life. My fortunes changed because of a Hall & Oates record. And not even a particularly good Hall & Oates record.

By the time I finished at university, the British economy was in decline again. With no architecture jobs on the horizon, I pointed my trusty Honda motorcycle out of Bath and started the two-day journey back to my old stomping grounds in Norwich on England's east coast. I quickly found a flat and my first full-time job as a photocopy clerk with the Sewage Division of the Anglian Water Authority. It was, aptly enough, a shit job and, after being scolded by management for recycling, I quit and looked further up the food chain for executive employment. Which is how I came to be standing in a dusty yard hidden at the top of the main shopping street in Norwich.

The yard was owned by Welles Taxis, the only company in the city that ran real London black cabs. On the day I wandered in looking for work, I was able to negotiate a simple and mutually useful deal with the owner of the company: I needed work and he needed drivers. All I had to do was show him my licence and buy a map of Norwich and I was hired.

I went to work that night. One of my first pickups was a rowdy Scot who worked on the offshore rigs and had spent his night back on the mainland turning his generous earnings into fluid refreshment. He reeked of booze and got down on his knees in the back of the cab so he could talk into my ear and give me precise directions home, which I thought was awfully decent of him. And then I smelt the warm odour of piss and realised that his position in the back of the cab was not to facilitate a friendly discourse with his driver but to allow him the chance to offload the pints that were straining his bladder. I pulled over and ordered him out, gesticulating furiously at the torrent flowing into the gutter. He chuckled, threw a fiver at me and disappeared into the night. I got on the radio and shared my conundrum with Reg, the controller. "Come back to the yard and we'll sort you out," he commanded.

Back in the yard Reg turned on a hose, threw open the door and thoroughly sprayed the back of the cab till it was clean and ready for action again. "The floors are curved downwards from the middle of the cab towards the doors, so they'll drain out in seconds. See? Happens all the time."

Reg spoke with a broad Cockney accent and, unless he was on the air, said "fuck!" and "cunt!" every ten seconds. Reg smoked constantly; his fingers and moustache were yellow from the nicotine smoke swirling up from his Woodbines. He was the best controller we had: he knew all the quickest back routes and all the regular customers' quirks and needs. Reg worked the night shift, shuffling his hands between the endless cups of Nescafé and the next Woodbine as he leant in towards the mic. Reg shared all his stories from his times working as a cook for British Rail to his time as a milkman and then his years on the cabs fleecing old ladies, arrogant businessmen and innocent American servicemen.

"One night I pick up this fucking Yank outside the Royal Hotel, and the cunt is so drunk he can hardly stand up straight. 'Driver!' he says, 'How much to take me to the Royal Hotel?' 'Twenty fucking quid,' I said. So the cunt says, 'OK,' climbs into the cab and I drive him round in circles for 20 fucking minutes before I dropped him off at the same fucking spot I'd picked him up from. Cunt gives me the 20 quid fare and then the cunt gives me a five quid fucking tip! Ha-ha. Cunt!"

He had a hundred stories like this, and the worse they were, the more I lapped them up. "Twenty-nine years I've been doing nights. One day my wife says to me, 'Reg, what would you do if you came home one morning and found me in bed with another man?' And I says, 'I'd shoot his fucking guide dog!' Ha-ha-ha. Cunt!"

Change was in the air and I felt it. Things weren't too good on the high streets of Britain; unemployment was rife and the natives were getting restless. As the bands that I loved — Yes, Emerson Lake & Palmer, Pink Floyd, Led Zeppelin — walked onto bigger stages with larger, fancier sets, the spotty kids on the streets felt more and more disenfranchised from these newly minted millionaires who drove large cars, made more money than company executives and recorded music which had more in common with dead composers than sexy three-minute rock and roll. So, the spotty kids rebelled, improvised and diverted their unemployment cheques towards the cheapest guitars they could find and set out to break all the rules. Suddenly a lack of musical ability was no longer sneered at — it was celebrated. The pop music scene in the UK exploded in rebellion, safety pins, acne, bondage pants and hundreds of amazingly catchy two- and three-minute songs: "The Damned can now play three chords. The Adverts can play one. Hear all four of them at..."

Suddenly my record-buying habits expanded from bands with names and attitudes that referenced Tolkien and the American Delta to a whole collection of brittle and angry monikers: the Stranglers, the Damned, the Jam, Sham 69, the Clash, X-Ray Spex, the Rezillos. I bought everything I could find by Elvis Costello and scoured the pages of *Melody Maker* to read about the punk explosion happening on the streets of London. It was going to be an exciting summer.

I liked the music, but I was not destined to become a punk: I was balding and far too polite and easy-going to become a working-class rebel. Worst of all, that summer I had a moustache and wore flared jeans. Still, I dipped my toes in the waters: I started wearing badges and buttons and bought myself a leather jacket as well as every single by the Clash and the Stranglers I could find. I also had that earring ... which was about the time I played that Hall & Oates record.

I'd given up my cab-driving gig and was drawing safety diagrams for Amoco's gas platforms in the North Sea — the closest I ever came to using my architectural skills to make a living. The money wasn't good, the prospects were awful and I could tell that my contemporaries were in the early stages of settling down, finding serious girlfriends and cutting their hair in order to look more presentable at job interviews. I had two choices: follow their lead or break out.

I was reading a lot of Zola that summer and then opened Orwell's *Down and Out in Paris and London*. It all sounded so romantic and perfect — that life of struggle and hunger! I hatched a plot to move to France, where there was surely a shortage of English-speaking rock fans, somehow snag a job in showbiz and eventually make my way back to the UK, where I could move up the ladder somehow. As plans go, it was poorly thought out and doomed to failure, but I'd convinced myself that some snooty French promoter would hire a bloke from England just because he knew the difference between Pink Floyd and the Pink Fairies.

But then, one gorgeous summer evening I was riding home through the Norfolk countryside on my tiny Honda 125 and, as the smells of the warm summer floated through my helmet, doubt set in. I decided that moving away would be a mistake. I needed to knuckle down and get a proper job.

I got home to my tiny room and put on a record before bedtime. I chose Hall & Oates' *Bigger Than Both of Us*. It's got a ludicrous sleeve and, apart from "Rich Girl," a lot of filler. But none of this mattered as I sat in my chair and adjusted the headphones, because I knew my plans to leave England were idiotic and foolish. I needed to man up and seriously plan my future.

And then, without realising it, I reached track four on the album ("Do What You Want, Be What You Are") and these words pierced my new dreams of a white-collar future: "The strong give up and go away, the weak give up and stay..."

I'm not much given to the idea of bolts of light from the heavens, but I immediately realised that Daryl and John had kindly interrupted their busy touring schedule and were reaching out to me across the oceans to say, "For fuck's sake, Nigel. Are you mad? Get out of there!" I have no doubt that if I'd played a different album that night the rest of my life would have been quite different.

I handed in my notice the next morning and sold my motorbike. Six weeks later, my buddy Ed Howard drove me to the station, and I boarded a train to France.

CHAPTER 4

If It Ain't Stiff It Ain't Worth a Fuck

MY EXPEDITION TO FRANCE WAS DOOMED before I ever left Dover. My savings were paltry; I had no idea of where I would stay in Paris and only a limited grasp of the language. On the other hand, I had a couple of addresses of Paris-based promoters, my trusty guitar and the element of surprise on my side.

My plan was to deposit my meagre savings in a French bank, arrange an interview with one of those promoters and play my guitar on the streets of Paris so I could keep the francs rolling in while my new boss and I negotiated the terms of my employment.

By lunchtime on the first day, I knew I was buggered. The banks refused to let me open an account as I was not French, and both promoters I had addresses for were on holiday. Like Hitler, who'd invaded Russia without ordering his troops winter coats, I'd invaded Paris without realising it was August — when every sane Parisian goes south on holiday and shuts up shop for a month!

I reverted to Plan B. I went back to my attic room for my guitar and went underground to earn my living on the Paris Metro. I quickly learned that you had to find a station where two or more lines intersected. And, in that station, you had to find a tunnel where passengers walked past in at least two directions, preferably three or four. There aren't many good spots like that in the Metro, so you had to get up early, find your pitch, fight to secure it and hope *les flics* had more important business to attend to. Though it wasn't illegal to sing on the Metro, if the cops didn't like the cut of your jib or your finger-picking style they would tell you to move on and walk slowly behind you to make sure you boarded a train and went off to annoy tourists in another part of the city.

My time in Paris wasn't turning out like I'd hoped. After a couple of months, my funds were running perilously low. The summer was ending, my French wasn't improving and I certainly wasn't breaking into showbiz. Coming back from another day's busk on the Metro I walked past a newsagent's stand on the Champs-Élysées and stopped in my tracks. The cover of the latest *Melody Maker* had a photo of five ridiculous looking musos, with a huge headline over their heads: FIVE LIVE STIFFS! I owned records by all of them: Elvis Costello, Wreckless Eric, Nick Lowe, Ian Dury and Larry Wallis. I couldn't afford to buy the issue, but I read the front page — they were all going on tour together.

I'd lost all touch with what was happening in the music business back home and suddenly realised I missed it desperately. I knew *that* was what I needed to be doing; *that* was where I needed to be. I had reached rock bottom, so I spent my last francs on a ticket back to London, unaware that the image on that *Melody Maker* cover was my destiny in ways I couldn't even dream of.

Back in London it immediately became clear to me that I was bound to wind up there sooner or later. Why had I been so blind? I found a place to live and went looking for work. I scoured the papers for likely employment opportunities that matched up to my world-conquering ambition, but the kind of jobs I was looking for didn't seem to exist. I watched what remained of my savings evaporate.

I was walking along Oxford Street on the way to a job interview one day when a tall, spindly figure strode towards me. He was dressed from head to toe in black leather and seemed about eight feet tall. His boots jangled with metal chains as his long stride took him through the city. But what singled him out from the rest of the world was the look on his face. The eyes seemed somehow vacant and yet full of dark and malevolent thoughts. He instantly struck me as a taller, straighter, more drugged-out version of Mervyn Peake's Flay, like an alien living in plain sight, desperate to get back to the planet on which he belonged while walking among Earthlings in full knowledge that he didn't belong among them. He frightened the shit out of me. Whoever the dude was, he looked more like Keith Richards than Keef did himself; quite plainly he was from Planet Rock. He carried nothing — no guitar or book or bag — and thus had to be a singer in a band.

I was mystified. I read *Melody Maker* from cover to cover every week. I was a walking encyclopaedia of current musical trends and of the lineup of every outfit that moved up and down the country. How come I didn't recognise this man? He was every rock and roll singer distilled into a tall leather cocoon and then somehow magnified for dramatic effect. The gaunt figure marched on and disappeared up the street as the shoppers cleared a path for him, terrified that his pure rock essence might somehow invade their safe English afternoon.

I didn't know it yet but the figure disappearing into the crowd was Nick Kent who, along with his pals at the *New Musical Express* (a.k.a. the *NME*), was helping create the great schism in musical tastes that was breaking Britain in two. In the movies they would have called this moment foreshadowing, but how was I to know that Mr. Kent and I would cross paths further on up the road?

After flunking the interview, I walked back along Oxford Street, thinking about that tall, striding alien. Maybe I wasn't rock star cool like he was, but I felt I knew more about his alien planet than the one I was standing on and had been trying stupidly to be a part of all this time. Since I felt like an alien, I needed to see if the alien nation would accept me into their midst.

I went home, rang up the *Melody Maker* offices and asked the nice lady who answered the phone where I could get a list of every record company in town. She turned out to be a lifesaver: she had a list and would photocopy it for me.

I rang all the record companies in London. No one was interested, and a lengthy future in the lower ranks of retail management looked increasingly likely. I'd avoided ringing Stiff Records, home of the five misfits I'd seen on the cover of *Melody Maker*, because they seemed far too cool and the label too small. But when Stiff became the only name on the list I hadn't rung, I took a deep breath and dialled. It turned out they had urgent need of a motorcycle messenger. I told them I had a motorcycle licence, and Cynthia Lole, the lady I was speaking with, told me to come by the next day for an interview.

I was a little more than 24 the day I went to see the people at Stiff. Not a single item of clothing I wore was black, and my balding haircut wasn't even remotely fashionable. I still had my moustache. Even worse, I had a degree and owned far too many Emerson Lake & Palmer albums.

I had three things in my favour: a huge enthusiasm for music, a good selection of punk singles and an earring. Looking back, I don't think the earring did me much good, and I don't suppose anyone gave a shit that I actually owned any of Stiff Records's meagre output, so we'll have to assume that my enthusiasm saved the day. Besides, who else was going to work 60 hours a week for £14 a week *and* provide their own motorcycle?

Stiff's offices were in a tawdry shopfront in Alexander Street — a middle-class residential street in West London. It was an unlikely location for the World's Most Flexible Label. The half-hearted attempt at window dressing consisted of a few single sleeves lying in the window area and a half-bent, life-size cardboard cutout of Elvis Costello with his Fender Jazzmaster staring out onto the street. Conveniently, Elvis's new release, "Watching the Detectives," was flirting with the lower edges of the Top 20. I'd never seen the offices of a record com pany before; this one looked like shit and I loved it on sight. I took a deep breath and walked inside.

Two women were sat behind a tiny, beaten-up desk. The blonde, ebullient one with brightly coloured clothes was Cynthia Lole. The thin, dark-haired one was dressed entirely in grey and black and wore a minuscule miniskirt and cowboy boots. She introduced herself as Phillipa. I later discovered she was the sister of Elvis's drummer, Pete Thomas. I owe Cynthia my break into the biz and I owe Phillipa for saving me from being booted out in the first month.

After a few minutes, I was bustled downstairs into the basement and met two talkative types who, luckily enough, were also wearing jeans and nothing black. They joked and laughed a lot and introduced themselves as Alan and Paul. Luckily, they didn't seem to have a problem with moustaches.

Alan Cowderoy and Paul Conroy were to become lifelong friends of mine. Paul had been a social secretary who became an agent and had looked after the early years of both Genesis and Queen. He then graduated to band management and had shepherded the Kursaal Flyers through their most successful period, including their time in the charts with "Little Does She Know." His father was a jovial ex-policeman who had retired and now spent time visiting record stores and distributing Stiff posters and flyers. Alan had started his career as a guitar player in an early prog band called Gracious whose greatest moment had been playing the *Isle of Wight Festival* supporting Dylan and Hendrix, though he later told me, "An inconsistent power supply meant that the mellotron had a conniption and we lost our way!" If the generator had been up to it perhaps his career may have led in a different direction, but Gracious never managed to trouble the charts, and Alan slipped quietly behind the scenes to work for Phonogram Records, where he looked after Thin Lizzy and was credited on their albums as "Nala."

They asked me some questions which didn't involve any of the things I felt were crucial — how the rise of pub rock had given way to punk or whether ELP's career had tailed off badly after *Trilogy*. Instead, they laughed and cracked jokes. I liked them both on sight but worried I wasn't making a good impression. A few minutes later, however, I was back on the street outside Stiff with a smile on my face and a spring in my step. I'd just secured my first job in showbiz — I'd been hired as Stiff Records' new motorcycle messenger.

Now all I needed was a motorbike.

It was a Thursday. On Friday, I quit my temp job at a department store and found a shop that sold motorbikes. A new one was out of the question, and I wanted something bigger than the Honda 125 I'd sold before the abortive expedition to France.

I spotted a bright red Suzuki 380GT. There were other more affordable, more sensible bikes available in the shop, but my heart was instantly set on owning that 380GT. Though I didn't care about such mechanical niceties, it was unusual in that it had three cylinders (not one or two or four like other bikes). The left cylinder had a shiny chromium pipe that went down the left side of the bike, the right cylinder had a shiny pipe that went down the right side, and the middle cylinder had an exhaust that split into two and went down both sides of the bike. The four shiny tailpipes made it resemble a bright red fighter plane on two wheels. I had no money, but I had to own it. The salesman knew he had a buyer and put it on hold for me while I figured out how to raise the cash.

And so, the following Monday morning, I started my first day at Stiff as a motorcycle messenger ... on foot.

I was sitting in the shop front with my shiny new copy of *London A–Z* when Phillipa handed me a package and told me to deliver it to an address in E17. That was all the way across London, and I had only an hour or so to get there.

Rather meekly I shared with Phillipa the embarrassing fact that I didn't have a bike yet. "No problem," she said and, raising her voice, shouted, "Dave? Can Nigel borrow your car?"

From the room at the back a voice replied instantly in an angry Irish brogue, "Who the fock is Nigel?"

And that's how I met Robbo.

On my arrival at Stiff in the fall of 1977 the company was barely a year old and, though I didn't know it yet, things weren't looking too healthy. In record company parlance, a stiff is a record that won't sell, so calling your label Stiff Records is a bit like calling your travel company Plummet Airlines (which, as it happened, was the name of one of the label's first no-hope acts), and Stiff was living up to its name in the most unfortunate way. Having read every copy of *Melody Maker* religiously for the last ten years I knew all about the foundation of the label, which was owned and run by two men — the exuberant and cheeky Jake Riviera (real name Andrew Jakeman) and the blunt, and for now more mysterious, Dave Robinson (universally known as Robbo).

Robbo and Jake were mavericks, guns for hire, blaggers, mischievous planners who had endeavoured to debunk the accepted way of doing things when they cooked up Stiff, supposedly funded by a £400 loan from Lee Brilleaux, the singer in Canvey Island's wonderful Dr. Feelgood.

Jake was from North London and had been a manager for Chilli Willi and the Red Hot Peppers and Dr. Feelgood. His hair was slicked back in a kind of mini quiff, and he dressed like a tasteful spiv from a John Waters movie. He had a quick wit and would probably have made an excellent game show host. The week I joined, Jake was the frontman of Stiff Records — the one who was always quoted in the press.

Robbo was cut from a different bolt of cloth. If Jake looked like he meant business, Robbo looked like he meant trouble. He'd grown up in Ireland, been Jimi Hendrix's guitar roadie, moved on to work with Van Morrison, had run London's Hope & Anchor pub (home base of the pub rock movement that predated punk in the UK) and — if he'd died then — would still have earned a very large footnote in the history of rock and roll by having masterminded the biggest stunt the music business had ever seen ... but you'll have to read Will Birch's wonderful *No Sleep Till Canvey Island* to find out about that!

There was no sign of Jake the morning I started work at Stiff, and

Robbo was obviously in a bad mood when he yelled, "Who the fock is Nigel?"

"He's the new bike messenger," Phillipa yelled back.

"If he's the new bike messenger, why does he need my car?"

Phillipa pointed to the door of the back room, "You'd better go and explain."

I poked my head around the door and found Robbo in a position I would become very familiar with. With his hair still wet from his early morning shower, he was leaning intently over his desk diary, scribbling with a pencil. Another pencil was tucked behind his ear. He was wearing a silver Graham Parker and the Rumour tour jacket which Cynthia called "the baked potato." Master tapes were piled high in the alcoves on either side of the unused fireplace; their spines revealed the names of every band that defined pub rock: Brinsley Schwarz, Ducks Deluxe, Eggs Over Easy, Kilburn and the High Roads, etc. Robbo looked up from his desk diary and sneered at me. I would later find out he had a wonderful smile and could be very charming. But today was not one of those days.

"Do you have a driving licence?"

I showed him my licence.

"Dick? From Stiff Records, eh?" He smirked, handed me back my licence, reached in his pocket and held out a set of keys.

"Don't crash it."

My second errand was taking Stiff artist Wreckless Eric to the doctor, and my day ended with a visit to the accounts department two doors down the street, where I was quizzed about my viability as the beneficiary of a loan from a struggling record label who would front me the money for the red 380GT. I was going to earn £14 a week; between my rent and the repayment schedule on the bike, it looked like my diet was going to be even more meagre than it had been in Paris.

Stiff wasn't the only entertainment company on Alexander Street. Directly above Stiff, sharing a staircase and a toilet, was a large room that housed Blackhill Enterprises, which was run by two well-spoken gents, Andrew King and Peter Jenner. They were managers who, as well as previously looking after the affairs of Marc Bolan and the Edgar Broughton Band, had already scored two notable mentions in the rock and roll almanac — they organised the Stones' famous free Hyde Park concert (the gig they played just a few days after Brian Jones had been found floating face-down in his swimming pool) and managed Pink Floyd during the first few years of their success.

The toilet at the back of the Stiff/Blackhill offices was, as in all houses of its era, an exposed three-walled room stuck onto the backside of the building. The plumbing was rudimentary, the facilities were desperately unhygienic, the flooring was aged, cracked linoleum and the place was always bitterly cold and smelly — the inevitable price to pay for one toilet being shared by up to 20 people at a time. But that toilet held an incredible fascination for me. Against one wall were haphazardly piled the normal kind of toilet reading you'd expect at a record label — old copies of *Sounds*, *Melody Maker*, *Musicweek* and *Record Business* — and here and there you'd find a discarded letter to Keith Christmas or Kevin Coyne, tour posters from long-forgotten gigs, telexes and food wrappers. One day, while I was taking a dump, the pile had cascaded onto the floor in front of me, revealing prodigious quantities of rejected colour transparencies from long-forgotten picture sessions. Over my next few visits, I made my way through the transparencies, trying to identify the various combinations of musicians: Pete Thomas with long hair, Martin Belmont before the GP tour jacket. One day, at the bottom of it all, I found the outtakes of the picture session for the Floyd's very first album, *The Piper at the Gates of Dawn*!

For months afterwards, as I sat on the loo, I wondered what would happen to those precious Floyd negs — until I thought, if they were so precious, why had they been left to rot in a drafty toilet on a London backstreet? I eventually liberated some of the negs and added them to my collection of rock trivia. A righteous man might describe this as stealing; I felt that "archiving" was more appropriate.

On the Friday of my first week at Stiff I took delivery of the red 380GT. I should have been ecstatic, but I was already worried that my time in the music business was about to come to an end. The day before, it had been announced that Jake was leaving Stiff. Even worse, he was taking Nick Lowe and Elvis Costello with him as well as Cynthia, who had given me my entry into showbiz.

By my second Monday at Stiff I'd established a routine. Phillipa would hand me a pile of packages that needed delivery up in the West End. Once I'd completed that task, I'd find a payphone and call back to the office to see if anything needed picking up. (If only cell phones had been invented back then my life would have been so much easier.) And so, somewhere in Soho, I waddled up to a payphone in my motorcycle gear and rang the office. A strange voice answered.

"Stiff Records."

"It's Nigel calling for Phillipa."

"Nigel who?"

"Nigel Dick, the motorcycle mess..."

"Dick? DICK? DIIIICK? Ha-ha! FUCK OFF!" The phone slammed down.

That's how I met Captain Sensible from the Damned. I learned to dread when the Damned weren't gigging because the Captain had nothing better to do than hang around the office and answer the phone. "DIIIICK!" he'd shout at the top of his voice, tell me to fuck off yet again and slam the phone down. I'd have to keep calling until he got bored and let Phillipa patiently explain what my next task was.

One of my jobs was to drop off the day's mail at the post office. I would show up with sacks of album mailers 30 minutes before closing time and they would lock the doors behind me as the poor mail clerk slowly weighed and stamped the mail-out. He would look at his watch and sigh till the last envelope was stamped. One night, he showed me a Pitney Bowes machine and explained that, if the company bought one, I could stamp the mail at the office, avoid the lines, drop off the sacks of mail at the post office and save both his time and mine. Pretty soon there was a brand-new franking machine at the office, and a shiny red scale to weigh every package and calculate the postage. This became my favourite end-of-day job, which I would enjoy with a cup of tea and a piece of cake from the corner shop.

One of the road crew who frequented the offices asked to borrow the scale. He disappeared into an office and locked the door behind him. Sometime later, he opened the door and handed it back as he rushed out the door with his briefcase. It must have been dusty in that office, because a strange white powder had fallen into the small dip in the centre of the scale where a screw held the weighing plate on the plunger. I brushed it away and continued with my work.

A few weeks later, after many borrowings of my scale, the roadie pulled me into a corner, held out a piece of paper and whispered, "I need you to go and pick up a package for me from this address." It seemed a bit strange that the pickup was not in the heart of the city, where most of my errands were, but somewhere out near the airport. I was just the messenger boy, and asking questions was not part of the job description.

It was raining outside as I climbed on my bike, pulled all the Velcro fasteners on my blue waterproofs tight and rode out west. Half an hour later, sopping wet, my visor steaming up, I finally found the address, a shabby post-war semi-detached on a rundown housing estate. A broken children's toy missing a wheel lay on the mud in the front yard that was once a lawn. The curtains were drawn. I double-checked the address and knocked on the door. Nothing. I knocked again. The mail slot clanked open, and a pair of bloodshot eyes stared out at me. "I've come to pick up the package." I held up the note with the address on it.

The slot clanked shut again. The sound of locks turning followed, and the door opened as far as the safety chain would allow. A tired-looking, unshaven man checked me out and glanced quickly up and down the street. "You're early — wait here!" He slammed the door, and I could hear him climbing the stairs. There was nowhere to shelter, so I sat on my bike and felt the rain dripping off my helmet as I wondered what was going on.

Ten minutes later I heard a whistle. Mr. Tired-Looking was standing in the open door, holding a battered plastic bag from Tesco and waving at me. I rushed back to the door. He handed me the bag. "Keep this dry. Throw that address away and forget you were here." The bag felt weighty, even though the package was quite small. I unzipped my suit and tucked it inside my shirt, zipped up and rode back toward the city, fighting the plumes of spray from the trucks and cabs racing into town.

I was naïve about drugs, but halfway back to the office, as I waited at a red light, it finally dawned on me that the cloak and dagger, the tired-looking mystery man, the rolled-up Tesco bag feeling clammy against my belly, the white powder on my GPO-endorsed weighing scale added up to one thing — I was likely an unwitting drug mule, currently ferrying enough cocaine to put me in jail for an entire album-tour-and-three-singles marketing cycle. A shiver ran down my clammy spine. Oh well, I was working for a record company. What did I expect?

The lights turned green, I kicked the bike back into gear and turned north towards Westbourne Grove vowing I would never run another errand for that roadie.

Stiff was on thin ice after Elvis and Nick Lowe left. Nothing was selling. By the following spring, however, the rock and roll winds were suddenly blowing in our direction. Ian Dury's *New Boots and Panties!!* was starting to sell.

That first week at Stiff, before I got my bike, I used Alan Cowderoy's car, a green VW Golf that I would later inherit. In the glove box of Alan's car were cassettes of new releases, two of which caught my eye. The first was an album by Clover, a band from Marin County, California, who were managed by Robbo and had been signed to Phonogram. They were extraordinarily gifted musicians, layered delicious harmonies over every song and featured a harmonica player named Huey Lewis. But they'd arrived in London to promote their album at precisely the wrong moment. With their long hair, California-cute denim wardrobe and Americana/rock material, they stuck out like a sore thumb against a city filled with mohawks, nose-rings and butt flaps. In an effort to keep them working, Robbo and Jake hired them to be the backing band on Elvis Costello's first album. In a strange coincidence, Clover bassist Johnny Ciambotti would become my chiropractor many years later when I moved to L.A. — around the same time I shot a video for Huey Lewis for a single that never reached the charts.

The other cassette that caught my eye was Ian Dury's *New Boots and Panties!!*

Ian had grown up in the Home Counties, the son of a limo driver and a woman who came from a different background; therein lay the magic of his charisma. He talked like a real Cockney bricklayer, but he was very knowledgeable and had studied fine art under Peter Blake, the man who art directed the Beatles' *Sgt. Pepper's Lonely Hearts Club Band* sleeve. He was an unlikely rock and roll hero — though quite handsome, his body had been ravaged by polio as a boy and he limped and shuffled around with the help of a stick. One side of his body was withered and weak; to lift the mic from the mic stand, he would lower his shoulder and with great purpose lift and swing his whole torso so that his arm would fly up. He would grab the mic and growl into it in that deep voice young women found so alluring. Like Wreckless Eric, he was not what anyone in the opera business would call a singer, but his charisma and wordplay were so marvellous that he was on the verge of a great career.

As I slipped Dury's first solo album into the Golf's cassette deck and sped off into the city, I was innocent of what marvels lay in store. The sun was out and, as it was the last of the summer warmth, I wound the windows down. I was in London, I was in showbiz and life was good. The lights at Marylebone Road and Baker Street turned red and I slowed to a halt as "Blockheads" faded out. I casually looked to my left as an attractive middle-aged lady in a sports car pulled up in the lane next to me. She glanced my way and smiled. I smiled back as the stereo in my car suddenly thundered into life and Ian bawled out the intro to "Plaistow Patricia": "ARSEHOLES, BASTARDS, FUCKING CUNTS AND PRICKS..." The middle-aged lady's face was a picture of horror and disgust. The lights turned green and she was gone while I nervously fumbled for the volume control and turned bright red.

Thanks to "Plaistow Patricia" and Dury's wondrous wordplay, *New Boots and Panties!!* was soon leaping up the charts. In the nick of time, Stiff had a hit album, and bills were being paid.

Dave Robinson was quite unlike any man I had ever come across. He seemingly took advice from no one, directed all the battles from his office and was riding high on a series of successful manoeuvres that everyone predicted would end in disaster but had somehow turned in his favour. He ruled with a steely glare, took no dissent from anyone and shouted a lot. Robbo came to be known to us underlings in the office as "The Fuhrer." Like Hitler, Dave had a long-suffering girlfriend and a dog he doted over, but he also had a lot of Yoda-like qualities that made working for him mesmerizing. Amid the ranting and raving he would dispense aphorisms that made us all laugh at their ludicrousness:

- I foresee no problems.
- You've got to boss to be the boss.
- Don't tell me your problems and I won't tell you mine.
- It's easy for an Englishman to say no.
- When you're hot you're hot. When you're not you're not.

We would chuckle behind Dave's back when these sayings were trotted out and roll our eyes and tut-tut as one does while listening to a grumpy old relative who needs moving closer to the fire — but what I didn't realise is that these ludicrous sayings, spoken in his distinctive Irish brogue, contained pearls that I was just too inexperienced to grasp. In time I would not only learn the wisdom behind Robbo's sayings, but I would start using them myself.

I'd like to say that being a bike messenger for Stiff was glamorous, but it wasn't. It was slave labour with a side-order of danger — I came off that bike three times in six months and nearly froze myself to death racing round London in the semi-dark of an endless three-day week caused by the miners' strike. Hurtling round town on a red Suzuki in the sleet and snow carrying artwork and test pressings and illicit packets of cocaine for roadies was the most rebellious thing I ever did. Dave Vanian of the Damned thought he was a rebel because he slicked back his hair and sang punk songs in defiance of Genesis, Yes and Emerson Lake & Palmer — big deal! I was risking my life on the Marylebone Road fighting lorries in the pissing rain so that Ian Dury's artwork would get to the printers on time. While the punks thought they were brave because they strutted down the high street with egg white in their mohawks, I was pissing myself with fear wondering if I'd make it to 25 with both legs intact. What I was doing was insane, but I truly didn't care because I was the guy in the joke who complains about working in the circus, shovelling elephant shit every day and, when asked why he doesn't find a new job, responds, "What? And give up showbiz?" It was mad and dangerous, but I was having the time of my life. But glamorous? No.

What made Stiff Records so special? Every one of the oddball characters who worked there had steered a path away from corporate rock towards something more vital. They each had a story, and every one of those stories was pure gold — sometimes more fascinating than the artists we were there to promote. From the outside, the company appeared to be a factory of vital images that were pumped out into the hinterland of popular culture on a daily basis: ads in the music press, the latest singles sleeve and posters pasted liberally across the fences and back walls of the city by night.

With the benefit of hindsight, Stiff was perhaps more rebellious — and indeed "punk" — than any of the bands who fronted the punk revolution. While the Clash, Sex Pistols and their ilk talked a good game about changing the system, they were happy to sign with major labels and cash the large cheques they were offered. Meanwhile, Stiff consistently broke the rules that had been laid down over the years. If they didn't break the system, Stiff certainly helped to reinvent it. Prior to Stiff, full-page ads in the music press for singles were unheard of.

Predating the MTV era by years, Stiff made videos for every artist on the label, and marketing stunts that were offensive, borderline insane or possibly illegal were common. Stiff may have been something of an industry joke at the outset, but by the end of the '70s there was not one label in London that hadn't nicked some marketing idea from the cheeky misfits on Alexander Street, and every record exec in town had had their assistant ring up to blag a free "If It Ain't Stiff It Ain't Worth a Fuck" T-shirt to establish their credibility.

CHAPTER 5

Be Stiff

ONE WET AFTERNOON, as I snaked between lines of traffic on the Edgware Road overpass, a lorry driver intentionally doored me. I slid off my bike and nearly disappeared under the wheels of another truck. "Serve you fucking right!" he yelled as I picked myself off the tarmac. After more near-misses, I sensed something had to change, so I was delighted when I was promoted off the bike and into the office to be Paul Conroy's production assistant.

Working for Conroy was fun. He had an excellent sense of humour. As he couldn't drive, I wound up spending a lot of time as his driver. Otherwise, I would be handed a host of other jobs as problems came up that needed sorting out, one of which landed me in hot water with Stiff's new signing, Devo.

The band were coming to the UK to promote their cover of the Stones' "Satisfaction" and my job was to find them lodgings close to the Stiff offices. I tried a number of likely places, but got laughed at when I said how much we had to spend. I eventually found a run-down hostelry round the back of Bayswater.

John Kalinowski — known to everyone as Kellogs, or just Logs, and a tour manager of some repute — was hired to look after the band during their UK visit. He met them at the airport and took them straight to the hotel I'd found. The band took one look at it and refused to even get out of the van. Kellogs and the label were embarrassed, I was named as the fall guy and the band were booked into the much nicer (and far more costly) Post House in Bayswater. The band spent a few days in London and then Logs drove them up to Manchester to appear on Tony Wilson's *So It Goes* TV show.

On the morning of the broadcast, Kellogs called the Stiff offices in a panic asking for me: "Look, Nigel, about that hotel thing, perhaps there's a way for you to unblot your copy book. I'm in the Granada TV studios in Manchester and Devo are supposed to go on the show live in four hours."

"So, what's the problem?" I said. Kellogs took a breath. "Well, they've left their Devo suits in the Post House back in London and they're refusing to go on without their outfits. Any chance you could pop round the corner, pick them up and dash up the motorway with them?"

"But that's a 200-mile trip."

"Yes. You'd better leave now."

Four hours later, I was racing towards the elevators at Granada in Manchester, having broken into the band's room in Bayswater, driven like a madman up half of England somehow avoiding speed traps and accidents, found my way to the studios, parked the car and breathlessly explained to the security guard that I needed to go to the *So It Goes* studio *NOW!* Riding up in the elevator, I studied the "suits" — cheap yellow hazmat knockoffs with stick-on letters that spelled DEVO. I'd risked my life speeding up England's most dangerous motorway for this?

Logs was pacing up and down like an expectant dad. When he saw me running towards him, he put his hand over his heart and sighed. "Bravo, Nigel. Well done!" He turned towards the band sitting like robots — motionless and unimpressed on a bench in the corridor.

"Hey, guys, say thank you to Nigel. He just saved our bacon." They said nothing, grabbed their yellow suits and five minutes later were in front of the cameras. I didn't expect, or want, to become mates with Devo, but having literally risked my life and driving licence for their five-dollar suits, I felt a thank you or at least a smile was in order. As I drove back south I didn't ask for or expect any kind of retribution for the band's behaviour — I just grumbled a lot. Perhaps one day I would get my revenge.

In the meantime, there was work to be done — and lots of it. Robbo, Dave and Paul had cooked up another massive wheeze to blow away memories of the previous year's *Five Live Stiffs* tour: the *Be Stiff 78* tour. Devo had provided Stiff with its temporary theme song, "Be Stiff," and the new jaunt — which would feature a knees-up of the Devo tune at the end of every night — was planned to promote the careers of Wreckless Eric (again) and new Stiff signings Jona Lewie, Rachel Sweet, Lene Lovich and Mickey Jupp. However, there would be no jaunty singalongs in the tour bus this time — everyone was going to travel by train. British Rail had been cajoled into providing a special service: tattered carriages that had been sitting in long-forgotten siding and given a fresh coat of paint upon which various sponsors were encouraged to adorn their logos in support of the tour.

The run-up to the tour was full of life-changing moments. I was one of the lucky folk who dressed up in colourful suits to appear on the cover *The Wonderful World of Wreckless Eric.* (That's me in the last row, sporting a stand-up bass.) I even had two of my photographs featured on the back of the album sleeve — a first for me.

Another album sleeve moment occurred when I drove Rachel Sweet to Brighton. The photographer pulled my leather jacket off and handed it to Rachel; the shot of Rachel wrapped in my jacket made it to the album cover. I later chaperoned Rachel and her sister Lia to Paris for a weekend because it was known that I'd lived there briefly before working for Stiff.

One evening, Paul, Alan, I and other Stiff luminaries were told to don our Graham Parker and the Rumour tour jackets and report to a tunnel under Hyde Park, where we were lined up against a wall and instructed to sing along to Lene Lovich's first hit, "Lucky Number," as the cameras rolled. It was my first cameo and music video experience.

On a subsequent afternoon, I was handed car keys, shown to a shiny new Jaguar and told to pick up its owner, Dave Edmunds — he of Love Sculpture and one of my all-time heroes. I was to drive him down to the south coast, where he was due for a recording session with Mickey Jupp. The car had a hundred miles on the clock, but Dave was too tired and emotional to get behind the wheel, so I gingerly drove his new motor southwards while Edmunds slumbered in the passenger seat and uttered nary a word on the whole trip.

Weeks later, with the Stiff train back in its siding, the *Be Stiff* tour was being geared up for a series of dates at New York's Bottom Line. Much to my surprise, over a generous portion of bangers and chips in a diner one night, Robbo said to me, "How do you fancy coming to New York on the tour?" It was a freebie: no work was expected of me. And I'd never been to America. I accepted.

A few weeks later, the motley Stiff entourage staggered out of the Customs Hall at JFK. Robbo was there to guide us onto a gleaming chrome and wine-red tour bus. It was dark and the streets were damp from melting snow as Robbo fiddled with the stereo. Suddenly, Graham Parker's as-yet-unreleased *Squeezing Out Sparks* was pounding out of the speakers at a brain-rattling volume so loud that all talk ceased. During the opening bars of "Discovering Japan," I saw the Empire State Building and Manhattan across the river in all its Christmas glory for the first time. Nothing in my life had ever seemed so magical. My rock and roll dream of guitars, gigs and girls hadn't come to pass the way I imagined it, but this would do nicely.

The next day I went to the Empire State Building with DJ Charlie Gillett and Les Chappell from Lene Lovich's band. I posed for a picture on the top wearing my silk motorcycle scarf, my omnipresent motorcycle jacket and a woolly hat à la Springsteen. I was prepared for the chill, but not the cold, not New York cold. I shivered every minute of my trip till I landed back in London.

As I'd heard guitars were cheap and plentiful in the U.S., I went in search of a guitar shop. Finding a small one, I wandered round the store looking at rows of Les Pauls and Strats. An older man, probably the owner, came over. "Hey, can I help you?"

"Just looking, thank you."

"Then get the fuckouddahere!"

It was my first taste of the real New York.

CHAPTER 6

12.5 on a 10 Point Scale

AT THE START OF the *Be Stiff 78* tour, a new face walked into the Stiff office. Andy Murray, the former editor of *Circuit,* a magazine for university concert bookers, had been hired to do press for the tour. By the time it reached New York, Andy and I had become firm friends. We had discovered a mutual fascination with guitars and rock trivia, though it has to be said that Andy was a far better guitar player than me and his arcane knowledge about the history of rock put me in the shade. After I picked up a Korean bass for 50 bucks in a pawn shop in Maryland on a subsequent trip to the States, we started writing songs and talked about forming a band.

Robbo, who was getting married, was planning a gig for the reception, so we coerced Alan Cowderoy to get his guitar out of storage, borrowed a drummer, Nick Garnett, from Virgin Publishing and placed beat poet Jock Scot in front on vocals, along with an attractive blonde who Andy knew. We dubbed ourselves the Stiff All-Stars, raided Chuck Berry's songbook and slotted ourselves on the bill between headliners the Inmates and a little-known ska band that Robbo's soon-to-be wife thought had a future. Thus, the Stiff All-Stars played our first-ever gig higher on the bill than future Stiff chart stars Madness and assaulted a packed hall which contained Elvis Costello, Phil Lynott and a number of other big names.

We weren't bottled off stage or welcomed by a number of comely maidens in the green room as we gasped for breath after our set but, against the odds, as we piled our gear back into our cars, we were delighted to find that we'd been offered a recording contract! Ted Carroll, another Irish punk record label owner, was in the crowd and thought it would be a good wheeze if he offered the Stiff Records house band a deal on his own label, Chiswick Records. Of course we said yes, and a short time later, Andy, Nick the drummer and I were in a studio, banging out our first single, "Maybe Tonight." To our amazement, the record, with an A-side written by Andy and myself, started getting airplay. One Saturday afternoon, sitting in my car outside the launderette, Andy and I heard it booming out of Britain's top station, Radio One. I couldn't have been happier. I have a copy of the record framed in my office over a fake plaque that reads: "This miserable piece of black plastic represents the dreams of a lifetime."

We didn't get into the charts, but we didn't give up, either. Nick was soon replaced by drummer Hugh Attwooll, who worked at CBS Records and had made a fortune for the label when he persuaded Julio Iglesias to make an album in English. Soon we had a keyboard player, Nicky Graham, who also worked at CBS in A&R but was a writer and producer who played on Bowie's *Ziggy Stardust* tour and subsequently went on to discover, produce and write hits for UK chart-toppers Bros. Our first guitar player was Jamie West-Oram, who didn't last long, as he declared one day that he was forming a "real" band and they were going to call themselves the Fix(x). He was replaced by Pete Glenister, who subsequently wrote and produced hits for Kirsty MacColl, Alison Moyet and others. I'm noting all this for two reasons. Firstly, to show off (my band had guys who played with Bowie and Tina Turner!) and secondly to describe how something that started out as a bit of a joke quickly became quite serious. Everybody in the

Stiff office pulled my leg, "Got another gig tonight then, Nige? Ha-ha." But, yes, we did have another gig and played all over the city, sometimes filling in at a moment's notice, but mostly booked in advance at proper rock venues like the Marquee, The Venue and the Hope & Anchor.

We subsequently released three more singles and even appeared on TV. We were ploughing a peculiar furrow through London's musical scene, playing a hybrid mixture of surf, West Coast rock and pub rock. We hit a high point when someone flew over from France to come to a gig and get that first All-Stars single autographed but, in the end, we had to admit that the Eagles were selling more records and were marginally better songwriters. However, I'd like to think that begrudgingly, behind our backs, our fellow record company acolytes were impressed by the fact that we tried to turn our dream into reality, released records, got airplay and impressed someone enough to make him cross the Channel. If only there'd been 100,000 more like him!

CHAPTER 7

All of the Day and All of the Night

WHILE TRYING TO TURN MYSELF into a rock star, work continued at all hours. One night, the phone rang as I was in a deep sleep. "Are you drunk?" It was Robbo. It was obviously a trick question, but when you're standing in the hallway in your jammy bottoms in the dark you don't think before you speak.

"Um. Not drunk."

"Good! Drive over to my house right now."

I looked at my watch as I got dressed. It was three o'clock in the morning.

By the time I was rattling across Battersea Bridge in the company VW Beetle I was conscious enough to start wondering what scheme Robbo had concocted for me. When I knocked on his door it sounded like a party was going on inside. His wife answered the door holding a glass of wine and was very surprised to see the company runner on her doorstep in the dark.

"Dave rang. Said he needed a hand."

"He's upstairs mending the toilet."

When I reached the top landing, there was Robbo kneeling on the floor, one arm halfway up the U-bend. He pulled his hand from the bog and gave me his car keys. "I've left my car in Soho. You need to find it and bring it back here." After a cab ride back across the river, I started to wonder why I'd been trusted with this mission; once I'd located his car and was driving back, I began to smell a rat. Back at Robinson Towers, Robbo appeared at the front door with bedhead as I presented him with his car keys.

"Why didn't you just take a cab into Soho this morning to pick up the car on the way into work?"

"Because, Nigel, last night, I'd had a few drinks and as I was driving round Trafalgar Square the wrong way, a copper stepped out in front of me and put his hand up to stop me and I drove over his foot, so I had to ditch the car in Soho and take a cab home. I needed somebody English, sober and with a clean licence to pick up the car for me in case the cops were after it." I must have looked shocked. "Don't worry, I would have bailed you out."

I Beetled my way across the river for the fourth time that night and climbed into bed about 15 minutes before the alarm was supposed to go off. Of course, I overslept. When I finally made it to work the first person I saw was Robbo. As always, he had a pencil tucked behind his ear. He sipped at his coffee as his eyes twinkled in a mischievous smile. "You were late to work this morning."

I was up early, shaving in front of the mirror of my tiny bedroom less than a quarter mile from Abbey Road, when the radio played two Beatles tunes back-to-back. That seemed odd; then the news came on. "John Lennon has just been murdered in New York City." I instantly went into shock.*

I woke up my roommate, banging on his door. I barged in, still holding my razor. "Wake up, Dave. Wake up! They've just shot my favourite Beatle."

* The news of Lennon's death broke that night in New York City. Being five hours ahead of the East Coast, the news broke in the early hours in Britain.

Many things made Lennon's death so wrenching: its suddenness, its senselessness and the damage it did to millions of fans around the world. But perhaps its most unique quality, one that is not often discussed, is the way it affected the news in the UK — at least the way I experienced it. On my first visits to America, I noticed that a story on the evening news about the President's latest press conference regarding world trade and the deficit would cut to a puff piece and a short interview with Peter Frampton or some other rocker playing the local arena that night. Such a thing was unheard of in the UK. In Britain, the TV news meant pictures of the PM stepping out of his or her car outside Downing Street intercut with opposition views from the steps of the House of Parliament; maybe later there would be a short documentary-style segment from the slums of Delhi or footage of another venerable Brit trying to sail the wrong way round the world. There wasn't so much as a sniff of a rock "moment" in the mainstream news unless someone like Elvis had pegged out in his glamorous home, in which case the segment lasted 30 seconds and inevitably failed to convey who he was or what he'd done.

That all changed the night Lennon was murdered. It not only made the news — it *was* the news. It was the top story and, when the breathless reporter finished his piece outside the Dakota, there were interviews with music journalists and other rock folk to hammer home how devastating this moment was. Those important announcements about trade deficits and the economy were quickly relegated to the "In Other News" segment. Do the math — on December 8th 1980, I'm guessing that the halls of the BBC and ITV, *The Times*, *The Mirror* and *The Guardian* and every other British news organ were peopled by intelligent reporters, producers, writers and presenters who were in their thirties and forties and who, like their seniors, wanted to file cutting-edge pieces about Whitehall and Washington and the dramas of the day but, unlike previous generations, almost certainly grew up in the '60s and had a Beatles record or five at home. Lennon's murder wasn't the sad death in a motel of some coked-up has-been muso — it was a MURDER of a bona fide cultural hero who had, with his three pals, pretty much defined the '60s, the decade during which Britain recovered from the previous 25 years of blood, war and financial trauma. For them, I'm guessing, it wasn't just a case of "if it bleeds it leads," it was a defining moment when they witnessed their youth dying. Perhaps for those people putting the news together that night it was the most personal news story they had ever covered.

The power of this awful coming-of-age moment was indicated by a quiet comment my mother made to me on the weekly phone call I had with my parents. For a brief moment, the usual sneering about throwing my life away working for a record label was gone and she quietly commented, "I'm sorry, I had no idea how important the Beatles were." I could hear the shock and confusion in her voice. She listened to Opera with a capital O and would grudgingly confess after a glass of sherry that she had a soft spot for Perry Como. But that weekend I think she finally sensed, in a very sad way, that maybe I was onto something after all.

That was the saddest day I ever spent at Stiff. We were all in shock. On my way home, I saw the *Evening Standard* one-sheet outside my local newsagent which read in stark words, JOHN LENNON SHOT DEAD. I ripped it from the easel outside the shop, had it framed and it hung in my house for years. No matter how many times I stared at it, I still couldn't believe its stark four-word message. I avoided facing up to the fact that Lennon's death, and its aftermath, somehow validated my rock and roll habit, legitimized on the evening news and the front pages of every paper in the country.

CHAPTER 8

The Up Escalator

STIFF HAD HAD A CONSISTENTLY brilliant cadre of press officers pass through its offices. B.P. Fallon had been in the mix in the early days — he'd moved from Ireland to work with Derek Taylor and the Beatles and then moved on to handle Led Zeppelin during their glory years. A small, intriguing man with a large head, who seemed wily and always had a mischievous look in his eyes, B.P. mainly looked after Ian Dury and was cut from the same cloth as Glen Colson, the first press man for everyone else at the label. Glen was equally mischievous, with a Cockney charm and a smile that never left his face. He always had an immaculate pair of suede shoes, and every story he told seemed to end with a guffaw and the same phrase, "...and then I told him to fuck off! Wanker!" Glen had also worked for the mighty Zep for a while, though his time with the band had involved setting up Bonzo's drum kit. I always admired Glen for his savvy and street smarts, especially when it came to blagging stuff with the press. Years later he shared his secret technique with me: "They'd give me a box of singles, and I'd take 'em round the press and just hope for the best."

The first full-time PR person we had was Pete Frame. Unlike Glen and B.P., Frame was tall and had been teleported to the Stiff offices from 18th century France: he had a pointed beard that any of the Four Musketeers would have been proud of; when he smiled, he looked like he could have been Errol Flynn's older brother. And along with him came an encyclopaedic, if rather musty, knowledge of the history of rock and roll. Frame had started a rock magazine, *ZigZag,* but his greatest claim to fame was the Rock Family Trees he created, which showed in meticulous detail how the careers of a dozen bands entwined. If you're remotely interested in music, buy his *Rock Family Trees* book — you'll be swept away for hours.

When the plan was hatched for the second Stiff tour and Andy Murray arrived, I noticed he was younger than Frame yet seemed to have even more trivia about band genealogy inside his head than Frame did. Our label was all about punky new wave artists from humble British backgrounds, but Andy would somehow always bring the conversation back to Little Feat or some other exotic American outfit that, by being Stiff staff, we were supposed to detest. Andy's credibility was also helped in my eyes because his brother Neil was a bass player who actually made money from it, eventually becoming a member of Whitesnake and a sometime performer with Sabbath, Clapton, Jeff Beck and Peter Green.

And then there was Kosmo. Kosmo Vinyl had been a roadie for Graham Parker but had taken a sideways career step into PR when Glen Colson hired him as an assistant; he was the world's biggest Clash fan and didn't let his day job as Ian Dury's lone PR man get in the way of his adulation for Joe Strummer and the Clash and anything they said or did. Kos was a tidal wave of chutzpah and noise. You felt him coming about 60 seconds before he appeared; his voice rose above all others, searing the air with a savage Cockney blast. I swear Kos could blag anything. He was shameless and exuded confidence like no man I have ever met before or since. I was jealous of his swagger and the way that girls looked at him. I was shy, polite, honest, too well-spoken. I don't think Kos was any of those things. In time Kos would leave Dury's side; my last sighting of him was in Scorsese's *King of Comedy*. When the Clash appear on a sidewalk, there was Kosmo photobombing the movie, all swagger and flash.

When Andy announced that he was leaving to work at CBS Records, it was somehow decided that I would be Stiff's next PR person. I was happy to get the promotion but privately terrified because I shared nothing with any of my predecessors apart from a lot of time spent in Andy's flat playing guitar.

On my first day I had to ring up a journalist at *The Times*.

"Who's calling?"

"Nigel Dick from Stiff Records."

"Dick? From Stiff? Yeah, right. Bugger off!"

SLAM.

Clearly my time in the press office at Stiff wasn't going to be all sunshine and roses.

At that time in the UK, there were four papers around which the entire world as I knew it rotated. *Melody Maker*, *Sounds*, *Record Mirror* and the *NME* churned out packed issues every Thursday without fail. I'd been weaned on the *Melody Maker* and had read every single issue cover to cover since I'd discovered it as a young teen. By the end of the '70s, however, it was past its prime and its journalists were no longer on the cutting edge. That they still operated out of the Nissen hut, a prefabricated wartime shed on the south side of the Thames, where I had first obtained Stiff's phone number said it all. *Sounds* specialized in heavier rock and harder punk outfits and had coined the terms "New Wave of British Heavy Metal" and "Oi" to describe these two genres of music. *Record Mirror* skewed to the poppier side of things and was more lightweight. Both *Record Mirror* and *Sounds* operated out of the same building in Longacre, close to Covent Garden.

And then there was the *NME*. The *NME* thought the sun shone out of its arse and was not going to be told by anyone who was the next big thing. Though owned by the same publishing company as *Melody Maker*, the *NME* distanced itself from every other rag and had its offices on London's fashionable Carnaby Street.

There were three other mags every music biz press officer also had to worry about. The recently launched *Smash Hits* was in colour and featured song lyrics of the hits of the day. It was run and edited by David Hepworth (who I knew and respected) and had future Pet Shop Boy Neil Tennant as one of its writers (who I didn't). And then there were the two august music biz mags: *Record Business* and *Music Week*. In many ways, getting all the info about your latest releases in *Record Business* and *Music Week* was the most important goal of the week because — in those pre-interweb days — all the retailers would read one of these two mags to learn about record releases. But, out in the real world, what mattered most were the four music papers.

I had none of the theatricality or chutzpah of my predecessors. I hadn't run my own paper or worked at an agency. I wasn't even outgoing — I was just a fan who'd got lucky. I looked in the mirror one morning and reasoned that what I lacked in gall and balls I made up for in enthusiasm. I started fashioning my own approach to the press, which involved stealing the *Rock Family Tree* template from Pete Frame, borrowing Andy's witty rock trivia knowledge and, adding my architectural drawing skills, creating press releases which were mostly light, humorous and filled with solid information on Stiff's latest release.

Robbo was passing my office one day when he leaned in the door and said, "Great news! We've just signed Alvin Stardust. Take him round the papers and get him some press!"

Alvin Stardust? My heart sank. It was obvious the label was desperate. Alvin was old news. He was already on his third name, his second wife and we were going to be his fourth (or fifth) label. Alvin was not cool or hip, if he ever had been, so how was I going to walk into the papers with him and not have everyone laugh at me?

Alvin's birth name was Bernard Jewry. He'd grown up in the north of England and roadied in the early '60s for Shane Fenton and the Fentones. The band broke up when teenaged lead singer Shane Fenton (real name Johnny Theakston) died. The Fentones had previously sent a demo tape to the BBC, which (unaware Theakston had croaked) offered them an audition in London. The band wanted that gig badly and persuaded Jewry to become its new lead singer and take on the dead boy's *nom de rock*: he was now Shane Fenton.

That audition at the Beeb must have been a success: Shane Fenton and the Fentones had some minor hits on Parlophone before giving up the ghost sometime in the late '60s. Jewry, still using his Shane Fenton alias, disappeared from the charts for a few years while doing small gigs with his wife Iris (a onetime girlfriend of two Beatles and the sister of Rory Storm of Rory Storm and the Hurricanes, whose first drummer had been Ringo Starr).

Bernard Jewry/Shane Fenton changed his name once more and appeared in the charts in 1973 as Alvin Stardust with a number-two record ("My Coo Ca Choo"). Soon after that, he improved his strike ratio and had a number-one with "Jealous Mind." Glam rock was sweeping Britain at the time; T. Rex and their ilk ruled the charts. Alvin, however, did not follow the trend and dress himself in silver, but went for a gay biker look involving black leather jacket and trousers, long sideburns and a high black quiff. His image, cooked up in a backroom somewhere, was a sort of demented Elvis clone from a rerun of a second-rate *Rocky Horror Show*. But it worked because Alvin totally embraced it. He even tweaked the whole look by lowering his chin, looking evilly over the mic while holding it at a strange angle with a black leather driving glove.

Alvin was successful for a few years, touring and releasing more records, but gradually the singles no longer made the charts and the arrival of punk made it appear that the only thing the future held for him was end-of-the-pier shows and late-night TV appearances. Whatever cred Bernard/Shane/Alvin ever had in the music biz was gone. So, when Robbo leaned in my door and told me we'd signed Alvin, I knew I was screwed. I was the press officer at a hip record label and now I had to get press on a guy who was pushing 40 and doing cabaret? What was the world coming to?

I put off the calls to the press for days until I knew I couldn't delay any longer. I decided to get the most difficult call out of the way first and called the features editor at the *NME.*

"Um ... we've just signed Alvin Stardust and I'm wondering if there's a chance you could perhaps, maybe, if there's space, put in a small piece about the signing in next week's paper?"

I clenched my teeth and closed my eyes with embarrassment waiting for some kind of put-down. So, I was shocked at the response. "Alvin? That's great news. I tell you what, why don't you bring him over next week, we'll grab lunch and I'll interview him myself and we'll see if we can do a nice piece on page three for you."

The cynical old hack who usually would not take my calls and gave me monosyllabic answers when he did had revealed his true colours as a friendly gent who was happy, if not delighted, to break bread with Alvin and me. Relieved, I rang all the other papers and received a similar response from every one. I was mystified — there was something going on I did not understand.

We met the journo for lunch in the West End a few days later. Alvin enthusiastically shook hands with him and asked how his wife and kids were. Surely the kids were of college age now? What careers did they have in mind? He remembered everybody's name, and for the next hour the journalist glowed as they swapped tales together and laughed about the good old days and some of the more ridiculous moments from Alvin's career. As I paid the bill and we walked out onto Wardour Street I realised we hadn't mentioned a thing about Alvin's article in the *NME.* But, as we bid farewell, the journalist promised he'd put something in the following week's paper. As I hailed a cab for Alvin, I breathed a sigh of relief. Getting press for Alvin proved to be a doddle. Everyone wanted to talk to him — it appeared he had a rolodex somewhere with the name of everyone's wife, offspring and hobbies — and at every interview he was constantly both charming and humble.

When the papers came out next week it was as if we'd signed someone with the cred of Bob Dylan. The *NME* even featured Alvin's signing as the top news story of the week. His first release on Stiff, "Pretend," reached the Top 5. Over the years I have shared this story with every grumpy pop star I have ever worked with. I have no idea if any of them bothered to learn anything from Alvin's lesson, but I know that I have: always be like Alvin.

Alvin was singing right to the end — he died from cancer aged 72, six days after his last gig.

When Robbo discovered Graham Parker and assembled his backing outfit, the Rumour, from the dying embers of Brinsley Schwarz, he brokered a deal for them to sign with Mercury Records/Phonogram. Graham, or GP as most of us called him, was not a big man but came off as a tough, scrappy urban fighter. He wasn't a punk per se, but he didn't mess around with soppy love songs, either. His songs were constructed from used razor blades and brittle steel, and you sensed his anger and outrage in every syllable — he appeared to have a giant chip on his shoulder, and he knew how to work it. You didn't put on a GP album if you needed soothing at the end of a hard day, you played it because you weren't going to take it anymore and you wanted to get even. As the office wasn't only a record label but also a management company for GP, the Stiff staff were fans of GP and the Rumour as much as they were fans of all of the Stiff artists.

But Robbo became increasingly disappointed with the way Mercury/Phonogram handled GP's career, and I remember one testy exchange when Robbo yelled down the phone, "We could sell more copies of a Graham Parker record with nothing on it than you've done with GP's last album." The relationship reached its nadir when GP recorded a song called "Mercury Poisoning" — "I've got Mercury Poisoning, the best-kept secret in the west!"

Ultimately Robbo, GP and the Rumour and Mercury agreed to disagree. Mercury/Phonogram dropped them, and Robbo signed the band to Stiff. Robbo had put things on the line, and we had to back up our boast with results.

GP had a new album to promote, *The Up Escalator*. At most labels, a forthcoming release would merit a marketing meeting with heads of all departments in the same room discussing plans for coordinating ads, press and promotions with the album and single release. As head of UK press, I don't ever remember being involved in any such meeting. In the run-up to the release of *The Up Escalator*, Robbo simply called me into his office and told me he wanted GP on the front page of the *NME* and a big piece in one of the Sunday colour magazines the weekend the record came out. But the release of the album was just four weeks away, and one of his demands was not so much difficult as impossible — the colour magazines had a six-week lead time, so the chances of getting a journalist to interview GP and insert his work into any of those mags to coincide with the album's release were absolutely nil. Robbo sneered when I told him the colour magazine idea wasn't going to happen and fed me one of his stock phrases, "It's easy for an Englishman to say no!" He harrumphed as he pulled a pencil from behind his ear. "I need that front page on the *NME*. Make it happen!" Robbo then upped the ante by demanding that the article be written by rock's most revered writer, Nick Kent.

By now the lines of battle between my office and the *NME* were clearly drawn — they were going through a phase of disliking Stiff and made it clear they were not to be mistaken for being willing partners in the age-old record company/music paper dance. They'd liked us when we were a true punk label (which in fact we never had been), but all respect for us went out of the window when we started issuing singles by people like Jona Lewie, and they now reserved the right to look down their noses on how we conducted our business. I understood and respected this policy but wished that, at the very least, they wouldn't sneer so much when I called. I took another deep pre-*NME*-phone-call breath, dialled the paper and asked what the chances were of Nick Kent coming out of the darkness to write about GP and his latest disc. To my surprise, features editor Roy Carr didn't start laughing. He even agreed that it was high time the *NME* ran an article on GP and then delivered the shocking kicker that, indeed, Nick Kent would be the perfect writer. I couldn't believe it. I'd blagged it.

Over the following days the line between my office and Roy Carr's desk at the *NME* lit up as a series of suitable venues for the meeting of the two great men were discussed, evaluated and discarded. My inquisitive mind began to wonder more and more about Nick Kent and who this man was who had so much respect but was proving to be so difficult to pin down. As we narrowed in towards a likely date, I even began to wonder what kind of man he could be. I'd never seen a picture of him. Every journalist I'd met from the *NME* came across like the poor cousin of every young journalist you've seen in a movie — not so much Nick Kent as Clark Kent. The one exception to this rule was Mr. Carr himself, who was older, had a distinctive comb-over and looked like he had once been a member of Acker Bilk's jazz band.

Finally, it was decided that the interview would take place at the Stiff offices, as Mr. Kent would be "in the area" on that day. GP arrived early as usual and I set him up with a coffee as the phone rang, "Nick Kent is in reception for you." I rushed out to meet the man I'd heard so much about.

Holy crap! Standing in front of me was none other than the eight-foot alien from Planet Rock who had strode so purposefully past me four years ago on Oxford Street as I'd gone for a job interview. As if to make sure that I absolutely recognised him, Nick had helpfully turned up in exactly the same outfit in which I'd last seen him — black motorcycle jacket, skintight black leather jeans and boots that jangled. I could tell that this was not a good time to share my story of the part Nick had played in my showbiz career and ushered him in to meet GP. I quietly slipped away, happy that I had managed to make this happen. GP was ready to spill the beans with rock's coolest writer.

Fifteen minutes later, I wandered toward the lobby and found GP quietly drinking another coffee and reading the paper. There was no sign of Nick Kent anywhere. "What are you doing out here? Why aren't you doing the interview with Nick!"

"He's left," came GP's casual reply. "Said he had a 3:30 appointment at the methadone clinic up the road!"

To my relief, GP got a two-page article in the *NME* the following week. It wasn't a front page, wasn't exhaustive and perhaps didn't portray the passion for GP's music that Nick Kent's legendary Stones pieces had, but it was everything that Robbo had asked for. My job was safe for another week.

For many years afterwards, I regarded Nick Kent, for all the respect he held as a rock writer, as a desperate soul who'd lost the plot. I was not well disposed to the man. In an interview with *The Guardian,* he bared his soul: "I was four years on heroin and ten years as a registered methadone addict ... I was in the right place at the right time on the wrong drugs."

One morning in Heathrow Airport, I picked up a copy of his memoir, *Apathy for the Devil*, and found myself glued to its pages as I flew across the top of the world on my way home to Los Angeles. His resurrection in my eyes was complete when he shared his views on Joni Mitchell's sublime *Hejira* album, "For my money, this remains the most intimate and breathtakingly beautiful album released in the '70s bar none."

And so say I.

For the bulk of my time at Stiff, Kosmo Vinyl was Ian Dury's own PR man. The press office would take care of a request for a Dury album from an out-of-town paper, but Kosmo handled everything else to do with the press side of Ian's career. Then Kosmo went off to work with the Clash, and Dury's albums weren't selling in the same numbers as they had before, so my office got to pick up the slack.

I was nervous about working with Ian Dury * — he had a reputation — but I was happy to embrace the challenge. My most memorable encounter with Dury was because Stiff had signed Dirty Looks, a three-piece from Staten Island, New York. The band consisted of Patrick Barnes (handsome, slim) on guitar and vocals, Peter Parker

* Ian Dury is the only person I have known to have had a movie made about him and I was very nervous about who could pull off playing his persona and difficult physical peculiarities. I can't vouch for the accuracy of the story, but in *Sex and Drugs and Rock and Roll*, Andy Serkis absolutely nailed Ian Dury. For a good read and more about the life of Ian Dury I also highly recommend Will Birch's *Ian Dury: The Definitive Biography*.

(taller, tough) on drums and Marco Sin (rotund and laughing) on bass. Like all good bands they had a little bit of a hundred others in their DNA, yet they had a distinct sound. Their songs were three minutes long, with gritty guitar solos and great harmonies, and I loved them. I wanted them to be massive. And so, when the white labels of their new album landed on my desk, I set about writing the best press release I'd ever constructed. It took a couple of hours but, when I finished it, I sat back and re-read it and smiled proudly to myself. I thought it combined the right combination of zeal, enthusiasm and hard facts. I even made a point of describing Barnes' vintage Gretsch Chet Atkins model as his weapon of choice. In a world of Les Pauls and Strats and Telecasters, I felt this was a clever way of the band saying, "We're different."

I sent out the press release with albums and pictures to the papers and waited for the reviews. *Melody Maker*, *Sounds* and *Record Mirror* were all polite enough, but the *NME* — my bête noire — slated it. In the review, Paul Morley went one step further than merely hating the record: he waxed lyrically about the way Stiff had lost its way, was no longer run by people who cared about music and hired impressionable press lackeys who thought vintage guitars were cool. Morley, who later masterminded the "Frankie Say" campaigns, hadn't spared the bullets but off-loaded his entire stash of ammo in my direction.

I was gutted. I read it again and again and then I got angry and did something a publicist is not ever, ever supposed to do — I wrote a letter to the editor. I didn't care that Morley hated the album, that was his right, and though I was a bit miffed that he took issue with my press release, what really hurt was his barrage of insults against the people at Stiff — the artists who worked hard and stuck with Stiff because it was family, the foot soldiers, the generals and even Our Dear Leader — who worked six and seven days a week, regularly pulled 12- and 14-hour days, loved their work and, despite what Morley thought, were passionate about their artists in return. Morley had pissed all over us and I wasn't going to take it. Perhaps I should have waited to let my anger cool; perhaps I should have asked for advice from people who knew better. But I wasn't going to let my fellow slaves be maligned. I licked the stamp, banged it down hard on the envelope and thrust it purposefully into the letter box.

There then followed seven days of total regret. I knew I should have kept my mouth shut. To lose my temper with the *NME* was a deeply unwise thing to do.

The following Thursday I grabbed an *NME* the minute I saw one and flipped the pages till I found the letters column. My letter had been printed in its entirety, followed by a short, flippant, sarcastic reply, which read something like, "Ooh, did we touch a nerve? We're so sorry — Ed." I shouldn't have lost it, but I was glad that we'd stood our ground. I took a deep breath and returned to my work.

A few hours later, bent over my desk, working on another press release, I heard an uneven footstep in the hallway and a strange crinkling sound. I ignored it and kept on typing, but it got louder and then stopped. I felt a tap on my shoulder, turned around and was confronted by an enormous bunch of flowers quite literally larger than the person holding it. What in heaven's name...? Then Ian Dury's large head appeared behind the crinkly cellophane that contained the roses, daffs, tulips and more. He smiled.

"Lovely letter to the *NME*. Thanks for doing that. Nice one, Nige!" Dury handed me the massive floral bunch and hobbled out of my office.

CHAPTER 9

Do It Yourself

AFTER THE SUCCESS of *New Boots and Panties!!* Ian Dury & the Blockheads went back into the studio to record the follow-up. As Ian finished his album, a particularly novel marketing ploy was hatched, and I found myself mixed up in a dangerously bold crime that could have easily landed me in jail.

I always thought the title *Do It Yourself* was inspired by the first track on Side Two, the third verse of which starts with a typically wonderful Dury lyric: "Home improvement expert Harold Hill of Harold Hill..." Kosmo Vinyl claims that it was Ian's response to punk rock and the independent labels that flourished back then. (The album reportedly had a provisional title, *Durex*, which was a Dury nickname as well as a popular British condom brand. Stiff was renowned for its cheekiness, but perhaps promoting prophylactics was a bridge too far.)

Barney Bubbles, who designed the album cover, decided it should feature some of the ugliest wallpaper you've ever seen in your life. This piece of genius was taken to a further extreme level when someone decided there shouldn't be one sleeve but dozens of different ones. Eventually, the Crown Wallpaper company provided over 30 different patterns so that the album you bought and the album your pal down the street bought had completely different covers.

Stiff was not shy about releasing records in different formats: for example, different colours of vinyl or various 7-inch, 10-inch and 12-inch formats. It was a way of persuading fans to buy the same record twice or even three times. But producing 33 (or was it 34?) completely different looking sleeves was certainly pushing this gag to the limit. To bolster the marketing push for Ian's album, boxes of Crown Wallpaper's hideous product soon started arriving at the Stiff door.

A fiendish plan was hatched. Acres of wallpaper would be plastered all over the capital; on the morning of the album's release, London would resemble the sitting room of homes up and down the country. What's more, record stores around the country would be shipped a roll of the paper and asked to hang it on their wall the week of release. In another genius move, cans of "tartan" paint were produced and sent out.

And then Kosmo came up with an even better idea. "Why don't we plaster the walls of the *NME*, *Sounds*, *Record Mirror* and *Melody Maker*?"

...which is how I found myself shaking like a leaf beside a chain link fence on the south side of the Thames at five o'clock one morning with a ladder, a roll of wallpaper, a can of paste and a brush. There were three or four of us wearing white boiler suits, Doc Martens and sailor hats — an outfit Kos later described as *Clockwork Orange* meets *The Navy Lark.*

The chain link fence surrounded a miserable plot with unmowed grass and a shabby looking hut left over from the war years: the offices of *Melody Maker*. It seemed likely that the *MM* was again going to play a crucial part in furthering my career — this time as a jailbird. The plan was to hop over the fence, break in and plaster the office with the wallpaper. "Um, but, er, how can I put this? Wasn't this going to be breaking and entering?"

We got over the fence or around it — Kos thinks we had bolt-cutters with us and cut our way in — and we approached the seedy little building. A cab raced down the road beside the hut and sirens could be heard in the distance; luckily, they were racing to a real break-in in another part of the city and the sound faded in the distance. I was shivering. Was it the cold or the fear of being handcuffed and bundled into a cop car?

Kosmo's Kommandos approached the door, which was locked; this was a good wheeze, but it was starting to get serious and again the issue was raised, "Aren't we breaking and entering?" Kos replied, "Of course not. We're promoting!"

The only way we were going to get into those offices and do our business was to break the door down. Realising that we weren't extras in *The Italian Job* or *Guns of Navarone*, Kosmo finally saw sense and realised we couldn't promote Ian's record from a jail cell (though it did cross my mind that it might generate more column inches than splashing some wallpaper on a wall. I kept that thought to myself.) Kos came up with an alternative: "Let's wallpaper all the windows and every time they look out the windows they'll see it."

Fifteen minutes later we were slinking back over the river. I'd had enough and made my way back towards Stiff, but Kos and the rest of his Kommandos were built of sterner, cheekier stuff and went on to raid *Sounds*, *Record Mirror* and the *NME*.

In Kos's official report of the raid, he recalls, "The *Melody Maker* was not amused. The editor had gone ballistic and had a total freak-out; the staff had spent the morning working with all the lights on as if it were nighttime! As far as 'Britain's Longest Running Music Weekly' was concerned, I was Public Enemy Number One. I don't know if anyone went back to take it down, but I did not show my face in those parts for some considerable time."

I'd like to report that I had the balls to earn my stripes as a fully paid-up member of Kosmo's Kommandos and follow him on further raids across the city, but one sortie was enough for me. In shame, I was asked to return my boiler suit and cap (I had provided my own Dr. Martens) and was never asked to go into battle again.

CHAPTER 10

Another Nail

ROBBO HAD SHOT A MOVIE with Madness about their early days and understandably, as I had no contacts in the film world, had hired a "proper" PR outfit to handle the launch of the film. I was still working the music press side of things. I put on my best togs for the launch party, but attending a "do" where I was supposed to make sure everyone had a smile on their face and a fresh drink in their hands was, for me, about as enjoyable as a trip to the dentist. I took a big breath, grabbed a beer and launched myself into the room where the party was being held.

I didn't have the balls to walk up to strangers, so I concentrated on groups and individuals who I already knew, which is how I found myself in front of Don Snow, who was chatting with someone I didn't recognise. Don had been on tour with Lene Lovich playing keyboards, but I didn't know what he'd been doing since then.

Me: Hey Don, nice to see you. What are you doing now?

Don: I've just joined Squeeze.

Me: Really? That's fantastic news! I love, love, love "Another Nail in My Heart."

Apart from being another excellent tune from the band's writers, Chris Difford and Glenn Tilbrook, "Another Nail" was unusual in that the guitar solo occurred immediately after the first verse and chorus, rather than after the second verse and chorus. The solo itself was 26 wonderful seconds of six-string perfection, not because it was flash but because it had a perfect beginning, middle and end.

My nervousness at trying to be the soul of the party got the better of me, and I launched into an enthusiastic breakdown of the record, the unusual placing of the solo and Tilbrook's extraordinary solo. I sensed Don shifting from foot to foot; his drinking pal was sighing rather a lot and looking around the room for something else to do. I couldn't help myself. "And that phrasing at the end where he climbs upwards? Amazing! It's the best part of the record!"

Still not done, I foolishly left my best plaudit till the end: "And who knew that Glenn Tilbrook had that in him? I certainly never rated him as a guitar player before."

Don stopped glancing around the room for help and looked me right in the eye as he indicated his friend, who looked like he had accidentally swallowed three chunks of ice. "Nigel, meet Glenn Tilbrook!"

As the blood drained from my face, they turned away and went to chat with some attractive girls across the room. I felt as if I would piss myself.

CHAPTER 11

We Got the Beat

STIFF HAD SIGNED THE GO-GO'S, and I was going to be their press officer. The single "We Got the Beat" was lively, the cover was colourful and, even better, the band would be coming to Britain to tour with Madness. Instead of ringing up the papers trying to blag interviews for eccentric and introspective boy musos, I could dangle attractive girls from California in front of the weary press corps.

The band landed at Heathrow and made their way directly to the Stiff offices. Including manager Ginger Canzoneri, there were six of them, heavily jet-lagged and almost in tears. The band had a British co-manager; the deal was that Ginger would handle the logistics and the costs of their work in L.A. and the Brit would handle everything once they arrived in London. Just before they left California, he broke the news that he would not be coming and that he had not arranged so much as a cab or a single hotel room in the UK.

With no time to organise a backup plan, the Go-Go's were now in London — and up the creek. The beginning of their tour with Madness was a week away, at which point there would be a budget for food, per diems and hotel rooms. But how would they cope till then?

An emergency meeting was held in Stiff's production area. One brave soul in the Stiff team volunteered space for three of them and, being more generous than sensible, I put up my hand and said the other three could stay with me.

My apartment was a tiny two-room space above a butcher's shop just off Abbey Road, a half-mile from the famous studio. My flatmate David Whitehead, a future manager of David Bowie, had one room and I had the other. Mine was exactly the width of the length of my single bed; the remaining space was filled with guitars and my boxes of albums and singles. The three Go-Go's I was dealt — Ginger, Belinda and Charlotte — slept side by side on the floor and quite literally took up all the available space. Taking a trip to the bathroom in the middle of the night meant literally stepping over three slumbering bodies and then squeezing open the door to the minuscule hallway. Somehow, we all made it through the week. On the final morning, Ginger told me how grateful they all were and if there was anything I ever needed in the future all I had to do was ask.

A year later, they were racing up the charts and back in London headlining their own shows. I rang up to ask for two tickets for the London gig and was denied.

That's life in the rock and roll fast lane for you.

CHAPTER 12

Kitchen at Parties

STIFF HAD A REPUTATION for signing quirky artists, and Jona Lewie fit the bill. Early in his career, he had enjoyed endless trips up and down the length of Britain with second division outfit Brett Marvin and the Thunderbolts. Like the Rolling Stones, Eric Clapton and many other bands of their type, they'd risen from the outlying suburbs of south London playing the blues — a bunch of lower-middle-class English white boys trying to emulate the sounds of the Mississippi Delta.

Jona's arrival in the band didn't change their fortunes much; it seemed their big claim to fame was going to be a support slot on a British tour by Derek and the Dominos — until Jona wrote a song called "Seaside Shuffle."

"Seaside Shuffle" was a classic Jona Lewie composition and recording: three chords, some kind of squeezebox, various peculiar pieces of percussion and Jona's south of Croydon blues-wailing. Most of all, it was fun. "Seaside Shuffle" had what it took to be a hit record, but it initially flopped. On a second release, it clicked and peaked at a giddy number-two in the charts.

What made this all rather confusing for those of us who studied the arcane trivia of early '70s pop was that, while the performers on the track were the usual Brett Marvin and the Thunderbolts, the hit was credited to Terry Dactyl and the Dinosaurs. While Brett's career was on the slide, it seemed that Terry's was on the rise — though, of course, this being rock and roll, there was no one in the lineup whose *nom de rock* was either Brett Marvin or Terry Dactyl.

Jona went solo, signed with Stiff and watched his first releases disappear without trace. Robbo then called in ex-Brinsley Schwarz keyboard player Bob Andrews to breathe some magic into Jona's next release. Bob was not Dr. John, though deep down he wanted to be. Like Jona, he was a white boy who could play a rockin' barrelhouse piano and had a ready smile. Robbo had connected two very English men who played piano, who'd travelled up and down the M1 a thousand times going to gigs and who wanted to break into the charts. Bob ploughed through Jona's demos and was particularly taken with an unusual tune called "You'll Always Find Me in the Kitchen at Parties."

The opening line captured what it was like to be a lonely guy at a party: "I'm no good at chatting up, and I always get rebuffed," and the chorus concluded with "You'll always find me in the kitchen at parties." In a few short seconds the heartbreak, stress, confusion and unrequited lust of a million singleton partygoers had been encapsulated in song. Jona and Bob's love of barrelhouse was still somewhere in the mix, but rather than an old piano sound from the 1930s, it was played on a bubbling, urgent, modern synthesizer. There was an outside chance this could be a hit.

The British music scene at the time was ruled by the charts, and the fortunes of every label in town pivoted on the fulcrum of a Tuesday morning deadline when the BMRB (British Market Research Bureau) would publish the list of the previous week's top-selling records. Over at the BBC, all the label pluggers would wait like excited children outside the office of a man named Michael Hurl.

Hurl was arguably the most powerful man in the British record business at the time because he was the producer of *Top of the Pops*, the TV show that was watched religiously by every man, woman and child in the country who had even the vaguest interest in popular music. The show was broadcast all over the British Isles on Thursday evening; whether you lived in the north of Scotland or at the southernmost tip of Cornwall you could watch the hottest bands of the day mime to their latest hits. On this particular Tuesday morning, Sonnie Rae, Stiff's bubbly blonde plugger, was waiting outside Hurl's office when word came through that, thanks to a lot of radio play, Jona's record had jumped from nowhere into the Top 20. Michael Hurl wanted Jona to appear on *Top of the Pops*, and what Michael wanted Michael got (unless your name was the Clash, in which case you told him to piss off).

Jona's invite to appear on that week's *TOTP* was great news for Jona, Bob and everyone at Stiff. But Sonnie had a problem. While Jona was in the country, ready to rock and booked on *TOTP*, which would be recorded in the BBC Television studios in Shepherd's Bush the very next day, the bad news was that Jona didn't have a band.

Phone calls were made. Bob Andrews would play the boogieing synthesizer, Bob's pal would play drums, someone's girlfriends would sing the backing vocals and Jona would be in the kitchen at his party. But who would play bass?

What they needed was someone who could play bass, wouldn't cause a fuss, was available the next day, could make his own way to the BBC studios, was a member of the Musician's Union and had his own instrument. What happened next made me weak at the knees and realised an impossible dream that never ever, in my wildest thoughts, had I imagined would come true: I was hired to appear on *TOTP* with Jona, Bob, Bob's mate and the two cute girls. All those years of miming to records in front of the mirror pretending I was in a real band had finally paid off — I was going legit and would be miming to a record on national television as if I were in a real band. And if that wasn't enough, I was also going to make the outrageous sum of £65 for my troubles — the MU minimum for such an appearance.

The next afternoon, I found myself in the *Top of the Pops* studios as dumbstruck as any fan. This was the very same studio from which I'd seen performances by the Beatles, the Dave Clark Five, the Shadows, Tremeloes, Swingin' Blue Jeans, Rolling Stones, Dusty Springfield, Cilla Black, Small Faces, Free, Elton John, David Bowie, T. Rex, Mott the Hoople, Alvin Stardust, the Sweet and a thousand others. And now it was going to be me up there, too.

I knew I was faking it and not a real member of the band. I hadn't done a real gig with Jona and didn't even know the part properly. I didn't have spangly pants or a problem with drugs, but I truly didn't give a fuck. Such was my immersion in music that all that mattered was that I was going to be on *TOTP*. How or why I'd gotten there was completely and utterly irrelevant. I'd dreamed a dream and amazingly, miraculously — if accidentally — it was all coming true! I hadn't got there on my terms, it wasn't one of my songs, it wasn't even my band, but I didn't give a shit. I was going to be on *TOTP*, and I was going to give it all I'd got.

We did some run-throughs for Mr. Hurl's cameras. We were herded around the place like so much cattle, and I was in heaven. The tatty stage we played on, like all the stages there, was about the size of a postage stamp, but who cared? I put on my best pair of jeans with Jam-like turn-ups I'd sewn myself, a clean black shirt, a stupid white tie and some shades. No one was there to tell us what to wear — we all supplied our own wardrobe. I even got sent to makeup: two minutes in the chair with some nice ladies who'd seen it all and had pink fluffy pads that put powder on your face. Like greeters at a wedding, they smiled nice and kept the line moving, kicking you back out into the corridor very fast as there were other bass players who needed some work before *they* appeared in front of the nation's public — and some of those guys were actually in real bands.

I don't remember much about those frantic three minutes of my TV debut, but I tried to look as totally cool and completely legitimate as I possibly could. Foolishly, instead of channelling the spirit of Donald "Duck" Dunn or Paul McCartney or Bill Wyman, I was trying to look as if I fitted in on *TOTP* along with that guy from Mud or that bloke from Paper Lace. In the end, I don't suppose anyone but my closest friends and my parents noticed — I was in the back behind the drummer, behind the cute girls, behind Bob and behind Jona. But I WAS on *TOTP*.

The minute the song faded we were ushered off stage into the darkness, where we milled around with all the young girls who always danced unconvincingly to undanceable songs on *TOTP*. One came up to me, blushing, with her pen and autograph book. She was giggling helplessly.

"Can I have your autograph, please?"

"You want Jona's autograph, not mine. I'm just some bloke who works at the label."

She looked confused and stopped giggling. I was about to launch into a long description about how the business of show business really worked and then realised she didn't care a toss. Here was my 15-year-old self in female form wearing a dress and holding an autograph book. In her eyes I was a pop star and she wanted my autograph. Who was I to deprive her? Instead of scribbling the illegible half-second scrawl of the seasoned pop-star who has to fight his way through fans at such events I composed a thoughtful and reasoned mini-essay and signed it carefully. My cover was blown — real pop-stars didn't act this way, and my biggest fan was getting impatient — I was stopping her from getting a signature by some dude in a spangly suit who really did have a problem with drugs who was passing by. She grabbed the book and was gone.

In an instant nothing had changed but everything was different. Instead of fighting off the groupies in the BBC bar afterwards I'd enjoyed a quiet drink with the rest of Jona's band before driving home alone with nothing but a big smile on my face. Next morning, I was back in the office, and Robbo wanted his 65 quid appearance fee back. I said no, and to my surprise he relented. I knew now that, whatever happened in my life, I had enjoyed one great moment and, if obscurity called, I could handle it. I didn't really want to be famous so much as I wanted to do thc stuff that other successful musicians did — playing gigs, recording music and being on *Top of the Pops*. In my own way, my dreams were being realised. I suppose when I look at it now I did something that even the Clash never did. And how cool is that?

And then the impossible happened. Over the next two weeks, Jona's record climbed and climbed again and 14 days later my return to obscurity was delayed as we all made our way back to Shepherd's Bush and did it all over again. Now I was a blasé, seasoned pro. I waved a friendly wave to the man in the uniform at the Beeb's car park like I'd been doing this for years and joked with the ladies in the makeup room. I *was* a bit miffed when no one asked me for my autograph — word must have gone around: that chap with the bass guitar isn't really in the band you know, don't waste time with him.

I don't remember much about the second appearance either except that one of the cute girlfriends was replaced by another cute girl, Kirsty MacColl.

Jona had another hit, and it was a monster: "Stop the Cavalry." A scratch band needed to be put together to support Jona on *Top of the Pops* — but this time with a twist. Bob Andrews' production featured a tootling brass band, and it was decided that the band would be assembled — not from real brass players — but from various rock and rollers hanging around the Stiff offices. And they would all be kitted out in World War I uniforms. Unbelievably, I was headed back to the BBC studios once more. There were no girls this time; the lineup featured Bob sternly pounding a keyboard, Will Birch from the Records and the Kursaal Flyers on cornet, John Otway on snare, Walter Hacon from Wreckless Eric's band playing trombone, Simon Climie on horn and yours truly tootling on a huge tuba. I hadn't gotten lucky during my first two appearances on *TOTP* but at least I'd been wearing tight jeans and had had one interaction with an autograph hound. Now I was dressed like an old soldier and wearing a uniform made out of itchy and smelly old blankets, so the chances of chatting up girls in the bar in the interval were nil. But I did get one lingering close-up in the middle of the recording, and rather than look like a serious player from a proper brass band I foolishly decided to channel Benny Hill. After it was all over, I quietly pocketed my 65 quid MU fee, again refusing to return it to Robbo, and drove home to tell my friends who were very impressed that I was somehow becoming a bit of a regular on Britain's foremost music TV show.

Incredibly, the gods of light entertainment were not done with me, and my career on *Top of the Pops* was not yet over. Nor had it reached its nadir: for around the corner, hidden till this point from view and lying in wait, was a band called the Snowmen.

No one seems to be clear how the Snowmen came to be on Stiff; I suspect that everyone involved is simply in denial. We liked to believe we were involved with promoting the careers of credible artists forging the new pathways of popular music. But then one day you show up to work, and you're asked to promote the Snowmen's new recording of "The Hokey Cokey." You groaned as you played it for the first time, for it was that most terrible of things — a novelty record — and the worrying thing about novelty records is that they have a nasty habit of becoming hits. I sighed, set to and wrote a press release and invented names for the three Snowmen — Bob, Blob and Splodge — and rushed them off, in their Snowmen suits, to the park to take some snaps when a convenient snow shower fell on the capital. I sent the pictures and the press release off to the papers and washed my hands of the whole affair as, quite obviously, the record was crap and no one would buy it.

Except everyone did. It went in the charts, and the Snowmen were invited to appear on *Top of the Pops*. The chief Snowman was delighted to accept Mr. Hurl's invitation and decided that a three-piece Snowmen wasn't going to cut it on TV. A fourth member had to be recruited tout de suite. And that's how the televised lineup of the Snowmen became Bob, Blob, Splodge and Dick. The WW I outfits we'd worn when promoting Jona's "Stop the Cavalry" itched, but at least you could see what you were doing. The Snowmen outfits, which had probably been stitched together by someone's mum, looked good from the outside but were lacking thc crucial and practical eyeholes. As I accepted my mission to once again Beetle over to the Beeb and perform on *TOTP* none of this seemed to matter until, as I was slipping into my Snowman suit, I learned that I was expected to dance and learn the choreography the other three Snowmen had perfected. As it was dawning on me that I wouldn't even need my two minutes of powdering with the lovely ladies in makeup, I was hit by the realisation that I was going to look like a complete idiot on TV in front of half the nation, stumbling around, looking like a huge marshmallow with a plastic carrot for a nose. My first appearances on bass with Jona now seemed akin to playing with Springsteen at Madison Square Garden. I was quite happy that no one would know who that fourth Snowman was. "The Hokey Cokey" ("Hokey Pokey" in the U.S.) usefully explains the choreography as it goes along, "You put your left foot in, your right foot out..." This might have been the solution to my problem, but when the cameras rolled there was clearly a Snowman on the right who didn't have it together at all. When Bob, Blob and Splodge put their left foot in, Snowman number-four was desperately trying to figure what position "in" was.

After our three minutes of TV time were through, we were asked to leave before we melted. It wasn't till I got home and looked in the mirror that I realised I was covered in white fluffy polyester furry bits and obscurity was pulling me back into its warm embrace. I never appeared on *Top of the Pops* ever again.

But Jona wasn't done with me yet. Little did I know that he would play a crucial role in the next phase of my career. Bob Andrews was no longer in the producer's chair, and Jona was slipping back to his old ways. He had penned a number called "I Think I'll Get My Hair Cut," which Pete Silverton reviewed in *Smash Hits* and described as "unexciting." It had some of the same ingredients as "Kitchen at Parties," but that wasn't going to be enough to get it into the charts. Alan Cowderoy pulled me into his office. "Nige, you like taking photographs, fancy making a video for Jona?"

For some reason, I had developed an attitude about people who wanted to direct, which was stupid and a bit like the guy at the merch table harbouring resentment about the lead singer in the band he worked for. But Alan was one of my bosses, and his lighthearted offer was really an order. What the hell, perhaps it would be nice to step away from the merch table and get in front of the band.

The only problem was that I didn't have the faintest clue how to direct. Luckily, there was a men's hairdresser across the street from my flat, so filming commenced in there. Jona sang his song, and the barber pretended to cut his hair. Our second location of the day was a club south of the river. Being short on experience, I leaned heavily on cameraman Chris Morphet, who was shooting the video for me. "What's happening here?" Chris asked me. "Well, er, um ... there's Jona ... and then ..."

"I tell you what," said Chris. "I'll pop a zoom on the camera and we'll do some handheld stuff while he sings. How's about that?"

"Yeah, that's brilliant! You read my mind."

And so it came to pass that my first directing job, "I Think I'll Get My Hair Cut," is now available on YouTube. However, if there'd ever been a credit roll it should have read "Directed by Chris Morphet (with agreement from an indecisive newbie film producer who had no clue what the hell he was doing)."

CHAPTER 13

Welcome to the House of Fun

MY CAREER IN THE PRESS OFFICE had been a mild success. I was diligent but frankly uninspired. As work piled on, I obtained an assistant, Fiona Grimshaw, who was wonderfully inspired, enthusiastic and energetic. The minute she walked into the office I knew my career as a press officer was cooked. Another label reached out — did I want to become their press officer? There would be a nice raise in pay. I turned them down. I knew PR work was not my career path, but apart from staying with music what was I going to do?

Robbo supplied the answer. One Thursday afternoon, he told me I would now produce the videos he was directing. Come Monday, I was a film producer on set, working on a video for Madness.

The making of videos at Stiff, long before the advent of MTV, had occurred organically. Presciently, Robbo had figured out that by making a video clip he could control how an artist's new release could be presented to the public in a new and powerful way. Also, for a small company without access to serious funds, it was a clever way to promote its investment. Stiff's records were being released around the world on a number of labels, and our stalwart International Manager Alan Cowderoy presided over licensees in Europe, the Far East and Australasia. Trying to control the new release of a Damned single in Greece or a Jona Lewie album in Sweden was a task requiring infinite patience and much tact. For a start, there were no e-mails, just the bulky telex machine, hidden in a dank corner of the office, which churned out rolls of bumpf at all hours of the day and night. At some point, it became obvious that when a new record was released it had to be released simultaneously worldwide.

It was always a great help if the artist could appear on TV to promote the record in its first week. Of course, you couldn't get Madness into a TV studio in Melbourne, Sydney, London, Paris, New York, Munich, Amsterdam and Athens all in one week unless you had a time machine or some film and, in the end, it was cheaper to make a clip than it was to fly seven mischievous young men around the globe. For Stiff, the music video was not so much a luxury as a vital necessity.

Robbo was directing most of the clips Stiff produced and, after using various outside production teams, had decided to take that in-house as well.

Madness were the most notable beneficiaries of Robbo's policy and directing style. Their Marx Brothers demeanour and his unique approach created some of the first remarkable moments in the history of music video.

And, so it was I showed up on Camden High Street to work my first day as a "Film Producer."

Silly me. I had no clue what a film producer did apart from something I'd read about some bloke who'd produced some '60s epics, in which he'd said, "A film producer's job is to make sure the crew get hot meals on set." As I shuffled over to greet the crew on that Monday morning, I had no idea how the film crew had been assembled, who did what or how much they charged. And I certainly had no idea how I was going to get them hot lunches that day. The minute I showed up, a lively young fellow introduced himself as the camera assistant. "Robbo's ready to shoot. Do you have the stock?"

What the hell was he talking about? "Stock? What's that?"

"Stock! You know, film stock ... the stuff that goes in the camera."

"Oh! Is that what you call it? Don't you bring that?"

In two years as press officer I'd overseen dozens of stills shoots, and that kind of cameraman always brought his own film. These guys were obviously lazier and had someone do it for them. Jeff Baynes, the director of photography (DP), muscled in on the conversation and solved the issue. He had an unexposed roll of 16mm film in his car. We could start with that. Meanwhile, I was given the address of the Film Stock Centre in Soho and some useful technical info as to what all those numbers on the yellow paper stuck to the side of the can meant. I raced back to my car, having learned my first important lesson.

Being thrown in at the deep end is a trite phrase that doesn't usefully grasp my naïveté about filmmaking on that morning, but it was typical of the way things were done at Stiff. You could reasonably say that much of what we did in those days was amateurish, but you learned fast, and if you didn't learn you were quickly spat out of the exhaust pipe. Rules were being broken constantly, but fresh new ideas were appearing and, though there were battles ahead with the standards folk at the BBC and other institutions, our lack of knowledge was also our greatest strength. I look back at my early work now and see far more adventurous ideas being attempted quite simply because I didn't have a clue how difficult it would be to try and execute them. Experience can be the death of innovation. I can't tell you how many times, while trying to come up with an idea for a video, I have killed the idea at birth because I've thought, "We'll never get that done in a day." Sometimes you don't know until you try.

Once I bought the film stock, that first video I worked on, "Cardiac Arrest" by Madness, was completed without fuss and made its way to TV sets around the world. My first few weeks in the film biz had been a steep learning curve, but I didn't have to speak with the *NME*, so that was a huge bonus. I felt a lot happier.

"House of Fun" by Madness was next on the slate. The song details the tribulations of a young man who has just come of age, is feeling lucky and needs to purchase some prophylactics: "a box of balloons with the featherlite touch." Robbo planned to shoot for a day in Great Yarmouth at the fun fair — to which I was not invited for some reason — and in London's Camden Town. There was no script, treatment or shot list, just some scribbles on a piece of paper in Robbo's pocket and a bunch of ideas in his head, some of which he chose to share with me, most of which he didn't. As we finished one scene, Robbo turned to me and said, "We'll be shooting in the chemist's shop next. Where is it?" What chemist's shop? I had 15 minutes to find a location — preferably within walking distance.

I rushed outside, took a gamble and turned left, ran down the street, turned left again and crashed into an old lady coming out of a chemist's shop on the corner. If not for the old lady I'd have run right past it. I ducked inside and breathlessly approached the man with greying hair in the white coat behind the counter.

"Can I help you sir?"

"I'm looking for a film location. A chemist's shop. Just like this one."

"When are you thinking of filming?"

"Er ... um ... in 15 minutes?"

"And what will that entail exactly?"

"Not much. Just a bloke with a camera, a bloke with a sound machine and ... um ... a pop group!"

"Well, as long as we can remain open."

"How much would you charge?"

"A thousand pounds."

"A THOUSAND POUNDS?!!!"

"Fifty?"

Delighted that the shop owner had talked himself down in two seconds from a grand to a reasonable 50 quid, I peeled off five tenners and went to find Robbo and the band.

"House of Fun" shows Madness at their best, and that has everything to do with the band and the way Robbo directed them. By this stage of the band's career, each member had developed an on-camera personality and, as a consequence, achieved something very few bands can accomplish — they were entirely original, wrote their own songs and appealed both to hip scenesters and five-year-old kids, who adored them. They were the people's band, massive all over Europe. "House of Fun" became the band's first number-one record. (If you look at the video carefully, you can see the owner of the chemist's looking a bit miserable, walking through the background, checking that no one in the band had half-inched a bottle of cough medicine.)

The video was a real success, yet I still had no clear idea what a producer did. I was in charge of fetching sausage rolls, sourcing costumes, finding locations and props, buying film, driving it to the lab and producing tenners from my back pocket as required. The most confusing part of a production was the conversation with the chap from the film-lighting company deciding whether we needed the small van of lights or the big lorry. Robbo wasn't just economical in sharing details with me, but also with cameraman Chris Morphet, who would try and help me decide what should be in the back of the van or the lorry. As there never was any advance discussion about budget it didn't really matter what choice we made, but we knew there would be hell to pay from Robbo if we got it wrong.

Just as crucial about what I was learning at this point was what none of us knew or cared about. Location agreements, release forms, insurance coverage, child labour laws, health and safety, union payments and company markup were things we'd never heard of. In fact, it was our ignorance of such things that made Robbo's work so wonderful: that kid wandering into the shot as the three Maddie boys trot into the liquor store, the laughing kids chasing the camera, the gran looking out the window are all wonderful moments that happened by accident and no one cared. Also, no producer or grip in his right mind would nowadays allow a cameraman to take a heavy film camera handheld on a fairground ride without a proper tether or a rehearsal of some kind — especially one that goes upside down! Filmmaking this way was, in many ways, literally madness. No film school was ever like this. It was enormous, if scary, fun.

And then came Madness's "Driving in My Car." There was a commercial on TV at the time which featured a Japanese man in a suit against a white background talking about the VW Jetta, "Number-one imported car in Japan. Tough as old boot!" As he talks, the car falls into the shot from the ceiling and bounces as it lands beside him. Unfazed, the man climbs into the car and drives off.

Robbo's idea was to recreate the car-dropping scene in the Madness video and have Lee, the sax player, emerge from the engine compartment playing his sax. "Driving in My Car" opens with the line, "I've been driving in my car, it's not quite a Jaguar..." so we decided that the car featured in the video would be a Morris Minor coupe, a reference to the early days of Madness's career, when they used two Morris Minor vans to transport their gear to gigs. So, as well as getting hot sausage rolls on set, I was now going to be the stunt coordinator.

During my time at Bath University there were many column inches in the local paper about a character dubbed Champagne Charlie. Charles Ware (his given name) was an artist and property developer who'd made his fortune, provided Roxy Music with a van to start off their touring career and then lost everything in the financial crash of the mid-'70s. He then took a peculiar career turn and started refurbishing decrepit Morris Minor cars — a passion he followed for the rest of his life. The Charles Ware Morris Minor Centre is still in business today, even though Charlie is no longer with us. So, when Robbo tasked me with dropping a Morris Minor from the roof of a film studio, I knew exactly who to call. Charlie and I came up with a quick plan — we'd need two outwardly identical Morris Minors, both painted white, one in working order and the other with no engine in it. The engine-less Moggie would have a T-shaped steel beam welded into place where the seats should have been with a hole drilled in the T at the car's centre of gravity. After the shoot, the engine-less car would be consigned to the scrap heap, and the working car would be sold back to Charlie Ware, minus a reasonable rental fee.

To film the car dropping from the ceiling of the studio we'd rented I needed two other things: a crane and a high-speed film camera. Rather than a camera crane, we got a building-site crane that would stick its jib in through the studio door and lift the engine-less car up to the roof. The high-speed camera came from Pinewood Studios with its own operator and would shoot up to 200 frames per second. The stunt had to be performed with some sense of urgency; otherwise, the camera would run out of film before the car could drop.

The bloke from Pinewood, who might have been called Geoff, was very experienced, had worked on a bunch of James Bond films and appeared with his camera and a side order of attitude. As he set up, he asked who was in charge of stunts and firing the quick-release bolt. Stunts? That would be me. Quick-release bolt? What's that? I had to explain that I had never produced a stunt before and had come up with a far simpler, if a little more rudimentary, plan. My idea was to put on the crash helmet I still had from my motorcycle messenger days, put a Stanley knife in my back pocket and shimmy up the crane jib from which the Morris Minor was dangling from a hook secured in place by a piece of rope. When I yelled, "Turnover!" Geoff's job was to turn on his high-speed camera while I sawed through the rope with my knife and let gravity handle the rest. It made perfect sense to me.

Geoff was appalled. "What? I want nothing to do with this, guv. Very unprofessional! I'll set the camera running and go outside. I'm brushing my hands of this. It's all very dangerous, very unusual."

As Geoff continued to grumble to anyone who would listen, I told everyone to leave the stage and put on my helmet. I huffed and puffed my way up the crane jib to where I could easily saw through that rope. I yelled at Geoff to turn on the camera. He yelled, "Rolling!" and sprinted outside of the studio, hiding behind the crane with everyone else. Now it was just me in the studio 20 feet off the ground with no safety net, a dangling car and a Stanley knife. I started sawing furiously but the weight of the car was pulling that rope super-tight and the knife was not making an impression. I sawed harder. I tried climbing the jib a bit. I was sweating now, frightened I'd drop the knife...

Suddenly, the strands started unravelling on their own accord, the line broke and the car plummeted earthwards, crashing onto the white studio floor with a loud bang, depositing rust everywhere.

There was silence. Nobody moved. I yelled "Cut!" and Geoff and the rest of the crew came running in. I yelled to Geoff, "Did we get it?" He gave me the thumbs up. I slid down the jib and clambered onto the ground. Geoff came running up to me and shook my hand. "We did it, guv! WE DID IT!"

We? I'm guessing that Geoff told that story a hundred times to the lads at Pinewood. And I bet he always missed out the part where he said, "I want nothing to do with this, guv!"

The next job couldn't have been more different. We were going to make a video for an artist who wasn't even on Stiff.

I had been given five pounds as a gift one school holiday and bought *Led Zeppelin II* and a black corduroy hat. I bought the album because I'd seen a boy at school with a copy tucked under his arm, and I bought the hat because Donovan wore one. When I got home, I pulled the album out of its sleeve, placed it on the record player and during the next five minutes and 34 seconds, as "Whole Lotta Love" played, my life was completely transformed.

I loved the Beatles and everything that the soundtrack of the '60s had brought for me but now I'd found a music that not only made me sing along and tap my foot but also spoke to me deeply. Perhaps there was a bit of teenage lust attached, perhaps some early rebelliousness creeping out, but most of all what I discovered in those grooves was an emotion that would define my musical tastes for years to come — a sense of yearning, a feeling of unattainable emotional nirvana just out of reach that would take decades for me to realise I would never find. I suppose now that what I had found in amongst those backward guitars, wailing vocals, awesome drumming and guitar breaks was the blues, and there was no going back. From that moment on music was no longer a part of my life — it *was* my life. I found that all of my frustrations and anger and yearnings could be expressed through music

— especially if it was played really loud!

Listening to Led Zeppelin, then Free and all the bands I discovered afterwards allowed me to become the person of my dreams that I couldn't be in real life. As I cranked the volume and closed my eyes, I could be as mystical as Robert Plant, as sexual as Paul Rodgers, as widdly on guitar as Jimmy Page, as cerebral as Paul Simon and as down to earth and rockin' as Rory Gallagher. At any moment, I could put on a record, and I was suddenly free of earthly constraints and gravity and could float away into a universe where I was a fabulous musician, a fantastic singer, girls adored me and everything made sense. That Zeppelin album had such a pull on me that my next purchase was the first Zeppelin album which, if anything, I enjoyed even more, and played it until you could practically see through the plastic to the other side.

As the band's career ploughed onwards, I bought every record they made but mostly felt it was an investment of diminishing returns. The rush from hearing those first two albums was so great that each consecutive dose of the Zep drug couldn't match the initial highs. Yet, even so, I remained a righteous disciple of the band.

And then Robbo told me that we would be shooting a video for Robert Plant, who was releasing his first solo album. Plant was a big fan of the Madness videos and wanted Robbo's magic touch to launch his solo career with the single "Burning Down One Side."

We had to go and meet the Golden God himself to discuss details. Robbo's car was out of action, so we climbed into the back of the van owned by Stiff's current art director, Simon, who moonlighted as a drummer. The vehicle had only one seat — for the driver — so Robbo and I slid around in the back as we made our way across London to a tasteful boutique hotel behind Shepherd's Bush.

I tried not to be too star-struck as we shook hands with Plant and went through details for the shoot. I asked if he had any special dietary requirements and if he would need a menu for food on set. "What will the crew be eating?" he asked. I told him, "McDonald's probably." Quick as a flash he responded, "OK. I'll have that then."

The meeting was over and, as we got up to leave, Plant asked us where we were going. Perhaps we could give him a lift? Robbo, Simon and I looked at each other in embarrassment and explained our van had no seats — hardly fit transport for a man who travelled on tour through America in his own Boeing 720 airliner known as the Starship. Plant pulled his coat on and delivered his verdict: "I used to work all day on a building site in Birmingham and then travel to London in the back of a transit van sandwiched between some amps and Bonzo's drum kit to do a gig before driving back up the M1 at three in the morning. You think I don't know what it's like in the back of a van? Come on. Let's go!"

From that moment, thanks to Robert Plant, I began to formulate my simple rule for gauging rock-star attitude. If you've done a real job before stardom beckons — brick-laying, working in a factory, cab-driving, pulling pints, policeman — you will carry your down-to-earth attitude with you as you hang with royalty, step out of limos at awards shows and fly around the world in private jets. But if you go straight from the schoolroom to the stage and success, you will have no idea what real life is like, and you will be forever doomed to looking over your shoulder for your assistant and whining like a small child.

One of the scenes in Plant's video would be shot in a restaurant, but when we got there we had a major problem on our hands. Plant's guitar player, Robbie Blunt, was indisposed and would not be able to deliver the scorching solo in the middle of the video. I can't remember if it was Robbo's idea or mine, but I was soon racing back to my flat to pick up my much prized £50 Jedson Les Paul copy. I was about to join Plant's backing band and deliver the scorching solo!

And so it was, dressed as a waiter, with bandages wrapped around my head, I found myself leaping onto the table and trying my best to mime to Blunt's solo. As I stood there playing my guitar, looking down at Robert Plant, I realised that for five minutes one of my impossible teenage dreams had come true: if that was Robert Plant and this was a Les Paul in my hands (OK a cheap one), then surely I had become Jimmy Page!

If you want something badly enough — really badly — it will come true ... but never in the way you imagined.

In the era before MTV, Madness made more music videos than probably any other band in the world. So, along with their greatest hits album, *Complete Madness,* Stiff would release a compilation of their videos, also entitled *Complete Madness.* Our normal record distributors, EMI, could not handle VHS duplication, so Robbo ordered me to track down the best facility in London that could handle the huge number of tapes we would need and, most importantly of all, could guarantee security of the master tape. Robbo had every reason to be concerned about security — videotape bootlegging was rife, and illegal copies of the latest hit movies were commonly available in street markets just days after they'd been released. For a small company like Stiff, the *Complete Madness* release was going to be a wonderful economic windfall. Robbo wanted the profits from those sales in the Stiff bank account and not in the pockets of market traders.

I made a list of every duplication plant within a hundred miles of London and, after eliminating some of the smaller ones, made a shortlist which I arranged to visit in person. One of the first was a subsidiary of a prestigious and very well-known firm in the British film industry.

After a short wait I was greeted in the lobby by a well-dressed man who was in charge of sales for the plant. He looked down his nose at my Doc Martens, my leather biker's jacket and my earring, but his manner changed abruptly when I told him we were intending an initial run of 60,000 tapes. When I voiced Robbo's concerns about security, he told me, "Mr. Spielberg and Mr. Lucas do all their duplicating with us, and I can assure you that security and quality are our two top priorities." As we toured the plant, I saw copies of the *Star Wars* movies and most of Spielberg's output, along with tapes of all the latest films. At every point in the process the salesman was eager to share that Mr. Lucas and Mr. Spielberg were very happy with how his firm executed their duplication work.

The process of duplicating VHS tapes was straightforward but time-consuming. From a climate-controlled booth a two-inch master fed the video and audio signal to a hundred numbered VHS machines in the adjoining room; they recorded the programme in real time. At the end of the programme, the hundred VHS machines would stop rolling and a worker would eject the hundred tapes, placing them on a trolley in numerical order. The tapes would then be trundled over to Quality Control where, in batches of ten, the end of the tapes would be tested for picture and audio.

The tapes would then be rewound to a random point in the middle and tested again and finally rewound to the start to receive a final audio and video test. If the tapes were good, they would be slipped into sleeves and shipped off to the distribution warehouse. If a tape was defective, the tape and the machine that recorded it would be double-checked and replaced or repaired as necessary. The Quality Control section was operated by a blue-haired lady in her sixties, a lovable granny figure, who looked as if she'd just stepped out of Central Casting.

As we walked through the plant, the Sales Manager explained the complex quality control procedure and how the hundred VHS machines operated and how the lovable granny double-checked the tapes...

"This is Dorothy who, as you can see, is now rewinding ten tapes to a random point in the middle of the programme to double-check quality. She'll see pictures on those ten screens and also this big monitor here. Mr. Spielberg's people were particularly impressed with our quality control when they first came through the plant."

At that point Dorothy hit a button and the ten VHS machines stopped rewinding. I heard a series of clunking noises as the ten VHS machines at her side started pulling the tapes around the drums. Suddenly the ten video screens in front of her shimmered as each screen played back images from the random point where the ten VHS machines had stopped. On each screen, an extremely fat, naked and very white woman was bent over a desk in an office while a tall, thin, naked Black man shagged her from behind with his pants around his ankles. As the lady's pendulous breasts rotated in circles over the top of the desk, she shouted enthusiastically, "Fuck me, fuck me! Harder, harder!" The Black gentleman was obviously very kind and obliged her every wish.

Dorothy seemed quite unfazed as she checked video and audio on every screen and then on the big monitor. I turned to the salesman and asked, "Is this one of Mr. Spielberg's films? I'm not familiar with this one!" The salesman quickly grabbed me by the arm and suggested we go through to the packaging department.

Despite my unfamiliarity with *Big Girls at Work* and my misgivings about its unimaginative cinematography, I decided that this was the best choice for our duplicating needs. I negotiated a good deal for our initial run of 60,000 copies, but Robbo hijacked my week of research and threw it in the bin — he'd met a guy at the racetrack, and his company would be taking care of our duplication needs.

CHAPTER 14

Lucky Number

IN EARLY 1983, I'd just come back from a chilly Christmas holiday in Philadelphia, where I'd spent every day watching a new cable channel called MTV. At Stiff, it seemed we were churning out videos every week. Robbo hired a second set of hands to work with me in the video department: John Mills, a lovely man with proper filmmaking experience. Utilizing that old ploy of hiring two people to do the same job but not letting either one of them know who was boss, Robbo obviously had some kind of plan for the future. But what was it? Luckily, John and I got on well, and the work got done without any manoeuvring for power. For a start, we spent one whole night building a prison set in the Stiff garage for the latest Madness video.

The next job was for Tracey Ullman which, thanks to John, was a carefully planned shoot. The morning after, John and I were chuckling about the previous day's dramas when my presence was requested in Robbo's office. I found Robbo crouched over his desk with a pencil behind his ear in exactly the same pose he had been in when I first met him five years earlier. He barely looked at me as he said 13 words that destroyed me: "You're going to be leaving us, Nigel. What are you going to do?"

There was no further discussion, no reason given for the firing. Fifteen minutes later I was out on the street, sick to my stomach. In many ways, working at Stiff was abusive but, like most people who find themselves at the end of a one-sided dysfunctional relationship, I felt lost when it was suddenly over and wanted back in. Working at Stiff had been hard, but it had also been enormous fun. A large chunk of my identity had been wrenched away from me when I walked out the door with a box of personal stuff into a miserably wet morning in Camden Town.

In five years under Robbo's harsh regime, there were times when I answered back and stood up for myself and called Robbo on his bullshit. On one occasion, Robbo complimented himself and the company for being able to churn out a music video for a very cost-effective ten grand. I'd added up the costs and, thanks to Robbo's determination to roll cameras all day long and expose and develop miles of film, I knew that the final tally was in fact twenty-six grand. I called him on it. Whether he was in denial or whether I'd failed to walk the party line it didn't matter — I drew a dark look from him. I was tired of the games and was speaking my mind. Robbo didn't like it, and now I was out of a job.

And then the phone rang. It was my buddy Andy Murray, now at Phonogram Records. Soon I was taking an interview with their legendary A&R guy Chris Briggs. Briggsy was aghast at the money his label was spending on making videos and had nobody who understood how the process worked. Would I fancy joining the company specifically to look after videos? Could I start in six weeks? I had been gifted a lifeline. But what to do for the next six weeks?

And then the phone rang again. Bruce Kirkland, the slow-talking Aussie who ran Stiff Records in America and managed Lene Lovich, had a vacancy for a T-shirt salesman on Lene's tour of the States, which was just starting and would last for six weeks. Within a few days I was stepping off the plane at JFK with a big smile on my face. I had a new job at Phonogram waiting for me with a decent raise and a shiny new car thrown in, making me one of the first people hired by a major UK label specifically to look after music videos.

I'd threatened to take Robbo to the Industrial Tribunal for unfair dismissal; we'd settled out of court, which had resulted in a few quid in the bank and a shiny new VHS player in my house. And now I had a gig to travel right across the U.S.A. It was a God-given chance to visit many parts of the States I'd never seen, and all I had to do was sell a few T-shirts.

It was a chilly March evening as I climbed onto Lene's bus in Poughkeepsie, New York, and learned why they'd chosen me to join them on the road. We all knew each other but, more importantly, as Bruce pointed out, we all had one special thing in common: the band, the road crew, the publicity woman, the road manager and the sound guy had all, like me, at some point in their career been fired by Robbo. It was a badge we wore with honour, and it would hold us together as the endless miles rolled ahead.

Lene's tour meandered around the East Coast for a few weeks and then moved southwards towards Texas and on to L.A. then up the coast to Seattle before my last gig with them at Western Washington University in Bellingham. The following morning at breakfast I experienced, for the first time, the horrible feeling of loss when you leave a tour. Last night you were an integral part (albeit a small one) of the team; this morning, even though you have yet to say goodbye, you are just a visitor, and the band have subconsciously already turned their backs on you. It is a sad moment.

I don't know how effective I was as an on-the-road T-shirt guy, but I didn't get fired, I kept the books straight and I seem to remember considerably fewer cardboard boxes to lug around in Washington state than there had been in Washington D.C. It was a wonderful way to see the country and gave me a new respect for life on the road and what it does to the body and the brain.

I flew back to England deeply grateful to Lene and her crew and excited about my new job. I was going to be working for a major label.

CHAPTER 15

I'm Still Standing

Stiff Records had been a devilishly mischievous independent record label. It did its first years of business in a disused shop front on a street full of apartment houses and a pub, then moved into a drafty space above a London cab company down a back street before relocating to an old hat factory in Camden Town. Even when the company was selling a lot of records these were locations you would not want to stand outside on a dark night for fear of being robbed.

Phonogram, however, was in the heart of London's West End, a stone's throw from Oxford Street. Its entrance was shoehorned in amongst fine jewellers and high-end tailors, estate agents and auction houses. The only robberies that took place on this street were in broad daylight and were the huge rents being asked by the property owners.

Phonogram was the "gram" part of the Polygram group. Polydor Records was the "Poly" part; Decca Records, Deutsche Grammophon and a bunch of other labels were also part of the group. All of the Polygram companies were located in one building but, for an impression of independence, Phonogram entered on the street from the west side of the block, Polydor got the east entrance and Decca the south. The offices were connected in the centre of the block in a warren of stairs and elevators.

Whereas Stiff had nurtured and succeeded with misfits, petty criminals and rebels such as Ian Dury, Elvis Costello, Lene Lovich, Lew Lewis, Madness, the Plasmatics, Wreckless Eric, etc., Phonogram boasted some hugely successful mainstream artists when I arrived: Dire Straits, Def Leppard, Tears for Fears, Elton John, David Essex, Status Quo, Thin Lizzy, 10cc, the Boomtown Rats, KISS, Steve Miller. The stakes were higher, the budgets were bigger and the pressure was on. There was only one guy in the video department now, and much was expected of him. That guy was me.

Chris Briggs, the head of A&R, gave me an assignment on my first morning. Big Country had made their first video, "In a Big Country," and he didn't like it. What could be done to rescue it? I rang the production company and was connected with a sophisticated female voice. The owner of said voice took me out to lunch to discuss our issues, and soon I was sitting across the table from the most elegant woman I'd ever met. She was cultured, well-spoken and, as I later learned, had had a very successful modelling career. Her name was Anne-Marie Mackay. As we shook hands, she held my hand long enough for me to be seduced — but firmly enough to know she was not to be messed with. At Stiff I had been used to dealing with roadies who'd done spells inside for robbery with violence. This was a distinct change in gears. After small talk, I explained Briggsy's concerns and asked what could be done. She reached across the table and touched my hand again. "Nigel, darling, nothing can be done — it's being finished right now in the telecine suite around the corner. Perhaps we should go and take a peek before I drop you back at the office."

Oh dear, it wasn't even tea-time on the first day and I'd already flunked my first test. Perhaps I could get something positive achieved before the end of the day. A call came down to my office — could I get a dub made of the latest Elton John video that needed be sent to a TV station in Germany pronto? This seemed a manageable task. After a secretive call to my pal Andy, I discovered that Phonogram did all of its dubs with Nick Maingay, a practical and efficient man with a dry sense of humour. "At last!" he cried when I called him up and told him who I was and what I was doing. "I've been begging them for months to get someone to control this video nonsense. What do you need?"

"Can you get me a dub of Elton's 'I'm Still Standing' by tomorrow morning please?"

"It'll be on your desk when you get to work in the morning, but it'll be a dub of a dub I'm afraid."

"Not good enough. It'll need to be a dub from the master."

"Aha — there's your problem, you see. Nobody has a clue where the master is."

"But surely..."

"Good luck with that master ... let me know how you get on."

I rang around the office and eventually was given a key to "the vault," which was in the basement, behind the boiler room.

The basement — filled with bric-a-brac, shovels and brooms — shook every time an Underground train passed directly underneath it. A bloke sat next to the boiler, smoking a cigarette, reading the paper and nursing a mug of tea. When I asked where the vault was, without lifting his eyes from the paper, he pointed to a door tucked in a corner. I had to move some boxes to get a clear view of it. I fiddled with the key, hauled open the door and was assaulted by fetid smells and dank air. I pulled a cord that dangled in front of my face, a light came on and I was presented with the sight of film library hell.

The massive pile of rubbish in "the vault" extended from my feet right up to the top of the ceiling at the back. On top of this sloping pile were the broken frames of rusting gold discs, an empty file cabinet, several cardboard boxes, a guitar case and the parts of two or three rusty bikes. As my eyes adjusted to the semi-darkness, I realised the pile of rubbish was not rubbish per se, but rather consisted of video boxes, video tapes, spools of film, audio master tapes, unsold albums and at least one dead rat. The filing system had been simple but effective: open the door, throw a video master as hard as possible at the back wall and slam the door ASAP before the pile of previously "filed" video masters tumbled towards you.*

It took me weeks to carry those tapes up to my office and start filing them properly. The collection was amazing: Thin Lizzy live at the Sydney Opera House, 10cc's "Good Morning Judge," Status Quo on some German pop show. They came in every possible format: 16mm, 35mm, PAL, NTSC, SECAM, two-inch tape, VHS, Beta, Video 8 and so on. The filing itself took me till the end of my first year with the company. That Elton John master? We never did find it. Nick Maingay later confided in me, "I think the master was sent to an Austrian TV show and is sitting gathering dust in a Viennese backstreet somewhere."

The people at Phonogram were much like those at Stiff: fun to work with and crazy about music. I began commissioning videos, but the first time I walked onto a set I was shocked. What were all these people behind the camera doing? As well as the producer, there seemed to be one person who was just looking after clothes, another person with an assistant who was handling the art department elements; there was someone called an AD (Assistant Director), another person taking stills, a locations person and, oh my god, the luxury, another person whose sole responsibility was taking care of snacks, lunch, coffee, tea, etc. They even had people called runners who did a lot of dashing off the set to pick stuff up and clean up at the end of the day. At Stiff, these were all jobs I'd taken care of on my own. I hadn't done it to save money or look for plaudits — I just didn't know any better.

I was gaining experience fast and learning as much about the hierarchy of the music business as I was learning about what happens on a real set. While I was dealing with the middle-range and lower-range acts, the really big ones like Elton John and Dire Straits didn't feel the

* Over the last 40 years I have frequently gotten calls asking me for footage of the various jobs I'm known for to use in a documentary or other production. Firstly, I have to explain that I don't own the footage and that the enquirer should contact the label. Inevitably, they call me back within a week or two asking if I have any idea where else the footage might be stored, as the label can't find it. At this point I share the story of the bloke reading his newspaper and the dark room in the basement with the old bikes and the dead rat.

need to deal with the video department at all — they went straight to directors and had the label pick up the bill. They not only didn't tell me what was going on, they made it clear I wasn't welcome. When I showed up at a preparatory meeting for our biggest act, the oh-so-successful guitar player who'd been raised on England's northeast coast asked who I was. "I'm your rep from the label," I replied. "Who gives a fuck?" he sneered, and a management person stepped forward to quickly usher me out.

The British Musician's Union had decided that they didn't like videos very much and insisted that anybody who played guitar on the original track had to play the guitar in the video ... and they were much happier if that guitar player was British. In addition, notice of filming had to be compiled onto an MU form and filed with the MU within 14 days of the shoot — if not, the video could not be shown on British TV. While this might have made sense to a trombone player with the Northern Dance Orchestra who'd been an MU member for 30 years, it made no sense in the modern world where the guitar player might have been a session guy in Los Angeles and the drummer was a Canadian who was now on tour with someone else in Australia and wasn't available to fly back to the UK just for a video. It was also likely that the session guitar player, while being a studio pro from L.A. who was able to dash out a killer solo in two takes, was not "camera friendly," and the band and label would much sooner use a slimmer, more dashing plank-spanker who lived in Basildon in the video. As a consequence, not knowing when a video was taking place and not being informed who had played on the track became constant thorns in my side. Some powerful managers saw me as a meddling desk jockey who was best avoided. I got the distinct impression that my contact at the MU didn't believe some of the information I was filling in on those MU forms — and he was right to be suspicious, as I was frequently forced to make it up. That part of my new job was not fun.

Brian Shepherd was our managing director; his second in command was a lovely man called Tony Powell — the kind of chap you'd want to have in your lifeboat if you'd just clambered off the Titanic and watched it sink. I imagine he would have said, "Never mind, Dicky, grab an oar! New York is only a few weeks paddle west of here, let's get cracking."

Tony called me into his office one day and played me a track by a Scottish band called Friends Again. "I have £2,000 squirrelled away that no one knows about, do you think we could make a video?" I did some quick calculations in my head and figured it would cover a cameraman, a sound guy, a few rolls of film, processing and an edit suite for a few days. "I could take them to Camber Sands for a day and bang something out." Tony gave me the go-ahead. Two weeks later I played him the video, and it was approved without any changes. I was soon making a low-budget video every month or so for some act that didn't justify a real budget. It was fun, and I was learning how to direct, but word got out, and it did not go down well in the now ever-more-professional and business-like music video community.

One night, while working as the client on a shoot for a new Phonogram artist being shot for us by the largest video production company in London, a belligerent young director who'd dropped by the set and had had too many drinks came blundering over to me and got in my face. "Who the fuck are you? You think you can direct? Fuck you! You're just a bloke from a fucking record company! Stop giving yourself all the jobs! Fuck you!" The shoot came to a halt as he was quietly dragged away by the producer, who came back to apologise. His point had been made, but as I was essentially using my Stiff experience shooting jobs myself that didn't have budgets, which couldn't have been made by third-party production companies, I felt he didn't quite understand what was going on. To his credit, the drunken director sobered up and later went on to marry a movie star and make some successful movies.

Brian Shepherd wandered into my office one Friday and noticed the painter standing on a ladder sanding the wall and prepping the office for a paint job. My desk and everything else in the office was covered with a fine white powder.

"How long is this going to take?" Shep asked.

I wiped some dust off my pants. "They've promised me it will be done by the end of next week."

Shep walked me over to his big corner office, the one with the huge desk, all those gold records on the wall and the amazing view down Bond Street. "I'm on holiday next week, make yourself at home till the painters are done. Here's the remote control system for the videos and the stereo." He called Stephanie, his secretary, over the intercom, "Nigel's going to use my office next week while I'm away. Look after him!"

"Shep, I can't use your office...." I was lost for words. My desk was a cheap office unit measured in square inches — his desk was plate glass and measured in acres. "Of course you can," he replied and gave me a conspiratorial wink. "Have some fun!"

On Monday morning I turned right out of the elevator instead of left and sheepishly said good morning to Steph, who asked if I'd like a coffee as I tiptoed into Shep's office and settled behind that vast desk. For the next few hours heads poked through the door, looking for Shep. I bashfully explained, "Shep's away, so he's ordered me to use his office while mine's being painted." "Lucky bleeder," they all said and grumbled away.

Steph's voice came over the intercom. "Anne-Marie Mackay on line one." It appeared that Anne-Marie was still talking to me after the embarrassing Big Country incident. She said she had great news.

"I have this fabulous new director in town from the States just for a few days and I'd love you to meet him over a nice lunch."

"Anne-Marie, you know I don't do that. Just send me his reel and I'll check it out."

"But I've told him all about you and he really wants to meet you. His name is Jerry Casale."

"Like the bloke from Devo?"

"Yes. He *is* the bloke from Devo."

Remembering Shep's conspiratorial wink on Friday night, try as I might I just couldn't resist the temptation. I looked at my diary, which was completely blank, and made an "I'm really busy" kind of noise.

"I have 15 minutes spare tomorrow at 11:30. Does that work?"

"Perfect!" she said, "We'll see you then."

The next morning at 11:25 the Stephanie's voice came over the intercom. "Anne-Marie Mackay and Jerry Casale here to see you."

"Ask them to wait, I'm on a call."

I wasn't on a call at all but made a point of spending the next ten minutes admiring the view down Bond Street and making sure that all those gold discs were perfectly vertical. While I gave that huge glass desk another polish, I remembered back to the moment I'd handed over those Devo suits to Kellogs after racing up half of England in a couple of hours and the way the band had marched off without saying a word. I also remembered the disappointment on Conroy's face when he told me that the band had refused to leave the van when they saw the outside of the hotel I'd found for them. Most of all I remembered the days and days driving Alan Cowderoy's Golf, filled with every copy of Devo's first release, across London so they could be specially packaged and then returning to drive every newly packaged disc, all 50,000 of them, back to the EMI factory for distribution.

I asked Steph to show Anne-Marie and Jerry into "my" office. We reached across that huge desk, shook hands and sat down. I had to assume that Jerry was at least a tiny bit impressed by my view down Bond Street and all those gold discs.

"Nice to meet you," said Jerry.

"Actually, we've met before." Jerry seemed surprised.

I related the story of the forgotten Devo suits and the young underling who'd driven like a Formula One champ up England's spine and hadn't even received a thank you from the boys from Akron. I didn't want to rub it in ... but, actually, I did want to rub it in, and I couldn't help myself from milking it.

We watched Jerry's reel, which was very impressive, but I never gave him a job. It wasn't revenge, it was simply that Jerry's work was very left-field; I couldn't think of an act on our roster at the time who would've benefited from his vision. I actually wished that I *could* have given him a gig.

For a time, I would tell my Devo story to anyone who would care to listen — always amping up the scenes where Jerry Casale, Mark Mothersbaugh et al. had treated me with such disdain and the time I wreaked my revenge. It was a very smug tale with an almost impossibly perfect ending and I loved telling it.

One night, years later, in L.A. I was invited to the Viper Room to see a show by Tal Bachman, whose chief claims to fame were the facts that he was Mormon, had about eight children and his dad Randy had sung "You Ain't Seen Nothing Yet" over and over again with his two friends, Turner and Overdrive. The younger Bachman was about to release a single on Epic and needed a video. Thus, my presence was requested at the infamous Hollywood hangout so I could watch TB rock and be inspired. At the required hour, I showed up at the Viper Room and tracked down the label person who said, "There's someone I think you should meet," and took me to a dimly lit corner where I soon found myself sitting in a booth with none other than Mr. Casale — the other director being considered for the gig. Any sensible human being might have been tempted to button his lip and watch the show, but I couldn't contain myself and felt it necessary to share the story with everyone else at the table while the unfortunate Mr. Casale sat next to me and was forced to listen to yet another telling of my days with Devo. To his credit, Jerry said very little and his slight smile when I was finished spoke volumes.

Jerry, if you should ever read this, I apologise. What I did at that gig was very tasteless of me and I've promised myself I'll never tell that story again.

I was starting to feel at home at Phonogram. Tony Powell was a wonderful man to work for; instead of being shouted at with orders that made no sense, I had an understanding boss who would discuss what we needed to do and was fulsome with praise if I got something right. Even better, he never once rang me in the middle of the night asking me to go and look for his car.

One day he called me into his office and asked me to sit down.

"We've got a bit of a problem with these low-budget videos you've been making for us." My stomach sank. "People are liking them more than the expensive ones you've been commissioning. How do you fancy doing some Quo videos?"

Status Quo were the UK's most unlikely superstars. Their career had got off to a great start in the '60s when they had a hit with "Pictures of Matchstick Men." Publicity stills of the era show them in mod jackets and trousers with carefully puffed haircuts that would not have looked out of place on Dusty Springfield or Cilla Black. For a brief spell, they were up there with the Hollies, the Swinging Blue Jeans, etc. They'd slowly disappeared from view until the '70s came along and they were suddenly back on the charts, though now completely unrecognizable. Where everyone else wore stage clothes, they wore real life: old sneakers, worn jeans and tired waistcoats nicked from Dad's wardrobe. Their hair was no longer long and puffed, just long and shaggy. Their songs were catchy as hell, totally derivative, completely lacking in any sophistication — and they were proud of it. In an interview once, lead singer/guitarist Francis Rossi said something like, "Every time I sit down to write a song, if I come up with something new or original I put down my guitar and wait for it to pass." If you had picked four navvies off a building site south of London, given them guitars and a Chuck Berry *Best Of* to listen to and told them to write songs, you could have come up with Status Quo. But they were brilliant. The kids loved them, and so did I.

I think that if a gas pipe had exploded on Bond Street at that moment, demolishing the building and killing me off, I wouldn't have minded a bit — my life would have been fulfilled. Status Quo weren't the Beatles, the Stones or even Freddie and the Dreamers, but they had more cred perhaps than any band of their era. They smoked ciggys, they drank, they wore jeans, they knew five or six chords — but never used four chords when three would do. They were hysterically funny and fun to be around and, more importantly, had a bullshit meter that could spot a numbskull at a thousand yards. Other folk learning their trade as a director might have turned up their noses at an offer to work with the mighty Quo. I saw it as a high honour.

I shot two videos for the band, and I'll admit neither of them are award-winners, but I was learning more and more with every job. And I got to blow up a shitload of Marshall amps on "Mess of the Blues." This directing lark was turning out to be a lot of fun!

But some jobs were easier to pull off than others...

CHAPTER 16

You Don't Love Me

IT WAS 7:00 P.M. ON A SUNDAY evening when Marilyn's manager called me at home.

Marilyn's image was half-boy, half-girl. He sported long blond locks and often wore a woman's shirt with perhaps something feminine over the top. From the waist down he frequently wore jeans. It was a brilliant and original look. He was known to hang out with Boy George and, as of that Sunday evening, had released two excellent singles on Phonogram. Neither had broken through and, in the previous week, I'd made several vain attempts to hook him up with a director to shoot a video for his third. On Friday his manager sighed in frustration, and we agreed to tackle the problem again the following week, as the release of single number three was just two weeks away.

On Sunday, Marilyn's manager had a new plan. "Can you shoot a video for Marilyn tomorrow?"

This was an impossible request. There was no studio booked. We didn't have a cameraman. We didn't have film purchased. We didn't have a cast. We didn't have a mag track of the single prepared for playback. Come to think of it, we didn't have a sound guy to play the mag track we didn't have, and we didn't have a makeup person, wardrobe, lights, catering, etc. Oh yeah, and one other thing — we didn't have an idea!

The manager's voice brought me back to the present fast. "Marilyn is flying to Australia on Tuesday afternoon. Perhaps you could go with him and shoot some extra footage while you're Down Under. We need to have a video completed by a week on Wednesday."

This was a ridiculous request. He was asking me to turn around a video in ten days and throw in a quick round trip to the other side of the world in the middle of it. And at 7:00 o'clock on a Sunday evening, in a world where cell phones still hadn't been invented, it was foolish to even think of starting a production before 9:00 a.m. on Monday. In short, it was insane and also impossible to pull off. I said, "No problem, I'll make it happen."

By 11:00 the following morning I had a small crew assembled in a studio and was looking at wardrobe options as a DP and gaffer set up lights. A messenger delivered the mag track, and my roommate and future film producer Phil Barnes arrived from Soho with a bunch of film under his arm. Without texting or e-mail, I'd somehow managed to get a location and a crew. We were setting up the first shot just hours after the manager's call. But I still had no idea what we were going to film — I was just going to have to make it up as I went along.

Twelve hours later, I drove the film out to the lab near Heathrow to get it processed. I got up early on Tuesday, packed a bag, raced to the office, cleared my desk of anything urgent and booked myself a round-trip flight to Sydney and Melbourne. The travel agent was very confused: "I think you've got the dates wrong. According to what you're telling me you'll only be in Australia for 48 hours before you fly back." Helpfully, she added, "It's on the other side of the world, you know." I reassured her I was not mistaken and got on another line to wake up a stranger in Melbourne who produced documentaries to ask if he could meet me at Melbourne airport in 36 hours and take me on a location scout to find a spot where I could shoot Marilyn.

"What exactly are you looking for?" he asked. "Don't have a clue, but I'll know it when I see it." I rushed out to take a meeting. When I came back there was a ticket to Australia on my desk. I grabbed my suitcase, ran out onto Bond Street, hailed a cab and told the driver to take me to Heathrow, where I met up with Marilyn.

Early the next morning I was woken by the harsh sunlight as we landed in Bahrain. After a layover in the desert, we were back on the plane. The next stop was Singapore, which we reached around 3:00 in the morning. I took a stroll around the airport and, having nothing better to do, bought a cheap Super-8 camera and some film in the duty-free shop. It was still dark when we took off for Sydney, had another layover and finally jumped down the coast to Melbourne. As we flew south on the final leg of the journey, I started shooting Marilyn gazing out of the window of the plane — it was my first gig as a director of photography.

We went through immigration and customs in Melbourne. Marilyn was delighted when we got outside the arrivals building and dozens of young fans rushed towards him with record covers to be autographed, asking to take pictures with him. I shot some more Super-8, shook hands with the confused Aussie documentary producer who had no idea who Marilyn was, climbed into his car and drove out of the city to scout locations as Marilyn was whisked away to his hotel.

I have no memory of what I saw in the next few hours. I'd just flown halfway around the world and briefly set foot in three countries and two continents I'd never visited before. I'd been wearing the same clothes for nearly two days, and I still had no idea what was going to be in the video.

I got back to Melbourne as the sun started to set. I staggered out of the doco producer's car, wheeled my bag into the hotel and bumped into Marilyn, newly rested and now beautifully dressed, going to an Australian showbiz do. I told him I'd found some great locations to shoot the rest of his video. "I don't want to do that anymore," he told me, waving his hands in the air. "Can't you just follow me around with your Super-8 camera?" I sighed in disbelief, staggered up to my hotel room and discovered I'd forgotten to pack any socks.

The next day, I shot Maz recording a TV show and doing interviews before we flew to Sydney, where there were more interviews to shoot. When Maz disappeared to sample Sydney's nightlife, I went to my room and collapsed. The next morning was Sunday. I woke late and had ten minutes to dash down the street to a small shop to buy some souvenirs before being picked up to go to the airport again to fly back to London. The shop was empty and quiet. The owner was busy behind the counter doing paperwork as I wondered which fridge magnet to buy. It was the first moment of free time I'd had since my phone had rung just a few short days ago and half-a-world away. The door opened and another customer walked in. He was tall and somehow familiar-looking. "Morning, Barry," said the shop-owner, and they started chatting. I looked closer. It couldn't be. Surely not? What were the chances? But yes, it was.

On my only moment of free time on my first trip to Australia in a quiet store around the corner from my hotel I'd somehow bumped into Australia's most famous export: Dame Edna in the flesh and off duty — yes, it was Barry Humphries! I took my fridge magnet and some other trinkets to the counter; Barry smiled at me and cracked a risqué joke about my purchases and the three of us laughed. Still not believing my luck, I left for the airport.

Exactly one week and one hour after that Sunday evening call from Marilyn's manager I walked into a London restaurant with my date. I'd just flown to the other side of the world and back. It was theoretically still the same day as it had been when I'd taken off from Sydney many time zones ago, but at least I was wearing clean socks again. I was totally exhausted but managed to ask my girl how her week had been. "Well, I hope you had fun on your holiday in Australia. It's been hell back here in the office."

And the video? It's a mess, but it was delivered on time and got a few plays. Sadly, Marilyn's third single didn't chart, and I felt sorry for him. Like his previous two singles, it was a great song but, for whatever reason, it didn't connect with the public. "You Don't Love Me" is still up on YouTube, where it can be seen in all its directionless glory — a memento of seven crazy days and an around-the-world trip I'll never forget.

CHAPTER 17

Do They Know It's Christmas?

ONE EVENING IN NOVEMBER 1984, the BBC News included an item from Ethiopia. I didn't see it, but Bob Geldof did. The report, by TV journalist Michael Buerk, described rampant famine sweeping across a country just a few thousand miles away. The footage purposely played on the emotions, showing children with distended bellies held in the arms of weakened and distraught mothers. In the background were masses of people dying from neglect and starvation. It seemed as if the reporter, so affected by what he saw, was daring the world to come up with an answer to this frightening and enormous problem. I'm sure that, as he filed his story, he never imagined that the man who would answer his call would be a shabby, loud-mouthed, opinionated but charming lead singer for a fading Irish punk band.

The Boomtown Rats had been, for a moment, the Beatles and the Oasis of their day. They'd had number-one hits and had reaped all the benefits that popular bands do: the babes, the limos and the bucks. But now their career was in the dumper. Bob Geldof was the most outspoken frontman of his time; journalists and the public had lapped up his bon mots and nicknamed him "Bob the Gob." He'd snickered and joked his way up the charts, dated the infamous Paula Yates and had even starred in a movie directed by Alan Parker. But he'd become a sort of cartoon character, had given his first daughter with Yates a silly name which made the press guffaw and stopped having hits. The public was turning its back on him.

At Phonogram, we couldn't turn our backs because Bob and the Rats were on our label and had a new album about to be released. *In the Long Grass* was supposed to be their comeback record. If the band had a manager I don't remember who it might have been because Bob was calling the shots. Like all good managers, he was on the rampage at the label, pushing us to get everything in line for the album's release. There were videos to be made (my department), a tour to be booked and press and TV appearances to be scheduled. Because the Rats were felt to be yesterday's news it was all an uphill struggle but, if anyone could do it, Bob could. I was thrilled when he asked me to direct the two videos he needed (even though I knew it was because the budgets he'd been given were paltry and no one else would do it). He even persuaded his partner Paula, presenter on the hottest music show on TV, *The Tube*, to twist arms and get the band on the show. Everyone knew it was hypocritical and nepotistic but somehow it was cool because Bob and Paula were larger than life and living together. And then he took an evening off and watched TV.

A day or two later, on my return from lunch, I was called into Tony Powell's office. Bob had apparently made the first of many passionate pleas that were to change the world. Tony explained the plan quite simply. "Bob saw this news broadcast about Ethiopia where thousands and thousands are dying from famine. He's going to make a record at the weekend, you're going to make the video which will be ready by Tuesday, the record will be available by next Friday and we're going to try and get it to number-one for Christmas. All proceeds will go towards famine relief."

It all seemed so simple: problem, idea, solution, result.

Bob must have had quite a morning. He had decided to make a

record for a song he'd not yet written and convinced his label, a staid German/Dutch multinational no less, to release it for no profit as a priority above all other releases to pursue the holy grail of British single releases — a Christmas number-one. He'd also found the time to ring Robert Maxwell, notorious publisher and owner of the *Daily Mirror*, to persuade him to guarantee the entire front page of the paper on the following Monday morning — a two-page spread inside was also promised. On that Wednesday afternoon, Bob sat in my office and explained the timetable once again. The backing tracks would be recorded on Saturday at Midge Ure's house, the overdubs would be done on Sunday with loads of stars, which is when I would shoot the video, and by the following Thursday (just eight days away) the video would be shown on *Top of the Pops* and copies of the record would be available in every record store in the country ready for the buying frenzy that would hopefully start on Friday morning.

He didn't have a band or anyone to sing the song he hadn't written. I didn't have a film crew or a budget for the video the BBC did not yet know they would be playing. There was work to be done. I had a spare phone in my office, and Bob used it to start what would become the most selfless, persuasive, determined and remarkable phone sales campaign that I will ever witness. He called presidents of labels and presidents of countries and blagged anything he could for free including, eventually, the use of the Suez Canal.

Bob was a tall man who seemed perpetually unshaven and sported an unruly case of bedhead that had remained out of control for years. He would pull his fingers through his hair, trying to force it behind his ears, as his piercing eyes lasered holes in your face. He wore wrinkled suits and embroidered red velvet carpet slippers. He'd quote facts faster than you could absorb them and say "fock" every three words and "shite" every five. He was earnest, passionate, sincere, conniving, funny and determined. He was the most alpha of alpha-males I've ever met, and he was like a dog with a bone. As you were becoming rather too impressed by him, he would laugh his ridiculous laugh from the back of his throat with quick and repeated intakes of breath that completely deprived him of his dignity. As a singer he had limited skills, but as a frontman he was supreme. Bob could be a pain in the arse, but he was also lovable — the perfect man for the job he'd just invented for himself.

As the weekend rushed upon us, all other work became secondary. I met Michael Kuhn, then head of Polygram Music Video. He told me that PMV would give me £10,000 to cover anything I couldn't get for free, but he hoped I would use as little of the money as possible. Everyone who was asked donated their goods or services completely free except Kodak, which was supplying the film stock. When Bob found out, he was furious and subsequently berated Kodak in public for being so miserly. (His anger paid off — Kodak became a major sponsor of *Live Aid*, the massive concert that took place simultaneously in Philadelphia and London the following summer.)

Charity fundraising records were an occasional novelty in the dying days of 1984. Everyone had heard of the *Concert for Bangla Desh* and *No Nukes*, but few people in London had been asked to donate their goods or services. To my astonishment, I found it easy to round up a crew of cameramen and assistants willing to work a day for free. My friend Dave Bridges would be the Director of Photography, and his company Tattooist would supply all the camera bodies and lenses. Visions, my favourite post house, threw in everything without question. So, apart from Kodak, I managed to put together the entire shoot without spending a single pound. It was really quite easy.

Bob had more to do and seemed to be finding it harder going. Midge Ure, onetime Ultravox singer and Thin Lizzy gun for hire, and Bob wrote the song. Linda Valentine from the Phonogram press office came up with Band Aid as a name for the project — but who was going to sing it? Bob was overwhelmed with maybes and if-I-cans, but the definite yeses were few and far between. Another concern was that none of the Black artists Bob approached were interested in participating. He didn't want to send a message that this was a bunch of overpaid white pop stars telling the world what to do — he wanted the message to be more universal.

In addition to rounding up the talent, Bob was stoking the fires of the PR bandwagon that he needed to give the project the necessary muscle. On Thursday, he rang Malcolm Gerrie, producer of *The Tube*, from my office. Malcolm was a hardheaded TV guy who later hit the headlines for being the guy Russell Crowe tried to beat up at the *BAFTA Awards*. As his partner and future wife was a presenter on *The Tube,* Bob knew Malcolm well, but he also knew that Malcolm was against the planned Boomtown Rats appearance that Paula had blagged for him on the show. Any negotiation for Band Aid would therefore need to be delicate.

Bob politely told Malcolm about the project and asked him to send a crew to cover the recording on Sunday. Malcolm was interested but needed to know who else would be there. Bob: "The BBC, ITV (news), CBS, ABC, NBC, Reuters, *The Times*, *The Mirror*, *The Sun*, *The Old Grey Whistle Test...*"

The Old Grey Whistle Test was the granddaddy of BBC rock shows. Malcolm's show, *The Tube*, was the hip, independent, mischievous antidote to *OGWT* and was on the enemy station. To ask *The Tube* and *OGWT* to cover the same event was like asking Putin and Zelenskyy to have their picture taken together. Malcolm balked, "If *OGWT* are covering it, then *The Tube* won't. It's us or them."

"Look Malcolm," Bob replied, "this is bigger than petty focking jealousies between rock shows, this is about life and death." Bob was getting upset and things were going to get ugly. Malcolm held his ground, "You know how it is, Bob. If they cover it, we can't. Of course we're interested, of course we'd like to help. This is a great thing you're doing but you'll just have to choose." For the first time, I saw Bob manipulate and gamble with all the chips for the greater good: "Listen Malcolm, Robert focking Maxwell has guaranteed Band Aid the front page of the *Mirror* on Monday morning and he's also promised me a focking double-page spread on the inside. On the left-hand page will be a list of all those people who've helped. On the right-hand page will be a list of all those who haven't. So far, you're the only focking name on the right-hand page!"

Bob slammed down the phone and leaned back in his chair. I cleared my throat nervously and looked at Bob. "Jeez, do you think that was such a good idea?" Bob shrugged his shoulders as my phone rang. "It's Malcolm Gerrie from *The Tube*. I need to speak to Geldof." Bob grabbed the phone and grunted, "Yes... OK... deal... absolutely. See you Sunday then." At the risk of alienating the only producer who would put the Rats on TV, Bob had staked it all to get the blanket coverage he demanded. He had managed to get *The Tube* and *OGWT* to cover the same event for the first time ever using the promise that when he later went to deliver the aid to Ethiopia, Gerrie would lead the only film crew to accompany him. Bob smiled as he put the phone down. "I've been waiting for some idiot to volunteer to do that!"

Come Saturday afternoon, I knocked on the door of an elegant house in Kensington. I was ushered through to the studio that Midge Ure had built for himself at the bottom of the garden. So, this was what pop stars did with their cash? Sting was there, Paul Weller, too. The track was taking shape rather nicely. There was nothing for me to do, so I slipped away, wondering what the following day would bring.

Sunday morning, the 25th of November, was clear and sunny as I arrived outside SARM studios. As a young rock fan I had pored over album sleeves, and this rather ugly building, formerly known as Basing Street Studios, was the Holy of Holies where many of my favourite albums had been recorded. Now I was being welcomed inside by Trevor Horn, who owned the studio. We had just passed through the summer of Frankie Say, and Trevor was the guy to have behind the desk if you were making a record. I was excited; I had passed some mysterious exam and had been allowed to participate in something at which many of my heroes might be present. But what if we were throwing a party and nobody came?

Once again, this was all Bob's responsibility, and he must have been worried. Pop stars are not the most dependable of folk, and who but the most optimistic and foolish of betting men would bargain on getting a bunch of moody pop stars out of bed to work for free on a Sunday morning? The tape was ready, the floor of the studio had been cleared, the press were congregating outside, and I had my three cameramen, their three assistants, a sound recordist and my long-suffering assistant Sarah Wills inside. All we needed was some talent.

Bob had primed his charges well. We got the call that Bananarama were approaching and dashed outside to get it on film. The initial dribble became a torrent as star after star turned up at the door — remarkably, many arrived alone, without managers, minders or other halves. The morning's arrivals included Paul Young, Paul Weller, Bono, Sting, George Michael, Marilyn, Tony Hadley and the Kemp brothers from Spandau Ballet, Simon Le Bon, Nick Rhodes, Andy Taylor and John Taylor from Duran Duran, Francis Rossi and Rick Parfitt from Status Quo, Jon Moss from Culture Club, Martyn Ware and Glenn Gregory from Heaven 17 and, of course, the Rats: Johnnie Fingers, Pete Briquette and Simon Crowe. Significantly, Bob had broken the white barrier he feared would tarnish the project — Kool and the Gang showed up along with Jody Watley. Bob was smiling in his newly printed "Feed the World" T-shirt. The first major hurdle had been cleared.

Everyone collected in the studio in a makeshift crescent in front of the mics as Trevor started teaching everyone the chorus: "Feed the world, let them know it's Christmastime again..." Within a short time, tape was rolling and work was progressing. With the chorus laid down, the press was allowed in to take pictures. I remember counting an incredible 72 reporters, photographers, cameramen and sound recordists there to get the tape, the picture, the close-up they all needed. We tried to hold them back as the tape rolled and the chorus mimed, but it was useless — everyone pressed forward trying to get a clear shot. I remember the Bananaramas looking worried as the snappers and shooters got within about two feet of them. I marked a line on the floor and shouted for silence. "Step over this line and I'll throw you out!" I yelled at the representatives of some of the world's greatest news organizations. "Ooooh!" murmured the stars, giggling at my rather stupid head-schoolboy-like threat. It was useless, and the press corps pushed forward until no one could get a clear shot. Eventually my assistant Sarah Wills and I raced across the street to a building site and stole a 20-foot plank to hold everyone back. We held it in front of the journos, who banged off their pics and were soon gone.

Less than 90 minutes later we were all sandwiched into the TV room downstairs. The lunchtime news on ITV featured the singalong and the story of Bob and Midge's effort as one of its lead stories. There we all were on TV already. Somehow it validated everything we were doing — if it's on TV it must be happening.

As it was lunchtime, stomachs were rumbling and one hapless pop star put our thoughts into words: "Is there any food, Bob?" There was silence as a cloud passed across Bob's face. We all stared at the hungry singer. "You're a fockin' millionaire and you want free food? There's a chip shop on the corner, buy your own fockin' lunch." The joy we'd all shared at hearing the voices sing that memorable chorus for the first time evaporated as we remembered why we were all here. The point was well made, and we returned to work.

Now began the job of laying down the individual vocals. Our first victim was Paul Young. The former frontman for the Q-Tips leaned into the mic: "It's Christmastime..." Midge suggested another way to sing the lines. Paul tried it again. Bob suggested another approach, and Paul tried it Bob's way. As I stooped alongside a camera at Paul's feet I heard Midge's voice over the talkback: "One singer, one song. Just do it the way you feel is best," and the formula for the day's work was decided.

Even then, recording studios were magical places — they allowed you to make the ordinary sound wonderful. Conversely, so many effects and techniques are applied to voices in the modern recording process that you lose sight of who can really sing and who's bluffing. Sitting there with the camera just feet from the singers who came in I heard all their voices unadorned for the first time. Paul Young's voice sounded strong, soulful and clear, just as you'd expect; Sting's seemed strangely out of tune on its own but then incredibly perfect in context; Bono's voice was like a wild emotional howl, unique and distinctive; George Michael amazed me with his control and quiet professional approach.

We'd been told that Boy George would be arriving in the afternoon — he was flying in from New York on the Concorde just to sing his two lines. There was doubt that he'd make it, yet suddenly he was there asking for a brandy to help his sore throat. His voice was a stupendous surprise, and I vowed to go home that night and check out my Culture Club records with a fresh perspective.

Most of the artists who stayed on for the afternoon's festivities were of a certain age and had enjoyed time in the charts during the past few years. As one, they all expressed interest in waiting for the arrival of one man who was scheduled to be the only musician to play that day: Phil Collins. I'd known Culture Club drummer Jon Moss since my time at Stiff and asked why he was hanging around so long in the afternoon. "Phil Collins is coming. I'm not leaving until I see Phil play."

With the lead vocals complete, Phil's kit was set up in front of the control booth, and he came inside to listen to the track. Heads dutifully bobbed as everyone grooved (or pretended to). Terse musical comments were made to establish a kind of rapport/pecking order. Phil was all business, no smiles, settled down at his kit and the tape and the cameras rolled.

There's much talk nowadays about living in the moment. I'd never heard the phrase in 1984, yet I can remember doing just that for the first time in my life. *This is an incredible moment I'm witnessing,* I thought. *Something this remarkable may never happen to me ever again. This is my "Woodstock moment" — remember how it feels.* I was sitting just inches from Phil Collins as he banged away in only the way that he can. As my cameramen circled his kit, Malcolm Gerrie's crew circled on the other side. There they are in the video — true to their word, they'd showed up and decided to do a special on the Band Aid recording, thereby trumping their rivals at the Beeb.

We wrapped at 11:00 p.m. Dave Bridges left for the *Daily Mirror* printing plant to shoot the front-page story coming off the presses that opens the video. All the footage we'd shot was processed overnight; on Monday morning, I made my way to Soho, and we started transferring the dailies to tape. That evening, I sat down with editor

Dave Gardener to start on the cut but, as the film was still arriving in dribs and drabs, we had to leave holes in the edit hoping that a missing close-up by George Michael, Sting or Boy George would arrive in time. Bob came by with the mixes of the track, and I was overwhelmed with emotion as I heard his final message on the B-side. In keeping with that emotion, I included a similar message at the end of the video. We finished the cut by breakfast on Tuesday morning. As the boxes were being labelled, I stumbled into the dawn and hailed a cab to take me home to bed. It was just over five days since I'd been told to make the video.

At 7:00 p.m. on Thursday evening, five minutes before the broadcast of *Top of the Pops*, the Beeb interrupted their normal programming. David Bowie appeared on the screen and introduced our video. I was stunned and, in that moment, pride got the better of me — for a second this wasn't about saving lives, this was about Bowie introducing a piece of my work!

Victor Hugo famously wrote, "There's nothing as powerful as an idea whose time has come," and Bob had certainly touched a nerve. The record raced to number-one and stayed there for weeks, becoming, at the time, the largest-selling single in British history and making millions of pounds. Before long, every country with a recording studio and a star was recording its own famine relief disc. Bob was asked to fly to L.A. to attend the recording of "We Are the World" by USA for Africa. He returned with a scowl on his face and told me that the session was well organised with backstage passes and the like, but he was distressed by the celebrity grandstanding and the huge tables full of catered food, which he felt was not in keeping with the spirit of the cause.

Bob's life was changing before our eyes. The Rats were touring, passing buckets into the audience at gigs to collect yet more cash for the Band Aid fund. Bob's passion and vision for his cause was turning him from a scruffy celebrity into a powerful spokesman who told the truth. As the Rats' career slid inexorably further down, Bob flew to Africa to check out the problems firsthand. On his return, he addressed the EEC in Brussels; news cameras caught him as he left the meeting still dressed in his velvet carpet slippers. Maggie Thatcher was seen on television shaking hands with the new darling of international politics. What they hadn't bargained for was a well-briefed, intelligent young man with a bug up his arse about the way Britain and Europe were idly sitting by watching millions die on the other side of the Med. Their conversation went something like this: "Mr. Geldof, we're all so terribly proud of what you're doing," she said, smiling that sickly, condescending Thatcher smile, but Bob wouldn't let her hand go.

"What are we going to do about the butter mountain?" he asked. "With your permission I could have all the butter stored in Europe made into biscuits and shipped to Africa within days."

Thatcher's smile was slipping. "It's not quite that simple, you know, Mr. Geldof, and I don't think this is the time or the place for this, do you?"

"Why not? People are dying as we speak!" I suppose people talk to Prime Ministers like that all the time — but you don't see it on TV. Bob was doing whatever it took to achieve what he wanted, and he didn't care who got in his way or who he was speaking to — his view was no one had voted him in so there was nothing to lose, he could say what he liked.

As the cash rolled in, Bob founded the Band Aid organisation, based in London, to help him get the money directly to where it needed to go. He avoided the usual agencies like Oxfam and was soon purchasing trucks to drive the supplies from the docks right to the heart of the famine. The trucks were then left in the area to assist in creating local work. Bridges were built; wells were dug. By the following Christmas, when the Band Aid record was released again, Bob asked me to do a new cut of the video using footage shot in Africa of the supplies being delivered. I added captions over the pictures, detailing the impressive list of accomplishments that the Band Aid money had brought to fruition.

Bob's newfound power was particularly noticeable when I next visited my parents. On a previous trip, I had arrived on their doorstep proudly sporting a newly acquired silver and black Graham Parker and the Rumour tour jacket. My mother looked down her nose at me and sneered, "So, I suppose you're a punk now!" not knowing that her bald, denim-clad son looked nothing like the mohawked, bondage-outfitted scions of the Kings Road. But now she worshiped Bob and all things Bob — the scruffy Irish singer was her new knight in shining armour. She'd showed her devotion to his cause by buying not one but two copies of the Band Aid single. Later on, when Bob's book *Is That It?* was released, she was first in line to buy a copy and hailed it as a great read. Quite what my mother, a woman who thought sex was an appalling invention, thought of the first line of Chapter IV ("Mrs. Armstrong from down the road was my first fuck.") was never discussed.

In the spring, Bob had another brainwave. He was going to promote a concert that would take place simultaneously on both sides of the Atlantic with a huge array of stars. TV stations would pay hand over fist for the rights, dial-in pledge lines would be set up and, again, all the profits would go into the Band Aid pot. The concert would be called *Live Aid*.

Once again, artists were afraid to commit. It was the summer of Springsteen's massive *Born in the USA* jaunt through Europe, and it appeared that everyone who Bob asked to appear on *Live Aid* replied, "If Bruce is doing it, then I will, too." Months on the road had worn Bruce down, and he, too, turned Bob down. But, realising he could start the ball rolling, Springsteen made a deal with Bob. He could tell everyone that Bruce was going to appear to make them commit. Then Bruce's name would be quietly withdrawn from the list of acts; hopefully, no one would notice. In addition, Bruce, who would play Wembley Arena the week before *Live Aid*, would leave his massive rig and staging up for Bob to use at no charge.

Bob was using the phone in my office less frequently, but one day he called President Hosni Mubarak of Egypt from my desk and secured the use of the Suez Canal for free in order to get some food through without having to pay the stiff canal duties. Bob was calm, persuasive, relaxed and got what he wanted — it was as if he was asking the local constable to help out with the school fête.

Bob wanted Hall & Oates for *Live Aid.* They were hot stuff in that summer of '85, and their manager, Tommy Mottola, refused to let his boys appear for free ... unless they could headline. Bob agreed instantly. Tommy smelled a rat (!) and asked why Bob was so eager to grant what must have been the spot everyone was asking for. "I've been looking for weeks for the band stupid enough to want to go on after the reformation of Led Zeppelin, after Mick Jagger and Tina Turner, after Queen, after Bob Dylan..."

I went to see Springsteen's gig at Wembley. He played for hours, and I shouted myself hoarse. Foolishly, I decided not to go back to Wembley six days later for *Live Aid.* Instead, I watched the show on TV. David Hepworth, the music magazine editor who served as the BBC's co-presenter of *Live Aid*, expertly guided the British end of things as we cut from the U.S. stage to the UK stage and back. Things seemed to be going quite smoothly, and the music was great. But, as Hepworth smoothly filled in a gap between artists, Bob was having none of it. He swore on live TV, rammed his finger hard into the table in front of him and yelled, "Give us your money now!"

Various revamped versions of the song and the video we shot have been made over the years. Each time, a little bit of the sheen has been rubbed off the original; the enthusiasm for trying to help those in need has diminished. Bob called it "compassion fatigue" and eventually refused to be a part of anything like Band Aid or *Live Aid* again. A new generation of critics have come along who sneer at the original song, especially Bono's line, "Thank God, it's them instead of you." In December 2016, I opened *Billboard* to find a review of the record by Andrew Unterburger: "Band Aid's 'Do They Know It's Christmas?' (is) an ultra-hyped act of '80s celebrity selflessness that comes off today as an exercise in coke-fuelled arrogance and imperial ignorance — but shit, what an outro!"

I wrote to him, chastising him for his baseless drug reference. To his credit, he apologized. But, for me, he'd caused great harm.

I've even heard that Bob himself does not think much of what he achieved that wintry day so long ago, but I have to disagree with him and all the other critics. Is it so bad to want to try and help? Who knows how many lives those millions saved? If it saved only one life, and it was surely many more, then we did a good thing. It is possible, probable even, that some mistakes were made distributing that money. By all accounts, many walls had to be climbed or knocked down, but I believe it was as efficient and well-managed (if not more so) an effort as what many relief agencies at the time provided.

In 1997, my dad sent me a clipping from the *Daily Mail.* It read, "Thirteen years ago, Band Aid asked the world to feed Ethiopia. Now Ethiopia is selling food to the EC. The African nation has developed so much since the biggest names in pop music came together for a benefit record and concert that it now has a grain mountain which is threatening to drive world prices to rock bottom ... Ethiopia's remarkable turnaround was due to Band Aid and *Live Aid*'s financial assistance, practical aid, good rains and the fall of state monopolies, which made equipment cheaper and fertilizer more readily available." I don't know what struck me the most — the fact that Band Aid had helped to turn around the fortunes of an entire country or that my dad, the retired squadron leader who was not a lover of any music recorded after 1945, had sent me the cutting.

Thirty-seven years after that crazy day in Notting Hill I was invited to take part in a Zoom call as part of Band Aid's publicity for the billionth viewing of their YouTube channel. Midge Ure, one of the other participants, told us that Band Aid was still making around $250,000 a year, which was going to schools and other projects, and that, after all this time, the organisation, while borrowing other people's conference rooms and hijacking photocopiers, had still never opened an office or paid for its own telephone.

I haven't seen Bob Geldof for years. At times I found him to be a difficult, stubborn man who was opinionated and loud. However, I doubt I will ever meet a person for whom I could have more respect. As later events have shown, his capacity for forgiveness and compassion is beyond description. His determination was astonishing, and his selflessness was so blind it destroyed the career of his band. Saint Bob? Sir Bob? Just Bob? I don't know which moniker is most apt, but whenever I'm asked what video I'm most proud of, I mention Band Aid. Perhaps it's not beautifully shot, and maybe it's not the best directed or edited video in the world, but it saved lives and put food in the mouths of thousands and thousands of starving children. Every other video I've ever directed has only put food in my mouth, which we can agree is not quite so noble an achievement.

CHAPTER 18

Everybody Wants to Rule the World

ONE OF THE FIRST BANDS on Phonogram that I met were Tears for Fears. They were the darlings of everyone in the office, but I dreaded meeting them because I'd heard their first album (*The Hurting*) and didn't like it much. Someone had tried to excite my interest by saying they were rather like Pink Floyd when you saw them live, but the only image that stuck in my head was of Curt Smith, the slightly smilier one, looking glumly out a window and whining about how it was, all things considered, a very mad world.

Going into a meeting with Curt and Roland Orzabal (the other one, who really did seem to be miserable) with a chip on my shoulder the size of an LP wasn't going to go very well if I couldn't find something in common with them. Further examination of the details revealed that they were both ten years younger than me; in my eyes, they were practically children. Oh, hell — it was getting worse. But I also read that they practiced screaming a lot and had issues with their parents, so maybe it wasn't such a lost cause — and we did have something in common after all. Then I made a breakthrough. Curt and Roland came from Bath, and I'd spent four years at university in the same city. We were practically cousins!

Curt and Roland never seemed to give a damn about whether I'd spent my whole life in that fine Georgian city. They concentrated entirely on how brilliant their next video was going to be, which, under the circumstances, was perfectly reasonable behaviour.

I'm a very nuts-and-bolts sort of guy, and Curt and Roland ... well, they weren't. They saw mystical ideas, they saw vistas, they saw unique visions and they were making an album which Roland explained had something to do with a big chair. I furrowed my eyebrows together hard and tried to wrap my brain around that one but, honestly, by that point I was much more interested in albums called *Jailbreak,* which talked about rockin' and chicks.

But as our meetings progressed, I got to like Curt and Roland. Though I felt that *The Hurting* was a pretentious load of angsty bollocks, I didn't care anymore because they were fun to be around. Curt may have had a silly haircut, but he was just one of the lads and liked a drink. Roland, when he wasn't being unbelievably intense and doing his funny dance, had a winning smile and an amazing voice. They had a new single coming out called "Mothers Talk." It was going to be the next release from this album about the big chair and it needed to leap to the top of the charts, thus the video for the single needed to be brilliant. What do you think, Nigel?

I wanted to show that I understood their artful demeanour so, rather than line them up with one of the successful directors of the era, I suggested they meet Laurie Lewis, a talented photographer who'd done a lot of work for Robbo when I'd been at Stiff and who'd recently started making music videos. My main reason for suggesting Laurie was that he was a nice chap and slightly pretentious about his art. As I didn't hang out with pretentious people much I hoped he and TFF would get on famously. And so they did. Laurie came up with an idea that was dark and moody. Curt and Roland were excited, and we could make the numbers work, so Laurie was hired and we were soon ensconced in a studio shooting the video.

Let me rephrase that. We were soon ensconced *outside* a studio, waiting and waiting while Laurie was inside shooting something that didn't involve the band for the "conceptual" part of the video. I did the crossword with Curt while Roland paced up and down and the day dragged on. At periodic intervals I would go inside to try and hurry Laurie up. I was "the client" after all. But Laurie wasn't to be hurried, and in fact didn't like very much that I was trying to hurry him up. I'd go back outside with the guys and raise my eyebrows, "Artists! Don't worry. I'm sure it's going to be brilliant!"

Eventually, the band, very tired and rather upset, went in front of the camera in the late hours. Thanks to Laurie, I was learning one of the most important lessons of my future directing career — don't keep the artist waiting.

But as the night ended, Curt and Roland were much happier, excited by their day's work. It was going to be a killer video that was going to knock the socks off anything they'd done previously. They couldn't wait to see the first cut.

They hated it. There wasn't anything they liked about the video. They hated every single frame of it and were pissed they'd been made to wait so long to perform. I didn't think the video was so bad, but the band didn't like it and didn't want it released. I had to find a solution.

The video had cost £25,000 which, at the time and even today, is a considerable amount of money. The single was coming soon, the band were very important to the label and something needed to be done quickly. I had a very clear idea of how the label would sort out this problem — they were surely going to fire me. It was the obvious thing to do. That Dick fella has hired one of his mates to make the TFF video and we don't like it. Let's get rid of him. That's what I would have done.

But my boss, Tony Powell, was made of sterner stuff. He called me into his office. I stood quaking in front of him. What was I going to do without a company car and a wage? I'd just bought my first flat and would be screwed without any money coming in. I looked out of the window searching for help: I needed to be manly and not whine and cry. Curt was right: it was proving to be a very sad world after all.

"Dicky," Tony said in his chirpy voice, "They don't like the video, and we need to make another one. What are we going to do?"

We? I thought. *That sounds promising.* I'd created this problem, but here was someone not pointing the finger but effectively putting his arm around my shoulder and offering help and support.

"Don't know Tony, got any ideas?"

"I do, actually. There's £5,000 left in the budget. Curt and Roland have seen that video you did for Julian Cope for £4,000 and wonder if you could do something for them that's like it?"

Wow. The flat was safe, I could keep the car, it was a very wonderful world. I saw trees of green. By trying to do my best for the band, I'd failed miserably but had unwittingly created an amazing career opportunity for myself.

A few days later I was climbing up on Solsbury Hill with Curt and Roland and a small film crew. Solsbury Hill is a large mound that rises above Bath to the north and, as well as being lyrical inspiration for one of Peter Gabriel's earlier hits, it was also adjacent to the farm where Curt was living at the time.

For their part, Curt and Roland bore me no ill will, and between the three of us we had come up with a number of ideas that could be easily shot and incorporated into a video. Roland explained that the song had been inspired by an animated film he'd seen called *When the Wind Blows* about the coming of nuclear war. We were all in agreement that, with our five-grand budget, the chances of recreating Armageddon were slim, so we settled for Curt and Roland singing on top of the hill, playing guitars and for it to be intercut with some footage that — how can I say this? — I had "borrowed" from the TV.

The couple of afternoons that we spent shooting the video proved to be immense fun and I recall being quite relaxed about it all. At one point we walked casually back to keyboard player Ian Stanley's house, where they were still recording the album about the chair and I drank tea and relaxed in the corner while Roland cut some guide vocals for a song that had eleven choruses, went on and on for about six minutes and was about shouting and letting it all out. "Not much chance of that being a hit," I thought.

The second video for "Mothers Talk" went down a treat and I was back in business at Phonogram. Only one problem — the single flopped. I was called into Tony's office again so he could play me the band's next single. "Listen to this, Dicky!" he said triumphantly. "It's going to be huge." The single was six minutes long, it had something like eleven choruses and it was all about shouting and letting it all out.

As the final notes died away, Tony turned to me with that big smile of his. "What do you think of that, then?"

"It's going to be massive!" I said.

"I'm glad you like it, because Curt and Roland want you to make the video."

"Righto, I'll draw up a list of directors for them to have a look at this afternoon."

"No, no. They want YOU to make the video!"

"They do?"

Roland sketched out the idea for the "Shout" video for me. The band would play in a studio surrounded by fans, rather like the Beatles had done for "All You Need Is Love," and some conceptual stuff would be shot down in Dorset at a mythical beach area called Durdle Door. I had a real budget, so the video had to be good. The song was double the length of the longest video I'd ever made, and it had those eleven choruses. I sat down to write out a plan. But I had no idea how to storyboard anything and no real idea how to tell a story, so I pinched an idea from another director I'd been working with.

Michael Brady was a tall, quiet man who made beautiful films. I'd hired him a couple of times to make videos for Big Country. I'd noticed that he'd take four pieces of paper and tape them together to make a much larger piece of paper on which he'd write out the words to the entire song. Over various words he'd write or sketch an idea of what needed to be shot to tell his story.

I took four pieces of paper, stuck them together, wrote out all the lyrics from "Shout" and made copious notes of what needed to be shot. My sheet of paper didn't look as impressive as Mike Brady's had. I had to find a way to stick everything together — but that would come later, much later.

The next Sunday evening I drove down to the Dorset coast and checked into the hotel I'd found for the band and myself to stay in. The following morning we were down on the beach shooting. Dave Bridges was hired to shoot the video. The soundman was a Liverpudlian rascal named Steve Jones who everyone called Scal. The crew was fleshed out by stills photographer Clare Muller; makeup artist Miranda Joyce, who'd been the sax player in the Belle Stars when I was at Stiff; and my pal and future producer Phil Barnes. There was no gaffer or grip that day and no craft service or a porta potty on the beach. If we needed a drink or a toilet we had a long climb to the top of the cliffs to see what we could find up there.

I only had one clear idea, and that became the opening shot: we would pan off a view of the cliffs to a close-up of Roland singing the opening couplet and then pan away to find Curt. While Curt sang the second couplet, Roland would move behind Curt and we would pan over again and see the two of them together. The clifftop was pretty crowded with a camera assistant, Dave, Scal, Miranda, me, Phil Barnes, Curt and Roland, but it seemed to work, and we knocked it off in a couple of takes. I drove back up to London feeling quite smug. It seemed I had done something that was "creative" — and it actually worked. It wasn't exactly the opening shot of *Touch of Evil,* but it was a start.

We shot the performance section back in London in a studio south of the river. Roland insisted I insert myself into the crowd. I said I would only do it if I could cut myself into the video clapping out of time. While I was at Stiff, my boss Paul Conroy had married and had a baby, and I'd become the boy's godfather. So, my godson Drew and his mum Maxine appeared in the crowd, along with a number of other friends and Phonogram employees. I did a rough cut in a basement room in Soho, finished it at Visions and, with teeth rattling together, played the finished video for my bosses at Phonogram. I nearly collapsed with relief when they declared they liked it.

The single went in the UK charts, the video got played and Tears for Fears' career was back on track — but not all was well. A few weeks later, the band's American A&R man flew in from New York, and I was summoned to a meeting with Tony Powell, Brian Shepherd and the New York honcho to play the newly finished video. As those six minutes seemed to go on forever, the New York guy moved restlessly in his chair. "I like the song," he announced at the end, "but we'll have to remake the video for America. Kids over there won't get this at all!" I was dismissed and went across the street to bury my sorrows in a cup of tea and a slice of cake.

"Everybody Wants to Rule the World" was the next single. It seemed Curt and Roland approved of me, so I was going to make a third video for them. Given the American A&R guy's huffy attitude to the "Shout" video, it was decided we should shoot it in the U.S.A. and make it look as American as possible. No one disagreed, but Roland said he wouldn't be going abroad, so we would have to shoot the whole band in London and shoot conceptual stuff in the States with Curt on his own. Scal and I pitched a number of ideas to the band, one of which included a nuclear missile being driven across the desert. That got a unanimous thumbs down.

I felt the song was classic driving music and pitched an idea involving Curt in a sports car driving through the desert. Like me, Curt loved sports cars. I went to L.A. to scout locations, rented a Ford Bronco and for the next five days drove a long circuit toward Palm Springs, south along the Salton Sea, over the hills towards San Diego and then back toward L.A. It was a stupidly long route; nowadays, I would never allow myself to stretch production that far and that thin. But it was raining back in London, and in California the sun was always shining. Like so many Brits before and after, I was falling in love with the desert.

There was a lot going on back in London, and I was about to embark on my first shoot in Los Angeles, so I did the sensible thing and hired a local production team. I spent the early hours of each morning on calls back to the UK, making sure things were proceeding well there before going scouting. This was going to be the first time I'd ever directed where I wasn't also the producer, and it lifted a huge weight from my shoulders. The L.A. producer and I decided that we should shoot over a weekend, and that the only way to make the budget work and visit all the locations was for the cast and crew to travel through the desert in a motorhome, using it as our production base, dining facility, bathroom and mobile hotel. So, on the Friday night, Curt, Dave Bridges, Scal, the moho driver, the U.S. producer and I bedded down in the parking lot of the Wheel Inn, a few miles short of Palm Springs. I can think of a few artists who might have balked at the sleeping arrangements — six of us piled into the moho that night — but Curt impressed me greatly by volunteering to sleep on the floor for the duration of the shoot.

The next morning, after breakfast in the Wheel Inn, we set up for the first shot, which would involve Curt driving up in a British Racing Green Austin-Healey 3000, getting out of the car and making a phone call. While Dave Bridges set up the lighting, Curt and Scal climbed into the rented Austin-Healey and took it for a spin. When they returned 15 minutes later, looking very cheeky, the car was covered in dust. It wasn't until later that I learned Curt had taken a corner way too fast and had spun off the road into the desert, narrowly avoiding a very nasty accident in an aging open-topped car with no roll bar or safety belts. If luck had not been on our side, Tears for Fears' career might have ended right there and then, and I would have had a lot of explaining to do back in London.

We shot the scene in the phone booth with Curt dialling 74688 (which corresponded to s-h-o-u-t on the phone pad) and then hit the road. We were nearing Palm Springs when I noticed a huge sandy bluff off to the side of the road filled with weekenders on ATVs and motorbikes. The hill had been deserted when I scouted during the previous week, but now it was filled with weekend revellers. I suggested we pull over and shoot something amidst the excitement. “Mad World” had been a big hit in California, and people started to recognise Curt. We asked them to ride towards the camera on their bikes while Curt sang the bridge. Then Dave shot some B-roll of other revellers riding around while the gear was piled back into our truck. One guy overcooked his wheelie and tumbled off his bike. He lay on the ground, lifeless, for what seemed like an age. He eventually got up, climbed on his bike, chuckled, rubbed his head and rode off. Another disaster averted.

The moho pulled up beside a dock on the edge of the Salton Sea that night. As we sat beside the inland lake drinking beers, I suggested that perhaps we could shoot Curt by the lake at sunrise the next morning. Alarm clocks were set, and we drifted off to sleep.

None of the alarms rang in the morning. I was the first to wake. Dawn was coming fast, so I kicked and screamed for everybody to get out of bed. Still in his bare feet, Bridges set up his camera while Curt got dressed. I dragged Scal out of bed to roll sound. I was shouting directions this way and that. Less than six minutes after first waking up, we got the shot (which made it to the video) in which Curt sings “Holding hands while the walls come tumbling down.” I was so happy we'd got the shot and couldn't understand why everybody was laughing so hard. I turned around and saw Scal sitting cross-legged on the ground, his Nagra tape recorder in his lap and his headphones on, ready for a second take — wearing only his underpants.

While we were having luck grabbing shots that weren't in my plans, the ones that I did have planned were proving hard to get. Too much was slipping through the fingers of the U.S. production team. Curt noticed, too; unbeknownst to me, Scal and Bridges had also been mumbling about it together. By lunchtime on the second day a definite us-and-them mentality was breaking out on set. The final nail in the coffin occurred when we came to the dance sequence.

ZZ Top's “Gimme All Your Lovin'” was a huge hit at the time; the video showed the band standing beside the road, watching the Eliminator car drive by. Our plan was to take the piss/show homage (take your pick) to their video by showing three Black guys do the same thing in "Everybody Wants to Rule the World" before breaking into a hip dance routine.

We arrived, behind schedule, at the deserted petrol pump scene and I asked the producer to get the three dancers on set. "We have a problem," she announced. "Only two of them have shown up." Turns out she'd known since early that morning that we'd be one man short but hadn't told me or tried to find a replacement. I was furious and Curt was mad. From that day onwards, I have always told my crew that if something's going awry, let me know as soon as possible so we can come up with a solution. If I'd known earlier in the day, there would have been time to get a third dancer to drive out from L.A. or for me to rethink the scene. Instead, we were ready to shoot, and I only had two dancers. We pressed on, and I guess it worked out OK, as Eddie (the dancer on the right) became good friends with keyboard player Ian Stanley and the rest of the band.

It was getting dark as we reached our final location. There was only time for a closeup of Curt singing before the sun set. The final scene that was never shot was the whole point of the video — Curt driving through the desert making calls and getting directions to visit a junkyard where he would find a spare part for his beloved Austin-Healey. In the end, no one ever asked what the video was about; they just liked the visuals. But it still bugs me that Curt never found that spare part for his car.

As we wrapped, Curt, Bridges, Scal and I climbed into my rental car and drove back to L.A., moaning about the production. I vowed if I ever shot in California again I would not allow things to go so badly. The next day, as we packed our bags and prepared to catch the overnight flight back to London, Dave introduced me to a U.S. producer friend of his named Steve Golin, who he promised would do a much better job if I ever came back to L.A. He seemed like a lovely man, funny too, and I had no idea that not only would Steve and I be working a great deal together, we would later found, with four other guys, a hugely successful production company.

Back in London, we shot the performance section of the video in the same soundstage where we'd done "Shout." The plan to insert footage of Curt driving through the desert in the blue dot at the back of the set didn't work out, but I may be the only person who remembers that part of the original plan.

With "Everybody Wants to Rule the World" complete, Tony Powell had great news for me. Despite the warning from Mr. Hotshot New York A&R man, the "Shout" video was being played on MTV and starting to do great business. The label was very excited about the upcoming release of "Everybody Wants to Rule the World." I was instructed to start planning a multi-camera live shoot for the band at London's Hammersmith Odeon on the last night of their UK tour. It was going to be the biggest production I had ever worked on, and it was taking place in a gig I'd been to many, many times to see a huge range of artists: David Bowie, Tina Turner, Ry Cooder, Tom Petty, Ian Dury, Madness, even an early version of Tears for Fears. Doing a live shoot there was going to be something special.

Despite my concerns about the way things had gone in L.A., I had seen the benefits of not being the producer and the director on the same job. As I'd never shot a live show before, I hired a local producer to take care of business for the London show. She knew what she was doing and arranged permits, booked a recording truck, secured a whole team of cameramen and assistants, hired catering and everything else we needed. The only advice I had to give her was to make sure we had non-appearance insurance.

Eventually, show day at Hammersmith dawned. I was nervous. I'd never directed a live concert before, and I had one shot at this. But I'd seen TFF live a dozen times and knew the show inside out. I was sure I could pull it off. My camera crew and assistants, dozens of them, were milling around the craft service table, the talkback to each camera station was being tested and a wall of monitors had been set up for me backstage. Soundcheck rolled around, the band sauntered onstage and I heard the usual sounds: snare hits, a kick drum, an odd guitar chord, some "one-two-one-two"s and a stab from the keyboards. The taped intro from "Shout" echoed round the building; the band approached their mics and started singing. Within seconds, Roland was waving his arms. He looked like shit. He motioned at his throat, tried to say something, handed his guitar to his tech and disappeared. A few minutes later someone from management appeared, sucked their teeth, shook their head and said, "Show's off. Roland's got the flu and he's lost his voice."

My producer and I were shell-shocked and speechless. Eventually I turned to her and said, "Good job we got that cancellation insurance." Her skin turned pale white in an instant. "Oh, fuck!"

A few weeks later I landed in Toronto. Tony Powell had covered my arse yet again and found a way to pay the £50,000 cancellation fee. I was now going to take a second bite at the live show, shooting the band at the famous Massey Hall. Just to make things more exciting, I was simultaneously going to shoot a video for the fourth single from *Songs From the Big Chair*, "Head Over Heels." Roland had presented me with the complete concept. He walks into a library and starts singing the song to the cute librarian while Curt, dressed as the cleaner, talks with a chimp. Other band members appear as a biker and a rabbi before four-leaf clovers fill the screen and the band play the outro. We return to Roland and his librarian paramour, now his wife, who are in older age: funny how time flies! The idea never made much sense to me but that wasn't my problem. My problem was to execute it AND make sure the band would be able to play a gig in town that night — a gig that I would be filming. As if that wasn't enough on my plate, I was also looking after other projects in the works in London, exec producing a shoot in Istanbul for Vitamin Z and overseeing another shoot in New York for Dexy's Midnight Runners, all of which meant a lot of calls to four different time zones before leaving for set in the morning. Somewhere in the vaults is an interview with me shot by MTV, who had flown into town to do a story on the band. I'm sitting on the stairs outside Massey Hall and unsurprisingly I look exhausted.

The local producers — Sean Ryerson, Steve Howard and Steve

Surjik — had managed to get all the pieces we needed to make the "Head Over Heels" video. We had a library, a cute librarian, a pile of books for Roland, a rabbi's outfit for Manny, cleaner's togs for Curt, a leather jacket for Ian and, most importantly, Zippy the Chimp, who had been brought over the border into Canada and was earning more than anyone on the set. To complete the scene, Sean Ryerson, Steve Surjik — later to become a successful TV and film director in his own right — and I dressed up as the string players.

There was a surprise awaiting the band during the shoot. I think it was tour manager Andy Cheeseman who walked up to Curt and Roland and whispered in their ears. Both of them yelled at the top of their voices with sheer unbridled joy; "Everybody Wants to Rule the World" had just gone to number-one in the States. I was so happy for them and could not contain my own delight. Quite by chance, I now had four videos that had been hits on MTV and around the world: "Everybody Wants to Rule the World" and "Shout" by Tears for Fears, "Things Can Only Get Better" by Howard Jones and "Do They Know It's Christmas?" Out of nowhere I suddenly had a hot director's reel.

At lunch one day during the shoot, a friendly, smiling man introduced himself to me. Mark Freedman ran a small production company in L.A. The producer there was Steve Golin, the friend of Dave Bridges whom I'd met at the end of the "Everybody Wants to Rule the World" shoot. Mark had flown to Toronto from L.A. and wanted to represent me in the U.S. I'd had no offers from anybody else, there was an impatient AD over my shoulder telling me I had to get back to set, and Mark seemed like a nice guy, so I said sure, why not?

Looking back, getting representation in the States was a big deal — especially as I'd never had representation anywhere before. My method of getting work up till then had been entirely passive — my phone rang at Phonogram, a voice told me a video needed making and I got on with the job. There was no pitching involved, no stressful freelance worries. I was given a problem and a deadline to meet and got on with it. Most directors would have spent hours, months and years planning their careers — gone to film school, studied films, understudied on sets and somehow made their first shorts then, taking their hearts in their hands, gone looking for someone to represent them, probably having door after door slammed in their face before getting lucky. Me? I had no plan. I'd somehow stumbled into a job I enjoyed. I had a company car and a paid parking space in the centre of London. I was 32, much too late to start thinking about embarking on a directing career but, as there was no plan to direct full-time, I had no idea I was breaking rules. If I was offered something that sounded like fun, I simply said yes.

What I remember most about that short meeting in Toronto with Mark Freedman was that I was exhausted and petrified. It was a sunny day but there was no time to stroll around Toronto and enjoy the warmth. The "Head Over Heels" video was a big production and, now the band had a number-one record in America, had to be good. I didn't fully get Roland's idea, but I threw myself at it, figuring that intense involvement would somehow make up for my own lack of vision. But what scared me most was the live show I had to shoot.

I have since shot dozens of live shows all over the world. I plan meticulously and write out every bar and every word of the show and know when every solo starts and finishes, where every drum fill occurs and who is singing every backing vocal moment — and it's still terrifying on the night, as you have just one chance to get it right. I had none of that experience the night I shot Tears for Fears in Toronto but, on the other hand, I didn't know what I didn't know. So, I just ploughed into it with the only thing I had in my favour: I knew every song in their set by heart. As the band walked onstage, I sat down in front of a bunch of monitors without a single note and winged it.

Back in 1985, shows were shot on film and recorded on tape, so there was no on-the-fly line-cut to watch the next day. Consequently, in the morning, I breathed a sigh of relief, ate a big breakfast and climbed onto the band's bus for the drive to Ottawa and Montreal and the chance to shoot more B-roll footage for the long-form video we were planning. I found myself chatting with Roland, who asked for my honest opinion of the lighting and production of the band's stage show. As they were about to tour the States, did I think it was good enough for American audiences? I told him that it didn't feel big-time. They were now a number-one act in the U.S. — perhaps they should add some extra bells and whistles? Roland seemed to agree with me, and I thought nothing more about our conversation.

Back in London, I started work on cutting "Head Over Heels" *and* putting together the first cuts of the live show, which was now turning into a full-length documentary with additional road moments from Canada and Germany and behind-the-scenes footage of a Japanese crew shooting the band performing "Shout" outside Winston Churchill's family seat of Blenheim Palace. I was starting to feel burned out as the work piled on. I hadn't taken a day off in months, so I decided to take a break in California that wasn't going to be a break at all. Tears for Fears were mixing the live footage; they wanted to make a video for "I Believe" while I was there; and I wanted to drop into Mark Freedman's office to see if this directing malarkey was something I should consider taking more seriously.

I landed in L.A. and Steve Golin handed me a tape by a band called Smash Palace. Before I knew what was happening, I was shooting a video for the band all over downtown L.A. Then we started casting for the "I Believe" video, which was going to be shot in Seattle. En route to the casting session, I made a quick dash to McDonald's in the Mustang convertible I'd rented. Turning into the McDonald's on Vine Street, I was rear-ended. I pulled over and exchanged information with the young lady who'd run into the back of my car and, by the time I'd picked up my burger, was running late for the session. I raced back down Vine to Mark's office, parked the dented rental in the lot and ran up the stairs with my burger. As I walked into the offices, now filled with dozens of lovely L.A. ladies nervously chatting loudly and wanting a part in the next Tears for Fears video, I found myself facing an impatient Steve Golin, who asked me why I was late. Still upset from the shock of the fender bender, ignoring the girls, not thinking what I was saying, and answering much too loudly, I explained: "Sorry I'm late, but some stupid fucking bitch drove into the back of my car outside McDonald's."

Steve guided me into one of the offices. I gobbled down my lunch and, as the last French fry went down my throat, he opened the door and ushered in the first dancer. I just about spat up my lunch when she took one look at me, put her hands on her hips and angrily announced, "Remember me? I'm the 'stupid fucking bitch' who drove into the back of you outside McDonald's!"

She didn't get the part.

We shot "I Believe" in an aircraft hangar at the Seattle airport. For the second time in a couple of weeks, I got to see Steve Golin and his partner, Joni Sighvatsson, in action. I really enjoyed the experience. They were both graduates of the American Film Institute and seemed to know what they were doing. With the video in the can, we shot interviews with the band on the tarmac outside, then flew back to L.A. the next day.

I was invited to a dinner with Curt, Roland and their manager, Paul King. We filled a big table at some swanky place. There was much to celebrate — glasses clinked and toasts were made. Paul King ordered more wine. One bottle in particular seemed very expensive. The waiter poured Paul a taste and he approved but asked the waiter to just leave the bottle on the table, which seemed strange.

A while later, Paul picked up the bottle and proceeded to pour every single drop of it over my head! The talk at the table stopped instantly and everyone looked at me as 200 bucks of fine red wine dripped from my nose to join the puddle in my crotch. "Thanks a bunch," said Paul. "You just cost me £65,000!" It appeared that my casual conversation with Roland on the tour bus in Canada had resulted in him going to management and demanding that the lighting rig for the U.S. tour be upgraded — because Nigel said so.

I never got to see that sexy new rig, but I felt the shame as I sat at the table for the rest of the night and had the remains of the fine claret slide down my spine and into my underwear.

The only ambition I'd ever had was to play guitar in a band. That hadn't worked out, but I'd stumbled into the music business, and that had changed my life. Now that I was commissioning videos at Phonogram and producing and directing, I was simply trying to do too much. I was getting to a point where I had to make a choice. Like everyone I knew at Phonogram, I really cared about my job and the artists we worked for, so we put in the hours — lots of them. At the same time, the lack of respect we received back was sometimes jaw-dropping. One of the bands we looked after was Soft Cell. One day, I turned up to the set of the latest video to keep an eye on things and was physically prevented from going into the location by the band's manager, Stevo, who made me stand outside in the garden of the house where the band were shooting like a naughty child. I give full credit to director Tim Pope, who made a point to come outside and give me a progress report, but the message I'd received was clear. I no longer went out of my way to speed paperwork across my desk if I saw Soft Cell's name on it and did the absolute minimum. If they didn't want my help they weren't going to get it.

Stevo wasn't the only one. A number of the band managers I dealt with saw me as the enemy, which seemed beyond foolish to me. Wouldn't you want to cultivate a good relationship with the people who worked at the label to which your artist, your bread and butter, was signed? I was getting tired of it. I loved the people I worked *with* but the people I worked *for* were often full of contempt. In addition, the folk at Polygram's corporate level had asked me to take a meeting about working for the young video division full-time. They were offering a nice fat pay raise and I'd floated the idea of having six weeks off every year to direct, but I was already sensing that this would never be enough time and, I had to confess, I was enjoying this directing lark rather too much. Also, did I want to go another step up the corporate ladder? I had also been offered a job at another entertainment company that promised good pay and interesting prospects, and it was tantalizing. I mentioned the Polygram offer I was considering and they were happy to wait for me if I needed more time.

So, here I was in L.A. and, even though my trip was coming to an end, I had just been sent two tracks to write ideas for by other labels —

and, to my delight, one was by Aretha Franklin. How was I going to fit all of this in AND return to my job in London AND continue directing? It was another sunny morning. I had a rented Mustang convertible outside, and the day beckoned as I stepped in the shower at the Motel Tropicana on Santa Monica Boulevard and pondered my options.

For every artist I loved working with there were others who were not so much fun. For every Status Quo there was a Soft Cell, for every Tears for Fears there was a Dire Straits. I don't think any of us expected hugs and personally signed Christmas cards, but we all cared about our work, we loved our jobs and we wanted our artists to do well. We wanted, perhaps naïvely, for someone to occasionally say thank you. In all my years in the business I don't ever remember anyone at the labels I worked at ever saying, "Let's see if we can screw this artist and mess up his career." We always tried to do the best thing. Of course, we were often wrong, our enthusiasm was misplaced and we made stupid decisions — such things happen — but, in my experience, it was never malicious. At the end of it all, if I was going to be hated and despised, I wanted the artists and managers to hate me personally for what I was doing for them — not just hate me for being one of the drones at the label. If I wasn't going to get respect from the band or their managers, then at least I was going to get my self-respect back. I was going to be doing something for me.

Once I'd had the thought that perhaps there was life outside the labels, it became an annoying bug in my head that wouldn't go away. I couldn't help thinking that maybe, just maybe, I should figure out what my future would be.

As the water pounded my back I thought about returning to London, where I would be asking other directors to work on ideas for the artists at Phonogram. I knew about the whispers behind my back: the label guy who thought he could direct, the label guy who was stealing some of the good jobs for himself — even though I'd made a point of letting my bosses make that decision for me. I had some money saved up and had two other promising job offers in the pipeline if things didn't work out. Mark Freedman and Steve Golin were on my case about getting a visa and moving to L.A. to direct full time. I was 32 and already late to the directing party — if I was going to give this a whirl, now was the time. I decided to roll the dice. Not only was I going to quit Phonogram, go freelance and direct full-time, I was going to move to America.

When I'd climbed out of bed ten minutes earlier, I was not even thinking of a move or a career change. As I stepped out of the shower, I never gave it a second thought. I got dressed, rang London and tendered my resignation.

But first I had to go back to the UK and finish off the Tears for Fears film. Phonogram offered me more money, and I turned them down. More surprising was the reaction from some of my co-workers, one of whom said to my face in a sing-song voice, "Ooh, Nigel's going to Hollywood! We'll see how that works out." I ignored it and carried on clearing out my desk. A few weeks after my move to the States, I secured my first job as a freelance director ... and it had to be shot in London!

I was living in a poky apartment off Sunset Boulevard when I was summoned to the Columbia Pictures offices in Burbank. Eddie Thomas (a.k.a. Eddie Jnr.), one of those two dancing guys from the "Everybody Wants to Rule the World" video, had cut a wonderful song with Roland and Ian Stanley called "Fish for Life" and it was going to be featured in the movie *Karate Kid Part II.* The gent behind the Columbia Pictures desk asked me if I'd seen Peter Gabriel's "Sledgehammer" video. Of course I had. "Good," he said. "Can you do something like that for 'Fish for Life'?" Foolishly I told him it would be a piece of cake, which was daft, as the budget was a tenth of the "Sledgehammer" budget and we didn't have weeks but two days. Roland was a no-show for the video, so it was just Eddie and Ian Stanley playing a cheap Telecaster that I'd bought two weeks after moving to Hollywood. I got some wind-up toys from a shop on Melrose, the art department came up with some lovely, tiny paintings which became backdrops and editor Scott Chestnut and I drove all over town with a video camera, shooting neon signs of fish and other crazy moments. We were just making it up as we went along, but somehow it all works and I feel no shame when I come across the video nowadays.

A month or two later, Tears for Fears were going to release "Mothers Talk" again and were going to shoot a third video of it especially for the U.S.A. — was I interested?

I had already figured out that nothing goes on forever and that there was every possibility I would not work with Curt and Roland again. For both them and me, that might actually be a good thing. I already had a big project in the works (my first feature film), so I had to turn the job down. But it hurt. I'd grown to like Curt and Roland a lot. When the new "Mothers Talk" was finished I couldn't watch it. It was like running into an old flame at a party who was hugging her new man. It hurt. A lot. I knew there would be many more occasions like this up the road and I would just have to deal with it.

When the follow-up album, *The Seeds of Love,* was due for release everyone started asking me if I was going to be shooting videos for the new album. I think I surprised a lot of people by telling them that not only had I not heard from the band but that I thought it was a good idea for them to try other people and get new ideas flowing. Because of my involvement with it, *Songs From the Big Chair* had become a personal favourite, but *The Seeds of Love* proved to be a huge improvement. I played that thing to death; it's unquestionably my favourite album of the '80s.

As it happened, TFF weren't done with me yet. Sometime later my good pal Andy Murray, now the Marketing Director for PolyGram Video International, told me they needed another long-form video from the band. He explained that the band were going through a rough patch — Curt and Roland weren't talking. Perhaps I could go and see them on tour in America and convince them to record and shoot a show? I flew to Denver and saw them at Red Rocks. After I spoke to Curt and Roland separately, they agreed to let me shoot and record a show at the

Santa Barbara Bowl. At the time I was trying out intercutting lots of film textures, so the finished piece has colour, grainy black and white and footage shot off the TV screen. It looked great at the time, but I don't think it's held up well. Now it feels gimmicky, though the show itself was wonderful. I later cut together a video version of "Famous Last Words."

I have no doubt that, without Tears for Fears, my career might never have happened. I'll be forever grateful that they asked me to shoot the video for "Shout." Back then, I was not shy about remarking that, apart from my Phonogram wages, the only payment I got was £40 expenses for a shirt that was ruined during production. Looking back, what I have subsequently received from them in turns of enjoyment and help up the directing ladder is beyond calculation.

Thank you Curt and Roland, I am so grateful.

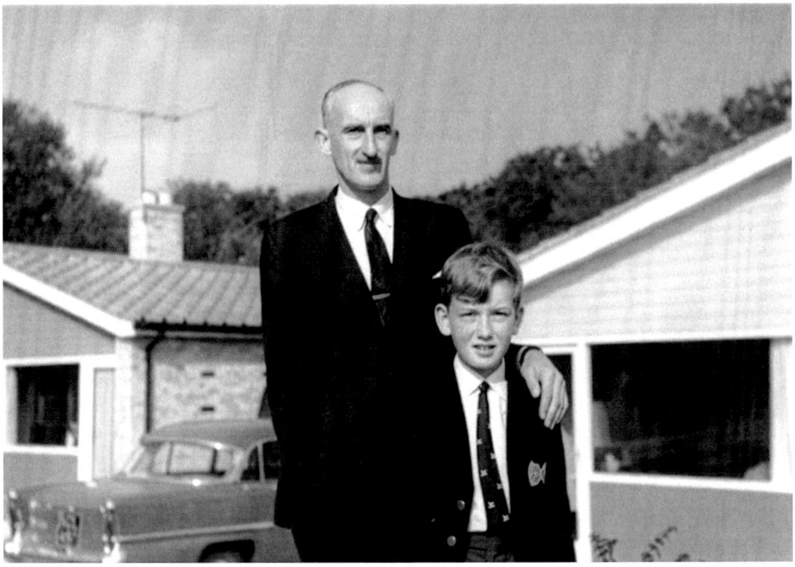

My dad and myself the morning I was sent to boarding school (with his battered Vauxhall in the background). I wouldn't see him again for almost a year.
Photo by my mother.

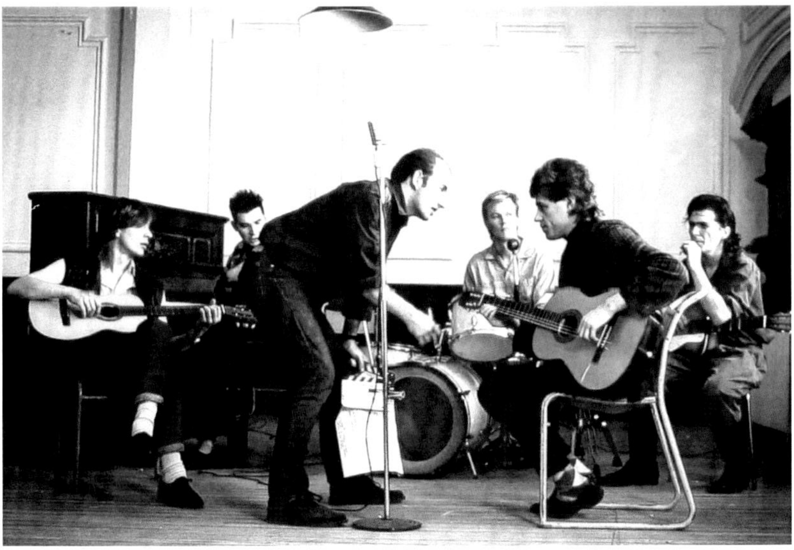

Directing Bob Geldof and the Boomtown Rats on the set of "Dave," a video that few people saw. Our next job together would be seen by millions, court controversy and save many lives. Photo by Clare Muller.

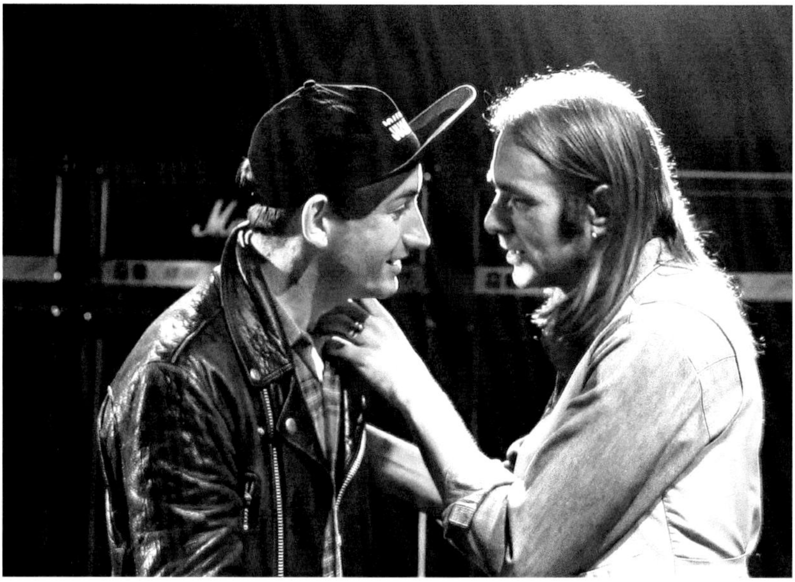

I've just told Francis Rossi of Status Quo that I'm about to blow up all his amps on the "Mess of Blues" video shoot. Photo by Clare Muller.

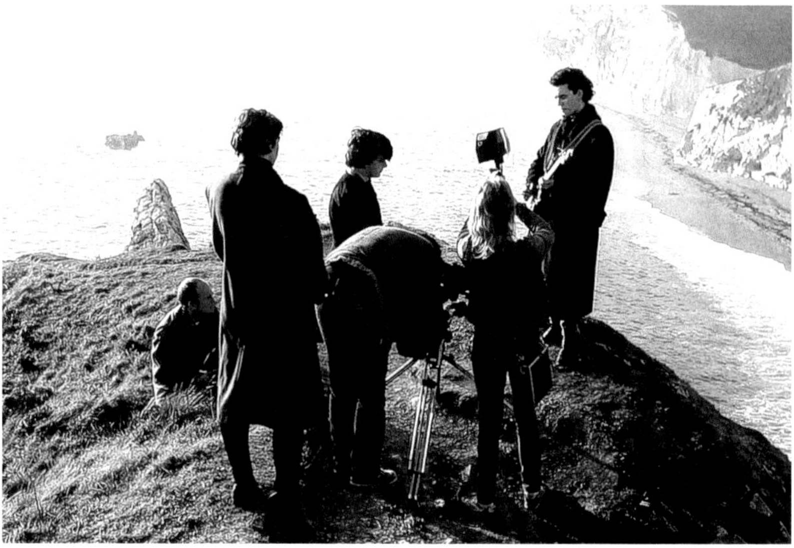

Roland Orzabal of Tears for Fears plays the solo from "Shout" perched on a rock above Durdle Door on England's Jurassic Coast, watched by myself on the left, Miranda Joyce (makeup), our camera assistant, Dave Bridges (bent over the camera) and my pal Phil Barnes. Photo by Clare Muller.

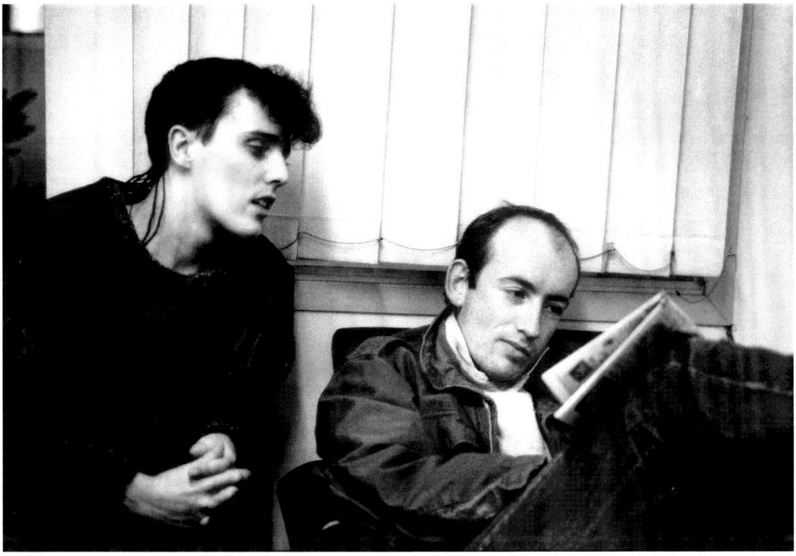

Curt Smith of Tears for Fears and I do the crossword during the long wait outside the set of the first "Mothers Talk" video shoot. Photo by Clare Muller.

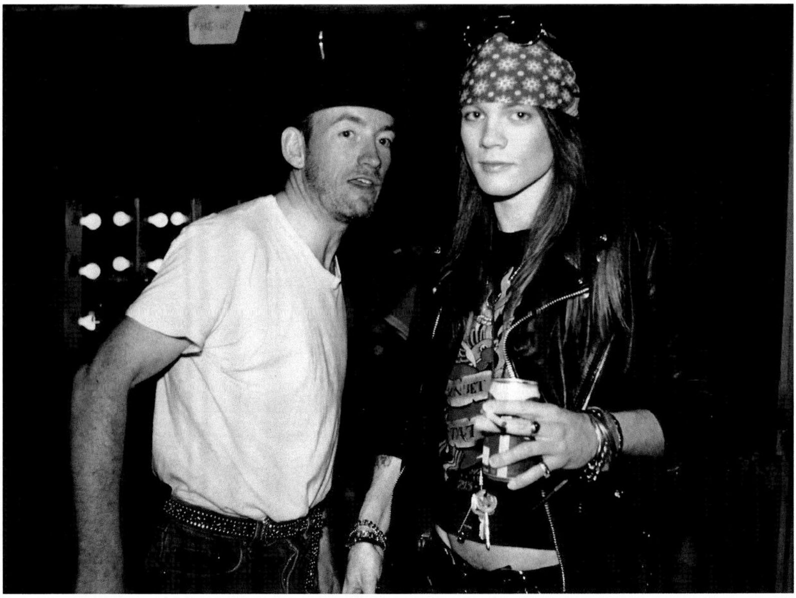

With Axl Rose on the set of "Sweet Child o' Mine." (Note the offending bracelets on Axl's wrist.) Photo by Gene Kirkland.

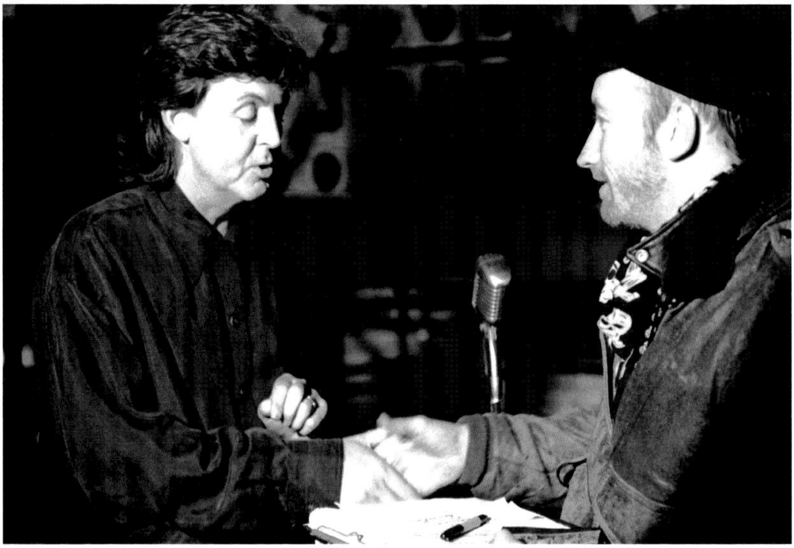

Shaking hands with Paul McCartney on the set of "All My Trials" just after he autographed my McCartney CD "To Our Dick!" Photographer unknown.

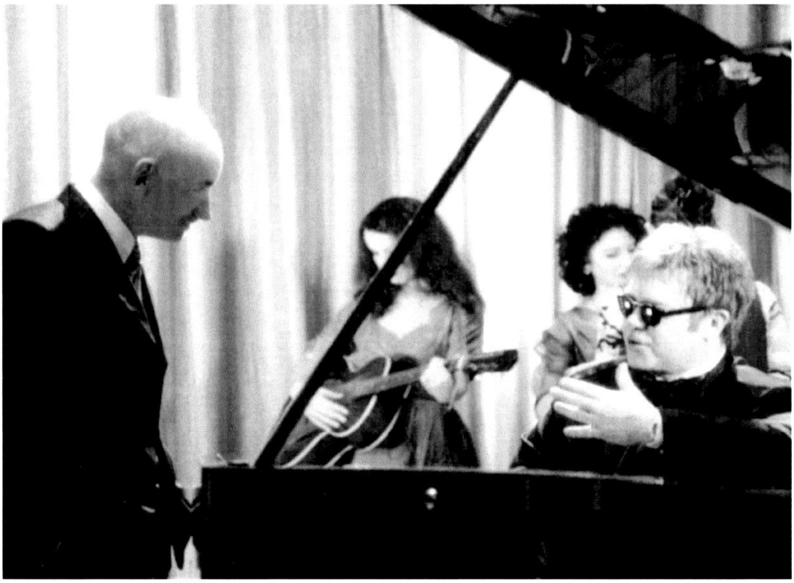

By wearing a suit and discussing every track on *Tumbleweed Connection,* I managed to calm Elton John down on the set of "The Heart of Every Girl" after his morning tantrum. Image from a film outtake.

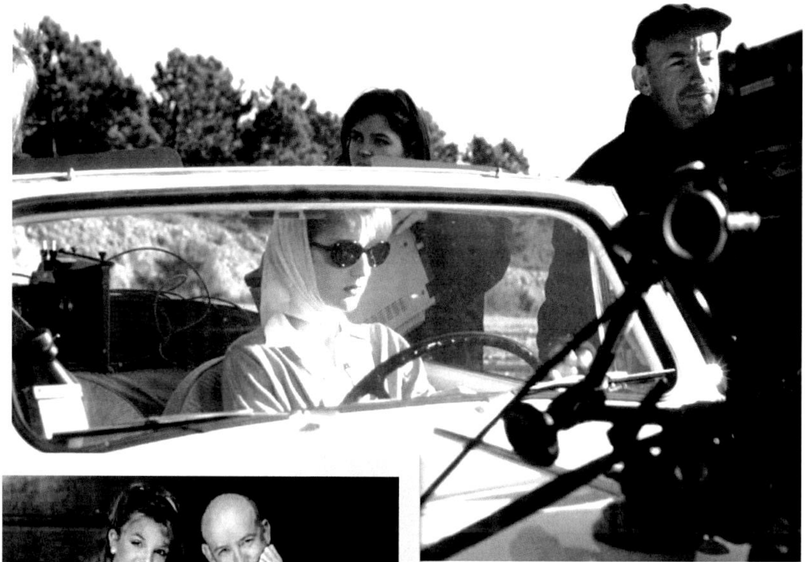

With Celine Dion on the French Riviera shooting "Falling Into You."
Photographer unknown.

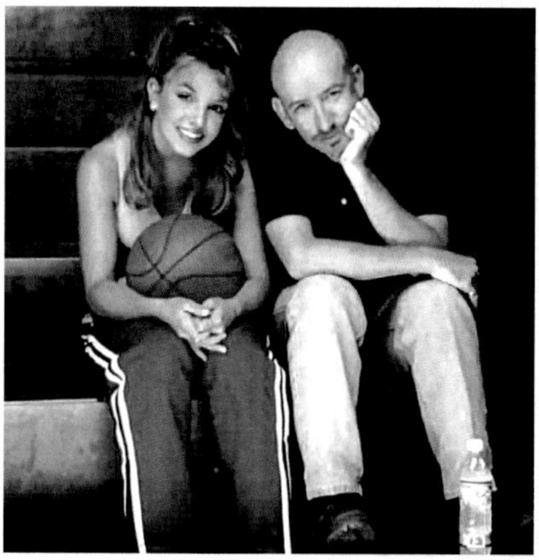

Sitting in the bleachers with Britney Spears shooting "...Baby One More Time."
Photographer unknown.

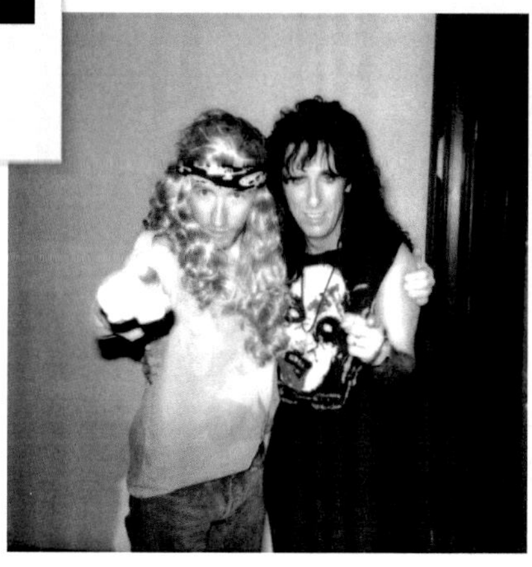

Mugging with Alice Cooper between takes on the set of "Poison." His hair is real... mine isn't.
Photo by Vance Burberry.

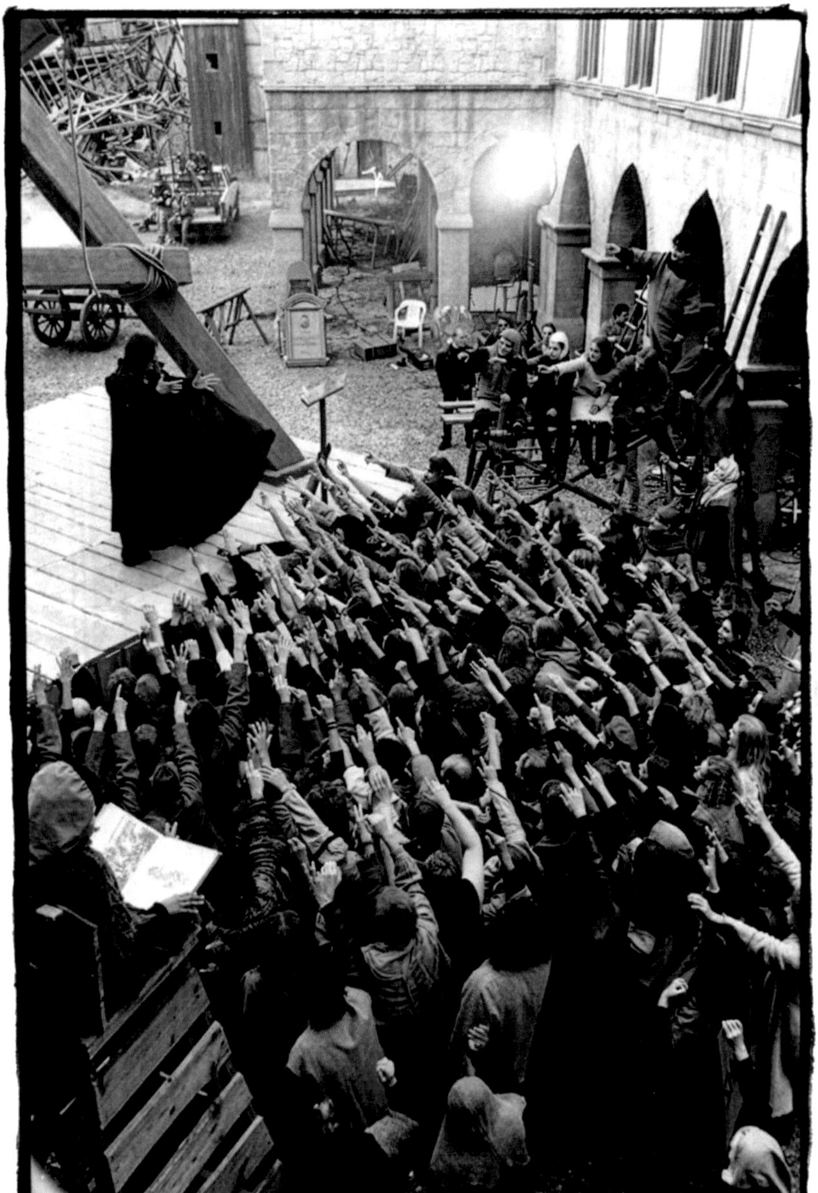

A fraction of the “Ozzy 200” worship their saviour on the set of “Back on Earth” outside Prague. Photographer unknown.

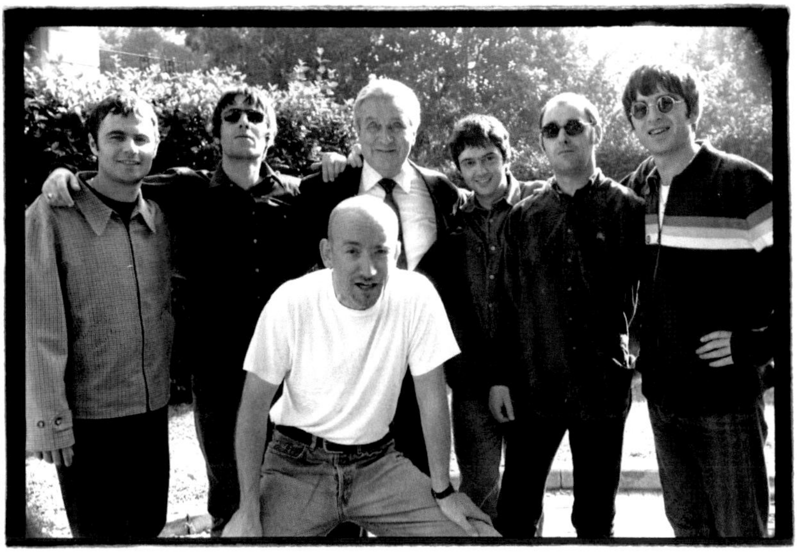

Possibly wearing the same T-shirt I wore with Axl, I hog the picture with Oasis and Patrick Macnee on the set of “Don’t Look Back in Anger”... and Noel Gallagher is smiling. Photo by Johnny Buzzerio.

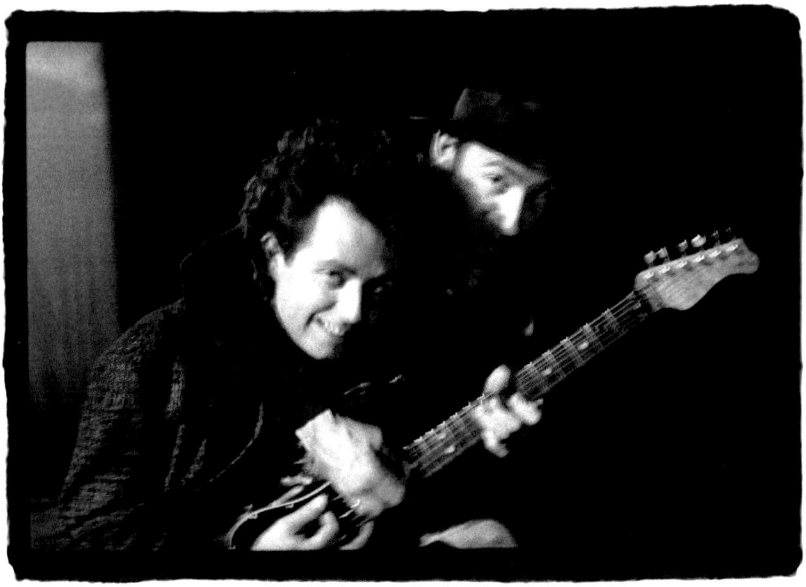

After working with Toto for the first time, I begged Steve Lukather for a picture together. One man in this shot is an extraordinary musician who has played on over 1500 albums ... the other is a Dick. Photographer unknown.

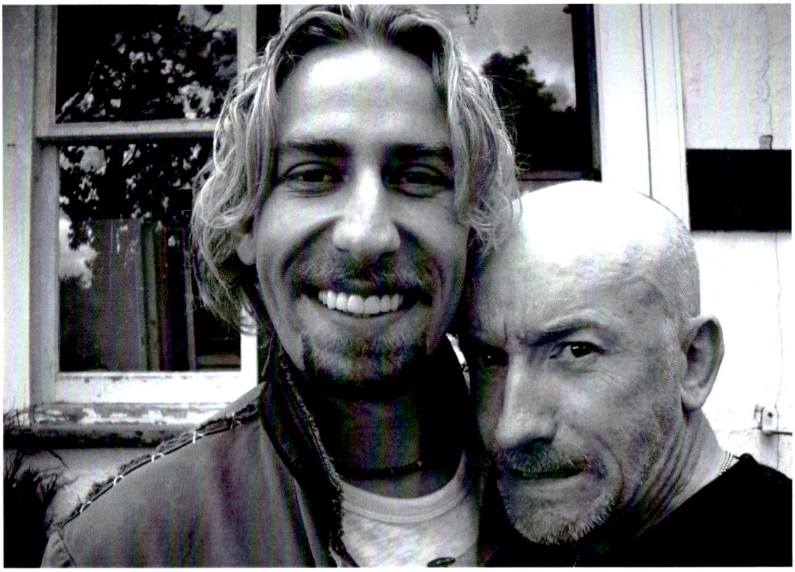

At the end of the "Photograph" shoot I cuddle up with Nickelback's Chad Kroeger. I have shot more videos for them than any other artist. Photo by Russ Swanson.

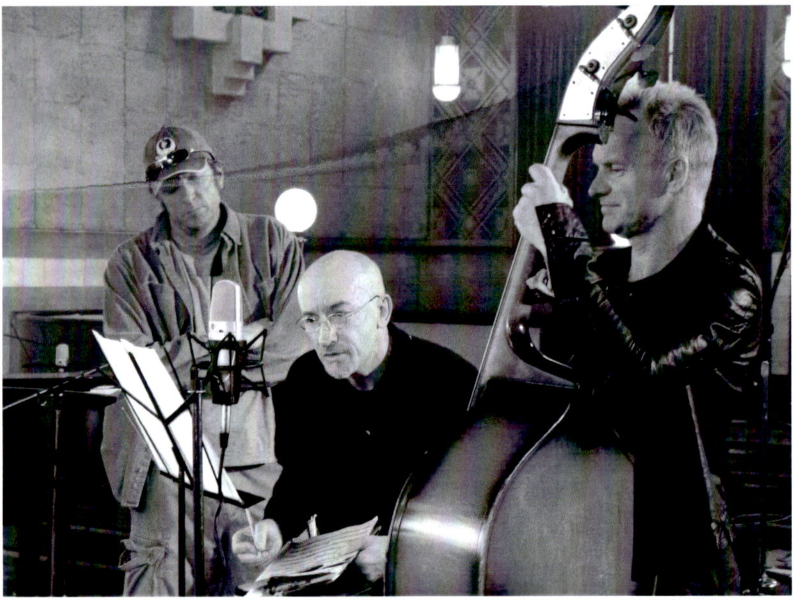

AD Lennie Appelquist looks over my shoulder while we chat with Sting about whether that's an F# or a G♭ on the set of "Always on My Side," his duet with Sheryl Crow.

CHAPTER 19

Welcome to the Jungle

I MOVED TO HOLLYWOOD in late 1985. I climbed aboard the plane in London known as a record company guy who thought he could direct. When I stepped off the plane 12 hours later, I told anyone who asked that I was a film director. It was a conscious decision to rebrand myself; in time everybody fell for the ruse — even me. When Steve Golin and Mark Freedman asked me to come to America, I figured I'd stay in L.A. for a couple of years and then move back to London when everyone had forgotten the time I'd put in as a record company guy. But one thing led to another, and I never moved back.

Mark and Steve started pitching me for work, and in short order I had my first gig as a freelance director. I was going to shoot a video for Robin Gibb ... back in London. Other work came in: a video for the Temptations, a threesome of videos for movies, one with the Turtles, another with John Parr and a third with Ben E. King featuring River Phoenix. Happily, Phonogram commissioned a couple of videos from me, too, and were trusting enough to send the bands to me without any label folk or management to interfere.

With Steve Golin's help, I started the long legal process which would eventually lead me to becoming an American citizen. I bought a car and found a tiny apartment on Gardner, near the Guitar Center. Little did I realise that, not a hundred yards from my new home, on the other side of the Sunset Strip, five tussle-haired youths wearing tight leather pants were rehearsing and partying hard and, in a few months, would change my life. And I, in my way, would change theirs. I was driving into the mountains to ski at weekends and having fun. But even though the work was improving as I honed my skills, I was worried that I hadn't had a hit since leaving London. Then I met a tall man in snakeskin boots who made me laugh.

In his second great rock and roll history book, *Uncommon People*, David Hepworth kindly credits me with creating the opening sequence of Guns n' Roses' first video, "Welcome to the Jungle," in which Axl steps off the bus for the first time in Hollywood, a blade of straw in his mouth; Izzy offering him drugs and a hooker asking him if he wants to party. I would like to take full credit for coming up with this sequence, but sometimes the smartest thing a director can do when someone offers him an idea is to simply say, "Sounds good. Let's do that!"

I have a policy about starting a new project: keep your eyes and your ears open and figure out who on that job is wielding the most power. Keep that person on your side, and you'll make your life a lot easier. Sometimes it's the lead singer, sometimes it's the record company/film company boss, sometimes it's the actor's agent, sometimes it's the guitar player's wife and sometimes it's the lonely record company gal with an axe to grind. In Guns n' Roses' case, it was Alan Niven, their leather-jacketed manager. And it was Alan who'd pitched that memorable opening sequence to me, except that Alan's style wasn't so much about pitching as telling me what we were going to do.

In June 1987, I shot a video for the ill-fated Great White. "Rock Me" was not exactly a groundbreaking song, but it was to be my first-ever ROCK video for a ROCK band, and I got into the spirit of the exercise with great excitement. The finished video featured a tall blonde babe with a spear gun, a massive pool and a huge stage with many flashing lights. If anything, the video I made was even less original than the song.

Great White's manager, Alan Niven, was deeply suspicious of rock videos and their expense, but we seemed to hit it off anyway. We'd both been brought up in England in military families and loved the sound of Paul Rodgers' voice — but that's where our common ground seemed to end. Alan managed a highly derivative though very successful rock band and dressed for the part as if he'd been assisted by the costume designer of *This Is Spinal Tap*. His tall, bulging frame was always forced into tight black leather pants which finished in a pair of snakeskin cowboy boots; a flamboyant shirt lurked underneath his black leather jacket, and a pair of lightly tinted aero shades hung on the end of his nose. His hair was thinning but long and dirty blonde; his fingers and wrists flashed with silver and turquoise. Whatever my misgivings about his fashion sense, I couldn't help but like the man a lot. (It also helped that he was very generous, flattered me endlessly and called me Maestro.)

When we'd first met and agreed on the "Rock Me" idea, Alan looked over the top of his glasses and asked me what time of day I'd need the band on set.

"Eleven in the morning?" I said, guessing.

"What? This is a rock and roll band! They don't like early starts. But if that's when you need them, I'll make it happen. But, I warn you Nigel, if they have to start that early, don't under any circumstances make them wait. None of us will be very happy about it."

When he said "none of us" I sensed that the person who would be most annoyed was Alan himself.

Everything started out according to plan on the morning of the shoot. At 10:59, the doors of the vast hangar we were shooting in near Long Beach opened and a bunch of scraggly individuals in black leather walked in. They were on time, the stage was set and last-minute adjustments to the massive lighting truss were being made.

Suddenly, the stage went dark for a second. My AD came running over and whispered in my ear. The generator had farted, and when it kicked back in, the lighting director was horrified to realise that all the settings he'd been refining for the last three hours on his computerized lighting desk had been lost. He'd have to start again. Mindful of Alan's veiled threat that there would be fireworks if we didn't start on time, I spent the next two hours hiding and avoiding him. Alan was a large and imposing figure; I had no doubt that the inevitable dressing down he'd give me in front of my crew would be a supreme exercise in humiliation.

Ninety minutes later, my AD found me hiding in the production room. "I suggest we break early for lunch and get the lighting director to work through his meal break and then we can start for real once lunch is done."

Happily, Alan was nowhere to be seen, so we broke for lunch. I filled my plate with food and went over to sit with the band and properly introduce myself. After half an hour of chit-chat another tall, long-haired figure in a black leather jacket entered the hangar and rushed over towards us, breathing hard and looking panicked. Lead singer Jack Russell looked nervously at the newcomer and said, "You'd better go find Alan. He's been looking for you and he's pissed." The newcomer gulped and rushed off.

"Who's that guy?"

"He's our bass player. He's late and Alan's going to kill him!"

Then it dawned on me why it had been so easy to avoid Alan for the last two hours. While I'd been avoiding him because I had no lights, he'd been avoiding me because he was missing a bass player!

Two days later, I was in a small, dark room in Hollywood transferring the dailies when Alan marched in. As luck would have it, a freeze-frame of the hapless bass player was up on screen when he arrived. Alan tapped his finger on the screen.

"You see that guy? I don't want any closeups of him in the video!"

"Why not? He's awesome."

"He was two hours late for the most important date in this band's career. He's been fired. He's no longer in the band. No closeups!"

If I'd been in any doubt who was the person with power, the person to please on this job, I now knew.

Alan seemed to like the "Rock Me" video a lot. Pretty soon after, as we were planning another video for the next Great White single, "Lady Red Light," he asked me to listen to a song by a new band he managed called Guns n' Roses.

"Welcome to the Jungle" was quite unlike anything I'd ever heard. I didn't get it. To my eternal shame, I understood what made Great White tick but G n' R were the first sign that I was no longer on the sharp end of all things musical. Great White loved the sound of Led Zeppelin and all the bands I loved. All they wanted to do was sound like Led Zeppelin — and did a passable job of just that. Guns n' Roses were Zeppelin fans, too, and also cited the Pistols (who I liked) and Aerosmith (who I didn't), but they wanted to take those influences and leap forward into the future. I wasn't yet ready to take that leap with them.

I listened to "Jungle" a few times and told Alan I couldn't or wouldn't do the video. I was also busy doing videos with Was (Not Was) and the Japanese metal band Loudness. Knowing I had another Great White video coming, I already had enough on my plate.

Alan wouldn't take no for an answer. It wasn't just that he thought that I was the right guy for the job, he seemed to think I was the *only* guy for the job. Other directors had apparently been considered but had either not passed the test or had turned the gig down flat. Whether it was true or not, he begged me to do him a favour and direct the Gunners' first clip because, "You're the only person I know who could handle them."

Having someone beg me to do them a favour and wrapping it up in a big bow of flattery is always a good way to get me motivated. He sealed the deal with, "Of course, you'll have to meet with them first, and they'll have to approve you," so there was a challenge connected as well. Sorry plankton that I am, I was now determined to get the gig. A meeting with the guys was hurriedly arranged at their SIR rehearsal space. I was told to go alone, watch them play and not to expect too much as they'd be just returning from a funeral in San Francisco. Apparently, a close friend of the band, who already had a notorious rep, had ODed and I'd be the first person they'd meet after they stepped off the plane returning from the wake.

In everyone's life, there are situations where, at worst, you feel unwelcome and at best you just don't fit in. I've often felt this condition has defined my life: I was the only boy at a school of wealthy young heirs whose parents drove a secondhand car; I was the only one of my contemporaries who never had a steady girlfriend; the only driver on the cab rank who had a degree; the only person I knew in London who didn't drink or do drugs; the only person in America who had no clue who the Brady Bunch were; the only person in the film business who didn't watch obscure French new wave movies for inspiration. The list was endless. You eventually realise that most of us feel that way a lot, but I have never felt more like the fish out of water than the day I met Guns n' Roses.

I'd seen pictures and heard stories. I didn't have long hair anymore (it had mostly fallen out); I hadn't grown up in Indiana or L.A. or hung out with Joni Mitchell as a kid; I hadn't done speed or drunk copious amounts of Wild Turkey; I wasn't much of an Aerosmith fan. But I did have my old leather jacket from the Stiff messenger boy days. I pulled it on, arrived at SIR feeling quite unwell and sat alone in their rehearsal space for 40 minutes before they arrived, solemn and quiet. We talked for a while. I was soon back out into the afternoon sun; they hadn't played me a note.

Alan rang when I got home: I'd passed the test! We'd shoot Great White's "Lady Red Light" on the Thursday and Friday in San Pedro and G n' R's "Welcome to the Jungle" on Saturday and Sunday in Hollywood. If nothing else, I was going to make a nice load of cash for four days' work.

Alan and Axel (as I then thought his name was spelled) had come up with an idea which involved Axl stepping off a bus in Hollywood and hanging out in a motel room with the other guys and some babes. Axl would see himself on a TV screen in a shop window strapped to a chair and screaming, *Clockwork Orange* style, as he watched violent newsreels. All of this would be intercut with performance footage of the band playing in a large room in the Park Plaza Hotel. When I typed out the treatment for everyone to approve it barely filled one side of a page of paper.

Videos, like most pieces of film, are frequently made without enough money to pay for the ideas that are going to make them work, so we picked an empty store across the street from our offices on La Brea as our prime location and filled the shop window with TV sets. The shop front was soon tricked out to double as Axl's chair set and the room out back was filled with cheesy furniture to look like a motel room. A loop of lurid TV footage had been obtained from a stock house. We were ready to roll.

Axl sat in his chair and screamed his head off. I was too inexperienced, nice and, well, English to suggest he should get wild, but he didn't need any prompting from me — he went nuclear, cutting himself badly on the wrist restraints the art department had built for his chair. I wasn't directing Axl — he was directing himself.

Meanwhile, across the street where our motorhome was parked, nothing was happening. Slash, obviously bored, thought it would be fun to take the moho for a spin. Without warning, it lurched into life, did a screeching U-turn on a busy city street full of Mercs and Jeeps doing weekend shopping and started off up the street towards Sunset before Slash was relieved of his self-elected driving duties and the motorhome came to a halt. I saw Alan dragging Slash by his collar, barefoot, back across the road like a scolded child. It seemed that the master guitar player was getting into character and, like the wino he played in the video, had already been at the sauce.

The morning of day two found us at the Park Plaza Hotel — a location used for dozens of features and hundreds of music videos. In my time I've shot Elton John, Mandy Moore and a dozen other acts there. Among its other notable elements, it faces MacArthur Park, where Richard Harris famously left his cake out in the rain. We were preparing for the performance section of the video — what I like to call the skeleton — when Slash came bounding up, all contrite and full of smiles. He apologized profusely for taking the motorhome miles away from set the night before, up into the Hollywood Hills, before completely wrecking it in a canyon. I accepted his apology, appalled at the damage he must have caused on this second car-jacking spree. I hunted down my producer, Lisa Hollingshead, to find out what the damage had been and learned that there had been no second spree at all — apparently, the original U-turn and 100-yard dash up La Brea had seemed longer and far more colourful and disastrous to Slash than it actually was. The motorhome was currently in the parking lot — shiny, new and undamaged.

I'd reminded Lisa that having alcohol on set was a no-no in California and made her promise that the band would not be able to get at the hooch while we were filming on the second day. Slash's apology, it turned out, was not so much a plea for forgiveness as a prelude to asking that I lift the embargo and let him get at the sauce before lunchtime.

Before the crowd of extras arrived later in the afternoon, we were going to shoot close-ups of the band which we would later intercut with the crowd shots. First in front of the camera was Axl. I'd heard him telling someone earlier that he was going to tease his hair into an enormous fright wig — something he'd obviously done before — and that after the video was shot he'd never do it again. Sure enough, he came out with the massive do that would later define a musical genre: hair metal. After one take — which is usually not worth the celluloid it's printed on, as the crew and the artists find their feet — Axl mumbled something about being freaked out and disappeared back into the depths of the building. He was not seen again for another two hours. As plans go, my plan for the evening was now burning in flames. While I prayed for Axl's return, we pressed on with close-ups of Slash, Izzy, et al.

I went home when the night was done, exhausted and confident that my time with the band would not be repeated, as we clearly had nothing in common. Climbing into my VW Golf, I saw the band disappearing into the night, followed by a horde of willing and nubile young things.

The edit was subsequently completed to everyone's satisfaction and sent off to MTV, who promptly rejected it. Unnoticed by me (and everyone else), we'd included a piece of stock footage which very briefly, like a frame or two, panned past a Coca-Cola machine whose logo was just about recognizable. MTV didn't condone advertising unless it was connected with large amounts of cash paid directly into their coffers. Video effects back then were in their infancy and costly, but Geffen authorized an overrun and the errant Coke machine was transformed into an anonymous red blob. The video was resubmitted and rejected again. And fixed again. And then the really bad news arrived — MTV simply didn't want to play the video at all. Too edgy, too heavy, too real, too violent, too loud, too sexy? Who knew? They simply didn't want anything to do with it.

With the important Christmas sales season coming up, the label pulled out the heavy guns. David Geffen: "I called my friend Tom Freston [at MTV] and said to him, 'Just play it in the middle of the night. Don't report it, just play it and let's see if there's a reaction to it.'" *

Tom Zutaut, the A&R man who signed G n' R: "Sometimes there's that one thing that pushes someone's exposure ... and in this case that one thing that David did made all the difference in the world ... from a band that was dead at 200,000 to a band that sold almost a hundred million." *

And so it was agreed the video would be played once a day but only after 9:00 p.m. The hair metal craze was off to a very jumpy and problematic start.

I forgot about Guns n' Roses and concentrated on that Was (Not Was) video I was planning. Then Alan Niven called again. Christmas had passed, "Welcome to the Jungle" was still being played and it seemed something might be happening out there in MTV land. There was

* These remarks are documented in the PBS American Masters show *Inventing David Geffen.*

going to be a second video called "Sweet Child o' Mine." Axl was dating Phil Everly's daughter Erin and was rumoured to have written the song about her. This was the second G n' R track I'd heard, and I didn't like this one much either, though I thought the guitar solo rocked. Instead of presenting me with an idea for the video, Alan suggested I meet him for lunch at a swanky L.A. watering hole. He would bring Axl.

I've occasionally been asked what this musician or that celebrity is like because I've worked with them. My usual answer is I haven't a clue. The beauty of the business I've been in all these years is all the wonderful people I've met and become friends with all over the world, but those people have mostly been camera folk, casting directors, producers and editors, grips and gaffers, art directors and location scouts. Going to lunch with the lead singer of a band was quite unusual.

The Axl I saw at lunch that day was a happy, funny young man. He had some ideas for "Sweet Child o' Mine" which were quite dark. I also feared the ideas were expensive, but I nonetheless promised to write them up into a treatment. The video would open on a newspaper headline which said TOUR CANCELLED and pan down to a frame of Axl from the "Welcome to the Jungle" video — this picture would be captioned BRAIN DEAD? We'd see an ambulance racing past and then depositing Axl in a mental home wearing another white straitjacket similar to the one in "Jungle." In a room full of male mental patients Axl would look through a window at an adjacent room full of female mental patients. Eventually, he would be transfixed by the image of Erin Everly, who would be equally transfixed on the other side of the glass. The treatment suggested Elvira and Jack Nicholson might do cameos. I suggested Maud Adams, who told me she wanted to be in a music video when I'd shot a feature with her.

As the lunch progressed, we mostly talked about Queen and the Electric Light Orchestra. In the end, that lunch with Axl produced an agreement between us that "Mr. Blue Sky" was a perfect pop moment and an open verdict on whether *Out of the Blue* would have been better as a single album.

Over the five videos I did for Guns n' Roses, this was the only social interaction I had with anyone in the band. I'm not resentful or upset by this — this is the way my business has been. I'm part of a service industry, and my service is to provide great film. When I ask the plumber to come over to my house to fix a leaking tap I don't expect to hang out and share my life story with him — I want him to fix my tap and then leave.

The treatment I'd written up was rejected. Alan rang me back — they simply wanted a performance video, and he had a location in mind: an old ballroom above a bank in Huntington Park. We could have the band rock out and shoot ourselves shooting the band, invite Erin and friends down and cut the whole thing together. The only problem we'd have to solve was clearing out the prodigious piles of pigeon crap we found in the building when we went to check it out.

The first attempt to shoot the video was cancelled at the last moment. When the plug is pulled just hours before work commences, the crew gets paid. I got half my fee and smiled all the way to the bank. A few weeks later, the shoot was postponed a second time: drummer Steven Adler was "ill," and you can translate that anyway you like. Once again, the crew got their cancellation fees, though I think, as I'd already pocketed a couple of thousand bucks from the first cancellation, I nobly (but foolishly) volunteered to put this delay down to experience and not submit another invoice.

Consequently, when, at the third attempt, we actually got our gear in the building I was not really optimistic that we'd roll any film — especially as Alan warned me that the band would appear on time but that Axl would arrive late and have to check out the building and see if the "vibe was right" before he'd agree to join in and take part. This was not good news. A rock band without a lead singer is no fucking use to anyone, least of all me.

But I had noticed that a promising change was in the air. Firstly, someone from MTV was going to be on set with us. The young lady had specially flown in from New York and Alan had concocted a piece of simple blackmail. He wanted to put her on the dolly and have our "behind-the-scenes" film crew shoot her operating one of the cameras. If we used that footage in the video, then surely MTV would play the video, if only to show one of their own hard at work. DP Vance Burberry and his crew rolled their eyeballs, but we all understood that, though we saw ourselves as "creatives," we were in the business of selling small round silver things, and if that's what we had to do, we'd do it. When we'd shot "Welcome to the Jungle," I couldn't recall seeing anyone from the label on the set, but there were lots of people from Geffen here, many of them wearing high heels and short skirts.

Suddenly a whisper went round the set. Axl had been spotted outside and was said to be climbing the stairs into the building. Everyone pretended not to notice but watched nervously as he prowled around, checking that everything was to his liking. An emissary was sent my way. Axl approved, and we were ready to shoot. Sighs of relief were audible around the building. The ADs scurried to and fro, getting everyone ready for camera.

A short time later, I was sitting in front of my monitor and I was concerned. Well, not so much concerned as shitting myself with worry. The whole point of having a director on the set of a music video is to make shots that look amazing and cool and sexy. Of one thing I was certain — this first shot was none of these things, it was just godawful and dull.

In the early '80s, film cameras had finally been built that could operate without cables. And then some genius came up with the idea of placing a small video camera in the film camera's eyepiece so that directors, and then their clients, could see exactly what was being filmed and make useful comments about it in real time. On one of the first jobs I ever directed, when I asked the grumpy English camera assistant to plug in the monitor for me, I heard him loudly complain to the cameraman, "It's taken us decades to invent a camera with no bloody cables coming out of it and now three years later they're fucking back again."

Over the years, people have commented that they like the way I hunch over the monitor as it suggests to them I'm watching the filming take place with great intensity. I may be doing that, but it's more likely that I'm terrified as to what people will see on the screen and I'm trying to hide it. If the shot sucks, people will notice. If people notice, they start talking amongst themselves. And then they complain and people agree with them and before you know it everyone has a better idea on how the shoot should proceed — and your authority to run the set has evaporated.

This was one of those times. Axl was finally on set, film was finally rolling and at last we were making a video for "Sweet Child o' Mine." A trio of those high-heeled women from the label were looking over my shoulder; surely, they could tell this was horrible, and I knew they'd be making a comment.

And then one of them did.

"Oh. My. God!" she said. "This is so fucking cool!"

"Isn't it?" murmured her pal. "Ax is so fucking hot."

I'd been looking for vindication and I'd found it. Yes, this was fucking cool and, come to think of it, Axl did look fucking hot, and everything was going to be alright. But then it wasn't.

Axl had suggested that it would be a cool idea if, just before the solo, he ripped off his leather jacket so he could really rock out in his T-shirt in the second half of the song. I concurred but asked if he could please remember to do it in every take at exactly the same point in the song. Axl said that would be no problem.

So, why now, halfway through the first take of the shoot, was Axl flailing his arm like a windmill with his jacket hurling around through space like a lasso? I yelled "Cut" at the top of my voice and everything stopped.

Axl — just like any self-respecting rock star would — had festooned his wrists with myriad bracelets, and the bracelets had got caught in the lining of the sleeve of the jacket. We figured out a solution and started over.

In the middle of take two it happened again. And take three and take four and take five. We were an hour into filming, and I hadn't gotten a single run-through in the can. Alan wandered over and shooed away the women in their high heels. He leaned over me and whispered, "For god's sake, get a full take now whatever happens. Axl is going to walk any minute."

On take six we got lucky; from that moment onwards things proceeded according to plan. We'd started shooting at 4:00 p.m. and wrapped somewhere around 2:00 in the morning.

But we weren't wrapped at all. Axl had other ideas. He was having so much fun he wanted to keep going. And so we went back to work. By 4:00 a.m. we'd completely run out of film. I pulled the plug and we all went home.

I had started regularly working with a wonderful editor named Michael Heldman, who was to become a lifelong friend. One thing we had in common was a love for the music of Pentangle, the English folk-rock band that had been a huge influence on Led Zeppelin. We also both had degrees which served us no useful purpose in our chosen careers. Mine was in architecture. His was in classical Greek!

The two of us set about cutting the hours of footage into the "Sweet Child o' Mine" video you know today. There was one problem — like most music video sets, no one was recording any audio, so when we cut in the shot of the panting dog before the music starts, we had no panting dog sound. We found a microphone, we rolled tape ... and Michael started panting like a dog. We also didn't have the sound of Slash plugging in his guitar, so I went home, cranked up my tiny practice amp and recorded the plugging-in guitar sound on my cassette four-track. Not exactly high fidelity, but no one has ever complained.

The next big issue for me was that Axl shimmied from side to side with an unusual snakelike move that struck me as effeminate and lame. It wasn't rock and roll or tough. When Michael showed me the first cut, I instructed him to take that move out, every single shot of it. And then a woman in our office wandered into the edit bay and saw 30 seconds of the cut.

"What do you think?"

"I love those shots of Axl doing that sexy side-to-side dance of his. He's gorgeous!"

I realised she fancied him. But, more importantly, I realised that what I hated was something that others seemed to really, really like. When she left, I turned to Michael. "All those shots of Axl shimmying from side to side — you know the ones I told you to take out? Put them back in — all of them. And see if you can find some more!"

Whether it was the shimmying, the gratuitous shot of the MTV employee pretending to operate the camera or the fact that people, a lot of people, were now buying copies of *Appetite for Destruction,* MTV was very enthusiastic about the video and there was no 9:00 p.m. restriction on this clip. It went into heavy rotation and was suddenly the hottest thing on the channel.

A few weeks later, Alan Niven called with a radical suggestion. "Why don't we make a second version of the video using all the shots that we didn't use in the first cut, and transfer all the footage in black and white?" Was this a clever ruse to extend the life of a video which was being played to death on MTV and in danger of overstaying its welcome or a cynical marketing ploy to squeeze more sales out of the video's airplay? Probably a bit of both. Michael went back into the edit bay and version number two was soon on the airwaves.

I've often been asked what's the most important decision you can make while making a music video. My response has been quite simple: pick a hit. Some of my proudest work has been for songs that no one ever heard and were thus videos that no one ever played. But if the song you shoot a video for is a hit, then people will certainly see your work and, if you do good work, the phone will start ringing.

After "Sweet Child o' Mine," my phone started ringing. A lot. Sometimes this caused problems, one of which affected the next G n' R video, "Paradise City." Alan's plan this time was a clever one. The Gunners were touring the States opening for Aerosmith, who were also on Geffen. They had a date at Giants Stadium in New Jersey, so why don't we go and shoot them there and "borrow" the huge Aerosmith crowd to create the impression that G n' R were already massive enough to draw tens of thousands? Within a few months, the band would be able to draw a crowd of that size on their own, but for now it was a bit of a white lie. If we pulled it off, it would become a self-fulfilling prophecy. For me, the lure of this job was much simpler — it was to be the biggest budget job I'd ever done — a massive $200,000. I'd never had so much money to spend, though a very large chunk of it was going to pay the union workers at the stadium simply to get our gear in through the door.

The icing on the cake was that, immediately after the Giants Stadium show, the band were going to fly by Concorde to England to appear at the Donington Park heavy metal festival. I would get to go back to England with the band, on the Concorde no less, and shoot more footage there in front of another massive crowd.

Around this time I'd become friends with a lighting director with a broad Australian accent. Vance Burberry was born in England but had emigrated to Australia while still quite young and, after some adventures, wound up, at 15 years old, working in a theatre and doing lights for local garage bands. He'd fallen in love with stage lighting and, after stints with Cold Chisel and AC/DC, followed the rock and roll yellow brick road to America, where he went on the road with Tom Petty, Diana Ross, the Go-Go's and dozens of others. He adopted a hard-paced lifestyle that put most of his employers to shame. If he was perhaps a wild and crazy man, he was also a warm and generous soul with a huge appetite for work and a wild cackling laugh that I loved. He made shooting fun, though often nail-bitingly tense. Vance had been the gaffer on "Welcome to the Jungle"; shortly afterwards, after much pleading, I offered him his first chance to be a Director of Photography. It had worked out well, so I'd asked him to shoot "Sweet Child o' Mine." By the time we got to "Paradise City," Vance was a part of the team and my first choice to shoot the show.

I was working constantly now, and my regular producer was a small feisty lady, Lisa Hollingshead, who had once been a ballerina. By the time I met her, she was a producer of considerable talent, and I described her as a terrier — a description she didn't like much — but we made a good team. I was English, polite and sometimes had trouble speaking my mind; Lisa was tough and wouldn't put up with fools. With Vance as our DP and Michael our editor we made a formidable team and would spend the next few years travelling the world together.

Even with a generous budget, there was not enough cash available to shoot the show in 35mm. Vance insisted we use Panavision 16mm cameras which, though quite rare and only available from Panavision in Hollywood, did have the advantage of large magazines, which meant we could shoot longer sections of G n' R's live show without reloading — a definite practical plus when shooting a concert performance on film.

Flights and hotels had been booked; a plan was made to ship the boxes of camera gear to New York. Then Geffen A&R man Tom Zutaut called, asking for a meeting. This seemed unusual, as I normally dealt exclusively with Alan Niven about the Gunners, but I headed over to the Geffen office on Sunset, where Zutaut dropped a bombshell in my lap. The shoot with G n' R in New Jersey was still on, but he had another job for me. He'd signed a band named Rock City Angels, and they needed a video quickly. I was the man to shoot it, and it had to be made in the old Sun Studio in Memphis, where Elvis had cut some of his most iconic early records.

Being cherry-picked by Zutaut to shoot this crucial first video for his new signing was certainly an honour, but it came with a catch: the video had to be shot on a Saturday and Sunday. And not just any weekend, but the very Saturday and Sunday immediately before the Monday when I was scheduled to shoot Guns n' Roses in New Jersey. Not only would this mean I wouldn't be available for some crucial scouting and B-roll shooting in New York, it also left the thorny problem of how I was going to finish work in Memphis at 10:00 p.m. on Sunday and be available for duty in New Jersey at 8:00 a.m. the following morning.

I pleaded with Zutaut to help me out. I suggested that he was making life difficult for himself and jeopardizing the biggest job of my life, which he was also paying for. Obviously the gig at Giants Stadium couldn't be shifted, but surely the Rock City Angels job could be brought forward or delayed? His response was bizarrely not in his own best interests: "It's your problem, you sort it out."

I rang Lisa, who came up with a solution. She and Vance would fly to New York; the Panavision cameras would follow. On Saturday and Sunday, Vance would meet up with Slash, Izzy, Duff and Steven with a Bolex (a spring-wound clockwork camera) and shoot them hanging out in Manhattan before the Aerosmith gig. At the same time, I would be flying to Memphis to prep and shoot the as yet unheard-of Rock City Angels. Friend Michael Wells, the producer for the job in Memphis, and Lisa both scoured their budgets for some extra cash and found enough money — just enough money — to have a private jet waiting for me in Memphis after wrap on Sunday night to whisk me to the East Coast. In New Jersey, a car would meet me at the airport. A hotel had been found close to the stadium, so I could get a few hours of precious sleep and still be in time for the gig at Giants Stadium on Monday morning.

There was, however, a downside. With two important videos that both needed to be turned around double-quick for the same label, there was no time — and now no money — for that extra seat on the Concorde. Vance would fly back to England in luxury with the Gunners, the Bolex at his side, while I would make my way back to a small dark room in Hollywood to start the editing process.

I accepted my fate and got on the plane for Tennessee. Rock City Angels were cut from the same cloth as G n' R — they wore tight trousers and had piercings and tattoos in all the right places — but didn't have a spark. Their song was bluesy and derivative, whereas "Paradise City" was driving and unusual for a metal rock and roll record of its type. It had a fiendishly catchy hook that I couldn't stop singing. Shooting Rock City Angels in the Sun Studio was certainly special, but I felt 1,500 miles away from the action. After the first night of shooting, I rang Lisa in New York to make sure everything was ready for my mad cross-country dash the following night — only to learn that a disaster had been averted in Manhattan.

The FedEx truck had pulled up outside Lisa's hotel in New York on Friday to deliver Vance's camera order. One by one, 120 flight cases containing cameras, lenses, magazines, film, eyepieces, tripods, camera heads and other gear had been unloaded. The hotel lobby was filled with them. As it was a small boutiquey kind of place, they had to be moved fast. When Lisa and her production manager arrived that night, the two of them brought all the cases up to their room. With white camera cases piled to the ceiling, they changed into their pj's and collapsed on their beds, satisfied they'd never have to do anything that physically exhausting ever again. Seconds later, the phone rang. The occupants of the room below had noticed that the ceiling of their room was bending and making cracking noises. The gear probably weighed around a ton, and the floor of this small hotel was built to accommodate a couple of European tourists and a suitcase or two — not the weight of a truck. It was only a matter of time before gravity did its work and the camera gear sought a lower elevation. Lisa and her production manager changed out of their pj's and proceeded to distribute the camera gear around the hotel.

Sunday morning in Memphis was incredibly hot and stuffy. We had moved out of Sun Studio and, stealing a page out of my "Welcome to the Jungle" book, had turned a disused shop into a bedroom set that would eventually be trashed by the band in true rock and roll style. It was so hot that we'd brought in a mobile air conditioning unit, but it didn't seem to be making much headway. We had a lot to do, but I was confident that we'd be done by the 10:00 p.m. cutoff time. I was upset that I'd not get to ride in the Concorde, which had long been an ambition of mine, but at least I'd get to fly back to New York in an executive jet. How fucking cool was that?

Lunchtime came and went in a blur. I spent it in a roasting phone booth down the street, pitching an idea for another job and catching up with Lisa, who was tying up loose ends before the next day's shoot. When I ran back to set, the crew had thoughtfully put aside some food for me, but it had been placed on a chair next to the struggling A/C unit. The room was still hot and sweaty, but my lunch was stone cold. I threw it away and got back to work. Feeling peckish an hour or two later, I wandered over to the craft service table but all that was left was peanuts — not something I enjoy — so I drank another coffee and carried on.

Rock City Angels weren't going to put Pacino or De Niro out of work, but they were enthusiastic and eager. I had every reason to believe we would get the day done when my producer, Friend Michael Wells, whispered in my ear that I had exactly five minutes to finish the job because he was going to drag me away from the set.

"WTF? You said I could shoot till ten, and it's not even seven yet. Why are you doing this?

"We need to leave for the airport now!"

"But I haven't finished here. I have another scene to shoot and then we have to trash the hotel room!"

"I'll explain in the car. Now you have four minutes."

We rolled camera and I told the band to go for it and trash the hotel room set. "Make sure there's nothing to clean up but sawdust."

The band complied. As the dust was clearing, I frantically shook everyone's hand and saw the looks of confusion as I raced out the door, telling the band their video was suddenly, miraculously, in the can.

Before I had a chance to close the car door we were already moving, skidding away into traffic. I was dripping with sweat, filthy and enormously hungry. I looked at Friend Michael Wells, who was also sweating bullets as we swerved around a slower moving vehicle and merged onto the Freeway.

"What the fuck is going on?"

"The private jet thing isn't happening. I've managed to get you a seat on the last commercial flight I could find to JFK tonight and it's going to be a really close shave."

"No private jet? Why?"

He explained that the accountant at my company, a company I was a part owner of, had refused to pay the deposit on the jet hire, which would buy the jet fuel and secure the rental, until he'd cleared it with two of my partners — who were out of town and not answering calls.

The private jet company had told us to make other arrangements, which is why we were racing across the city like madmen to catch the last scheduled flight out of Memphis. As I lowered my head in my hands in frustration and righteous anger, I swallowed a lungful of appalling body odour … MY appalling body odour. Twelve hours in that fake hotel room in this heat with an A/C unit that was only good for cooling food had left me in need of a bath and a clean set of clothes.

"Where's my bag? I need to change clothes if I'm getting on a commercial flight."

"The PA took it to the airport half an hour ago. He's waiting for us at the check-in and trying to hold the flight for you."

We skidded to a halt in front of the terminal, and I leapt from the car. I ran to check-in, where the PA was waiting with my ticket. Before the horrors of 9/11, all I had to do now was race for the plane. I oozed yet more sweat as I sprinted through the terminal and found my gate. A flight attendant was waiting for me. She pointed to the jet bridge as I heard her yelling into her phone, "He's coming right now."

I stepped on board, the door closed behind me and an entire planeload of weekenders stared angrily at the perspiring mess who'd delayed their flight. However, their anger was nothing compared with the look of disgust on the face of the neatly dressed gent in Business Class who was horrified by the bedraggled, panting and rank individual who sat in the empty seat beside him and pulled a pencil and shot list out of his pocket, gasping for air, as we were told to watch the safety video.

As I was incredibly ravenous, I was glad to be in Business Class; the food would be decent. You can imagine my horror when the flight attendant told me there was no food on board.

"Perhaps you'd like some peanuts?"

It was one o'clock in the morning when I arrived at the hotel that overlooked Giants Stadium and discovered that, of course, the kitchen was closed. The Night Manager smiled as he handed me my room key. "There are snacks in the mini-bar, perhaps you'll find something in there." Yup … peanuts.

I consumed everything available in the hotel's breakfast room the next morning before waking the accountant in L.A. who'd scotched the private jet. He was unimpressed by my anger and to this day I imagine he thinks it was a ploy to bask in luxury at 30,000 feet at someone else's expense, when in fact it was the only sane way of working on two jobs in two different time zones inside of ten hours.

Giants Stadium was sunny and bright. I was freshly bathed and had a full stomach. We were rolling film during soundcheck, and Slash was perched on the edge of the stage with his guitar wailing, wearing only shorts and boots.

The transition between jobs had been a mess but all was going well now. Lisa had pulled off a few miracles, and Vance was chuckling about the cool stuff he'd shot with the band in Manhattan. Alan Niven sauntered over and told me that Axl would not be available to talk before they went onstage, so was there anything I needed to know before show time?

Me: When will the band be playing "Paradise City"?

Alan: When do you want them to play it?

Me: Third song in would be perfect.

Alan: Why third?

Me: We only have four cameras. The magazines on the cameras should last through the first two songs, so if we change mags before the start of the third song, we can make sure that all cameras are fully loaded when they do "Paradise City."

Alan: I'll go and check with Axl.

Alan returned five minutes later, chuckling.

Alan: Axl said he doesn't know where "Paradise City" will be in the set. All he knows at this point is that it definitely won't be third!

Me: Seriously?

Alan: Seriously.

I rolled my eyes and went to the office at the back of the stadium, where my four monitors had been set up, and tested the talk-back system. At a live show you give each camera operator a headset and a transmitter/receiver so you can give them instructions on what you want them to shoot. Everything was working perfectly, and I paced nervously, waiting for showtime.

The cameras started rolling the minute the band appeared behind the massive stage, ready to go on. On my monitors, I saw Axl for the first time that day. He'd gone full Hollywood rock and roll in a white leather jacket and pants. Slash was wearing a Hard Rock T-shirt with a difference — instead of L.A. or New York or London, the location printed on the shirt read "Hell." I chuckled to myself and wished the crew good luck as the band raced onstage. Down in the guts of the arena I could hear the crowd roar and the first dull thuds as Steven Adler tested his kick drum. I heard the count-off for the first tune, the band launched into their set ...

... and all the monitors in front of me promptly turned to snow and static! We'd tested the video transmitters after soundcheck and everything had worked perfectly but, when that massive PA system started belting G n' R out to a packed stadium, the soundwaves were so powerful that the transmitters couldn't cope. Occasional images drifted in and out of the static as if the band members were in a hurricane on Mars. I tried my best to direct the cameras to shoot useful angles. I didn't dare look around, but I sensed Alan over my shoulder boring holes in my back. I still had no idea when "Paradise City" would appear in the set. This $200,000 job was turning into a white-knuckle ride in a snowstorm; I now knew what must have been going through the Big Bopper's mind as he and Buddy Holly took off on their final fateful flight.

And "Paradise City"? They played it third!

The next morning, Vance climbed on the Concorde and flew to England with the band and Alan while I headed back to the cutting room in L.A. A few days later, I showed up to the editing room to see how Michael was doing with the footage. He had a dark look on his face. "We have a problem," he muttered. "The recorded version of the song, the version that we're cutting to, is nearly seven minutes long. The version they played at Giants Stadium is faster and only five minutes long!" He sighed and gave me a nasty look as editors always do when they've been presented with a problem created by the director that they're supposed to solve. There wasn't much I could do but sit down beside him and do my best to help.

A day or two later I came home to find a weird message on my machine asking if I was alive and OK. At the Donington gig, the Gunners had gone on in the afternoon and delivered a blistering set. Rumours swiftly travelled back across the Atlantic that the massive crowd was so into the gig that there'd been a huge surge towards the stage and two fans had been crushed to death. One of the dead was named Alan Dick, and my friend who called worried that the papers had got the name wrong and it had been me who had died. I wondered if the gods had planned for me to die at the gig but, by my missing that trip to the UK, had picked on another poor soul with my name instead.

It wasn't till Michael had worked his magic and we'd finished the video and delivered it to MTV that we noticed, in the black and white footage that Vance had shot at Donington, a small face in the surging crowd disappearing from view with what seemed like a scream on his face.

I don't really believe in such things but sometimes when I can't sleep and it's three o'clock in the morning I wonder if Alan Dick took a bullet for me that day.

The months passed and Alan Niven called me again and announced that the band had made an EP and we were going to make a video for "Patience." The band had an idea that involved a recording studio setup and a collection of hotel scenes.

We shot the studio scenes at the Record Plant in Hollywood. Axl whistled his way through the tune; Slash slumped in a chair and let his hair fall over his face. I kept asking him to look up and reveal himself, but he ignored me and then was upset when he couldn't see himself in the final edit. The hotel footage was shot at the Ambassador on Wilshire Boulevard. I'd shot the Temptations there when I'd first moved to L.A. The hotel had still been open then, but now it was a neglected dusty mausoleum, a memory of a bygone glamorous age. In other words, the perfect place for a film crew to go about their business and make as much noise as we wanted.

As each bandmember had his own vignette, it became clear that the vibe between them had changed. When we'd shot "Welcome to the Jungle" there was a clear impression of them as a solid social unit — five lads together against the world. But now, with some success and thousands of road miles under their belt, they were five distinct organs all pulling in different directions, no longer with the same unity of purpose. It happens with all bands eventually, but I felt it was happening particularly quickly with G n' R.

There was a final hurrah with the band when we shot the video for "It's So Easy," which in the end did not show me in the best light. The idea called for Axl and Erin to be seen in various scenes involving bondage. Whips and gags were the order of the day; those moments would be intercut with live footage shot in Hollywood's Cathouse. When I delivered the treatment to Anne-Marie Mackay, now my rep at Propaganda, she refused to allow us to be associated with it. I'd like to say that I did the right thing but, as always, I wanted to get the gig and pressed onwards despite her objections. Looking back, I believe she was right, but it says a lot about my work ethic (or not, depending on your view) that I put the blinkers on and just pressed onwards to get the job done. The scenes between Erin and Axl were shot with Axl making most of the crucial decisions on set as I was too embarrassed to really get behind the idea. Axl eventually contacted Vance, my DP, directly to shoot the footage of him and two girls making out in the car.

The live footage at the Cathouse was shot during a crazy live show in a packed club with the P.A. cranked to the max. There were no monitors for me to watch, and my directing consisted of pushing through the sweaty bodies and pointing frantically to tell the cameramen what to shoot. My abiding memory of that night was sitting on the hood of my car talking to a crew member on the street after the show and watching David Bowie leave the club alone. He gave us a brief, limp smile as he passed and then disappeared into the night.

As we were completing the edit, Slash stopped by the edit room to check it out. He arrived carrying a beer bottle as if still in the role we'd first seen him play in "Welcome to the Jungle." After he approved the cut I walked him to the door of our office. He draped his arm around me. "Y'know Nigel, we need to go out and drink sometime." What could I tell him but the truth? "Slash, I don't really drink!"

As his arm slipped from around my neck and he stumbled for the door, I heard him say, "Weird!" **

We sent a cut of the video to the label, where it remained in limbo for many years before being released with the 30th anniversary edition of *Appetite for Destruction.*

For the next few years, a manager or label person would hire me to shoot their hair metal band and say, "Do for my lead singer what you did for Axl Rose." And I would accept the gig, knowing in my heart that I was involved in a fool's errand. For all their faults, the original Guns n' Roses were a magic collection of parts that created a greater whole. And no one was ever going to match Axl, let alone be a better version of him. God knows, I certainly tried to do my best.

Alan Niven was later fired, which I think was a dreadful mistake. He'd been hired to manage the band before Geffen released *Appetite for Destruction.* The label had concluded that the band needed a manager who understood the business and could keep them in line and look after them. I doubt they could have picked a better man for the job.

Alan was a tough guy who didn't mince words or actions. When he looked at you over the brim of those aviator shades you knew you'd better have a good answer for whatever question he had next. But he understood the business like no one I'd ever met. I think G n' R's career could have played out quite differently if only the band understood what Alan did for them. Without question, I think he's one of the best artist managers I ever worked with.

I get calls every few years from journalists wanting to talk about the videos I made for the band. I go on YouTube to watch them again

**I saw Slash again 30 years later when I shot some interviews for his blues project — he was charming, sober and lucid.

to see if there's anything I've forgotten. The final irony is that, when I watch the videos, I finally get Guns n' Roses. I didn't understand at the time what they were about; it seems I had to make the videos so that I and the rest of the world could see what it was that made them tick.

Slash was certainly right: Weird.

CHAPTER 20

Bed of Nails

AS A FREELANCER, one of the surest ways to book a gig is to book a holiday first. You sit down, take a look at the calendar, see a nice space opening up in your schedule and start reserving flights and hotels and making plans. Within hours, the phone rings and you have a choice: cancel the vacation or tell the person on the other end of the line you're unavailable. You really have no choice if you want your career to flourish. You have to take the gig. You have to show up.

And so it was when I first got to work with Alice Cooper. My old school friend Ed Howard was coming to stay with me in L.A. for a two-week holiday. I owed him so many favours that I promised him I would be completely available to spend time with him, and I kept that promise right up until the moment that Steve Einczig from Epic asked if I could write a treatment for Alice, who had a comeback album, *Trash,* scheduled for release. I'd seen a picture in a magazine of a Japanese actor tied to a vast sculpture, which inspired me. I dashed off a treatment for "Poison" and crossed my fingers. A few days later, I was invited to lunch with Alice and his manager, Shep Gordon. By the time coffee was served, I sensed the gig was mine.

We had everything we needed for Alice's shoot, but we didn't have a band, so we had to go and cast one. We set up a drum kit and some amps in a shitty rehearsal room off Santa Monica Boulevard and opened the floodgates. The line of hopefuls filled the waiting room and stretched out across the parking lot. I've done hundreds of casting sessions in my time, but none where the participants were so eager ... and so desperate! There were around 150 hopeful drummers and guitarists; perhaps ten percent were contenders. In one way or another, I loved every player that showed up that day. Even the most desperate and untalented players impressed me with their enthusiasm and eagerness. My heart went out to them because, as they strapped on their cheap guitars, I saw my own hopes and dreams. Like me, they'd spent countless hours in front of the mirror and out in the woodshed. This was their big shot and, bizarrely, I was the one to decide whether they would make it to the final selection. I don't know if I was the best or the worst person to be the judge that day.

For years I kept a VHS tape of that casting session; when friends came over, I'd throw it in the video player. It was sometimes hysterically funny to watch, sometimes heartbreaking. I remember one guy who walked in with a big smile and luxurious black curls halfway down his back. He was short and stocky and already carrying an impressive double chin, but he was full of pride as he pulled out the ugliest guitar I'd ever seen and plugged in. The guitar lead was far too short, so every time he threw some shapes, he would unplug himself, then jump around and desperately try and line up the jack plug with the amp's input. As he was shaking like a leaf, the air was rent with horrible squeals until he finally reconnected and started his performance all over again. It was *Spinal Tap* on steroids — only more tragic. But if memory serves, two of the players we picked that day became members of Alice's touring band for the next few years.

With the shoot only days away, I worried how I was going to break the news to Ed. Ed was a rock and roll fan, and we'd gone to many gigs together over the years. "School's Out" had been a huge hit in the UK, but when I'd turned left and gone into the music business, Ed had turned right and started running his father's farm. When I was driving a cab, Ed gave me one day's work a week on his farm to boost my earnings to a survivable weekly wage. I suspected he kept the really shitty jobs just for me; he would piss himself laughing when I emerged from a barn, covered in dust and gasping for air. But even so, such kindness was not to be forgotten, and I owed him a great holiday in the L.A. sun. So, I hatched a devious plan.

Ed was landing the day before the shoot. That evening, there was a dinner planned with Alice to go over the final details of the video. I picked Ed up from the airport, gave him time to take a shower at my house and then took him out to dinner with Alice. You'll have to ask Ed if this was a fun thing to do on your first night in Hollywood or whether it was a bit of a downer to find that your mate had reneged on his promise to be one hundred percent available on your inaugural trip to California.

I had a full-time assistant then, a lovely young actress named Connie Blankenship. As I would be shooting the next day, I asked her to take Ed to Disneyland or Universal Studios — whichever he preferred — but Ed decided it would be much more fun to come to the shoot, so I gave Connie the day off. By 11:00 in the morning, Ed had discovered the great truth of being on a set that you're not working on — it's terribly dull. "Hey Nige, any chance your assistant can take me to Universal Studios now?"

Working with Alice was fun. If I suggested a move or a nuance in his performance, he was all over it and gave me what I wanted and more. If I suggested something that wasn't appropriate, he'd say, "I don't think Alice would do that, but why don't we try this?" Whenever we needed him on set after a lighting change, he was back with us in a flash. During that first lunch he'd shared with me some eye-watering stories of the mischief he'd gotten up to in his earlier years, but that was obviously in his past. On set, he was clear-eyed and ready to do whatever it took to make the video great.

With "Poison" in the can, I got to shoot "Bed of Nails," which is my personal favourite. Keen-eyed Oasis fans might notice the female cello players, an idea I later cannibalized for "Wonderwall," and the silhouetted backgrounds which later showed up in "Champagne Supernova." With these two videos completed, I was asked to shoot Alice's live show in Birmingham, England. The budget was generous enough to grant us two nights. Then Alice came up with a brilliant suggestion — on the morning of the second show, why not play the previous night's show back through the PA and mime to it? It's something no other artist I've ever worked with has ever been prepared to do — let alone suggest. As a consequence, we got three performances out of Alice and his band for the price of two.

As showtime approached on the first night I asked if I could have a quick chat with Alice to wish him luck, but I was forbidden from going to his dressing room. Alice later apologized and explained that, before the show, he had to isolate himself so he could become Alice Cooper — the dark persona who chops off babies' heads onstage — and then he similarly needed time to decompress after.

During that first night's performance, as I called the shots from the wall of monitors backstage, I suddenly heard Alice's voice disappear from the mix I was listening to. His radio mic had crapped out. But Alice kept on singing and performing, moving to the side of the stage, where he swapped mics quickly for a working one. "That was pretty nifty!" I told Alice later. He smiled. "I knew that the first night was going to be the best for audio, so I kept singing so you'd still have the close-up if you needed it. I knew I could dub myself in later."

Back in L.A., we shot two more videos, "House of Fire" and "Only My Heart Talkin." The latter was done over a weekend. As we were nearing a wrap on Saturday, Alice asked me for a quick word. He sensed he was done for the day and asked if he could leave early. Also, would it be possible to arrive on set half an hour later than scheduled the next morning? Of course, I said yes. It wasn't till the next day that I heard that his wife had fallen ill and been rushed to hospital. He was flying home to Phoenix to be with her overnight. "Why didn't you tell me?" I asked. He put his hand on my shoulder, "I've noticed how hard you work, and I can see that it's a very stressful job. I didn't want to add more anxiety by having you worry about me."

Without question, Alice is the most professional artist I've ever worked with and a lovely man to boot. After that first video, I said to Shep Gordon, his longtime manager, "Alice is such a sweet man and such a pleasure to be around. Who knew? You should get him on *Letterman* or something and let people see the real Alice." Shep smiled at me, "We've spent 20 years refining Alice's dark public image. Do you think I'm going to blow all that for ten minutes on a chat show?"

CHAPTER 21

All Together Now

IT WAS STEVE GOLIN who first suggested I move to America and become a full-time director, and it was Steve who suggested to Mark Freedman that he fly to Toronto and sign me up to his company and, when I'd arrived in L.A., it was Steve and his wife Vilborg who took me under their wing and looked after me. Steve arranged my first U.S. bank account, got me an immigration lawyer, helped me find an apartment and supplied an endless string of hysterical stories to keep me laughing.

Shortly after my arrival, Michael Kuhn from Polygram asked if I would like to pitch an idea for a film. Polygram were looking to get back into the film biz, and he was looking for a script with a car chase, a love story and a crossbow bolt through the neck. It was Thanksgiving weekend and I had nothing better to do, so I sat down with my little Radio Shack laptop that could only remember three sheets of typed paper at a time and pounded out a treatment. I'd never been to film school, had directed maybe ten videos and a documentary about Tears for Fears, had never seen a movie script or read a treatment, but I'd seen a thousand movies and knew the basics. Guessing that you should write what you know, I made my lead character a young architect and described a scenario where, by chance, he gets involved with a bunch of bad guys who are selling drugs. The twist is they're all cops. I sent the treatment off to Kuhn and went over to Steve and Vilborg's house for my first Thanksgiving dinner.

When Michael called back, he had bad news and good news. He'd asked a number of people to submit scripts and ideas and liked none of them ... but he felt mine showed promise. Could we turn it into a script? Kuhn came to L.A., where I introduced him to Steve and his partner Joni Sighvatsson as potential producers of the film. With Kuhn's approval, Steve introduced me to his pals John Dahl and David Warfield, who set about turning my 17-page pitch into a script. Within six months I was stepping onto the set of my first film with my cameraman pal Dave Bridges, who'd first introduced me to Steve Golin. It was less than a year since I had handed in my notice and bought a ticket to L.A.

I learned that making a movie is intensely stressful, but Steve was at my side throughout the whole process. By the time we reached post-production, the film had been sold at a small profit.

In 1986, Steve told me that he and Joni were going to leave Mark Freedman Productions and set up their own company. They were going to partner with two directors I had once hired at Phonogram, Dominic Senna and Greg Gold, and an unknown director named David Fincher. Would I like to be the sixth member of the new company? I liked Mark Freedman a lot, but it was Steve who had driven my move to L.A. and been at my side the whole way through the film. Without a moment's hesitation, I said yes.

The company was to be called Propaganda and, as it was explained to me, we would all have an equal share. A temporary location was found on La Brea Avenue in the heart of Hollywood, and we went to work. I'd miraculously landed a directing gig on a second movie, so I wasn't around for much of the first few months of Propaganda, but it seemed that things were moving along nicely.

Steve alerted me that they were thinking of hiring a rep for the company. He wanted me to meet her to get my approval. I laughed out loud when he told me her name was Anne-Marie Mackay, the woman I'd met on my first day at Phonogram and who'd later brought Devo's Jerry Casale into my office. There was no question that I would approve of hiring her — it was a smart move — but we still met up for coffee.

Early on, the six of us — Steve, Joni, Greg, Dom, David and me —would hold regular meetings. While larger issues like the company logo needed to be approved by all of us, I felt that details such as who should be answering the phones should be left to Steve and Joni. Soon the meetings became less frequent — we were all too busy.

A cavernous space on a quiet street in Hollywood was chosen to become the Propaganda offices. Everyone loved it and, as we walked around the empty building, plans were made for the front desk here, the production office there, the directors' offices over there. The floors were concrete, the walls were brick and the overall approach was to be open-plan. My architectural training kicked in. I explained that with the hard floors and walls and dozens of people all on phones it would be noisy and tiring to work in there, and we should look into carpeting, sound insulation and roofs on the directors' offices. I was overruled. (Within a week of moving in, plans were made for those offices to get roofs!)

By now MTV was at its height. Greg was making videos with Smokey Robinson, Dom was shooting Janet Jackson, and David — who was suddenly proving to be a major talent — was shooting Madonna. Anne-Marie was doing fabulous work, and I was working with so many metal bands that we'd opened a subsidiary, The Foundry, run by Juliana Roberts, just to deal with hard rock. Propaganda was hip, cool and very successful.

Steve had told me that the six-way agreement would be worked out with the lawyers and I would be presented with the paperwork soon. I was so busy and had come to trust him so much that I didn't doubt for a second that it would all be as promised. When the paperwork finally arrived, I discovered that I was not getting a sixth share at all. Everyone else had negotiated their deals; I was being given what was left. I had been naïve and foolish. It was the first sign that the dream I had signed up for was to be found wanting.

CHAPTER 22

The Dutch Angle

ONE MORNING IN LATE 1978, Robbo called me into his office at Stiff Records and said he wanted to play me something. He put a 7-inch white label on the stereo and cranked the volume. As a onetime Hendrix roadie who I'd seen shoving his head inside speaker cabinets at gigs, Robbo was infamous for his battered hearing and the deafening volume he would use to listen to new releases. I was certainly no stranger to loudness myself, but I didn't like what was coming out of the speakers and suffered through the next three minutes and forty-eight seconds. When it was over, Robbo turned to me. "What do you think then? Is it a hit?" Foolishly I decided to tell the truth: "Who's going to buy a record that opens with 'In the deserts of Sudan'?"

I'd just been given an advance play of Ian Dury's "Hit Me With Your Rhythm Stick." Thankfully, Robbo ignored my commentary and released the record the next week. It not only charted but became Stiff's first number-one single and the source of much pride at our little shop-front label. If I was going to rise to dizzying heights in the music business, I clearly needed to sharpen up my A&R skills.

At the heart of the music business, certainly in the days I worked in it, there existed a deep respect for the alchemy on which the success of every label and every artist relied — the genius of the A&R man. Everyone who's ever worked in showbiz knows an unspoken law of success that follows you around like a stale fart, that nagging little devil over your shoulder constantly whispering in your ear what you know only too well: You're only as good as your last job. But for the savviest of A&R men, if the last job went well, it could keep you, and your label, afloat for years. However, for every guy who had "good ears," like George Martin, who signed the Beatles, there were a dozen guys like Bill Smith (name changed to save embarrassment) who signed Zodiac Mindwarp and the Love Reaction.

A good A&R man (they were mostly men back then) would not only spot talent but then nourish that talent, cherry-pick songs for them, select the right producer, help them find a good manager, cajole nonbelievers at the label into bouts of feigned enthusiasm, convince their CEO to allocate an enormous amount of cash on marketing, release their record at the most propitious point in the calendar and buy them huge meals at midnight after gigs and recording sessions before pushing them towards the door marked International Success. What made their task supremely difficult was that all too often, having pushed the artist through that door, a light would come on as it swung back into the A&R man's face, revealing that instead of International Success, the sign on the door actually read Failure & Obscurity. If you were good at it, I mean really good, you could demand a percentage of the subsequent profits on record sales which, if you were lucky, might mean you'd still be cashing checks long after your ears had failed you and you no longer wore tight trousers.

I never aspired to be an A&R man, but I had a shitload of records and an endless supply of opinions. Once I arrived in the music biz, I tried to soak up every bit of insider knowledge I could. Robbo once told me, "Musicians are like pebbles on a beach, but if you can find a decent singer with some good songs, then maybe you're on to something." Although my first brush with A&R had been a short and dismal failure, that didn't stop me thinking that perhaps, if I had another chance, I might get lucky.

And so, one afternoon Paul Conroy told me to cancel my date that night (as if!). I was going to be temporarily promoted and allowed to call myself an A&R man.

The task I had been given was simple enough. I was to report to a small club in Soho at the appointed hour and announce myself at the door. Impressed by my credentials, the doorman would whisk me inside, free of charge, where I would be shown all the respect and honour due to a member of the A&R department from the country's leading independent record label. If I was in the right mood and the band gave it their best shot, then maybe they would be on their way to superstardom, and I would be on my way to a massive expense account and frequent holidays in the Caribbean.

That was the plan.

Like many labels of its type, Stiff Records didn't have an A&R department as such. A&R was squeezed in during the day and in the evening by the three principals: Robbo, Conroy and Alan Cowderoy. Every night they would be traipsing around town or up and down the motorway looking for the next big thing. On one occasion, I'd driven Conroy to the airport for an overnight trip to see a band play in Dublin. The next day, I went back to pick him up from the airport.

"How was the band?"

"Brilliant. They're going to be massive."

"Really? So, we signed them then?"

"No. It'll take three albums to get them off the ground and we just don't have that kind of money."

How right he was. That band was U2.

And so, on the inaugural evening of my A&R career, as night fell and the Stiff offices closed, I unlocked my bike and cycled towards Soho, full of optimism and excitement. Perhaps the band would be truly great, perhaps I would have that moment of mystical vision, perhaps they would get signed to the label and perhaps my own career would benefit.

I pedalled into the street where the club was located and was intrigued by the fact that the band was playing in a club I'd never heard of. I locked my bike up against a railing, approached the door and found it closed. A handwritten sign said, "Doors open, 11 p.m." I had three hours to kill and just a few shillings in my pocket.

I walked towards Tottenham Court Road, found a cheap café and sat down to read my book. The hours passed slowly.

At 11 p.m. I was back at the club. There was no fabulous welcome for me at the door, just a surly man from the East End in flash threads who turned his nose up at my beaten jeans and leather jacket and begrudgingly let me in. Stairs took me down to the club, which was nothing like a rock and roll club at all — all mirrors and carefully placed lights. I found a corner to sit in. I wanted to buy a drink but discovered I couldn't afford any of them. I asked for water, which brought me an evil look from the waitress, and waited. And waited. The stage was empty, and the DJ played angular, obscure dance music as the night dragged on. The crowd were all sharply dressed and elegantly wasted. They had money for the drinks and occasionally someone would look my way and sneer. My first night as an A&R man was not going well. I was tired and whingy, weary of being stared at by people with more money than I had. Where was the fucking band?

It seemed like hours later when a bunch of overdressed fashion victims finally took the stage. There was not a guitar in sight — all they had were synthesizers, and they plonked at them like amateurs. I instantly took a dislike to them.

Generally speaking, I had nothing against synthesizers or keyboards. I was a card-carrying member of the Emerson Lake & Palmer fan club; a thrilling Keith Emerson solo involving rich electronic sounds whizzing from channel to channel and back at the Moog or a knife-wielding thrash at the Hammond organ as it rocked back and forth was just the kind of thing to excite me. And if a bit of classical music was being rearranged into a pounding 4/4 beat — so much so that the original composer was complaining in his tomb somewhere in Eastern Europe — I couldn't have been happier.

But tonight, the dead giants of classical music were sleeping soundly. It was way past my bedtime, this wasn't rock and roll, no one was putting their foot up on a monitor and promising to shag the young ladies in the audience senseless and my foot wasn't tapping. I couldn't afford a drink, and I was pissed off. After three numbers I left and started the eight-mile bike ride north as a heavy drizzle drifted over the capital.

Back at work the next morning Conroy asked me what I thought.

"Awful, I hated them. Not a single anywhere. They'll never amount to anything."

Conroy seemed a little confused and perplexed.

"Funny. I quite liked their demos. Oh, well."

Later that morning, Paul let down the band's manager. "We went to see them last night and didn't like them much to be honest. Good luck elsewhere, though."

And that was the last that was ever heard of Depeche Mode. I wonder what happened to them.

If we're counting, that's two attempts at being an A&R man. I had failed both tests miserably, but I wasn't going to give up so easily. At the time, the music papers were awash with a new genre they named NWOBHM — the New Wave of British Heavy Metal. Though I loved punk and Stiff and all its crazy oddball characters and had a large record collection that covered everything from T. Rex to Delius, my go-to bands were still Led Zep, Quo, Wishbone Ash, Thin Lizzy and such, so maybe this NWOBHM might have something going for it.

As I scoured the papers, I got wind of a young band from the north who were all 16 and 17 years old. They had a self-released EP out, were unsigned and desperate to come down to London and make it big. Through the Virgin Records store in Sheffield, I got hold of their manager, who blagged a ride down to London on the back of a friend's motorbike to see me at the pub at the end of my road. He gave me a copy of the EP, which had a bright yellow label that proudly announced Bludgeon Riffola Records. I played it at home that night and decided it showed some promise.

The next day, with butterflies in my stomach, I knocked on Robbo's door and asked him if he would listen to this new band I'd found. Robbo cranked the volume, and the pile of musty Brinsley Schwarz master tapes piled in the corner trembled. Halfway through the first song, there was that distinctive vinyl-ripping sound as Robbo pulled the needle from the disc, smiled smugly and handed it back to me. "The thing you need to understand about the music business, Nigel, is that you need to sign bands that are going to make you some money." Coming from the man whose label had signed Wazmo Nariz and Plummet Airlines, that was a bit rich.

The record he'd handed back to me was the first recording by Def Leppard. To date, they've sold in excess of 100 million albums. So, if I'd been a real A&R man, and if we're counting still, I'd have passed on a number-one UK hit and said no to Basildon's most famous band, but I would have signed a band that ruled the airwaves and MTV in the late '80s. I'm guessing many real A&R men would have been quite happy with that one out of three. But enough of my smug preening. In reality, I would have sucked at being an A&R person. The fickle mistress of showbiz had other plans for me — when I started at Phonogram, the first major video I was sent to oversee was Def Leppard's "Bringing on the Heartache," which was being shot by David Mallett in Dublin.

At Stiff, I often heard Alan Cowderoy say the craziest thing: "This record will sound great on the radio in the car in America." I thought he was mental until my first time in San Francisco and, driving into the city from the airport, heard Def Leppard's "Photograph" on the radio in the cab. He was right, it sounded bloody magic. That summer, "Photograph" and the album it came from was shipping platinum in America. The five lads from Sheffield (now four lads from Sheffield and one from London) had hit the big time and were rolling in it.

By the time I turned up in Dublin, Def Lep were massive, but you wouldn't have known it by talking to them. They were down to earth and, though I was the record company bloke on set, very friendly and approachable. I probably bored them to death with my story of how I'd tried to get them signed to Stiff. When I started at Phonogram, Chris Briggs had told me to find out why videos were so expensive and where all the money went. So, one night at the docks, I chatted up Mallet's much respected producer Jacqui Byford to get an idea of where the money was going. Were we still on budget? "Well, I always keep seven or eight grand in my back pocket in case David suddenly decides he needs a helicopter." I never did find out whether that seven or eight grand got spent, but I did fly back to London with the distinct feeling that Mallett didn't get rock and roll the way I did.

Def Leppard were managed by Cliff Burnstein and Peter Mensch. Burnstein I met only once very briefly but Peter Mensch would drop by my office frequently to park his bike. It seemed he always wore an army-green flight suit, and his eyes sparkled with mischief. He was very sharp; I liked him. When the "Heartache" video was finished, Peter asked what I thought of it. I told him that I didn't like it. Peter looked me straight in the eye and said, "Nigel, you wouldn't know a rock video if it hit you in the head."

Just a few months later, all of us at Phonogram were deeply moved when drummer Rick Allen lost an arm in a car crash and the band's career went on hold while they figured out how they would proceed. I was dispatched to Holland with a camera to shoot footage of them in the studio for use at a sales conference. On the wall was a chart listing the songs for the new album and which parts for each had been completed. There were marks for completed guitar parts, solos, vocals and backup vocals, but the drum column was completely empty. The band eventually stunned everyone in the business by saying Rick was not only still in the band but was still their drummer. A new kit had been designed especially for him and neither he nor the band ever looked back.

By the time I was living in L.A. and making Guns n' Roses videos, Def Leppard had achieved a rock and roll miracle. *Hysteria* was their second ten-million-selling album. Mallett was no longer making their videos; Wayne Isham, Jean Pellerin and Doug Freel were taking turns in the director's seat. I got to hear all the inside stories because my rep, Juliana Roberts, was dating Def Lep's bass player, Rick Savage.

In November 1988, I was in England shooting three bands — Big Bam Boo, Red Warriors and Bad Company — when Juliana called. Could I quickly come up with an idea for "Rocket" by Def Leppard? They were in Holland and needed to shoot a video a few days later. Seeing as I was already in London, perhaps I could bang something together quickly? The song includes call-outs to a host of rock stars (or their songs) — including Thin Lizzy, Lou Reed, Mott the Hoople, David Bowie, Elton John, the Beatles, Stones, T. Rex and Queen — and I had records by every single one of them. I quickly threw together an idea: a dozen TV sets dotted around a stage endlessly showing pictures of the artists mixed in with NASA stock footage to synch up with the NASA dialogue mixed in with the track.

Just hours later I got the green light — I had the job. But now we had to scramble to get the pictures together and edit the TV reel before leaving for Amsterdam in 36 hours. I rang *Melody Maker* and got permission to rifle through their picture library. Hours later, I was sitting cross-legged on the floor in a back room, surrounded by pictures of my heroes lit by someone's desk lamp as I snapped away with my still camera. As I worked away, I remembered that dark morning when I had attempted to break into their offices with Kosmo Vinyl and was relieved that now I was here with their permission. My editing pal Michael Heldman had come to England to work with me on Red Warriors and Bad Company; he pulled a late-nighter cutting the B-roll together.

Amsterdam was cold and wet, but we found a warehouse down at the docks where we could shoot the band. TV sets were located and hung around the space. Michael took charge of synching the audio playback so that every time we rolled camera the images would appear on the screens in order and at the right time. The additional drama we had was making sure that those screens stayed in synch in Holland (where the standard was 25 frames per second) and then transferring it and cutting it in the U.S. (24 frames per second). It was a technical nightmare, but Michael made it work.

Peter Mensch called me the night before the shoot. We hadn't spoken since I'd moved to the States. "I'm just calling to make sure everything's going to look great. I want it to look as good as those G n' R videos!" I couldn't resist, and responded, "Hey Peter, remember when you told me I wouldn't recognise a rock video if it hit me in the head?" The phone went dead, and we haven't spoken since.

The day of the shoot went well although I found it hilarious that, now I was shooting in Holland at long last, the local grip department found it very hard to get me a Dutch Angle on the camera! Without knowing it, the end of day had a touch of sadness attached as it was the last time I saw guitar player Steve Clark alive.

The video went straight into heavy rotation at MTV. When the channel listed their Top 10 most-played videos at the end of the year, "Rocket" was right in there with "Sweet Child o' Mine," "Paradise City" and a couple of other Dickfilms. Not bad for a guy who wouldn't know a rock video if it hit him in the head.

The band came back to me in 1996 to shoot "Slang" and "Work It Out." I had an idea for "Slang" in five minutes, but I didn't really get "Work It Out" at all. I tried hard to pass on that second song, but they insisted I had to shoot both songs or neither. "Slang" came out great and I love it, but "Work It Out" didn't work out and had to be reshot with a different idea.

And then, in 2006, I got to shoot "Rock On" for the guys. They wanted an idea that harked back to their past, so I shot them in a deserted Army base and gave it a *Mad Max* vibe — a sort of blasted land of memories with old Marquee gig posters peeling from the walls and blowing in the wind. Lou Reed even made an appearance. "Rock On" was basically a 2000s version of "Rocket," which I think worked quite nicely. I cut it myself. The band asked for just one shot to be changed, which in itself is a compliment.

In recent years I've shot guitarist Phil Collen again for another project he was working on. So, in some way or another I've been circling the Def Leppard universe for over 30 years. What's most noticeable about how much they've changed is actually how little they've changed. They're still down to earth regular guys which, considering the massive success they've enjoyed, is something of a miracle. I take my hat off to them. I'm sure they've had their moments over the years, as we all do, but I've always found them to be very friendly and fun to spend time with on set.

I love them — I just wish my old boss had signed them and I could have negotiated myself a hefty finder's fee!

CHAPTER 23

Until Forever Is Through

IN THE LATE '80s, like just about every other band, Toto wanted David Fincher to shoot a video for their latest tune. But he wasn't interested.

The world's music critics have always agreed on two things about Toto: the band consisted of some of the most gifted and accomplished musicians in rock and yet those same critics considered them to be totally uncool.

Me? I loved them.

So, when I heard that Fincher had turned Toto down, I begged to be considered. A meeting was quickly arranged; on my way out to see them, I was handed a cassette with two new songs: "Pamela" and "Stop Loving You."

The band met in high school. There were three Porcaro brothers — Jeff (drums), Steve (keyboards) and Mike (bass). Their father had been a studio drummer who played with all the greats of his day. Their school friend, David Paich, was a gifted pianist and son of film composer Marty Paich; the band was rounded out by guitarist Steve Lukather, whose father was an AD on *The Deer Hunter* and *Man-*

nix. By the time I met the band, original singer Bobby Kimball and bassist David Hungate had left; they'd recently hired another former classmate, Joseph Williams, to be the singer. Joe's father, John Williams, was another Hollywood icon, known the world over for scoring nearly every film that Steven Spielberg ever made.

Every member of Toto was precociously gifted on his instrument; they were highly respected studio musicians. Years later, when Lukather's father Bill assistant directed a job for me, he told me how Steve had been given a guitar as a child and had shown immense talent at a very early age. The elder Lukather approached a guitar teacher he knew through the studios and asked him to tutor his child. The young Steve — possibly rather like the grown-up one — was a bit of a handful, so his father was not entirely surprised when the guitar teacher said he needed to talk about a problem he was having with his student.

Bill groaned inwardly, concerned that Steve, with his quick tongue and wild sense of humour, had offended the teacher. Some kind of punishment would have to be handed out. And he was worried that the teacher would refuse to teach the young lad anymore.

"Tell me about the problem," said Bill.

"I quit. There's nothing more I can teach him," said the teacher. "He's the most gifted student I've ever had. At this point I'm learning more from him than he is from me!"

Steve was about 14 years old at the time.*

As I pulled into the parking lot of the dingy rehearsal studio in the Valley, I wasn't aware of the history the band had as school friends and brothers. I was only aware of the music that I cherished and had played over and over. While all my musician friends gushed about Jeff Porcaro's fabulous drumming, which was simultaneously rock solid yet somehow fluid and grooving, I was awed by Lukather's guitar work — not because it was fast and flashy (though heaven knows he was as fast as anyone) but because, at its most melodic, it was unbe-

* Lukather tells me this story is not true. Ha-ha!

lievably soulful and tweaked the yearning and longing deep inside me. His simple, straightforward solo on "I Won't Hold You Back" with that silver sound could reduce me to tears in a second. That solo said everything I couldn't articulate about all the pain and loss and desperate need for affection that I carried around in my young body. I wasn't clear how I was going to win these guys over, but I was very clear about one thing — I wanted to shake Lukather's hand and say, "Thank you!"

A roadie ushered me into a waiting room. It was sparsely decorated with a motley arrangement of chairs and sofas. With the smell of a thousand stubbed-out cigarettes, there were scores of old beer cans and rotting take-out food. In other words, the same hangout room that was in every rehearsal studio the world over.

Toto walked in and introduced themselves. Strangely, I don't remember meeting Lukather at all — what I do remember is meeting Jeff Porcaro, with his outsize glasses, his wide eyes, his slightly hunched-over build and his intensity. If there were artistic decisions to be made about the band, Jeff was going to make them, and I felt him locking onto me like a laser.

"So, Nigel, what have you got for us?"

I hadn't had time to come up with any ideas and stumbled for what to say. I remember being shocked as I heard these words coming out of my mouth: "I'm more of a fan of your music than any other director you'll ever meet. I've seen you play live and I own every record you've made. I've also seen all your videos, and I can tell you one thing about them. Every one of them sucks!" **

There was a whoosh as all the available oxygen was sucked out of the room, leaving a terrifying, lingering silence. I remember Paich recoiling as if I'd tossed cold water over him.

Jeff leapt to his feet. His face was glowing as he shouted, "He's our man, I love this guy!"

Fuck! I was in with a chance!

** I later learned that the last video Toto had made had been directed by Jeff himself!

A few weeks later, we assembled in a massive warehouse in San Pedro harbour. I was in awe of Lukather and tiptoed around him as we set up the first shot. He was goofing around, and there was a crack as he dropped his guitar on the floor. The screw that held that strap knuckle in the tail of the guitar had fallen out. He picked the guitar off the floor and held it up in the air, cackling. "Anyone got a screwdriver?"

An art department helper rushed over, and we checked out the damage. The guitar was quite famous — it had a reclining semi-nude robot painted on it. Most musicians are understandably highly protective of their instruments, especially hand-painted ones. The art department dude picked up the guitar as if he was about to drill a new hole in the tailpiece.

"Stop!" I yelled, "You can't do that!" I was convinced Lukather would have a meltdown.

"Ah, fuck it," he said. "It's only a piece of wood. Drill all the holes you like." He sauntered off to chat with his bandmates while the art dude set to work, and I loved him all the more.

That first day, something became apparent to me. Every other band I'd ever worked with seemed to put on their stage faces when the music rolled. Their brows would furrow, their bodies would go taut and they would assume the poses of wannabe rock gods ... and I would merrily push them on their way, loving the artifice that we were creating as I lived out my own rock and roll dreams through them. Toto were different. They were totally unpretentious in the posing department and would smile the whole way through, watching each other like hawks. Lukather's mid-solo face was not that of a man struggling to get all of the notes right, but of a man filled with the joy from his gift, sharing it with his brothers. Jeff would look across at Mike as they shared a groove that was sublime, perfect and human. They loved playing, and it showed. What gradually dawned on me was they loved life with the same kind of intensity. Miraculously, it seemed they liked me as much as I loved them. I'd met a thousand other musicians who weren't half as gifted and who looked down their noses at me because I couldn't play like they could. The guys in Toto were more gifted than perhaps any artists I ever worked with, yet they instantly made me feel at home.

I started learning the code that is hardwired into every band. Joe preferred Joseph, Mike and Jeff were all called by their first names (Steve Porcaro was not in the band at this time), Paich was usually Paich (sometimes Dave) and Lukather was Lukather or Luke but rarely Steve. It was fun to watch them, and it was fun to hang out with them.

At the end of the first day's shoot, we stayed in a cheap hotel down by the harbour. They invited me to have a drink with them and told me wonderful stories of working with Paul McCartney and Rickie Lee Jones and making Michael Jackson's *Thriller* album.

At the end of the second day of shooting, when the work was nearly done, I noticed Lukather sitting quietly on a chair. I went over to talk.

"We're nearly done!"

He sighed and looked up at me, "Can I ask you a favour?"

"Sure, anything you want."

"If I give you my phone number, will you call me so we can hang out?"

If it seems, having lived the life I have, that I would do nothing but spend all day hanging out with famous people, the reverse is true. Normally, I only see the rock stars and famous people in preparation for a shoot and the day of the shoot — in fact, it's not uncommon for me to only meet the artist the morning of the shoot and then wish them farewell for good that evening when we wrap, never to see them again. But over 30 years later, Luke and I are still friends. To this day he's never once let me buy him lunch.

I've learned many things from the musicians I've worked with, but one of the most important things I ever learned I learned from Toto: how to hug another man. As an Englishman, I was never very good at hugging, but Toto changed all that. You've never had a hug until Lukather wraps his arms around you and slams you in the back and tries to give you a big hairy kiss on the cheek!

I became their video guy, and it was an honour to work with them. Tellingly, they gave me more freedom than perhaps any band I'd ever worked with. We went on to do a video for "Straight for the Heart" which I thought turned out very well — it intercut a great, energetic performance with a beautifully shot story of a younger man having an affair with an older woman. They didn't particularly like it but totally supported the idea and let me run with it. They trusted me.

My old friend and Stiff All-Stars bandmate Andy Murray came to stay with me for a few months and got himself a job at Elektra. In the evenings, we would get our guitars out and play like we'd always done. He thought we should record some tunes, so we booked a session at Sound City, the famous studio Dave Grohl made a documentary about.

We needed a drummer. "Do you know any drummers?" Andy asked.

"Well, I know Jeff Porcaro."

"You wouldn't dare ... would you?"

I did dare, and Jeff didn't blink an eyelid. As long as I'd pay for the drums to be brought to the studio he'd play them for free. Andy and I were speechless. The guy who'd played on "Beat It" was going to rock out with the Stiff All-Stars!

In the studio with Jeff and Andy, I had a demo for Jeff to listen to, but he demurred and simply asked me to play the song for him on acoustic guitar.

After one play-though, Jeff sat down at the drums and scribbled a musical note with the number 64 beside it. And he was ready.

We laid down the song in one take, and it was perfect, I didn't have to count the bars between verses; thanks to Jeff, I just knew when to come in, a slight push here, a tasteful lick there and I knew instantly where I was in the tune. So, *this* is what it was like to play with a real drummer!

In the summer of '91, Toto manager Mark Hartley called. Joseph had left the band. A new singer had done some tours with the band and then he had been ditched. Lukather would now be the singer, and the band, searching for a new audience, was going to take a heavier approach.

Mark had hours of footage from a concert shot in France by the BBC which featured the old singer. Could I create a viable concert film out of the footage and lose the missing singer completely? I looked at the footage and said I could do it if I had some extra footage to paper over the gaps. Mark said he couldn't pay me a cent to shoot the footage, but he'd fly me to Europe with the band for ten days and pay all my hotel bills if I'd bring a camera and shoot the footage myself. Would that work?

An all-expenses-paid summer holiday in Europe with Toto? Are you kidding? When do we leave?

At its worst, going on the road to shoot a band can be a giant pain in the arse and an expensive mile-eating game of cat and mouse where, every time you lift the camera and start rolling, the band members turn their back on you, slam doors in your face and refuse to emerge from their secret inner sanctum until just before showtime.

So, I was a trifle nervous. Would I be allowed into that inner sanctum or would I be a pariah — just another hanger-on, albeit one with a job to do? The first show was the *Roskilde Festival* outside Copenhagen. I had total freedom to roam with my camera before, during and after the gig. As we climbed on the bus to go back into the city, Jeff Porcaro smiled his enormous smile, patted me on the back and said, "Great to have you here with us, Nige, it's like having another member of the band onstage with us!"

This was the highest of compliments. Though it was a wonderful gesture, I knew not to imagine for one second that I'd actually joined the group. I was simply doing my job, delighted to have the band's official endorsement. I kept Jeff's special thank you to myself.

We jumped across to Sweden and flew up to Lulau, north of the Arctic Circle, where they played a gig at midnight. It was the summer, so the sun never set. Afterwards, we walked through the town to our hotel and watched young lovers making out on the sidewalks in the broad 3:00 a.m. daylight. In Germany, Lukather showed his butt through the glazed walls of the hotel elevator as it slowly climbed four stories. Toto were second on the bill at *Rock in the Ring* in the

Nürburgring racetrack, and I shot 70,000 Germans singing along to every song.

All too soon, we were flying down to the South of France, where the band was scheduled to play in a massive tent on the Promenade des Anglais in Nice. I was just starting to have some fun, and now there was just one show to go.

Before the gig there were smiles and hugs and thank yous — it was my last night with the band, and I was gutted to be leaving for Spain the next day on another job.

It was hot in that tent. Three-thousand fans shook the place; in minutes the heat from the sweating mass reached the ceiling, condensed against the cold fabric and it started raining inside the tent. The diffused light shining on the band was heavenly, and I was determined to roll every inch of film stock I had left in my suitcase. While playing, Jeff shouted to his roadie for a bucket of ice and dunked his whole head in it.

As one number ended, Jeff got up from his drum stool, wandered to the front of the stage and started shouting at someone in the crowd. Jeff was pointing his sticks at a hapless punter; he seemed very animated, shouting and pointing and gesticulating. The gig and the band's momentum had ground to a halt.

What was happening? A fight maybe? I inched forward with the camera. Whatever it was, I wanted to get it on film.

Jeff leaned in over the crowd and pointed with his sticks again. I still couldn't see what was going on but I knew I should keep rolling.

A tall young man in the mosh pit was taking off his moist T-shirt. He handed it to Jeff, who gave the guy his drumsticks in return. There was a huge roar from the crowd, and the rest of the band were smiling.

WTF was going on?

Jeff unravelled the dripping T-shirt, looked at the front of it and laughed!

He started walking towards me. I kept rolling, peering through the sweaty eyepiece, which kept fogging up. I panned down and the logo on the front of the T-shirt came into focus. It read DICK MACUMBA!

Jeff had stopped the entire gig to trade drumsticks for the T-shirt which had DICK on it and presented it to me in front of the whole audience! I was stunned.

After a wonderful post-gig party I snatched a few hours' sleep, grabbed a quick breakfast and walked out of the hotel to the taxi. One of the road crew appeared, nodded silently at me, and disappeared into the hotel.

It was over. I was no longer in the band. But in my bag was a sweaty memento from the night before that I would keep forever.

I've been back to Nice many times since and stood on the spot where that tent was erected and thought back to that night and that T-shirt that Jeff-fucking-Porcaro stopped the gig, took a T-shirt from a fan and gave it to me.

But who would ever believe that story?

The Stiff All-Stars would sometimes rehearse in Andy's tiny flat in a back street round the corner from Island's famous Basing Street Studios. Among the songs we'd play was Warren Zevon's "Lawyers, Guns and Money," one of three numbers on *Excitable Boy* that go further, deeper and darker than anything I'd ever experienced. The title track is about a psychotic killer, while "Roland the Headless Thompson Gunner" betrays its darkness in the title. Once you've listened to that one there's no going back innocently to listen to "I Wanna Hold Your Hand" again.

So, imagine my delight when Jeff Porcaro asked if I'd like to shoot a clip for Warren Zevon's "Searching for a Heart," on which he'd played drums. Sadly, there was no further news of the characters who fought as mercenaries in Africa or worked as spies drinking coffees in late-night diners in this song: it was a straight-up love song. But it was a good one and again had that sense of yearning and longing that spoke so strongly to me. I signed up right away.

There was a twist. Jeff felt I should shoot the video myself — not just direct it, but be the cameraman, too. This was still in the days of film, a world where little flip-up screens didn't exist. You had to make sure that film was exposed properly by using a combination of a light meter (which I had) and experience (which I didn't). It was a bold idea for sure, but, hey, I was going to get to work with Warren Zevon. So, if throwing myself off the cliff was part of the deal, I would sign that part of the contract, too.

I don't remember first meeting Warren, but I do recall him being rather standoffish on the days we shot. That was OK — I think I'd have been disappointed if he'd been too friendly. Besides, I had a lot to think about, discussing with the gaffer and the camera assistant whether I'd got the lighting right. We'd made the choice to shoot in black and white, so that gave me a lot more latitude — if you screw up the exposure it's much easier to fix it in post if you suck out the colour.

Sadly, "Searching for a Heart" didn't make a dent in the charts, and few people saw the video, but I loved it and was proud to have worked with Warren. Years later, at a party in my friend Brian's house, he said, "There's someone in the kitchen who wants to say hello." It was Zevon. I thought we'd just have a short chat, but we talked for more than an hour.

The next day, I received an e-mail, headed "Should Old Acquaintance," which read: "Nigel, It was awfully nice running into you last night. I hope we stay in touch. I'll give you all my numbers and crap. Give me a call if you get a chance to go for a cup of coffee — although I think my character would drink tea. Fondly, Warren"

I e-mailed him straight back, saying I'd love to meet up but was getting on a plane that night to make a movie in Barcelona and would be gone for months, could we delay the tea date till my return? Four weeks later, he was diagnosed with terminal cancer and was gone by the time the film was finished.

Lukather was now the lead singer of Toto; their new album had a heavier, rockier sound, which I loved. "Don't Chain My Heart" was the lead track from *Kingdom of Desire* and it needed a video. Consequently, one afternoon, I was on a call discussing ideas with Jeff, who had just returned from a two-week holiday to Florida with his wife and three kids. He spoke animatedly about how good it was to hang out with his sons. Uncharacteristically for me, I said something very personal to Jeff, "You know something, Jeff — you're a really good dad."

I instantly regretted sharing that thought. Did I really know him well enough to say that? The moment passed. We agreed that we had some ideas worth thinking about for the video but nothing solid yet and would talk later in the week. Jeff was working in the garden and wanted to get back to it.

The following morning, I was booked into a telecine session at one of the post-production facilities in the Valley. I had spent so many hours in the bay at Unitel that not only had I become pals with the guys who worked there — George Cvjetnicanin, Cliff Laidlaw, Brian Linse and Mark Leiss — we had formed a band together that played gigs most weekends. We called ourselves the Transatlantic Rhythm Kings (TRK for short).

I picked up a coffee, wandered into the bay and sat down ready to work. Cliff — the TRK drummer — immediately appeared from the machine room, "I'm so sorry, Nigel."

"Sorry about what?"

"About Jeff."

"Jeff who?"

"Jeff Porcaro."

"What about him?"

"You haven't heard? He died last night! It's been on the radio this morning."

"Bullshit, I was chatting with him at 4:00 o'clock yesterday afternoon."

"Seriously, Nigel, you need to check it out."

I rang Toto's managers. Anita Heilig, their assistant, answered the phone and I asked about Jeff. "It's true, Nigel." She was crying and hung up.

Jeff had returned to his gardening but then felt unwell. His wife told him to take a break and relax in his drum room. He never made it to dinnertime, collapsing from a heart attack.

Jeff was 38. I couldn't believe it. I was so glad that one of the last things he'd heard was me telling him what a great father he was. Since that day, if I feel the urge to tell people something I think is important I don't hold back. You just never know.

Jeff was buried in Forest Lawn cemetery. The turnout was massive, and I cried like a baby through the whole thing. It dawned on me later I wasn't just crying for Jeff — I was crying for myself.

In the days after Jeff's death, the subject of that video we had talked about returned. The album was coming out, and the single would be released; there had to be a video. What were we going to do? I realised all that footage I'd shot of the band in Europe the previous year was a goldmine. Jeff had once introduced me to an Italian artist, Flavio Kampah, and it was decided to mix the Europe footage with Flavio's art and performance footage of the surviving bandmembers. Following Jeff's lead, I would shoot the video as well as direct it.

The day of the shoot was tough. How could it not be? But we pressed on, and there were big, meaningful hugs at the end of the day. The film was sent off to the lab, and I swallowed hard, knowing that I would get to spend the next weeks watching footage of Jeff as we cut the thing together. Two days after the shoot, I walked into the same room where I'd first heard of Jeff's death and there was more bad news. All the film we'd shot for the video was underexposed. It was unusable.

I have no idea what happened. There were frantic calls between me, the gaffer and the assistant cameraman. There were discussions with the lab. We went over every detail and had no reasonable explanation. But there was no denying that the director who thought he could also shoot film was quite possibly the culprit.

I rang Lukather and broke the news. He whispered, "You've got to be fucking kidding me." We had no choice but to get back on the horse, return to the studio and reshoot the video. To everyone's credit, they even let me shoot it again. As we set up the first shot again,

Lukather did that thing where he lowers his chin and gave me a look as if he's looking over the top of glasses he's not wearing. "You know this is Jeff's doing, don't you? He's fucking with you. He's fucking with all of us!" He smiled and we started shooting the whole damn thing a second time.

Two weeks later, the band and Jeff's mum and dad came to see the finished cut of the video. All I can remember is that I sobbed like a child and, afterwards, Lukather hugged me until it hurt. I cannot imagine the pain his bandmates experienced.

I have since worked with Toto many times, and it is always a joy to hang out with them. I have shot them in nine countries and recently shot their fortieth anniversary DVD in front of 17,000 fans in Amsterdam. As I've roamed the audiences of those shows with my camera, I've noticed the front rows filled with excited young fans singing the lines of every song — songs that were hits and then faded from the airways long before they were born. The critics still don't get it, but that doesn't matter. We all have bands that we love, guilty pleasures which make no sense if you try and analyse why you love them. But isn't that the point? Their music gets you in the heart, and that's where it matters.

Toto is my non-guilty pleasure and always will be.

"Until forever is through, I'll be over you..."

CHAPTER 24

Cherry Pie

I WAS STANDING IN THE WINGS watching glam-metal outfit Warrant rock out in front of a couple of thousand screaming fans in a theatre somewhere in Chicago. My rep, Juliana Roberts, and I had just flown in that afternoon to take a meeting with Extreme, who were supporting Warrant on a leg of Midwest dates.

After a useful chat with Extreme about their next video in the bowels of the venue, Juliana suggested we go upstairs and watch Warrant do their thing from the sidelines. She ran The Foundry, the heavy metal division of Propaganda, and knew everyone there was to know in that world.

As we stood in the darkness looking towards the stage, lead singer Jani Lane put his foot up on a monitor, lowered his mic stand and sang, looking right into the eyes of adoring girls reaching up to the stage and trying to touch his feet. Lights flashed as a thousand hands reached out towards the stage: Warrant were at their peak.

I seem to remember that the guitar player turned over his guitar and showed the audience the back of his instrument, on which the words "EAT ME!" had been painted. The crowd roared, the girls at the front laughed and he launched into a solo that contained far too many notes.

Breathing hard and covered in sweat, Jani ran towards the side of the stage and grabbed a towel to wipe himself down. As he opened his eyes, he saw Juliana. Over the wailing guitar, pounding drums and screaming fans, they had a brief shouted conversation:

"Juliana! Great to see you!"

"Fantastic show! How's the tour going?"

"It's a fucking mess. The way things are going I'll be back flipping burgers inside two years!"

He wiped his face again, threw the towel at a roadie, bounded back onstage, grabbed his mic and, as the solo finished, yelled at the audience: "Rock and roll, Chicago!" The crowd roared.

A couple of years later I crossed Wilshire Boulevard to do what I did every lunchtime — read a magazine and have a tuna melt at Johnnie's Diner.

Barbara, the waitress, knew my order. She popped a Coke with a straw down on the table and asked, "The usual?" I nodded.

I opened up *Rolling Stone*. When I reached "Random Notes," a short sentence caught my eye: "Jani Lane, lead singer of Warrant, seen flipping burgers in LA diner."

Years later Jani was found dead in his bed, in a Comfort Inn in Woodland Hills. He was 47.

CHAPTER 25

Chinatown

THE DOORBELL RANG, and I signed for the small package that had been urgently sent across town for me to listen to. I opened up the envelope and found a cassette inside. Nothing leapt out at me from the speakers, so I guessed I'd missed something. I rewound the tape and listened again. Still nothing. I tried a third time and still came up empty.

It was barely an hour since Anne-Marie Mackay had rung me. "I've just been sent a track by a new young singer," she told me. "She's the girlfriend of a well-known Hollywood producer, and the label are pulling out all the stops. They want a great video for her first release. Your name came up, so I'm sending a tape over and want you to have a quick listen. Can you ring me straight back when you've heard it? If you like it, they want you to take a meeting this afternoon!"

I called Anne-Marie. "I've heard the track and it's ... I dunno ... it's boring. She doesn't have much of a voice, the production is OK, but the song does nothing for me at all. Anyway, I've got those other two tracks I'm writing on today which you told me are urgent. I think I should take a pass."

She wasn't going to give up that easily. "The label really want to do a number on this, and her producer boyfriend is really quite a powerful chap. Are you sure you want to take a pass?"

"Unless the boyfriend is Bob Evans, I'm not interested."

"The boyfriend *is* Bob Evans!"

Forty-five minutes later, Anne-Marie and I were driving deep into Beverly Hills, climbing a canyon road where every gateway was surrounded by walls covered by winding tendrils of perfectly manicured shrubbery hiding security cameras. We parked in front of Robert Evans' famous house.

In his book *The Big Goodbye,* Sam Wasson describes Woodland as "a prime specimen of Southern California Regency, a relaxed stylistic descendant of eighteenth-century France." It was designed in 1940 by architect John Woolf, who had worked with many Hollywood legends, including Judy Garland and Cary Grant. After Evans purchased the place, he set about making it his own on the studio's dime. Wasson quotes Evans as saying, "An army of engineers, carpenters, painters, electricians [and] bricklayers built outbuildings and expanded the pool house into a screening room with state-of-the-art projection facilities. ... There were more deals made in my projection room than there were at Paramount during those days."

We were ushered inside the main house and spent a few minutes gawping at the beautiful artifacts, paintings and photographs of the famous before being shown through the immaculate gardens to the famous screening room. "Mr. Evans will be with you in a few minutes."

"Oh, my God!" I gushed. "This is the screening room where Evans first saw the dailies of *The Godfather*, *Chinatown*, *The Cotton Club*! Just think of the amazing people who must have sat in these chairs. Jack Nicholson, Roman Polanski..." Anne-Marie didn't say a word, she just looked at the posters hanging on the wall and the photographs of Evans with some of the most famous names Hollywood had ever produced. If you'd had to preserve just one room to demonstrate the history of Hollywood to show future generations and give them a sense of what it had been like back in the day, this room would have to be a major contender. Anne-Marie was concerned that I was freaking out about a bunch of chairs, posters and memorabilia. I was freaking out that a room could have such an effect on me. This place was right up there on my list with Abbey Road's Studio Two and the toilet where Elvis died.

The French doors opened, and Bob Evans walked in. He was tanned, dressed in one of his signature striped shirts, wearing his large glasses. He was accompanied by a young blonde woman, who I assumed was the singer, and two members of his entourage, who took one side of the table. Anne-Marie and I sat on the other. Introductions and pleasantries were exchanged. I shook hands with the singer, who said something with a European accent of some sort and never said another word. Bob smiled at me across the famous mahogany table and said, "I hear you have a great idea for this video. I can't wait to hear it!"

I gulped. Of course, I didn't have an idea at all — it was barely 90 minutes since I'd first dropped that cassette into my player and had been underwhelmed. I instantly regretted my stupidity in wanting to meet Bob Evans, because now I was going to have to blindly pitch him an idea across a table over which far more gifted writers, directors and producers than I had pitched well-rehearsed, well-developed ideas. There was every chance I was going to look like a fool. I glanced at Anne-Marie for help. She just smiled and remained tight-lipped. I turned back to Bob. "We find her in a hotel room..."

If it sounded like I was making it up as I went along, that was because I was making it up as I went along. But, in the absence of any solid ideas, I fell back on my oldest tactic — flattery. "As she reaches the first chorus, we start to realise what a fabulous singer she is; as that hook kicks in for the first time that's when we know this is going to be played over and over on MTV. The lighting is amazing, the dress she's wearing is gorgeous..."

Bullshit, bullshit, bullshit. Anne-Marie's smile never wavered, and Bob seemed to be at least somewhat impressed. His girlfriend, who was young but not exactly the most gorgeous girl I'd ever met, was doodling on a pad. As I laid on the adjectives, the French doors opened again and a tall, older, elegant man with smoothed-back grey hair walked in, sat down and chewed on some nuts that were in a bowl on the table. The stranger, who seemed vaguely familiar, appeared very comfortable in these surroundings and leaned back in his chair to listen as I droned on. I could feel the sweat under my arms. I was dying, and I knew it. An eternity later I finished and the room fell silent. Bob turned to the stranger, "Tell him your idea."

The stranger was everything I hadn't been: relaxed, eloquent, passionate — and had a huge advantage over me in that he actually had an idea. He spoke with an accent; I guessed he was probably German. "We are shooting in high contrast black and white. She is in an apartment, and she has just got home from work. She is dressed in elegant black clothes and stockings and heels. She starts to undress. Meanwhile, we cut to a man across the street who has a camera with a long telephoto lens who is spying on her. He starts taking pictures. She removes her jacket and we notice her breasts pushing forward under her shirt. She undoes her skirt, which drops to the floor, and we notice her long legs with the stockings held up by a garter belt and her tiny black panties peeking out under the bottom of her white shirt. She goes over to the kitchen and disappears from view for a second. When she comes back, she bends over to pick up something from the floor and the photographer shoots frame after frame of her beautiful derriere. And then she turns. Her black brassiere is bursting and, like the photographer, we want to see more. There is music playing and she starts moving, sexily, sensuously. She ties up her hair with a black ribbon and puts on sunglasses. She starts running her hands all over her body; it is deeply erotic..."

Blimey, I thought, this is a bit racy for MTV. They'll never play this. Bob was transfixed, Anne-Marie kept smiling, the singer kept doodling and, as the stranger carried on, I realised that his idea was no more original than mine. After all, I'd seen the images he was describing in a dozen Helmut Newton photo spreads. I seem to remember that someone in this new pitch was now masturbating — or at least simulating it — maybe it was both of them, the photographer across the road *and* the girl in her apartment. At any rate, the climax of the stranger's pitch was orgasmic. As he finished, the room held its breath.

"I love it!" said Bob and gave me a glance which hinted "loser" (or was it "amateur"?). At any rate, I knew I'd failed the audition. "I love the way you describe things," Bob said to his friend. "You have such passion, such vision." And then he delivered the kicker. "Helmut, you are a genius!"

And then it dawned on me. The reason he was ripping off Helmut Newton and his semi-erotic fashion photo spreads so convincingly, and the reason why he seemed familiar, was because he *was* Helmut Newton!

I had been outclassed and outgunned. Anne-Marie and I climbed into the car and drove back towards our little corner of Hollywood, laughing all the way. Helmut had checkmated me, but I didn't care — I'd pulled a fast one on Bob, got to hang out in his famous screening room for an hour with the man himself and even got to shake hands with Helmut Newton on the way out. I only regretted that I didn't have any of his books tucked into my backpack so I could have snagged an autograph.

A few years later, Newton climbed into his car at the Chateau Marmont hotel off Sunset Boulevard and, as he turned into Marmont Lane, had a massive heart attack and crashed into the wall opposite the hotel. He was pronounced dead at the hospital. Evans, who was married seven times, suffered a stroke at dinner one night, fought back from the edge and died at the age of 89 in Beverly Hills. And the girl? I can't remember her name. I heard that she got dumped by both Bob and the label and the video never got made.

But every time I see *Chinatown* or *The Godfather* I think about the hour that I spent in that screening room with the man who produced those wonderful movies.

CHAPTER 26

Alone Again, Naturally

THERE'S NO SENSE in sugar-coating it: after a few years at Propaganda, my career was going downhill faster than a freight train with no brakes. After a miserable six months working on a movie starring Michael Madsen, I'd returned to the Propaganda offices to find things were changing. Polygram had bought the company, and it was expanding fast. Films were being made, TV shows such as *Twin Peaks* were going into production and massive commercial campaigns were being directed by Fincher and new recruit Michael Bay. It seemed I no longer fit into this puzzle. The jobs I was getting were becoming smaller and less prestigious. I was fighting back, but the undertow was wicked — and became worse when I was called into the office of my rep, a young woman who was in charge of music videos now that Anne-Marie Mackay and Juliana Roberts had moved on. She showed me the reel of another director who the company was looking after and told me I needed to change my style. "This is the kind of work you should be doing now," she told me. I disliked this other director's reel and told her so. "That's not who I am," I explained. She pulled the cassette from the video machine, replaced it in its sleeve and looked me straight in the face. "In which case I can't represent you anymore."

I was furious and took my anger upstairs to Steve Golin's office. The commercials guy doesn't want to rep me, and now the Video Girl downstairs doesn't want to rep me either, I whined. "I'm a part owner of this company, a founder, and this girl is telling me she won't find me work? This is fucked. She needs to go!"

Golin sucked his teeth. "It's not that simple, Nigel. Things have changed." I left his office even more angry than when I'd walked in. I went home and pouted. Propaganda was becoming a very powerful company. The boat I'd helped build and create was now ploughing on through the Hollywood waves at great speed, and it seemed I had tumbled off the back and was disappearing in its wake. Everyone was so busy looking forward that no one noticed or cared that there was a man overboard.

I like to think I can control my pride, but when I reach a snapping point it's all over. I announced I was going to leave the company. Suddenly the phone started ringing. "You can't leave, you're the soul of the company," I was told. "Tell that to the Video Girl," I thought. My business manager, Steve Callas, was particularly worried. "Do you realise how much money you're making every time Fincher or Michael Bay makes a commercial?" I was very aware that I was earning more than six figures a year by just sitting at home, but I knew that if I stayed at the company and ran out my contract — another two years — my career as a director would be over.

(The Video Girl left the business not long afterwards, got married to a successful director and had a family. The director whose reel she showed me sank into obscurity. Propaganda, after some years of success, eventually started taking on water. In its final months I was offered the chance to return to the company. Now that they were in trouble, they wanted me back. I turned them down. I later heard that, on the day the company finally closed after weeks of the staff getting no wages, they were given 30 minutes to clear their desks and leave the building — at which point a near-riot broke out. People started ripping TVs from the walls and grabbing anything of value they could carry as a meagre substitute for their missing wages. It was a sad end to a beautiful dream.)

Within a short while I hoisted my flag at a smaller company called Squeak Pictures run by a well-respected producer, Pam Tarr. Squeak Pictures did not have the gorilla-sized clout that Propaganda had, but I felt this was a good thing.

The first job I got from Squeak wasn't exactly the solution I'd been looking for. In fact, it did not portend well for my decision to leave Propaganda at all: a video for Stuttering John from *The Howard Stern Show*. To make matters worse, I had to fly to New York to meet Stuttering John to see if he would approve me to create the video for his upcoming magnum opus entitled "I'll Talk My Way Out of It."

I'm glad I swallowed my pride and got on the plane, because something very useful came out of the trip. The morning before my interview with Stuttering John, I dropped in on the museum across from my hotel and saw an exhibition on the career of Frank Lloyd Wright. If you've ever studied architecture, as I had, Frank Lloyd Wright was one of those people you had to have an opinion about. What I learned from the exhibition was how little I knew about his career. I'd assumed naïvely that a graph of his career path had been a straight line starting bottom left and going upwards to top right, but I left the exhibition with new energy after learning that this great man's career had suffered many ups and downs — including walking out from partnerships which weren't working and a bizarre incident in which a servant murdered seven people in his house with an axe. While there was rarely more than one person in my house and I had no servants, I took heart from the knowledge that perhaps walking away from Propaganda would pay off in the long run and that this momentary lull in productivity would turn around.

I passed the Stuttering John test; though the video was no great shakes in the creativity department, I have to give Mr. John full marks for blagging Gene Simmons, Sting, Grandpa Al Lewis, Gilbert

Gottfried and Nuno Bettencourt of Extreme to appear in the clip. On *The Howard Stern Show*, Howard asked who directed it. "Nigel Dick? DICK? What kind of name is that?" When it was all over, he delivered his verdict. "The editing? I think it still needs some work." As I settled into my post-Propaganda career I wondered if Frank Lloyd Wright's lows had been like this.

CHAPTER 27

Tears of a Clown

ONE OF THE FIRST JOBS I got when I moved to Los Angeles was for a short-lived TV show called *Deja View*. The idea of the show was to make music videos for songs that had been hits before MTV came along. The song I got to shoot was the Temptations' "I Can't Get Next to You," and I was so happy when it was confirmed that both Eddie Kendricks and David Ruffin would take part in the video. As well as wearing the grooves out of "Papa Was a Rollin' Stone," I had solo hits by both of them in my collection. That moment in Ruffin's "Walk Away From Love" where the backing track subsides and he goes for the high notes to sing "Break my heart..." is just ... well, I don't have words to describe something so magical.

The video had an out-of-work actor played by Bronson Pinchot chasing casting agents, played by Kendricks and Ruffin, all over the Ambassador Hotel in Hollywood in the hope they would give him a gig — hence "I Can't Get Next to You." In one scene, Kendricks and Ruffin turn around by an elevator and sing the hook line. The first take was dull, so I stepped forward and suggested they do a slick move in time together as they looked both ways. "Like how?" they asked. I didn't notice the twinkle in their eyes as they asked the question, so I proceeded to show them what I meant. "Show us again." I did it again and then noticed that everyone, especially Eddie and David, were laughing at me. Eddie put his hand on my shoulder, "Shit. Don't you know we invented that stuff?" I started laughing, too. "Yup, that's me — the stupid English guy trying to teach the Temptations how to dance!" For the rest of the shoot, when things were getting dull, they'd ask, "How does that dance move go again?"

A few years later I got to work with Smokey Robinson, not once but twice. It was a real honour — not only because he was, well, Smokey, and not just because "Tears of a Clown" is one of my all-time favourite pop records, but because Smokey was by then an executive at Motown (or Tamla as we used to call it in the UK) and had real credibility as a businessman as well as being an artist. I felt his decision to hire me was doubly flattering.

The song "Love Don't Give No Reason" gave me the idea to set the video in a diner, where Smokey would sit in a booth as various scenarios that loosely fit the story line played out. Smokey's performance only took an hour or so to shoot, but he hung out on the set all day, keeping an eye on the other scenes we were shooting.

The diner was in Santa Monica. The craft service table was set up by the door; at one point, a homeless person poked his nose in and started putting cookies in his coat pocket. He was asked to leave by a PA. From the back, where we were working, I watched Smokey follow the man outside. He opened the door to his white Rolls Royce and invited the man to take a seat. Then they drove off. Someone beside me had also seen this happen, and we looked at each other, wondering what the hell Smokey was up to.

Fifteen minutes later, the Rolls returned and parked at the curbside again. Smokey climbed out, went around to the passenger door and held it open for the homeless guy, who climbed out, carrying a huge bag of food from McDonalds! The homeless guy sauntered off happily, while Smokey walked back inside to continue watching us work without a word.

I've always wondered what happened to that guy next. In my dreams I imagine he scoffed the food and that night settled down under the pier with his buddies, where the conversation went something like this:

Homeless Guy 2: How was your day, Jack?

Homeless Guy 1: Well, I was walking down the street and Smokey Robinson comes out of this diner and invites me to sit in his white Rolls Royce. He then drives me to McDonalds where he buys me one of everything on the menu and then drives me back to where he'd found me, opens the door for me and wishes me good luck.

Homeless Guy 2: Whatever drugs you are on — I want some!

I guess I'm mostly known for my "rock" videos, but it has been a delight to work with some of the artists who don't fall in that category and whose records I have played to death over the years. As well as the Temps and Smokey, that list includes Tina Turner, Little Richard, Quincy Jones, the O'Jays, the Hues Corporation, the Jacksons, Diana King, Kool and the Gang and my biggest hero of all, Stevie Wonder. When we did a commercial for a Tony Bennett duets album, I couldn't restrain myself from turning into a complete fanboy, gripping his hand and saying thank you for those four magic albums that came one after the other, *Talking Book*, *Innervisions*, *Fulfillingness' First Finale* and *Songs in the Key of Life*. I grew up in another society and another culture, so listening to those albums gave me a real insight into life in a part of America with which I had no contact. Of course, music is no substitute for experiencing the real thing but, growing up an ocean away, it opened my eyes and my heart. Every time I get to work with an artist from this era, I am so grateful to be able to pay back for all the moments I had as a kid with my ear stuck to the radio, wondering where this amazing music came from as my feet tapped uncontrollably.

CHAPTER 28

My Part in Margaret Thatcher's Downfall

IN 1990, RICHARD OGDEN CALLED. Back in my motorcycle messenger days, I often dropped off packages at his office in West London. Back then he was managing Motörhead, but things had changed — I was now making music videos, and he was managing Paul McCartney.

Along with a double live album, Paul was releasing a single, and somehow my name had come up as a possible director of the clip. My heart stopped beating and I gasped for breath. I tried to sound as relaxed as I could while we talked, but I knew my voice was quivering.

Getting to shoot Alice Cooper had been a highlight, but getting to work with a Beatle? I couldn't believe it.

When I first saw the Beatles on *Sunday Night at the London Palladium,* John had definitely been the one I admired the most. It was too early in their career to understand that he was the rebellious one and all that went with it, but I laughed when he made his "rattle your jewellery" quip. John was cheeky and I liked that.

But by the time *Abbey Road* came along, my loyalties had shifted. John had become sullen, resentful and bearded, while Paul seemed more upbeat and positive. His grasp of melody appealed to me more. I appreciated his musicianship far more than I did John's love of bed-ins and protesting the Vietnam War.

After the band broke up and the *McCartney* album came out, my desertion to the Macca camp was complete. "Imagine" notwithstanding, I was never completely on John's team ever again. Of course, when he died, like everyone in my generation, I mourned for weeks and knew that something magical had been extinguished — my childhood had been ripped from me — and it was a puzzle that could never be put back together again.

Whichever way I looked at it, it was an honour to be even considered as a choice for directing a video for McCartney, and I was going to give it my all. Richard suggested I speak to Paul.

"That's a great idea. Will someone arrange the call?"

"Well, he's in the car with Linda right now," said Richard, "Why don't you call him yourself?"

Managers are notoriously protective of their charges. Getting to speak with the drummer of an unknown starter group is right up there with getting a direct line to the leader of the free world. And yet, somehow, I was reaching for a pen and paper so I could write down the number for the man who wrote "Hey Jude."

Minutes later I could hear the broken-up sound of an English ringtone and then a rather familiar voice. "Ullo."

"Um, is Paul there? This is Nigel Dick calling."

"Ullo, Dickey. Paul speaking. Say hello to Linda, she's in the car with me."

It seemed like just another phone call with old friends. I had to control myself and not get too familiar. It was all so easy, and Paul made it so.

We talked briefly about his ideas for the video. He told me he thought it would be a good idea to shoot in black and white, roughed out some B-roll suggestions and left the details up to me. He and Linda were off to the shops and said we could speak later if necessary.

I still hadn't heard the song and, when I did, it was a disappointment. It was Paul's version of the old spiritual "All My Trials." It wasn't even a special reimagining of the old chestnut — it was, well, average. But it was Paul fucking McCartney and I didn't care. I took a breath and started writing.

Some months previous, I had received a tantalizing proposition. Would I like to shoot something for McDonald's?

All of us at Propaganda wanted to shoot commercials. Commercials were important, commercials had huge budgets, commercials led to bigger and better things.

And I wasn't making any. I was upset about this, very upset. I'd gone to plead my case with the producers and was told that agents weren't in love with my reel. We'd tried spec work and other tricks, but it had all come to naught. What made it worse was that crew members, cinematographers, writers and producers all said to me, "I can't understand why you're not shooting commercials. You'd be perfect for it." Clearly, the people who commissioned such work thought otherwise.

So, when the McDonald's call came along I jumped at the chance of a big breakthrough. But as the meetings took place and initial ideas were discussed, all was not as it seemed. The client from the agency was not a creative with a long list of great ideas but a producer who felt he needed to break out of his production mould and invent a new way to market the world's biggest burger-maker. We finessed his idea and came up with a plan for a series of 30-minute shows called *Glitsch*. The shows would be released on videotape and given away at McDonalds.

I shot two music videos for the show at budget prices. We auditioned for exciting young people who'd never been abroad, gave them some money and put them on a plane for Europe with an easy-to-operate videocam, telling them to film each other at every possible moment. What they came back with, which predated a number of TV shows, looked suspiciously like every selfie-cam moment you see on Instagram today, only with much worse picture quality. Looking back, the idea wasn't so bad and mimics a lot of lifestyle pieces we now see every day on the web.

It was right in the middle of shooting *Glitsch* that I found myself on the phone with Paul and Linda. Paul wanted to shoot his video in London at exactly the same time I was supposed to be shooting another segment for *Glitsch*. A scenario like this in the freelance world isn't so much bad luck as utterly normal. Jobs are like buses: nothing happens for ages and then two come along at the same time.

Something needed to budge, and it wasn't going to be Paul McCartney.

Lisa Hollingshead, my producer, shifted and begged and tugged and rebooked, and soon we had a plan. While another producer planned and prepped the shoot with McCartney in London, I would shoot some scenes for *Glitsch* in Los Angeles. At three that afternoon, I would be whisked to the airport and fly to London. I would land the following morning and go straight out looking for locations. The next day, a Thursday, I would meet Paul and draw up my shot list. We would shoot on Friday and Saturday; Sunday I would fly home and resume shooting *Glitsch*. It would be a tough schedule, but doable.

And so, on the Tuesday afternoon, I finished shooting a scene on a rooftop in Hollywood, raced down the stairs and climbed into a car that took me to LAX. A few hours later, I was sitting at the very front of a jumbo jet as it passed over northern Canada, an undeniably smug grin on my face. My producers, realising that I was going to fly to London to shoot the world's most famous living rock star and fly back again inside five days, had squeezed their budgets to get me into first class. Sitting on my own in the very front row, I had so much space to put my tiny carry-on bag I kept moving it around to different spots just because I could. There were so many films to watch I almost wished the flight would last a little longer; there was so much food to eat I was in danger of making myself vomit. One row back was Ronnie James Dio and his wife, obviously quite used to travelling in the front of the plane. Behind them was Jordan Cronenweth, the DP who had shot *Blade Runner*, on his way to England to work on David Fincher's

Alien 3. Like every other music video director, I was in awe of his work and had tried countless times to get that look in my videos.

I settled back in my seat and reflected on how extraordinarily lucky I was — flying first class across the Atlantic to spend two days shooting one of my heroes. I had to admit it didn't get much better than this.

Which is about the time it all started to go terribly wrong.

In the darkness, the jumbo jet banked to the right and started turning around. I knew something was amiss. I looked over my shoulder. Ronnie James Dio was fast asleep and snoring; his wife was reading a book. Back in the galley, I could see one of the flight attendants, a pretty woman with a black bobbed haircut, on the phone — she looked very serious and was nodding. She put the receiver down, flipped a switch so the cabin lights came on and picked up the phone again. "Ladies and gentlemen, the plane has been turned around due to a mechanical problem. We will soon be landing at New York's JFK Airport..."

A collective groan broke out in the cabin as passengers tried to figure out what this would do to their travel plans. I was worried — I would be very late for my location scout.

We landed in New York at 4:00 in the morning and were discharged into an empty departure lounge. A lone cleaner who was pushing her vacuum cleaner up and down the weatherbeaten carpet looked shocked when hundreds of weary passengers suddenly disturbed her late-night solitude. There was no coffee, no snacks and the natives were getting restless.

A bleary-eyed flight representative eventually appeared and was instantly besieged by a horde of anxious, angry, weary passengers. She picked up the mic and announced that a replacement plane was being found and we would be on our way presently.

Dawn broke and, around a breakfast time that came and went without any food or coffee, a replacement plane arrived. We boarded, breathed a collective sigh and settled in for the transatlantic hop. The plane pulled away from the gate and trundled slowly around the edge of the airport. Then it came to a stop. Nothing happened for 15 minutes, and then the captain's voice blared out of the speakers. "Ladies and gentlemen, I'm sorry to have to announce that we've got to go back to the gate. There's a problem with the navigation equipment and we can't seem to fix it." Back at the gate, we were turfed off the replacement plane — that navigational problem had proved to be terminal.

I sprinted for a phone, fumbling for my Sprint phone card (remember those?). I dialled Bridget Blake Wilson, my producer in London, and gave her the news. "I'll see if I can get you a flight on Concorde," she said. "Call me back in ten minutes." I walked to the back of the phone line and waited until I was at the front again. "Concorde's full. The airline says you'll just have to wait till tonight to get onto the next plane out of JFK, which will get you into London a whole day later than planned."

I ignored the person behind me who wanted to make an urgent call. This was a disaster — the 48-hour prep and scout window for the most important shoot of my life, which was already dangerously small, had just been cut in half. Furthermore, I was now worried about what delaying the schedule would do to the McDonald's shoot now taking place without me in L.A., for which the client thought I was still on set. I called McCartney's manager. I explained my predicament and suggested we call off the shoot and reschedule. There was a brief silence. Richard's tone changed from calm to icy cold. "Nigel, no one, and I mean no one, walks away from a job with Paul McCartney. Understand? No one. And certainly not you."

Feeling sick to my stomach, I walked off, found a vacant piece of recently vacuumed carpet, lay down and fell into a deep sleep.

It was getting dark when boarding started for our third attempt. As we weary passengers shuffled down the jet bridge, who was there to check our tickets but the pretty flight attendant with the bobbed black haircut from our first trans-Atlantic attempt, looking fresh and rested. Her smile dropped as she looked at a line of passengers she recognized. "Wait, are you all still trying to get to London?" We nodded our heads and she turned to another attendant, "Oh god, this flight is going to be hell."

It was grey and damp on Thursday morning when I finally made my way out of customs in Heathrow and met Bridget Blake Wilson and Director of Photography John Mathieson for the first time. In my absence, they'd had no choice but to pick a location for me: an old waterworks on the west side of London, thankfully close to the airport. I met the rest of the crew there and went through the details for the next day's shoot with them.

By early afternoon the meetings were done, and I was driven off to my hotel. I had not met Paul, I had not drawn up a shot list, and I had been wearing the same clothes for over 48 hours. I fell asleep in the bath and woke up with a start to find it was dark outside and the water was cold.

I got dressed and started work on my shot list. When I couldn't work anymore, I collapsed into bed, but the wake-up call seemed to come five minutes after I fell asleep. I found my producer outside the hotel, waiting in the dark to drive me to the set, where I got to meet Paul and Linda.

I felt like crap. I was jet-lagged, angry about the mechanical screw-up which had left me with even less preparation time than I needed and anxious about meeting one of my heroes and doing the best possible job I could.

I was also nervous about meeting Linda.

I remembered that Paul had dated Jane Asher as the Beatles' career skyrocketed. The pictures of them together were plucked from a fairytale: the tall, handsome pop star and his blonde girlfriend, who lived together in her dad's house in a swanky part of London, out on the town, smiling and in love. When they had parted it seemed to coincide with the arrival of the Fab Four's facial hair and songs that, if they weren't about drugs, were surely influenced by them. This was a turn of events that shocked my young teenage self. It hurt my feelings to read about Paul meeting Linda. It seemed she had zeroed in on him; she wasn't picture perfect; and, worse still, everything I read about her was less than complimentary, like the terrible stories about her "musicianship." The image of a headstrong spouse trying to wiggle her way into the Beatles' orbit was not one I could easily get out of my head.

So, I was completely caught unawares when she turned out to be friendly and not at all pushy. Paul, for his part, was also very easy to talk to. They instantly helped me to relax. But the trouble about meeting your heroes is that you know everything about them and they know nothing about you, so if you are tempted to ask them what it was really like doing gigs in Hamburg for four hours a night or whether the final rooftop gig above Savile Row was a bittersweet memory, you are likely to forget that thousands of people have asked them those questions before. Their butt cheeks will clench and their eyes will glaze over very quickly if they are kind enough to respond at all.

Instead, what you need to do is ask questions you already know the answers to, but no one ever asks. Like, "How old are your kids now?" You can almost hear your hero breathe a sigh of relief as he tells you what his kids are up to this week. The fact that you really don't care very much is irrelevant — your hero is put at ease and, like every parent, is delighted to share some information about their offspring of whom they are undoubtedly proud.

As the shoot got up to speed, I could not resist the temptation to ask Paul one Beatles question. He had recently made it known that he wanted to be credited as the sole writer of "Yesterday." While there had been a longstanding agreement between Paul and John that every song they wrote, individually or together, would be credited to Lennon and McCartney jointly, Paul was hopeful that a retroactive exception could be made to the rule. Yoko Ono, in charge of Lennon's publishing after his untimely death, had vetoed the idea. The resulting publicity about the request and its refusal had sparked a furious debate amongst Beatle fanatics and in the music business in general about the rights and wrongs of Paul's request and Yoko's refusal. For me, the hullaballoo reached its zenith when I read an article on the affair in which the writer made it clear that he felt Paul was in the wrong and suggested that Paul didn't really know John at all or understand how crucial John's contribution had been to every Beatles song that Paul had written.

I bit my lip and asked Paul if he'd read the story and what he thought of it. He smiled. "The thing that writer misses is that John and I were best mates for 20 years. And when John and I wrote all those songs he mentions, we were sitting alone together at the piano in my mum's front room. I don't ever remember that journalist being in the room with us. So, how can he claim to have any clue about what John and I discussed?"

Oh my god, there were a thousand more questions I wanted to ask but we had to go to work.

I arrayed Paul and his band around the huge water pump at the bottom of the pumping house. A gallery area two stories high circled the space and looked down onto the pumping area and the band. Somewhat understandably, every member of the crew who wasn't working on a shot, and I'm sure some friends and family as well, leaned over the balcony and watched as the day progressed.

As I was setting up the camera for Linda's close-up, I sensed she was nervous. I asked her if she would like me to tell the watchers to move away so we could work together in relative privacy, but she said there was no need.

During a big change in the lighting, I went outside to get a coffee and a biscuit while the crew did their business. As I poured my drink I found Linda at my side. "Can I ask you a question?" she asked.

"Of course."

"When you asked me if I would like to have all those people in the gallery moved away would you have done it if I had said yes?"

"Yes, Linda, absolutely. We do it all the time. We're here to make you look good and do whatever it takes to help you give the best performance."

Linda looked downfallen. "Oh, I wish I'd known that, because they were making me really nervous, but I didn't want to cause a scene or upset anyone!"

This was not the Linda I'd read about. The "pushy" girlfriend, now wife, was not pushy at all but shy and respectful and made Paul's public assertion that it was he, not Linda, who had insisted she be a part of Wings seem totally believable. Years later, I remember the exact piece of road I was driving along on the Santa Monica Freeway when I heard on the radio that she'd died and felt suddenly so sad for Linda and for Paul.

When the day came to an end, I sheepishly reached into my bag and pulled out my copy of Paul's first solo album for him to sign. He wrote in his distinctive hand, "To Our Dick, Paul McCartney. Ta"

The second day of shooting, at a football match and on the streets of London, went off without a hitch. Sunday morning, I was on the plane back to Los Angeles and my shoot for McDonald's.

Paul's video needed to be finished quickly, so my editor went right to work. Within a few days, we'd finished the cut, made a VHS copy and sent it off to London to see what Paul had to say. I was staying with friends that weekend and had told Paul's people where I'd be in case they needed to contact me. Over Sunday breakfast, the lady of the house picked up the phone, listened to a voice on the other end and said, "Yeah, right! Fuck off!" before slamming it down.

"What was that all about?"

"Someone calling saying it was Paul McCartney."

It rang again. I grabbed the phone before anyone else could reach it.

"Hello, it's Paul McCartney, is Nigel there?"

"Paul, I'm so sorry..."

"No problem, it happens all the time!"

To my surprise, he approved the video without a single change and said he was calling to say thanks for the great job and how much he and Linda had enjoyed the experience. With very, very few exceptions, no other artist has ever contacted me personally after a job to say thank you.

Later that day, the editor called. He sounded concerned.

"Nigel, I think you need to turn on CNN right away. They've got footage from the McCartney video and are saying they're going to preview it after the next break."

"But that's impossible. It's not finished yet. And how have they got the footage?"

"Turn on CNN."

I rushed to the TV and heard the presenter say, "In London, Britain's Conservative Party are rumoured to be pushing for a vote of no confidence in Prime Minister Margaret Thatcher's leadership. And Paul McCartney has announced that his latest music video reflects his view that it's time for Britain's first-ever woman Prime Minister to step down." They cut to the grainy black and white footage from the VHS we'd sent to Paul, complete with time-code numbers in the corner. Paul looked into the camera and sang, "All my trials, Lord, soon be over." Within three days Thatcher had been dethroned.

Shortly after my return to LA, *Glitsch* was abandoned and not a single frame of the show ever saw the light of day. One day an envelope appeared in my mailbox with a short handwritten note on Paul McCartney World Tour notepaper that is now framed in my cutting room:

Nigel,

Thanx for making me look "so" good.

X Love Linda.

Not long after, while shooting an unknown band, I discovered an unexpected benefit of having worked with Paul. As the shoot was nearing its end, the band's manager approached me and asked if the singer, 21 years old and plucky, could sit with me through the entirety of the edit. I said no, but the manager was not to be denied. "Y'know he's a very bright young guy — he's full of ideas, and I think you'll find having him there from the moment you start will be incredibly helpful. This band is going to be enormous; you might want to keep on his good side." I tried to explain that having the artist in the edit was usually more of a hindrance than a help and, besides, I'd earned my bones and didn't want to have five days of babysitting stretching ahead of me. When the manager tried a third time, I came up with the perfect answer out of nowhere.

"Look, I've worked with Paul McCartney who, as you know, has been quite successful in this business. When I did a video for him, he left me alone to look after the edit and approved the first cut. I'm going to treat the footage I've shot for your singer and his group with the same amount of respect, care and attention that I used on Macca's cut. And if Macca trusts me to do a good job, I hope your singer will give me the same respect."

The manager did not say a word and walked off. His band's video was approved after the first cut, the record never troubled the charts and I've never seen or heard of the singer or his outfit ever again.

CHAPTER 29

Long Distance Runaround

THERE IS MUCH TRUTH in the saying, "Be careful when you meet your heroes." It will often be a huge disappointment.

While working at Phonogram, I was asked to take a meeting with Van Morrison. I was not an instant convert to Van the Man — I'd found his voice unbearable, his demeanour unattractive and his songs impenetrable. But at university, I'd borrowed *It's Too Late to Stop Now*, his live double album, from my guitar-playing buddy Ian Sutherland and was won over. The opener, "Ain't Nothin' You Can Do," starts off with such a gorgeous groove that my anti-Van sensors were overloaded, and he slid right into my consciousness. One morning I woke up to find that I owned more Van albums than practically anyone else apart from Elton John.

Ulster's legendary misanthrope needed to make a music video for his latest album. Van, I was told, didn't like videos much; my task was to convince him to suck it up and get in front of the camera. At my meeting with him, I gave it my best shot and tried to be convincing. So, I was delighted when, as the meeting drew to a close, Van said he would make a music video after all, but with one condition: Orson Welles had to be the director.

A better man than me might have started dialling Hollywood, but I just sighed and let Van walk out of the door. Van has been notoriously difficult to manage over the years; he's gone through managers at the speed most of us get through napkins. At least two of my close friends have managed him and they were both fired unceremoniously with nothing to show for it but a slew of hilarious tales of a man who has turned being difficult into an art.

Which brings me to those gods of prog rock, Yes.

By the time the '70s rolled around, the bullies at school had moved on to fresher meat, so I looked out of windows, wrote crap poetry and dreamed of romantic scenarios with girls. Occasionally, I would try and focus on studying calculus and James Joyce's impenetrable *A Portrait of the Artist as a Young Man* but mostly continued my obsession with music. Hours were spent plonking away on the piano in the music room with an Elton John songbook and learning the John Pearse fingerpicking method on my guitar while memorizing the lyrics to every Donovan song I could lay my hands on. I made feeble attempts to mimic Zeppelin's riffs on my acoustic guitar and devoured *Melody Maker* every week.

And so, naturally, I formed a band — an acoustic duo featuring some of the numbers I'd composed. We landed ourselves a Sunday afternoon gig at the nearby girls' school. Whatever musical success we may have had, we agreed the gig was a miserable failure, as no girls fell madly in love with us. Contrary to popular opinion, trying to be the new Cat Stevens wasn't going to pull the girls in, so I figured a stronger, louder approach was required.

Conveniently, I was asked to temporarily join Ten Ton Tears. TTT was a fledgling outfit with a drummer called Dave (who had his own drums), a bass player called John (with his own bass guitar — Paul McCartney Hofner model) and a fearsome guitar player named Richard who had an electric guitar, an amp and every Free album that had ever been recorded. All three of them.

Ten Ton Tears were a power trio — but not a very powerful one, since they only had one amp — who had a gig coming up in the school hall. The set list Richard had devised required me to stand in for John and play bass for the Doors number "Five to One" (two notes played over and over) and, for the encore, to leap back onstage and play rhythm guitar in a romping version of Hawkwind's "Hurry on Sundown" that would push Richard's amp to the limit. There were now three of us trying to rock that Selmer Treble n' Bass 50-watt amp. As I had no gear of my own, I played a bright red Burns electric that Richard loaned me. In an age of low-slung Telecasters and Les Pauls, it was a tragic case of last year's model; as Ian Hunter was to remark a few years later, "And that's your instrument? I felt so ashamed!"

The other kids in the band had parents with money, so I had to swallow my pride. My guitar might have belonged to someone else and been desperately out of date, but sartorially speaking I was on the cutting edge of early '70s fashion — fresh from the back pages of *Melody Maker,* I was wearing the latest trend, loon pants: trousers with bottoms so large that your feet disappeared under them.

Loon pants or not, there were no babes to rush the stage as we butchered that Hawkwind classic in our all-boys school. But there was some benefit from the gig in that bass player John Holland and I spent a lot of time in heated discussion as to whether Clapton was God or Jimmy Page was the future of everything. John was a card-carrying member of Clapton's fan club, while my hero was Page, though I also believed that Rory Gallagher on a good day could outsmart both of them with just his battered Strat and a Vox AC30. Many hours of acoustic guitar riffing and argument followed as we debated the relative merits of our plank-spanking heroes and became good friends.

Musical disagreements aside, half-term was coming, and we had managed to hatch a fine plan. We were going to escape to London for the weekend. John was a "Day Boy," which meant he lived in a nearby village and was dropped off outside the gates every morning by his mum. He needed time away from the parents. My parents were far away in Germany, so I just needed to get away from school. It was a brilliant plan — London had the two crucial ingredients required for an amazing half-term break: girls and rock bands.

We had scoured *Melody Maker* looking for a gig to go to on the Saturday night and found only one within our budget: Yes at the Queen Elizabeth Hall. It was to be my first gig, and I was beyond excited — which, in retrospect, was rather foolish, as neither John nor I had ever heard a single note they'd played or knew anything about them.

Whatever I was expecting when Yes took the stage, I was not prepared for what I heard. Brought up on a diet of Beatles, Stones, Hollies and the like, I'd enjoyed a seven-year master class in three-minute pop songs with catchy hooks and choruses, bridges, middle eights, pithy guitar solos, perfect harmonies and, "I Am the Walrus" notwithstanding, mostly sensible and decipherable lyrics about lust and longing. My recent adventures with Zeppelin, Free and Rory Gallagher's band, Taste, had introduced me to the blues played four to the bar and the joys of longer guitar solos over the same three chords played over and over with a kind of mesmeric predictability.

Whatever Yes brought to the stage, it was none of these things — and yet it was all of them together. The opening number lasted nine or ten minutes and had the lot: harmonies, choruses, bridges, arches, doors, corridors, vistas and more besides. It was abundantly clear this band had never met a time signature they didn't like. I'd suddenly left behind a world full of songs about Liverpool, Manchester and South London; there was no trace of Memphis, Chicago or the Delta in what I was hearing — I was rocketed off to a distant ethereal planet where the conventional forces of musical gravity didn't apply. I found it fascinating. Subconsciously I'd been looking for a version of classical music to immerse myself in and I'd found it. Such was my joy I completely ignored the fact that the lyrics to every song stubbornly refused to make any sense at all and consisted of words apparently picked at random. No matter. I was dazzled and unknowingly stood at the gates of a whole new musical genre that was about to invade the bins of every record store across the planet — progressive rock.

Yes had a hit in America and started to issue albums with songs long enough to fill entire LP sides. I kept spending my cash on their output until they followed *Close to the Edge* with *Tales of Topographic Oceans*. I felt they hadn't so much as gone close to the edge as fallen right off it; I cancelled my membership in the Yes fan club. The band's lineup kept changing; bizarrely, one version featured Geoff Downes and Trevor Horn from the Buggles. A subsequent reincarnation featured South African guitarist Trevor Rabin making them possibly the only successful rock outfit to ever have two Trevors in its lineup. Rabin brought new blood to the aging rock giant, and his song "Owner of a Lonely Heart" returned them to the charts.

Then they took a break and, as bands often do in such circumstances — especially ones with troubled pasts — they all started making solo albums. One day Trevor Rabin rang up original singer Jon Anderson and asked him to come over and add vocals to a song he was working on. The song was called "Lift Me Up."

One hot Hollywood Saturday afternoon, I was doing what I love to do at weekends, which is work at my bench in the garage building things, when Trevor Rabin called, wanting to talk about this new Yes tune, the first single from their next album, which concerned something he felt very passionate about: homelessness. And so we cooked up an idea to intercut footage of homeless people (played by actors) with studio and concert footage of the band. I smiled to myself as I put the phone down. I was going to direct the video for "Lift Me Up" and meet my heroes.

Without anyone warning me, I'd wandered into a minefield.

Knowing more about Yes's recording history now than I did that sunny afternoon, I would guess that if you were to ask all the band's members how this album and tour came together, you'd hear eight different versions. On paper it was a masterstroke, but in reality it was a camel — a horse designed by committee. Yes were now signed to Clive Davis's Arista label, where someone thought it would be a good plan to take "Lift Me Up" and some other songs Trevor had written and combine them with pieces written and recorded by other Yes men to make an album. Furthermore, all the available and willing (or perhaps desperate) key ex-members of the various lineups were persuaded to go on the road together and promote the album. The tour and album were to be called *Union*.

It was a plan, but one that made about as much sense as putting Angela Merkel, Michael Schumacher and Adolf Hitler together on a speaking tour because they were good in front of cameras and were all German. For a start, there was too much of everything: two guitarists (Trevor Rabin and Steve Howe), two keyboard players (Rick Wakeman and Tony Kaye), two drummers (Alan White and Bill Bruford) and the original bass player and singer: Chris Squire and Jon Anderson. Even worse, there were at least five managers involved, and that's always a recipe for disaster.

Years later, I read Bill Bruford's fine autobiography, which described the tour's problems: "Arista executive Roy Lott, who had dreamed up this nightmarish scenario with [Yes manager Brian] Lane, was the man holding the purse strings ... I doubt all eight of us would have been able to get into a rehearsal room together — the lawyers alone would have filled most of the available space ... it was a synthetic and sentimental kind of party, performed largely for Roy Lott's benefit."

But of course, I knew none of this. All I cared about on that hot afternoon was that the next chapter of the history of one of my favourite bands was now my responsibility, and I'd better not screw it up.

It was decided that we would shoot for one day with the "homeless people" and the band on Stage 3 at SIR in Hollywood and the next night at their show at an arena in San Diego. As we planned our schedule, the cracks in the Yes *Union* façade began to show. We were informed that, under no circumstances, would all members of the band be available, or want to be available, at the same time. The drummers, Bill and Alan, were apparently good mates and would be available whenever, first thing if need be. The bass player, Chris, would not be available till 10:00 p.m. at night. Rick and Tony, the keyboard players, would be OK to shoot sometime late morning. Trevor, being the songwriter and most genial, would be available all day long. Original guitarist of note Steve Howe (who'd actually been preceded in the band for a couple of albums by Pete Banks) would prefer to perform only when Trevor Rabin was not present. Singer Jon Anderson would only be available at 4:00 p.m. We had to be ready to shoot him the second he walked into the building or there would be trouble. Producer Lisa Hollingshead and I joked that we were not trying to create a schedule for a music video but drawing up a table plan for a set of grumpy Eastern Bloc dictators who wanted to invade each other's countries. Making matters worse, I had been instructed to deliver shots in the video in which all members of the band would be present at the same time. How was that going to happen?

The day of the shoot dawned. First on set were the two drummers. Bill Bruford and Alan White were professional and friendly; their shots were quickly in the can. Next up were the keyboard players, Rick Wakeman and Tony Kaye. They, too, were easy to work with; Wakeman proved to have a wonderfully dry sense of humour. Perhaps this wasn't going to be as difficult as I thought.

I'd solved the problem of getting all the band members into the same shot. At the back of the set, we built a long dolly track that crossed the width of the stage and locked it down. We fixed the height of the dolly and marked a spot on the floor where each of the eight band members would stand. As each arrived on the set, I asked them to stand in the prearranged spot as the camera moved past them. The idea was to then stick the eight shots together in post and hope that somehow it would work as a long dolly shot of the entire band. Unfortunately, we didn't have the money for motion control — a programmable device that makes the dolly move with an accurate and repeatable speed — so the dolly grip would need to somehow make the same dolly move at the same speed at various times during the day.

By lunchtime, we'd shot the two drummers and the two keyboard players on their marks in front of the dolly track and were ready for the guitar players. Trevor Rabin had been with us all day and was polite and businesslike. I was happy with the way things were going, but the arrival of Steve Howe after lunch was my first signal that this was not going to be easy. It seemed that Mr. Howe was not a member of the Trevor Rabin fan club. I'd revered Howe's guitar playing for years; to see this side of him upset me, but we persevered, and soon he was done. We started shooting Rabin, who was eager to please. I glanced nervously at my watch as the camera rolled — Jon Anderson's 4:00 o'clock arrival was getting close, and I wanted to be ready for him as instructed. I asked the crew to prepare a setup for Jon's close-up so we could shoot him whenever he appeared.

At 3:50, with no sign of Anderson, I decided to squeeze in another take of Trevor Rabin. Halfway through, I felt a tap on my shoulder and turned round to find myself face-to-face with the legendary vocalist. I shook his hand and quickly explained we'd be ready for him within two minutes as planned. He didn't seem too concerned and wandered away muttering something about making a call.

The shot with Trevor was completed and we were ready for Jon. I looked at my watch — it was dead-on 4:00 o'clock. I called Jon over, placed him on his mark and explained what we were about to do. As I was talking to Jon, Lisa Hollingshead rushed over and told me there was an urgent call for me. I asked her to take a message as I was under strict orders to shoot Jon at 4:00 p.m. But she was insistent. I had to take the call which, before cell phones, meant leaving the set and going to the production office. I turned to Jon. Would he be OK with me leaving the set to take a call? He was very polite and told me it was not a problem.

I ran from the set, leaving Jon to chat with the AD, and pushed my way into the production office. The voice on the line was unfamiliar, and the connection was not good. "Hello. This is Jon Anderson's manager. I'm calling from Switzerland. Jon needs to go in front of the camera right now. It was made clear to you that you had to be ready for him at 4:00 p.m. and I'm very upset that this promise was not kept." Through gritted teeth I explained that Jon had indeed stepped in front of the camera at 4:00 p.m. and the only thing that was stopping me from shooting him was the fact that I was on this transatlantic call. I was instructed to get on with it and the line went dead.

I was not in the best of moods as I returned to set and suggested we get back to work.

The next morning, we drove down to San Diego to shoot the live portion. But I wasn't out of the woods yet. I'd decided I needed an opening shot for the video in which all eight band members really were in the same room at the same time — singing the opening chorus. It was going to be a simple group shot with the eight musicians arranged like a football team, all looking at the camera. It would literally take one minute to shoot. But getting the eight members to gather in one spot for one minute was a nightmare and, like that executive desk game with ball-bearings on strings hanging from a rack, as one band member entered through one door, another left through the other. Someone said, "If he's not here in half a minute then I'm leaving." It's at moments like these that you realise that herding cats or a class of five-year-olds on a school trip is infinitely easier than asking a collection of grown men in a rock group to congregate in a room for 60 seconds for the greater good.

After the first cut of the video was delivered, Trevor dropped in to oversee some of the changes and was appalled to see Jon singing one sequence. "What's happened here?" he asked. I showed him the list of notes we'd received which specifically asked for shots of Jon to replace shots of Trevor from the first cut. Trevor sighed deeply and put his head in his hands, "But I wrote this song. That's my voice. I'm the one who's singing there!"

More changes were made until all that remained was the final on-line, the process by which we assembled the shots from the master tapes in exactly the same way we had cut them together in rough form in the edit. Back then, the hourly cost of the on-line edit room was so expensive that this was left till the very end of the process.

The morning of the on-line dawned and I was slumbering in bed waiting for the alarm to go off when the phone rang at my bedside. "Nigel Dick? I have Clive Davis for you." Somewhere there is a chart of the most powerful men in the record business when it was at its zenith. Clive Davis was somewhere in the top three. He was known for his foibles and his uncompromising approach to artists and running his label but, undeniably, he got results. Clive didn't even say hello...

"I've just seen the Yes video."

(Fuck — I'm in bed in my pj's and Clive Davis is on the phone): "Um ... er ... good morning, Clive."

"Why are there badly dressed people with shopping carts in the video?"

"They're homeless people. That's what Trevor wanted."

"Homelessness is not attractive. I'm trying to sell records. Homeless people don't sell records."

"But Trevor told me it's a song about homeless people."

"I don't care. This is a love song — I want a couple kissing, rolling in the surf."

"Like that Burt Lancaster film?"

"Yes. Buy that footage and put it in the video."

"But ... that's going to take some time to arrange, and we have the on-line in two hours."

"I've just reached JFK. I have a plane to catch."

The line went dead. Whether it was the urgency to get the video on MTV or the prohibitive cost of buying footage of Burt and Deborah Kerr rolling in the surf, the video remained unchanged. Looking back at it now I have mixed feelings. I wonder would the video mean anything if you didn't know it was about homelessness? But I do know that if I was asked to make another Yes video I would.

I recently read a fascinating and hysterically funny interview with Rick Wakeman. The journalist asked what he thought of the *Union* album. Wakeman responded, "*Union*? I call it *Onion*, because every time I think of it it makes me cry."

CHAPTER 30

Free Man in Paris

I WOKE UP IN MY PARISIAN HOTEL ROOM befuddled and jet-lagged, threw on some clothes and made my way down to breakfast. Arriving in France was always something I looked forward to for the simple reason that French coffee and a baguette is about the best way in the world to start your day.

I was there to shoot Johnny Hallyday, the biggest rock star France had ever produced, and I was really looking forward to it. I poured my coffee, peeled open my baguette and spread jam on it. As I took a bite, I heard a horrible cracking noise and saw half of a molar tumble onto the plate in front of me with a sweet, tinkling noise. Was this an omen on how the job was going to go? It didn't seem like a good sign.

I finished *le petit dejeuner* and headed to the production office to get started on the job. The budget was too small to bring along a U.S. producer; Catherine Finkenstaedt, my executive producer in L.A., had asked if I would be OK working with a local producer. I spoke some French and, as we've established, loved a good baguette — of course I wanted to go! I was excited to work with the French Elvis.

The song was called "I Wanna Make Love to You," and I'd pitched having Johnny, framed in the window of a Parisian apartment, singing as he looked across a courtyard and watched an attractive young woman in her own apartment getting ready for the day. As with many video ideas, it was guided by the fact that I'd only have Johnny for one day. We were scheduled to shoot on a Thursday; he'd be jetting off on Friday to spend the weekend in the South of France with his gorgeous model girlfriend. I'd been told she needed to have a starring role in the video and was happy to cast her as the object of his affection.

The French producer looked down his nose at me. I wondered if he was miffed that a Brit who lived in California had been dispatched to shoot the iconic French rocker when there were plenty of French directors who could have done the gig. It also appeared that shooting music videos was beneath a man of such high and noble status. He made a big deal of being in the middle of post-production on a really important commercial. As we went through the details of the job, his final comment to me concerned the location I needed. "Zere is no such location in Parees!"

Was my vision of Parisian architecture so out of line that I'd dreamed of something which simply did not exist? I bought the largest scale map of Paris I could find and spent the weekend walking the streets, looking for likely buildings that seemed to have a courtyard. Not knowing the city well enough and not speaking the language adequately, I was unable to get inside any buildings and was drawing a blank. This happens all too often in our business — you have a job bearing down on you fast and, for some reason, you can't find a place to shoot it. We have a name for this situation: Location Hell.

In frustration, I went behind the producer's back and asked Sophie Herr, production manager on the job, if Paris had a location agency. Turns out she was also frustrated by the producer's intransigence and agreed to make some calls without his knowledge. That afternoon, we visited a location agency in what felt like a residential building. We were admitted to an office, where an elderly lady sitting behind a desk furthered the impression of being in someone's home. She lowered her glasses and asked what we were looking for.

I took a deep breath. Well, we were looking for an apartment with a room perhaps the size of her office with a window just like the one in her office. I stood up to point out of the window and continued that I wanted Johnny to look out of the window across the courtyard of the apartment building — in fact, just like the courtyard of her apartment building — to another apartment with its window open — in fact, just like that one over there. I stopped for a moment and looked around again as if something magical had happened. "In fact, this would be the perfect location!" She seemed unimpressed and started selecting folders piled on a cabinet behind her. "Is there a particular *arrondissement* you'd prefer?" It seemed there were many choices that matched my imaginary location, and she could offer us options all over Paris. So, the crazy Brit wasn't so crazy after all. By the next morning, we had selected and secured our location.

But that was only half the problem solved. Back in his office, the producer leaned back in his chair when I showed him the location pictures. "So, you have found somewhere? But you still have a problem," he huffed. "It will take ten days to get a permit." He smiled a sickly smile. "Now you will have to push the shoot back by a week."

I left his office wondering whose side that guy was on. I asked Sophie to do what she could to beg for a favour from the permit office and got into a cab. I was going to meet Johnny for the first time, and I wanted to be carrying good news, not bad. It was a grey afternoon, and my tongue wouldn't stop finding that half-broken tooth, which was starting to worry me. I was beginning to regret being so enthusiastic about accepting an offer to work with the French Elvis.

The cab negotiated its way into a gated community on a street lined with trees and dropped me outside a house with a bright red Italian sports job in the driveway. A housekeeper opened the door and took me into a tastefully decorated living room. Monsieur would join me shortly. I was drawn to the very good copy of an Impressionist master that hung over the fireplace and suddenly realised that it wasn't a copy at all. Was that really a Seurat?

Jean-Philippe Smet was born in Paris in 1943 to a French mother and a Belgian father. Mum was a model too busy to look after the boy, and Dad, a nightclub performer, soon disappeared, so his aunt took the boy under her wing. He learned to play classical guitar. He grew taller and his clear blue eyes attained their cat-like gleam. When he heard "Blue Suede Shoes" on the radio, something magical happened. He acquired an agent named Halliday who was born in Oklahoma; the agent, too lazy to call him Jean-Philippe, called him Johnny for short. He got a greaser haircut and released his first disc, "Laisse les Filles" ("Leave the Girls Alone"), in 1960. Two weeks later, while walking through the Metro in Paris, a bunch of kids came walking towards him, singing his song. "I thought, Shit! It's working!" said Jean-Philippe, *et voilà!* He became Johnny Hallyday, and a star was born.

He had hits all over Europe, came to America, appeared on *The Ed Sullivan Show* and in Vegas and cut records with the likes of Jimmy Page, Mick Jones (later of Foreigner), Peter Frampton, Steve Marriott and Ronnie Lane. He was Elvis, James Dean, the Beatles and the Stones all rolled into one tall, sexy French package. He went on to make 79 albums and was married five times. Stage shows featuring his extraordinary vibrato were spectacular; an appearance in the shadow of the Eiffel Tower in 2000 pulled between 500,000 and a million people (depending on who was counting). He smoked continuously and loved nothing more than putting on a leather jacket, climbing aboard a large Harley and riding across the arid deserts of the American West.

I was still studying the painting over the fireplace when I heard a noise behind me. There was Johnny — blue jeans, cowboy boots, an open shirt and a jacket. When he smiled, there was a charming sparkle in his eyes. We sat down to talk; his English was very good. I shared the casting pictures for his band, which he approved, went over the storyboards and finally proffered the location pictures, which he liked. "So, we shoot on Thursday. What is my call time?"

"Well, Johnny, we have a problem. I've been told it takes ten days to get a shooting permit in Paris, and we only secured the location this morning. Can we push the shoot back till next week?"

"Ten days? Pah! What's the address of the location?" I passed him the file, and he picked up the phone. "Jacques? *Comment ça va*?" A rapid conversation ensued. My French was not good enough to follow all the details, but I gathered Johnny was jumping over a few bureaucratic hurdles. He read the location address for Jacques. After telling Jacques he would see him that evening, he did that thing French folk do with their hands to minimize the difficulty of something they have just done. "*Pas de problème*," said Johnny. "It is all taken care of. We have a permit."

A huge weight slipped from my shoulders. But, so I could assure Sophie and her boss that the permit was sorted, I asked Johnny who he had spoken to. "Jacques? He is the mayor of Paris. We are friends. I will buy him a drink tonight. And now we must go to rehearsal — come with me."

I can't remember if Johnny's car was a Ferrari or a Lamborghini, but being driven through Paris by France's biggest singing sensation in an over-powered sportscar was quite a thrill. At every red light, Parisian pedestrians would cross in front of us, check out the fancy car and widen their eyes as they saw Johnny behind the wheel. "Johnneeee!" they would cry and wave happily.

The morning of the shoot, my tooth was starting to really annoy me, so I skipped the baguettes in the dining room and settled for a croissant. Sophie picked me up outside the hotel and we drove to the location. As we turned into the street where it was, we were stopped by armed officers who, when told who we were, let us through. "Oh my!" said Sophie, "I've never seen this before." The whole street had been blocked off; there were *gendarmes* everywhere. It seemed that knowing the mayor had many benefits.

Johnny was a delight. He was very relaxed and he even helped me by translating requests to the crew. When we broke for lunch, the AD walked me down the street to the restaurant where we were to be fed. There was a long table with starched white tablecloths reserved for the crew, but I was stopped in my tracks at the sight of a full glass of red wine at every place setting. I ran to find Sophie. "We have to lose the wine immediately. It's against the law to have alcohol on set — especially for the crew."

The ever-helpful Sophie vanished in a heartbeat and a tougher Sophie appeared. "*Non!*" she said. "In France it is the law. At lunch all crew members get one glass of wine and one glass only. If we lose the wine, you will lose your crew!"

During a break, I asked Johnny about his film career. Besides his considerable success as a singer, he'd also managed to carve out a decent career as an actor, not only in Elvis or Cliff Richard-style pop musicals but in creditable dramatic performances with well-known directors. He shared a story from one of his early films, which I recall him saying was a Jean-Luc Godard film.

The story ran like this: Johnny turned up on the first day of shooting excited and nervous, but the director looked up at the sky and declared it too cloudy. The crew hung around till lunchtime, when the director called a wrap and sent everyone home. On day two, the director showed up and said it was too windy. Wednesday dawned and the director was shivering — it was too cold. This went on all week and the next. Not a frame of film was shot. By now, the crew was used to hanging out in bars and coffee shops all morning; poker games were breaking out on set.

Come Monday morning of the third week, it was pelting down with rain; bullet-sized droplets were bouncing six inches off the pavement. As the crew were deciding which café would get their patronage, the director showed up and told the DP where the camera would be placed and where the actors would arrive and leave the scene. The crew were shocked. What about the weather? If the director had hated the clouds and the wind, surely the heavy rain made shooting a complete non-starter? The director shouted back, "Are you guys fucking crazy? I have only two weeks left to shoot this film. *Allez, Allez!* Hurry up!"

At the end of the first day of shooting, I thanked Johnny for his work and his help and wished him well on his trip. He explained that he'd delayed the trip and would come to set on Friday morning to watch. "And, anyway, I can help with translating your orders to the crew!" So, Johnny thought my French was that bad? I didn't care, it was a pleasure to have him around and work as my interpreter.

We wrapped right on schedule. As I was climbing into a cab to the airport, Sophie came running over with all the exposed film cans taped together. "Can you take these with you?" she asked. I was exhausted, I wasn't going to land in London till midnight, my tooth was killing me and now I had to carry all the film through customs at both ends without it being opened? I sighed, piled the cans on the seat beside me and left for CDG. I hand-carried the heavy rolls of film all the way back to London and made it home, nursing both my jaw and the precious negatives.

By all accounts, Johnny and his label were happy with the video. It wasn't till later that I discovered that Jacques, the mayor guy who'd bailed us out and secured our location permit, was none other than Jacques Chirac, the former President of France. I wish I'd known that when I told the you-still-have-a-problem producer guy we'd defied the rules and secured a permit to shoot. How wonderful it would have been to tell him, "You said I had a problem, so I went over your head and had the ex-President do me a favour." If only...

I'm often asked what was the most satisfying job I've ever done. Band Aid's "Do They Know It's Christmas?" is hard to beat because we saved lives, but I think Johnny's video comes a close second. I arrived in Paris to work with a production team I'd never met, had all kinds of hurdles thrown in my path and somehow managed to overcome all of them with the help of the artist and an ex-president!

And that tooth? I call the incident the $10,000 breakfast. Over the years that tooth caused me endless crowns and gum surgeries. Eventually I had the damn thing pulled out, leaving a huge hole. The cost of dental work I had on that molar far exceeds the money I earned on that job, but it was fun to hang with France's biggest star and see that twinkle in his eye when he smiled.

Johnny sadly died from cancer a few years ago. Three French presidents came to his funeral, and so many fans filled the streets that Paris ground to a halt. We'll not see his like again. If you've not seen his performance in *Man on the Train,* I suggest you check it out.

CHAPTER 31

The Hexagram of the Heavens

I CANNOT LIE — I have not been as generous to charity as perhaps I should have been. But I learned a great lesson when I shot the Band Aid video "Do They Know It's Christmas?": if you can't or won't give money, at least give your time. I also learned that, when you do a job like that, you get to enjoy an amazing life experience and the chance to meet a number of your heroes — and that's something that money can't buy.

After the city's riots in 1992, I directed a video for a charity record called "Stand and Be Proud." The song was co-written by David Cassidy and produced by Bob Ezrin to raise funds "to rebuild L.A." I wasn't a fan of David's work, but I liked working with him and was happy I'd accepted the gig. But it was a bigger thrill to work with Ezrin, famous for his work with Pink Floyd, KISS, Alice Cooper and others. I was struck by his passion for music and even more fascinated by his determination to create some good from the ashes and give voice to those in the city who'd long been marginalized. As part of the project, I interviewed teens who'd never left the inner city. One asked me if cows really ate grass and lived in fields. Another shared that she had never been to the beach and seen the sea — which was only 12 miles from where she lived — because she was convinced that she would be killed by gang members if she stepped out of the narrow corridor of streets which linked her home to her school and through which she was allowed to walk.

Ezrin's plan was to record the backing track in a studio then finish it at the Hollywood Bowl, with the Hollywood Bowl Orchestra and choirs of every denomination and skin colour from all over Los Angeles. I would shoot the climax of the video there.

Peter Ueberroth, organiser of the L.A. Olympics, fronted a newly minted outfit entitled Rebuild Los Angeles; with his help, we would try, for one glorious afternoon and evening, to create a vision of a unified front of people across the city in joyous celebration. I have no idea if it worked, but with the choirs and orchestra there were 1,500 people in the cast and crew. As the trucks rolled into the parking lot at call time one of the crew shouted out, "This job is so big it has its own zip code!"

The job had another entertaining twist to it. I rarely had access to the cool toys that every director wanted to use — Steadicams, multiple cameras, 35mm film and so on. I usually shot 16mm and only occasionally had the budget for two cameras. Perversely, because the job had no budget at all, I got all the toys I wanted — and more — for free. There were ten 35mm cameras with all the film stock I needed, two Steadicams, a crane, even a helicopter with a camera operator in it. Future film director Antoine Fuqua was my second unit director, and I was surrounded by assistants. There were so many people onstage that they spilled out into the auditorium. Apart from live shows, I've never shot a bigger production before or since. The finished clip was shown in theatres nationwide before feature films for a few weeks though, sadly, the film was transferred to tape, edited and then transferred back to film and looked awful.

A few years later I was asked to donate my time for a few weeks to work on a show for APLA (AIDS Project Los Angeles) to be produced by Elton John's songwriting partner, Bernie Taupin. I wasn't directing the show but would instead provide clips to be projected behind the artists as they performed at the fund-raising gala. I asked who would be appearing and, apart from Elton John, there was initially not much agreement on who would make it. I set out to source pieces of film for free, borrowed a camera and wandered the city late at night shooting flashing lights and time-lapsed traffic hoping that when the list of artists was confirmed I could find a home for it. I hoped that maybe working with one of those artists would make the job worthwhile.

There are some artists who, once you've heard one song, you have to compulsively purchase every record they've made, track down every demo they've recorded, watch every clip you can find on YouTube — and it's still never enough. I once climbed into a cab in London and noticed the driver's impressive stash of cassettes. There must have been a hundred. "That's quite a collection you have there," I told him. "Yup," he replied, "every cassette there is a live bootleg by Bob Dylan. You should see what else I have at home!"

I've also found artists who have made one record so powerful and mesmerizing that all the others in their canon don't come close. As you go deeper into their catalogue, you become afraid that hearing their other work will somehow lessen the power of that one great album, so you back away from the counter and allow that one record all the space it needs to resonate. One such record and artist for me is *Hejira* by Joni Mitchell.

Like many British music fans my age, I'd first heard of Joni Mitchell when "Big Yellow Taxi" had some success on the British charts in 1970. It was cute and hummable. I liked its green message and the way she laughed at the end of the song. I was going through my Zeppelin–Yes–ELP stage so I didn't look further into her career at that point. Then I started waiting at that restaurant in Bath where I briefly served John Phillips and Princess Margaret and heard *Court and Spark* booming out over the speakers for the first time. Every song on that record was deeper and more sophisticated than "Big Yellow Taxi," and I started to take notice. Keeping my feeble earnings for more important records like that Be-Bop Deluxe album I wanted, I made a cassette copy of a friend's copy of *Court and Spark*. When *Hejira* was released, I bought it and had my mind blown. At first it was her voice and the melodies that got to me, then the arrangements, then the Jaco Pastorius moment occurred, but it wasn't till much later that I really started listening to her words and my whole understanding of the world shifted on its axis.

I grew up in a household with a woman whose attitude towards men and sex was distilled into one stock phrase: "It's always the man's fault." As I was reaching an age when humans started to really interact with people of the opposite sex, I was sent away for eight years to a school where there was absolutely no interaction with women apart from Matron — a widow of some age who dispensed clean sheets once a week and treated any bruises and scratches with generous portions of witch hazel. As my university years were equally bereft of female contact, discovering those lyrics was akin to having a bomb go off in my head. Her lyrics weren't moon and June and silly love songs, they discussed — in complex and beautifully composed stanzas — emotions that were complex and seemed rather familiar to my own. I found this totally confusing. Weren't girls supposed to think differently than boys about such things? Wasn't it always the man's fault? Wasn't it men who only had one thing on their mind? With that one album, the fates had provided me with messages from the older sister that life had denied me.

The crux of this learning moment came with "Song for Sharon," which starts out as Joni boards the ferry to Staten Island to buy a mandolin. When she sees a wedding dress on a store front mannequin, it takes a sharp turn into thoughts about childhood in Canada and what marriage is all about, detours into an expensive visit to a fortune teller in Greenwich Village and then dismisses the prospect of a "world of noble causes and lovely landscapes" in favour of finding "another lover."

At this point she's only halfway through the song! It didn't take me long to take a step back and realise that Joni was painting more vivid pictures about her day shopping and about her life, her dreams and failures and about her upbringing, than any artist I'd ever heard. There was more lyrical meat in the first four verses of that one song than in an entire double album.

So, in late 1994, when I was asked if I would work on that charity show for APLA, I hoped that the confirmed list of performers would be special. Eventually, Bernie told me that Elton would be joined by Julie Andrews, George Michael, Terence Trent D'Arby, Melissa Etheridge, Marianne Faithful and others. Plus Joni. Perhaps I could create a collage of her paintings; if that was possible, Joni would like to be involved.

So, one evening, trying to keep my cool, I waited in a tiny editing room in Hollywood for Joni Mitchell. Many stars have an assistant appear to announce that said mega-personality is on the way. Arrangements have been made ahead of time for special parking spots, brands of approved still water and preferred room temperatures. Joni was different. She simply walked through the door, took a seat and lit a cigarette.

We had images of a number of her paintings on a tape and were going to create a montage that would play on a large screen behind Joni as she sang. I would be in the darkness somewhere up near the sound desk with a videotape machine and hit Play when she started performing. We would just have to hope that the cuts came at roughly appropriate points during the song, because there was no way to ensure that her live performance would be at the same tempo as the recording we had in the edit bay. I'm sure nowadays there are school plays in the poorer parts of town which use more sophisticated machinery than I had at my disposal for that show. I explained my concerns to her. She shrugged her shoulders. To my great relief, Joni didn't seem to mind.

As we worked, Joni shared a surprisingly hilarious story about how her house was under siege from a stalker. She'd hired some off-duty cops to keep the scoundrel/fan at bay but discovered they were from the drug squad. "So, now we have to go into the bathroom and turn on the shower to smoke a joint in case they can smell what we're up to!"

When I asked Joni if she'd be going on the road soon, she sighed and said she used so many special guitar tunings that it was difficult to organise a live show. Plus, she was starting to worry how strong her hands were — a knock-on effect from her childhood polio. I tried to keep my fanboy self under control but, as the session came to an end, I had to ask if she didn't worry that smoking would affect that beautiful instrument of hers — that voice. She took another puff from her cigarette, stared at it for a second and gave me a sideways look. "I'd rather be killed by a friend!"

CHAPTER 32

Down in a Hole

CREW CALL WAS 6:30 A.M. in the vast hotel lobby. There must have been 30 of us scattered on seats and chairs, but I was worried — one crucial person was missing. There was no sign of the Director of Photography, a fellow Brit with an impressive reel. I'd previously avoided working with him because he had a worrying reputation as a serious drinker, but I had been persuaded this time on the understanding that he would keep off the sauce. The day before, I made him promise he would go to bed early and be ready for a long day. We were going to shoot Alice in Chains live, and I needed him to be on his A game.

The pressure was particularly intense for shooting the gig at Memorial Hall in Kansas City, Missouri. An audio recording truck had come down from Chicago, extra lights had been trucked in from New York and most of the crew had been flown in from both the East and West Coasts. One cameraman had come from the UK. Between flights, per diems, hotels and travel days, an enormous amount of money was being shelled out. A shoot like this is much cheaper to produce in a major film centre, where the crew and equipment already exists and most of the crew can get to work via subway or car. For reasons lost to the mists of time, we had all flown to Missouri for the gig.

I have shot dozens of live shows; far too often, the client wants me to shoot a show in some remote city because the crowd there is so excitable and enthusiastic, arguing that it's worth navigating the difficult logistics and increased cost to get the wild fans down in the front row on film. Sadly, my experience has rarely matched the client's dreams. On one occasion, the acoustics were appalling and seriously compromised the audio. On another, the only place I could put cameras was on the side of the stage, and the artist was furious that all his close-ups were in profile.

But my worst experience was when the artist's A&R man insisted we shoot his band's live show in a small Midwestern city because the audiences there were always incredibly enthusiastic. He insisted that we capture wide shots of the stage since he'd spent a lot of money on a one-of-a-kind set. In the end, I felt the audience were no more enthusiastic than scores of audiences I have seen at other shows around the world, but the real flaw in his plan came to light when he saw the first cut and blew his stack.

"What the fuck is this? Where are the shots of my stage set? I specifically told you to get shots of the set. It cost me $50,000! All I am seeing are a bunch of lights. It looks like every other fucking show out there. Where's the set?"

On the night, I had asked the tour manager the same question. Why were there just a bunch of lights hanging from a truss like a million other live shows? Where was the sexy stage set? "Oh, it's still on the truck," he explained. "It wouldn't fit through the door into the gig. It's a shame you weren't available to shoot any one of the last three shows. It looked epic — much better audiences, too!"

Back in the lobby, there was still no sign of the Director of Photography. I asked someone to go and bang on his hotel room door. There was no answer. I turned to my pal "Frisby" Fraser, one of the camera ops who'd flown in from California, and rolled my eyes. Now I was really worried. Then the tour bus rolled up outside the hotel. "Well, at least the band's here."

My producer on the job, Tima Surmelioglu, went outside to chat with the band's manager, Susan Silver. Even though I was some distance away and inside the hotel, I could tell something was wrong.

"The gig's off!" I told Frisby.

He was confused. "How can you tell?

"Look at the body language."

Susan was slowly shaking her head. Tima's hand had gone to her mouth in shock. She was pointing at the crew in the lobby, all patiently waiting with their small cases of personal film gear, eager to go to set.

The discussion outside continued for some time. Finally, Tima and Susan hugged, Susan climbed back on the bus and Tima sat down beside me as the bus pulled away.

"The gig's not happening, is it?"

"Nope. The band broke up after last night's show. They've already been dropped at the airport and are flying home."

Tima shared more sobering details of what had occurred the previous night. It was clear that our journey to Missouri had been in vain. Tima told us all to hang tight and went off to ring the label, which had spent over a quarter of a million dollars getting us all to Missouri, paying fees, hiring trucks, buying film, etc. and would have nothing to show for it. So, they came up with a potential plan B. The support act on the Alice in Chains tour was a then little-known band called Rage Against the Machine. Perhaps we could shoot a live show that night with them instead? We were told to wait in the lobby.

Hours passed. The crew had taken off their coats, piled their camera bags and hand-carried equipment into mounds and were ordering food. Somewhere across town, a catering truck with 50 hot breakfasts was wondering why there were no takers.

Hours later, the Brit DP collapsed onto the seat beside me and a noticeable whiff of stale alcohol came in my direction. He had a big smile on his face and did not seem at all worried (or even aware) that he was four hours late for his call. Despite his earnest protestations of sobriety, I later discovered that he had been seen drinking heavily the night before and had left the hotel in the early hours in search of a club.

Rage Against the Machine were eventually located in their tour bus, sleeping off the previous night's show. Even though the label assured them it would not cost them a cent, they turned down the offer of a film crew eager to shoot their show.

The recording truck drove back to Chicago; the lighting truck got on the road to New York. The next morning, the airport was filled with a laughing film crew looking forward to hefty cancellation fees waiting for them when they got home.

Three months later, I was standing on the outskirts of Johannesburg, California, a tiny desert town two hours outside Los Angeles, knocking on the door of the same tour bus I had last seen outside that hotel in Kansas City. Alice in Chains were back together, had played the last night of a tour and been driven to Johannesburg, where they spent the night sleeping on the tour bus. I'd been hired to make a video for "Down in a Hole." The label wanted me to do what I failed to accomplish in Kansas City: get the four of them on film. The details of the brief I'd been given are a distant memory, but I do remember that the budget was tiny and my treatment, which is barely half a page long, starts: "ADVANCE WARNING! ... Anything could happen and probably will!" The treatment finishes a few sentences later with "We will have playback with us, but it seems unlikely that the band will do any lip synch!" The treatment is noticeably free of the normal bullshit promises of fabulous vistas or passionate performances — it might as well have read, "I'll get what I can, and you'll just have to like it!"

The band, who were obviously exhausted, stumbled out of the bus as I issued directions and handed them a bunch of film and the Super-8 camera I'd bought in the Singapore airport for that Marilyn video. We simply walked around the edges of town while we rolled film with a second camera and spent the afternoon in a ramshackle collection of rooms built around a trailer that we'd discovered. This unusual location belonged to a retired miner who'd spent his early years leading mule trains across the desert to Las Vegas and back. His name was Cowboy Frank Without a Horse, and he spent the afternoon sharing stories with the band. I got the clear impression they wanted to be somewhere else but felt obliged to spend the day making the video.

Nine years later, I was in Edmonton, Canada, getting ready to shoot a live show for Nickelback when Chad Kroeger told me there would be a special guest appearance by Alice in Chains guitarist Jerry Cantrell.

As my face fell, Chad asked me what was wrong. I told him, "He hates me."

Minutes later, I saw Jerry backstage. He smiled, gave me an enveloping man-hug and said, "So good to see you."

That's the crazy thing about this business — there's no shortage of surprises.

CHAPTER 33

Rock 'n' Roll Star

I'D BEEN LIVING IN CALIFORNIA for ten years when I realised something was happening back in the UK; I was not involved, and that made me uneasy. When I'd first moved to the States, even though I was not the coolest person in Britain, at least I knew who was. I wasn't the most fashionable person, but at least I could tell what was going on by simply walking down the street.

Within a few months of emigrating, I sensed I was losing my edge. Things in America moved slower, and every time I flew back to the UK, a new fashion trend had evolved behind my back; a new band had taken over the airwaves that everyone was talking about; a new TV show was all the rage; a dozen new buzz words and phrases peppered everybody's conversation. I had some catching up to do. I came to accept this as part of the deal I had made to live and work in America, but I didn't like it. In an effort to try and keep up with what was happening in the music business, I read imported magazines like *Q* and *Mojo,* but it was hardly a substitute for a quick stroll through the West End at lunchtime with your eyes and ears open.

I started reading about Oasis. People were talking about them, they seemed to be causing quite a stir, Britain seemed to be coming alive again and I had to check them out. I knew the basics of their story. They were brothers from Manchester. One had gone on the road as a roadie for Inspiral Carpets and came home to find his younger brother had started a band. Noel, the elder roadie brother, declared they were shite and would be a whole lot better if he became the leader and they did his songs. The bold and bloodless coup seemed to have worked. Oasis were racing up the charts. I bought the record and didn't get it. I saw a video that didn't impress me either. Perhaps they would come and go quickly and soon join the long line of one-hit wonders.

But the news stories persisted, the hits kept on coming and eventually I heard from Scott Spanjich at Epic. Scott had given me many jobs and had become a good friend. One of his many wonderful qualities was honesty about what he needed and why. On this occasion, his brief was as unusual as any I would ever get. "Look, we don't understand a word they say, and I figured that, as you're English, at least you'll know what they're talking about!"

I'd never met the band, but I'd read enough about them to know that hiring me just because I was a Brit made as much sense as sending over a French or Italian director. I was born in Yorkshire; they came from Lancashire. I was older, they were younger. I'd been sent to a posh boarding school. They were working class lads from Manchester. I wasn't going to be looking down my nose at them, but I suspected they would look down their noses at me. Being brought up in the same country was no guarantee of a successful collaboration, but I wasn't going to pass on the opportunity to work with the year's hottest band, so I kept my mouth shut and dutifully jumped on a plane to Minneapolis.

Oasis were playing a gig at Prince's club, and I arrived in time for the soundcheck. I stood off to one side and waited patiently for it to be over before saying hello — this is always the worst moment, you're a stranger from another planet dropped in by parachute to meet a bunch of young men who have been in the trenches together and are exclusive members of their own club. They're probably resentful that the record label have picked you to spend a lot of their money and you're nervous because of all of the above. I braced myself for the worst, so I was more than surprised when Liam Gallagher ambled over and introduced himself. His brother Noel had famously described him as "a man with a fork born into a world of soup," but he didn't strike me as miserable or difficult at all. He was friendly and talkative.

Liam introduced me to Noel, who pointed to the rest of the band — "Bonehead, Guigsy, Tony" — and then walked off. But something must have gone right because, not long after, I was back in England, at Cliffs Pavilion in Southend, shooting a video and a live show for them. The video was a U.S.-only version of "Rock 'n' Roll Star" shot onstage and at the fun fair with Super-8 cameras.

When shooting a live show, I always try to obtain audio of a previous gig on the tour and listen to it over and over while writing out every lyric and every bar of the show. That way, while sitting in front of a row of video monitors backstage, I can make sure that every nuance of the show is captured and that a camera is pointing in the right direction for every guitar solo or backing vocal. Normally, you have only one shot at getting it right, so being on your toes and knowing every drumbeat is crucial.

The Oasis show that night was so loud, so chaotic, so feral that, after three songs, I tossed my carefully prepared notes away and just concentrated on the screens to make sure we captured the essence of the show. Scott Spanjich had warned me that Liam did nothing onstage — he just stood there — but what I saw that night was incredible intensity and charisma. Yes, he just stood there, but you couldn't take your eyes off him.

Despite its complete lack of remarkable imagery, my video for "Rock 'n' Roll Star" went down well enough that I was subsequently asked to come up with an idea for "Wonderwall." The short brief I was given came straight from Noel: "I want something in black and white but with bits of colour in it." I sucked on the end of a pencil and wondered what in the world I was going to do. I was very aware that there were other, far more talented, people pitching to get the same job, so I had to come up with something special.

Many years later, I was interviewed by a radio journalist from Bogota, Colombia. He was very complimentary and rattled on about how artistic and creative I was, using the "Wonderwall" video as his example. My reaction was a polite thank you, but I realised what an elaborate smokescreen I had managed to create over the years about what I do. I don't see myself as artistic. My competitors are mostly people who went to art school and are often gifted fine artists in their own right; many of them are wonderful photographers who understand the fine details of painting with light; a number of them are deep thinkers and gifted writers with much to say about politics and the human condition. And, it must be said, I am none of those things.

Long ago, I discovered that the only way I can create a piece of film is to find something I can grab onto, an "idea brick" if you will. This idea brick could be a location, a photograph, a character, an instrument, a car, a fleeting image. Once I have that image in my mind, I can imagine other building blocks that go together with it. Perhaps it's a childlike process and nothing as sophisticated as the methods of others who make film, but it works for me.

So, Noel's request for "black and white with a bit of colour in it" was no help to me at all. That was certainly the final layer — the tarpaulin that would be laid over my building bricks — but for now I had no brick, no cornerstone.

Oasis were massive in Britain but had yet to make any impression in the U.S., which was both a help and a hindrance. On one hand, I had no idea of the buzz they were creating and no sense of the energy coursing through the veins of the British public, but on the other that allowed me to be free of any preconceptions about how Oasis should be presented. All I had to do was find that first idea brick.

It was well known that Noel was inspired by the Beatles, so, using Nick Lowe's mantra "If you can't think of a good idea, steal one," I opened up a book of Beatle pictures and started looking for images that inspired me. Amid the stills from *A Hard Day's Night* were images of the Fab Four playing against a white cyc during the sequence for "If I Fell." I knew Oasis would only be available for a few hours, so a white cyc set seemed like a good idea. There were also stills of the showgirls Paul meets in the theatre corridor, so I threw those in for good measure. "Wonderwall" had cellos (or something that sounded like cellos), so I threw in an image of a cello player I found from a book of photographs. The cellos were obviously treated in the mix — I guessed it was a sample — which made me think of people who played the saw with a violin bow, a sort of poor man's theremin. Out of nowhere popped an image of a musical hall clown — hell, why not two clowns? Finally, since I knew the band would get bored on set, I threw in a foosball table and a dart board to keep them amused.

I had my idea bricks. I stuck them all together, photocopied some photographs, wrote out a description, sent it off to the label and crossed my fingers. This is always a moment of great calm for me — good or bad, you have to grab hold of an idea and stick with it. My acting teacher Judith Weston always used to say, "To succeed you must be prepared to fail brilliantly." I would put my heart and soul into an idea, send it off and, if they didn't like it, fuck 'em.

They liked it.

Days later, I was on the plane back to London. My longtime pal Phil Barnes was going to produce the video. In short order, we found a studio location, two clowns, a couple of showgirls and two men who played the saw. What could possibly go wrong?

Phil had told me that his wife was pregnant. Upon landing in England, I discovered that she was due any day. The morning of the shoot Phil told me that there was a good chance his wife might go into labour at any moment, in which case he would have no choice but to leave the set. A good producer is a great asset on any shoot, if only for moral support, and I didn't want to be left alone on the set in the middle of this day — especially with Oasis in the room. But I had no choice — I had to press on.

The morning started off in a leisurely fashion as we shot the showgirls, the cello players and the swinging saws. The band arrived around lunchtime. At the request of the label, we had scoured all the fashionable shops in London and provided suitcases full of clothes for the band to check out. The threads were beautifully laid out on tables for the band to sample — perhaps they'd like to try on some of the clothes and wear them in the video? They sniffed at the clothes, said they weren't interested and made it clear they would do the video in the clothes they'd turned up in.

Scott Spanjich had warned me repeatedly that I should not on any account consider asking the band to "act." The director on a previous video had asked Liam to act, and a huge row had broken out. I took the warning seriously. I had five chairs sitting in a line and suggested that each band member take a seat. I handed them a newspaper and a guitar, told them to make something up and rolled the camera. They proceeded to act their little hearts out. There's a copy somewhere of one of those takes, which is a video in itself. Their arrogance and complete indifference to the camera — yet complete awareness of it — is just oozing with mischief and encapsulates for me every bit of the magic of Oasis at that time.

Things went off the rails fast. Phil's phone rang — his wife had gone into labour; he gave his apologies and ran off to the hospital. To get back on track, I decided to shoot a scene with both clowns, but it became obvious very fast that one of the clowns hated the other one. How could I know that they had some kind of professional clown code and that clown #1 would not lower himself to take part in a scene in which clown #2 was so obviously transgressing so many rules of the code?

Then Liam and Noel began shouting at each other. Within seconds, they were having a full-scale row right in front of the crew. The business of filming ground to a halt. The rest of the band walked away, obviously used to the fraternal bickering. I looked at my shot list and decided it was time for the big performance scene. I quickly pushed everyone into place. The band were only going to be on set for a few hours and every minute with them was valuable.

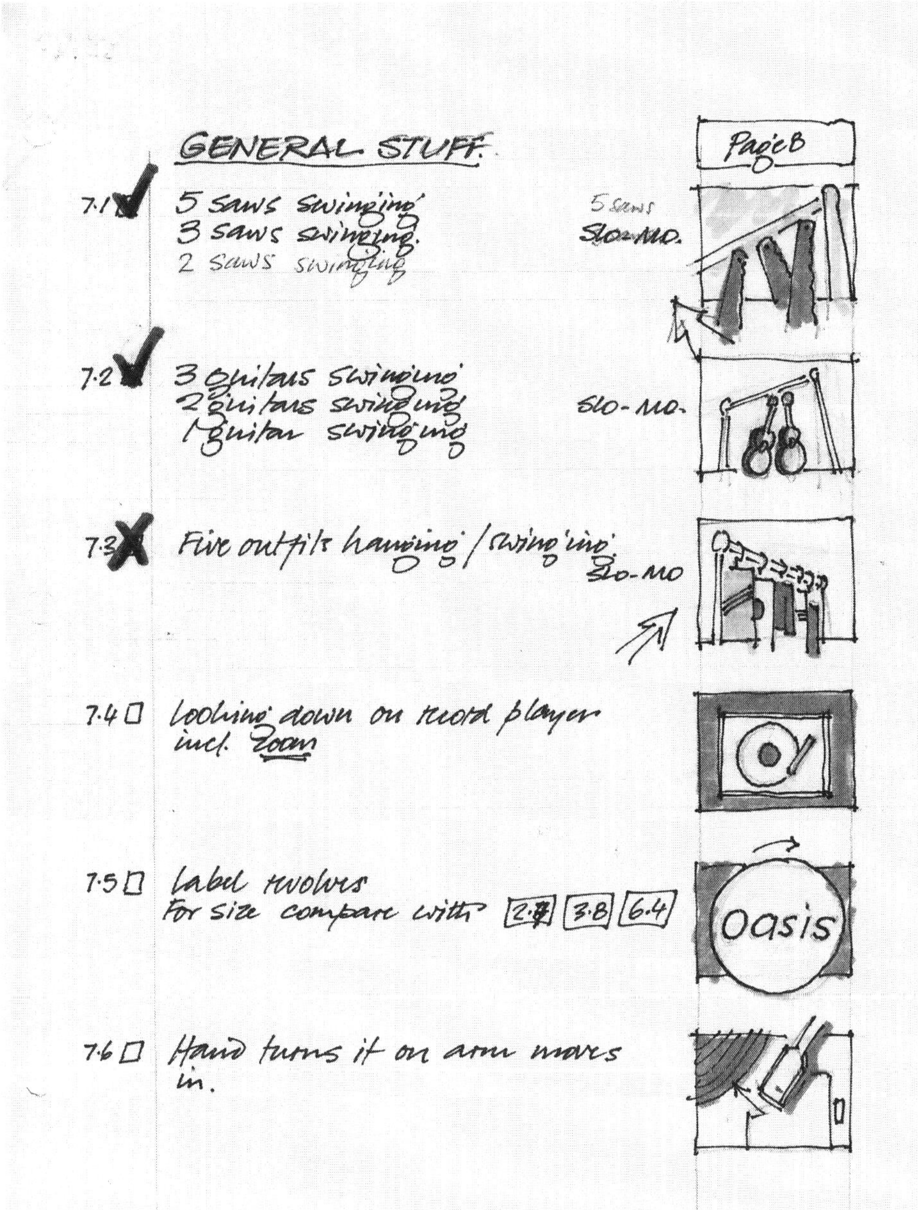

My storyboard for the opening section of "Wonderwall." By drawing storyboards before the shoot I am able to make decisions about elements in foreground and background, the DP has a clue on how I want the shot framed and lens size and the art department are able to ensure they have the correct props ready.

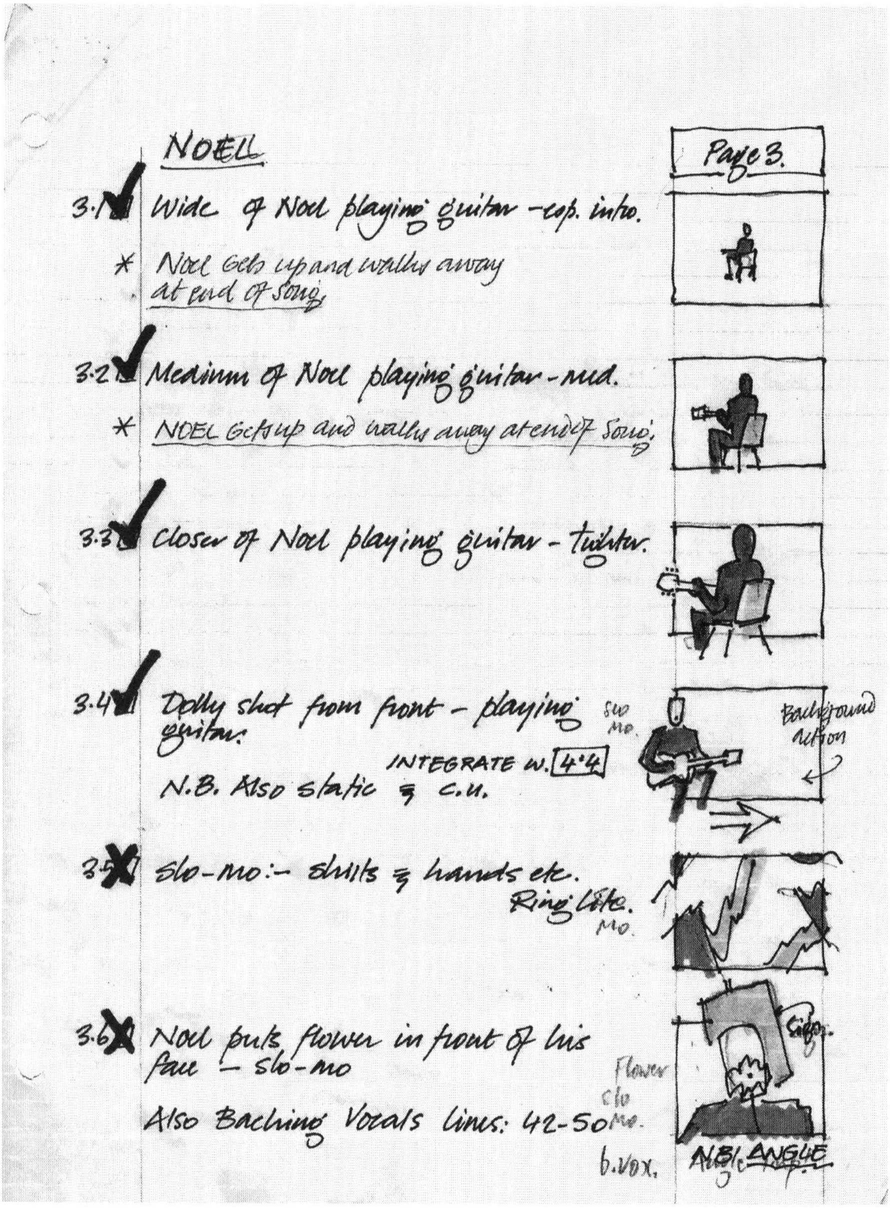

"Wonderwall" storyboard page 3 which shows frame sizes for Noel sitting in the chair — which will later be edited together in a mini sequence. This page also shows two scenes which I decided were superfluous and didn't get shot.

When the first take finished, I yelled "Cut." Nothing happened: The camera was still rolling and valuable film stock was being wasted. Sitting behind my monitor I yelled "Cut!" again and turned around to see what was going on. The AD, the DP, the art director and seemingly everyone else on set were talking on their cell phones. I blew my stack — now it was Oasis's turn to see *me* get upset. I made everyone put their phones in the corner of the room and concentrate on the job. There was a lot of grumbling and eye-rolling, but I didn't care. The crew could talk to their agents and wives later. We pressed on and finally exhausted my ideas. The band were ready to leave. As we wrapped, the band walked past that table still laden with the thousands and thousands of pounds worth of neatly folded clothes we'd found for them and took every last shirt, jacket and pair of socks with them.

I caught a cab back to my friend Andy's house, where I was staying. I felt exhausted as the rain fell over London in the darkness. In Andy's kitchen we cracked open some beers, and he asked, "How did it go?" I hung my head low, "Terrible." The next morning, I flew home, convinced I would never work with Oasis again.

Unsurprisingly, "Wonderwall" was a hit — it's a great song. A video sometimes makes a song a hit, sometimes the song makes everyone notice the video. I believe I got lucky: the video started playing everywhere. In the quiet of my house, I breathed a sigh as the video started playing on MTV and sensed I'd dodged a bullet.

Scott Spanjich rang me up again. Oasis needed a video for "Don't Look Back in Anger," and they wanted it fast. The band would be in L.A. for a day, could I bash out a treatment overnight? I needed my idea brick. Like Noel, I went back to the Beatles for inspiration. I'd plundered the early black and white years for "Wonderwall," so I needed to move on and come up with something a bit more *Revolver* for this next video. The foosball table had been very useful as a distraction on the "Wonderwall" set, so I thought maybe a host of lovely women might do the trick this time.

I was a member of BAFTA (British Association of Film and Television Artists) and had noticed in a monthly blurb that onetime *Avengers* star Patrick Macnee lived outside Los Angeles in Rancho Mirage and was looking for work. Perhaps we could get him in the video? I wanted the video to feel English, so I added a cab and a John Lennon-style mansion, and I had my idea.

A few days later, I was waiting nervously outside a large house in Pasadena as a limo drove up and Patrick Macnee stepped out, sporting his *Avengers* outfit of bowler hat and umbrella. I hadn't asked but hoped he would bring them "Everyone expects me to show up dressed like this," he told me. "I'd hate to disappoint them."

I don't think the band knew who Patrick Macnee was. They didn't pay much attention to him; in the end, I don't think they paid much attention to the women, either. Noel later delivered his critical appraisal of the video: "The biggest pain in the arse ever. Bag of shite, that. Waste of a fucking afternoon."

And yet they came back for more; this time, a treatment for "Champagne Supernova." "The song is about drugs. The video needs to be very druggy, but don't put any drugs in it," Scott told me. This was going to be a challenge. I'd had two joints in my entire life and had never popped a pill or taken acid — yet I had to create a video that represented an experience I had no firsthand knowledge of. The first thing that sprang to mind was the oil-wheel projector I used to have when I was a DJ at university: coloured oil sealed between two circular pieces of glass. The powerful beam from the projector heated the oil, which moved around as the machine rotated the glass. The beam, passing through the heated oils, projected coloured blobby images on the nearest wall. That seemed to fit the song. If *A Hard Day's Night* had been my reference point for "Wonderwall" and *Revolver* my reference point for "Don't Look Back in Anger," I was now moving into *Magical Mystery Tour* territory for "Champagne Supernova." I remember worrying that I would run out of Beatles reference points if this keeps on.

The song was seven and a half minutes long, so my oil-wheel gag was only a device. I needed a bigger idea. At the time, I was bicycling long distances every weekend and, like a long bike ride, I knew that

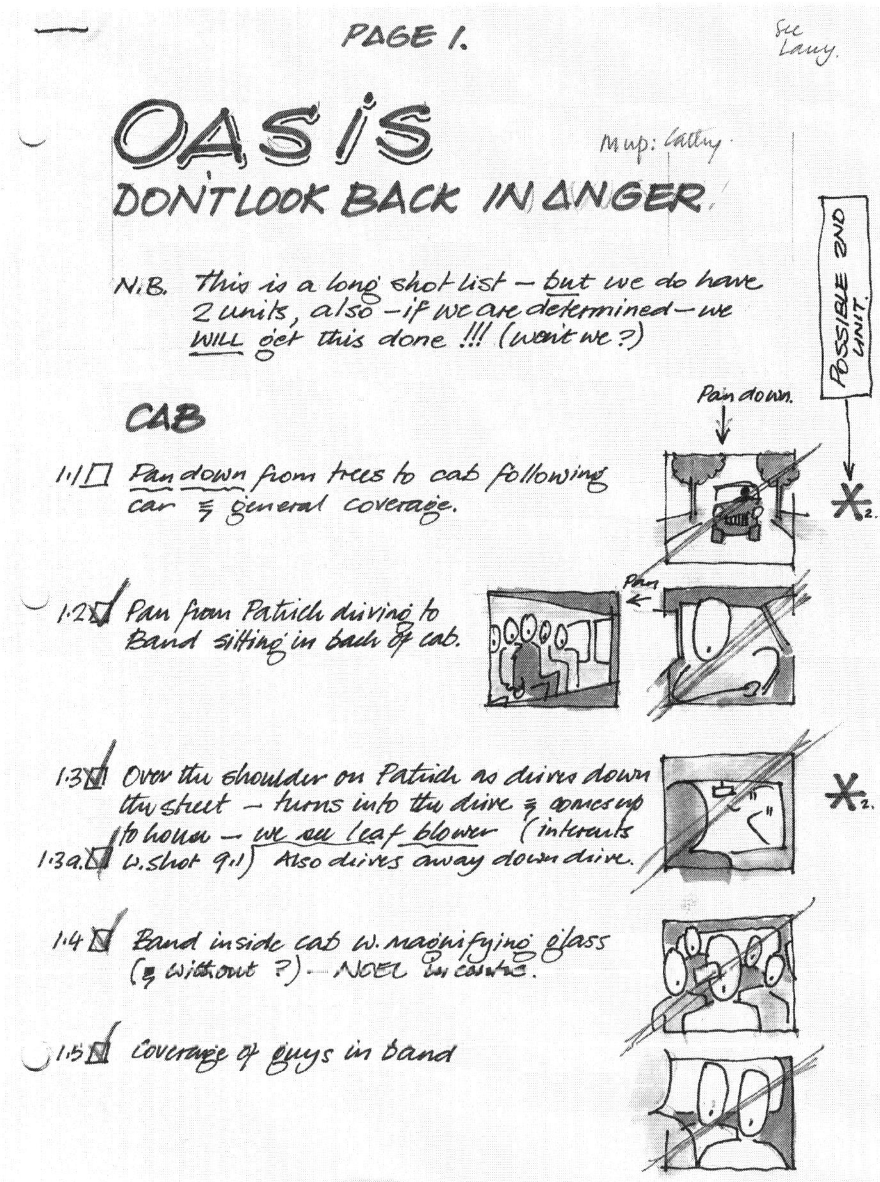

Page 1 of the "Don't Look Back in Anger" storyboard with my mantra-for-the-day to the crew: "We will get this done!!! (Won't we?)" In the end we ran into darkness (it was December), but we did get it done!

fixating on the song's length would be intimidating, so I broke it down into sections or acts: Liam and his TV, a stylized bedroom that becomes a performance space, a discotheque with go-go dancers, a psychedelic coloured *Yellow Submarine* floor and, eventually, Liam watching TV again in a silhouetted version of the bedroom with the walls reflecting the blue light from the TV screen.

DP Simon Archer came up with a fabulous idea as we scouted the London studio location that would pull the whole thing together — a lens left over from the '70s, little-used anymore, that rotated and distorted the image. Perhaps we could use it for the shoot? That lens became the glue that pulled the whole thing together.

A writer for *Rolling Stone* doing an Oasis piece was visiting the set, as was a rep from the record label to make sure things ran smoothly. When I discovered she had never met the band, I offered to introduce her. A terrified look washed across her face, and she shook her head frantically. The wrath of the brothers Gallagher was by now well known.

We settled down to work and the scene in the bedroom was going along well enough. The oil wheels were working their magic, the wibbly-wobbly lens was rotating efficiently, and I was happy with what we were getting when, in the middle of a take, Liam got up, walked off set and left the studio. I yelled "Cut" and waited for someone to go after him, but nobody moved. I ran outside and saw him strolling off down the road. I shouted after him, asking where he was going. "I'm going down the pub!" he replied over his shoulder and disappeared around a corner.

Back inside the studio, the band were snacking at the craft-service table. I told the label person that Liam had walked off the set but could tell she had no inclination to do anything about it; the manager shrugged his shoulders and suggested I speak to Noel. I told Noel his brother had gone to the pub and we couldn't shoot without him. "He's a cunt," he replied, "What do you expect?"

I once made a video for Third Eye Blind. The first thing singer Stephan Jenkins said to me was, "What you have to understand about

Third Eye Blind is that it's all about me." I was shocked. What an arrogant prat! But then, the more I thought about it, the more I realised he was absolutely right. In any band, if it's got any chance of being a success, it's all about the lead singer. No Jagger? No Stones. No Bono? No U2. The trouble with Oasis was that it was all about the lead singer ... but it was also all about the guitar player. And they were brothers.

My cousin Fran Parker — an Emmy-winning film editor — was visiting with her kids, standing quietly to one side. "The lead singer's just walked off the set in the middle of a take and gone down the pub," I told her. "Does that happen often?" she asked while comforting her kids, who seemed confused. I lied, "Yeah, all the time."

I reverted to the only option open to me and shot Alan, the drummer, for the next hour. When Liam finally wandered back onto the stage, we finished the scene on the bed. If I look at his performance now, I can't stop myself from wondering what's going through Liam's mind and separate that sullen look on his face from the way he stood up and walked off the set. In the final crane shot of the video, he picks up dominoes and arranges them on the bed to write "HELP." Was that a Beatles reference, or was that what was going through his head all day? Once again, Noel was not shy about sharing his opinion: "I fucking hate videos ... fucking bollocks. It's nonsense."

As my editor Bruce Ochmanek and I set about cutting the video, I heard that my mother was dying, dropped everything and flew back to England. After a long transatlantic flight and a 200 mile drive up England's spine in a rented car, I met my father, who drove the final 20 miles to the hospital. As I walked into her room, my mother glanced in my direction and delivered a final stinging verdict on her errant son: "Oh, it's you!" She died the next day. At the funeral in a windswept Yorkshire graveyard, I was stunned to see that Oasis had sent a huge wreath. There was something so perfect about that — the woman who hated rock and roll and all it stood for, who despised everything her son had become, had been remembered by the biggest band in the land — oh, the irony!

Just last week my Mother died
Funeral at eleven
Oasis sent my Mother flowers
Now she's gone to heaven

I had a final hurrah with Oasis: the video for "Don't Go Away." Having run out of Beatles references, I turned to Belgian surrealist Rene Magritte for inspiration. I went to meet the band, who were rehearsing, in England. The first person I saw as I walked through the door was Noel. "Hey, Noel, how are you?" "Older! Richer!" he replied and walked off.

Once again, I only had the band for a few hours. We were shooting in a studio in the East End on a hot summer's day. The band were playing football outside; when I called Liam to the set for his close-ups, he was hot and sweaty. His hair stuck to his forehead like rat tails. I called makeup over and asked them to blow-dry his hair, but he pushed them away. "Don't you want to look good in your video?" I asked. Impatient to get back to his game, he harrumphed, "It's not my video. It's your video!" It was no easier when it came time for Noel's close-up — he told me that a mutual friend, Simon Halfon, who I'd worked with at Stiff, had played him the Stiff All-Stars' first single. Noel smirked. "It's the worst fucking record I've ever heard." It seemed important to him that I knew what he thought of my musical efforts. This wasn't fun anymore. I decided not to ask him if the first record he'd made in a two-hour rush in a backstreet studio sounded any better.

As the shoot progressed into the evening we were slipping behind schedule, but I was determined to get every frame on my shot list. Noel had other ideas. In the middle of setting up a shot, he walked up to me with the other members of the band in line behind him and announced, "We've had enough — we're leaving!"

I can't say I ever enjoyed working with Oasis. It was clear they hated making videos, and they didn't try to hide the fact they didn't like me much, either. That was OK. They were a different kind of band,

and their indifference made me push myself harder and try new ideas — ideas that I might otherwise never have attempted. Deep in my soul I love the grit of the stage, a guitar lead plugged into a beaten-up Marshall amp and a flash guitar solo delivered by a sweaty rock star in a leather jacket. Oasis were never that kind of band, and I needed to leave my comfort zone to try something new. Melding a bunch of lads from Manchester with Magritte was something I only ever attempted with them; perhaps mixing Oasis with the work of a Belgian surrealist painter was, in the end, a step too far and Liam was right: "Me floating through the sky with a brolly? Nah! Never gonna happen." But I did make it happen, and I take great satisfaction in that.

In the end, that brief chat I had with Liam when I first met the band in Prince's club in Minneapolis proved to be the only pleasant conversation I ever had with Liam or Noel.

CHAPTER 34

Back on Earth

AT THE END OF 1995 I DECIDED to go on holiday over Christmas. Whenever I had time, I would go on a biking trip, usually one arranged by a company called Backroads. The original plan had been to go to Thailand with my pals Andy and Ed, but they'd dropped out. And so it was that, on New Year's Eve, I found myself up by the Golden Triangle where Laos, Thailand and Myanmar meet, staying in a gorgeous hotel on the banks of the Mekong River, enjoying a drink and playing my guitar. The holiday was nearly over, and I wondered what the next year would bring. The following day, I was at the Bangkok airport on my way home.

The 17-hour flight back would have been bad enough in a big seat, but I was next to a family with screaming children. I wished I'd splurged on something more comfortable nearer the front of the plane. At two in the morning, the customs officer at LAX suspiciously tapped the wooden elephant I'd bought in Chiang Rai, convinced that a stash of drugs was hidden in its tummy.

I got to bed at four, confused and jet-lagged. At eight, my other pal from Epic, Steve Einczig, called. "I need you to fly to Paris tonight. I have to shoot a video for Celine Dion before the weekend in the South of France. I'm sending you the track now. She has two days free in Nice. Can you write me an idea before you leave for the airport?"

In a befuddled daze, I bashed out a treatment, did a round of washing, changed sweaty cycling gear for warm sweaters and a heavy coat and prepared to make my way back to LAX less than 12 hours after I'd left it. I missed my connection in Paris and had to sleep on the airport floor while waiting for the final leg to Nice, where a cab dropped me off at a small hotel. The night man handed me my key at reception, and I staggered up three flights to my room on the top floor, where I collapsed on the bed, fully clothed, and slept hard.

The next morning, I met the local producer, Antoine Sabaros, who took me to breakfast at a delightful café down by the port and asked me what I'd been up to over the holidays. I explained about my trip from the Cambodian border to Bangkok to L.A. to Paris to Nice. "Are you crazy?" he asked me in his charming French accent, "Why didn't you fly direct? The flight from Bangkok to Paris is only 12 hours!" It dawned on me that, in the last two days, I'd flown two thirds of the way around the planet.

Antoine drove me up into the hills behind Nice looking for locations. I fell in love with a gorgeous village called Gorbio. Celine's song was called "Falling Into You," and the idea I'd thrown together while in my pyjamas fighting jet lag in L.A. was that Celine was working for a circus as the assistant to a juggler-cum-magician. She would absent-mindedly hand *le jongler* his props while dreaming of her beau, who she would eventually run off to meet at the end of the video. With two tiny town squares joined by a cobbled street that wound through the centre of the village, Gorbio, perched in the mountains above the Riviera, was the perfect setting for this timeless romantic idea.*

After our day in the mountains, Antoine took me down the hill again and we happened upon a circus set up in the port. Seizing the moment, we bought tickets and checked out the talent to see if we could find a juggler we could steal for Celine's video. I kept nodding off before being woken by applause and had trouble remembering which continent, let alone which country, I was in.

The next day, we went to meet Celine in a very expensive hotel in Cannes. I knew very little about Celine, and I always like to have a bit of homework in my back pocket before I work with someone. I was just going to have to busk this one. I respect all musicians even if I don't much like their music, but the thing that separates the men from the boys, the women from the girls, is who they are as people. And Celine proved to be just wonderful — charming, funny and cheeky. She was with her manager and husband, René Angélil, and I sensed him sussing me out as we shook hands. This job was moving at speed — we were already looking at wardrobe choices.

I was unnerved by the expensive surroundings, and the jet lag was sending shivers up my back, so I was very tentative as René and I watched Celine model outfits. She emerged from the bathroom wearing something simple and straightforward, but not right for the video. René quietly said, "I think it makes you look like a housewife" and turned to me. "Don't you think?" Celine, slightly surprised, said "Oh!" and gave me a glance before she disappeared back into the bathroom. A moment later, she emerged wearing something super-sexy that hugged her figure and stood coquettishly in front of her husband putting her hands on her hips. "Do I look like a housewife now?" She smiled and gave me a big conspiratorial wink. I turned beet red. René got to his feet, gave her a wonderful smile and said to me, "I'll leave you two together. I think this will go better without me!" She laughed as he left and went to try on another dress. It was a wonderful moment and a very touching insight into their relationship. That

* Once, while lecturing, a student asked me why so many videos followed the same storylines. I explained that your ideas often followed the lyrics or title of the song. Celine's song was called "Falling Into You." I have also directed videos with these titles: "Can't Stop Falling Into Love," "Can't Stop Loving You," "I Can't Stop Loving You" and "I Can't Get Next to You." And if you think that lot sound similar, try this lot: "Out of Love," "Outta Love," "In It for Love," "Don't Say You Love Me," "As Long As You Love Me," "Bring Me Your Love," "Long Way to Love," "Waiting for Your Love," "Save Your Love," "Give Love a Chance," "Sunshine of Your Love," "House of Love," "House of Broken Love," "Spy in the House of Love," "Highway of Love," "Love Around the World," "Love Will Lead You Back," "Love Kills," "Love Don't Give No Reason"...etc.

little moment made me instantly feel at home and hugely grateful to both of them. Any concerns I had for the video instantly evaporated. I could tell this was going to be fun.

As I was drawing my storyboards, Steve Einczig told me that he and René had decided that, when Celine ran off to find her beau at the end, it would be great to shoot a sequence from a helicopter of her driving along the Riviera coast just like Grace Kelly in *To Catch a Thief*. And, of course, that piece of road was just along the coast. Steve was going to find the money to do the shot, and I was delighted. Helicopter shot? Riviera coastline? Why would I refuse? But the more I thought about it the more I worried about what we would see from that helicopter. It was 40 years since the Hitchcock film, and I meant for Celine's video to have a timeless feel. I asked that we scout the road and said the only way to do that was from a helicopter. Eyebrows were raised, but a day later I was tying a harness around myself as we took off and scoured the coastline. It might have seemed like directorial excess to ask for an hour in a chopper to scout, but it turned out to be worth every penny. The stretch of road Grace Kelly had driven along was still there, but it was now a mess of telegraph poles and other up-to-date road furniture. In addition, the vintage car we'd chosen for Celine would look out of place amid the traffic. Another road on the far side of Nice was suggested, and the chopper pilot turned us around. Half an hour later, we found a perfect stretch of road that climbed gently from the coastline and seemed completely deserted.

The morning of the shoot in Gorbio dawned pale and misty. The little town square was quiet as I went to find some coffee. Celine was already on set and ready to go through hair and makeup, which I'd been warned would take three hours.**

I'd been introduced to Celine's makeup person, who was very well thought of, not cheap and hailed from some part of Scandinavia. An hour later, I found Celine at the craft service table getting herself a coffee. It was strange to see her there on her own. "How's makeup

** Three hours may seem like a long time, but it's about average for a female lead on a shoot like this.

going?" I asked. "Oh, I haven't started yet. My makeup person has a documentary crew following him around and they're doing a long interview with him this morning!" I couldn't believe that we were paying this guy, had flown him in from Paris and now he was making our whole production wait while he was interviewed for his own documentary! Five minutes later, Celine was in the chair and the documentary crew, chastened but still cheeky, were raiding the crafty table.

Working with Celine was fun and easy. It was delightful to see her find her light and not just perform the song but add subtext, so that each line gave more meaning to the pictures we were shooting.

The initial scenes called for Celine to sit on the steps of her circus trailer and then touch up her makeup in the circus tent while Chocolat the clown sat in the background. The big production number called for Celine's magician to perform his act in front of a crowd at night. We were in a small village, miles from anywhere. Where would we get a crowd? Simple — we invited everyone in the village to be in the video. That evening, there was a stream of people walking along the narrow street from one square to the other to be in the video. I was overjoyed that everyone had decided to join in the fun. But then a message came from the mayor's office that he would like to make a presentation to Celine. Drinks would be served and speeches would be made. Unfortunately, we had a schedule to keep and now the whole town was waiting for us at the end of the street. On the other hand, the mayor had been very kind to the production... What to do? What made it worse was that the entrance to the Hotel de Ville — the mayor's office — was on that narrow winding street that led to the small square where our next scene was to be shot. For Celine and the rest of us to get to set we could hardly walk past the mayor's front door without stopping by and saying hello.

Celine was wonderful. She cracked jokes and took pictures with the mayor. In the background, Steve, Antoine and I looked nervously at each other and checked our watches. As soon as we dared, we pulled Celine away and rushed across the cobbles to get our final scene of the day.

The next morning, we were on the deserted road I'd found. The sun had come out; by lunchtime, the scene was in the can. Many years later, watching a film on another transatlantic flight, I noticed that same road was used for the car chase in Rowan Atkinson's *Johnny English Strikes Again*. The spot where Johnny English's Aston-Martin runs out of gas is the very spot where Celine meets her beau.

After two weeks in Thailand and my unplanned trip to the South of France, I was looking forward to getting home and some clean clothes, but Steve Einczig had other ideas for me. In the town square the night before, he told me I wasn't flying home; he'd booked me a ticket to New York. He needed an Ozzy Osbourne video shot in five days' time.

Twenty-four hours later, I hailed a taxi in Manhattan and told the driver to take me to a bookstore. Google Images had not been invented yet, so I needed inspiration for the treatment I had to write for Ozzy's video. The treatment was delivered by lunchtime; by teatime the concept and budget had been approved. The next day, I went to meet Ozzy and his wife, Sharon. We were going to Philadelphia for the evening.

When I was a teen, my parents moved to Germany for the third time and would drive into Paderborn every week to go shopping in the NAAFI — the Navy, Army and Air Force Institute, a British version of the American PX — where British food, newspapers and records were for sale. On one visit back from school, I'd gone to the NAAFI with them and forked over some of my precious deutsche marks for the first Black Sabbath album, which immediately went into heavy rotation in my tiny bedroom in the farming town where we lived. Our street, which led to the cemetery, was called Heilige Seile (Holy Souls), and Ozzy and his pals reached out to the undead along that quiet country lane. God knows what the locals thought about the sound of Ozzy screaming, "Oh NO! Please God, help me!" coming from our apartment; it certainly had its effect on my mother. On my subsequent return to school in England and another round of lacklustre exam results, she wrote one of her long letters, going into great detail about my many sins, concluding, cuttingly, "If you spent as much time learning your French reflexive verbs as you do listening to that Black Sabbath record, perhaps we'd see an improvement in your grades." I still have no doubt how painful it must have been for her to have to write those two powerful words: Black Sabbath. Ozzy had a lot to answer for.

Climbing into the elevator in Ozzy's ritzy hotel by Central Park, I assumed this meeting would go differently than the one I'd had with Celine just a few days earlier. It wasn't till a few years later that their TV show, *The Osbournes,* came on the air, but what I got when I walked into their suite was exactly what you would now expect. "Shazza" was in control; Ozzy was bumbling about, trying to find a missing shoe and worrying about getting to the gig that night. In much the same way that Celine and René had made me feel at home, Sharon and Ozzy did the same though, heaven knows, the dynamic could not have been more different.

Ozzy's tour had reached the East Coast, so Ozzy and Sharon had bunked up in Manhattan. Every afternoon, they drove to the airport and were whisked via private jet to that night's gig, which, on this evening, was in Philadelphia. This whirlwind of travel since leaving my bike outside that hotel in Thailand just a week or so before was becoming even more outrageous — three transcontinental flights, a helicopter ride and now a private jet.

Backstage at Philly's enormodome, Ozzy rode his exercise bike and drank a horrid concoction made from wheat grass. In the auditorium, as the lights went dark, a huge screen was lowered over the stage to show a short film in which Ozzy appeared, Forrest Gump-style, in scenes throughout history. It was hysterical, and the crowd loved it. When Ozzy finally walked onstage the roar was louder than the encore at most gigs. He wandered up and down the stage, encouraging the fans to roar louder. The show was now ten minutes old, the crowd were going mental, and the band hadn't played a single note — a fabulous piece of theatre.

After the show, Sharon, Ozzy and I flew back to New York. Ozzy draped a towel around his neck and scratched his balls through his sweatpants. “Shazza, I’m hungry,” he moaned, so she pulled a tinfoil lump from her bag and unwrapped a baked potato for him. He was nonplussed. “What the fuck is this?” “Eat it up,” she told him. Ozzy turned to me, “I’m playing to ten thousand people a night and she won’t even let me have a fucking hamburger after the gig!” Sharon looked at me and smiled while Ozzy poked at his spud.

The shoot, two days later, went smoothly and I finally made it home two weeks after the urgent phone call to get on a plane for Paris. In my empty house, Stinker the cat was unimpressed by my tales of globetrotting and hanging out with the stars. He demanded food while I stuffed the dirty washing in the machine.

A few months later, Celine had a new single coming through the pipeline. “It’s All Coming Back to Me Now” was an interesting change of pace for her — dramatic as hell and over six minutes long. The song was written by Jim Steinman, famous for his work with Meat Loaf. Steve Einczig asked me for not one but six or seven ideas. I could tell right away that landing this job was going to be no easy task. I sat down and started throwing mud against the wall.

None of it stuck. I pitched more ideas, but eventually Steve rang and announced that we would be joined on the call by Jim Steinman himself. Jim, who never wrote a two-word song title in his life, got right down to it. He had an idea which he thought was original and would be perfect for Celine. It involved a motorcycle. Of course it did. If you’ve ever seen a Meat Loaf album cover from that period, you might be forgiven for thinking that an idea from Jim Steinman involving a motorcycle wasn’t such an original idea after all, but I kept my mouth shut.

I wrote up Steinman’s idea, but of course there were changes and modifications. New ideas were transmitted to me and alterations added here and there. The final shooting script, which I labelled Version 18iii, could be summarized like this: handsome young man (Celine’s lover) crashes his motorbike and dies in fiery carnage on a dark and stormy night. Celine, distraught at the loss of her lover, runs through her palatial mansion seeing images of her dead man as the rain falls and lightning flashes.

The story called for a dramatic execution and an epic location, so I thought of Prague. Just a few weeks earlier, I had shot a live show with Green Day at an ice hockey rink in Prague and had been impressed by the local production facilities, the eager crews and the fabulous locations available — though the hockey rink wasn't one of them. I pitched Prague as the perfect place to shoot Steinman's epic idea. Everyone approved and soon I was back on a plane for Europe. On arrival, the local producer, Tomas Krejci, took me to Barrandov Studios and my jaw dropped as I realised what we would have to play with. The studios had been built in the 1930s. When Hitler and his mob arrived, a number of massive stages were added, and one of them had been booked for us. Barrandov also had a huge props department. I could have spent hours wandering amongst the thousands of candlesticks, oil paintings and sculptures that we could use on our set. It seemed my choice of Prague had been a wise one.

But Prague came with one huge problem which I'd overlooked. This video was set at night. As I sat outside a local bar, relaxing with a beer and a book, I noticed that it was taking an awfully long time for the sun to go down. It dawned on me that it was nearly the summer solstice, and Prague was much further north than, say, New York or L.A. My grasp of celestial mechanics is not vast, but I knew enough to realise that we had a problem. Celine and her team and my crew would soon be flying in from all points of the compass for a five-day shoot that required darkness and there would only be six hours of night to work in. I suddenly lost interest in my beer and scuttled back to the hotel to figure out a solution. Of course, there wasn't one — I didn't have the budget to make the Earth change its trajectory around the sun — we'd just have to work around it.

Two days before leaving for Prague, I shot a video for another Canadian act. When I was awarded the gig, the record label rep alerted me that the band's female lead singer would need some direction in selecting her wardrobe. "She'll arrive at the wardrobe fitting insisting on using what she's already wearing in the video. It'll be dirty and it'll be something she's worn before. We have to make sure that she looks great this time."

They weren't asking for sexy or slinky; they simply wanted something flattering or, at the very least, new and clean. The budget wasn't big, but Agnes Baddo, our wardrobe person, filled a sizable hotel room with racks and racks of frocks, dresses, shirts, shoes and accessories. It was an impressive display, and I could only imagine all the effort Agnes had put into sourcing the goodies, piling it all into bags and lugging it up to the hotel room. The label would be impressed, and the singer would surely jump at the chance to sample this huge selection of clothes.

Wrong. She hated everything. "This is too skimpy," she said. "This is too long, this is too bright, this is too low-cut. I hate this neck. Don't like those shoes. I'd never wear that..." She had an encyclopaedic number of reasons why everything that had been picked from L.A.'s finest stores was wrong for her. Finally, she turned to us, pointed to her own unremarkable and rather tired outfit and said, as predicted, "Why can't I wear this?" Behind her I saw the label person gasp and put her head in her hands, very nearly in tears. The singer retreated to her room, and a few minutes later her dress was brought to us for dry cleaning. It also needed repairing.

On set the next day I introduced myself to the band. "So, you're the director?" said the guitar player. "We hate directors."

Steve Einzcig and I were sitting in the lobby of Prague's swankiest hotel watching rack after rack of clothing being wheeled up to Celine Dion's room. I shared my recent nightmare wardrobe-fitting story with him. We were worried because it was 9:00 at night and very late for a wardrobe fitting. In addition, it had now been Celine's turn to fly in from Bangkok. She'd performed there the night before and had just arrived in Prague. Now she was about to do a fashion show for Steve and me.

The outfit we were about to choose was virtually the only thing she would be wearing in the video, so it had to be fabulous.

We were called up to Celine's suite. She hugged and kissed us both. We inquired after the gig the previous night and the 15-hour flight across half of Asia and Europe. Surely, she was too tired for a wardrobe fitting? "Are you kidding?" she said. "Let's do it."

But first she wanted to try on a long, cream housecoat-style outfit that she'd had specially made but had not yet worn. She was excited to see if it fit and thought that maybe it would work for the video. She emerged from the bathroom with a smile on her face and did a swirl for us. "What do you think?" she asked. We were all smiling — it looked perfect. "I love it," she said. "Can I wear this in the video?" It was a unanimous decision — we'd hit the wardrobe target in five minutes. "That's it then," said Steve chuckling and clapping his hands, "We can all go to our beds and get some rest." "Are you kidding?" said Celine again. "Look at all these fabulous clothes. I have to try them all on!"

For the next hour and a half Celine kept stylist Annie North busy pinning a hem up here and tucking a waistline back there. At one point, a button undid itself and allowed a momentary glimpse of Celine's chest. Both Steve and I instinctively covered our eyes and turned away. Celine giggled and threatened to flash us again, "What? You've never seen boobies before?"

In the end Celine tried on every shoe, every bodice and every gown, giggling and cracking jokes the whole time. Her energy and her sense of humour was intoxicating, and it was probably the most enjoyable and fun wardrobe fitting I have ever attended. But after all that, we stuck with that very first outfit. As Steve and I wearily walked to the elevator and made our way back to our hotel I couldn't help but marvel at Celine. And I couldn't help but compare this fun lady, the youngest of 16 kids, with that other Canadian singer I had shot just 72 hours earlier who never smiled once and hated every frock we showed her.

There was only one other person in the video: her lover, a character we nicknamed Motorcycle Boy. Steve and I picked a good-looking young man from tapes and pictures we were sent from London. When you sift through pictures of models there's an instantly notable difference from looking at pictures of actors. Actor headshots will have "Joe Smith" or "Jenny Jones" printed at the bottom. Model headshots will just say "Joe" or "Jenny." The young man we chose to be in Celine's video was simply Alex.

Alex had arrived from London and was staying in my hotel. I suggested we have dinner so I could talk him through the script and find out what he was like. He was quiet and polite; I found myself telling him about one of my favourite photographers, Don McCullin. Born in the north of London, he left school at 15, bought his first camera in Kenya while doing his National Service and eventually got a job at *The Observer* as a staff photographer. Then he moved to *The Sunday Times*, where he forged a career as the leading wartime photographer of his generation. His pictures of the troubles in Northern Ireland, Biafra and Cyprus and the wars in Afghanistan and Vietnam define his career.

In his book *Unreasonable Behaviour*, McCullin describes how he became horrified by war but at the same time found the experience of being in the battlefield so addictive that he couldn't stop himself going back. This addiction took over his life and ruined countless relationships. The book cover, a portrait of McCullin taken by another war photographer, Nick Wheeler, shows an unshaven man, cool as any rock star, holding on to his Nikon and staring coldly at the camera, so damaged by what he's seen that he embodies both the phrase "if looks could kill" and "the thousand yard stare." I find the final paragraph of his book especially sad and haunting. I return to it often:

"...mostly (now) I'm alone in my house in Somerset. The ghosts in my filing cabinets sometimes seem to mock me — the ghosts of all those dead in all those wars..."

As Alex and I finished dinner, I told him about the extraordinary pictures McCullin took and how in some way they'd been as crucial to my youth as the records I'd played over and over again. I told him about that final paragraph and tried to quote it word for word, telling him how moving I found it. Alex took a sip from his drink, looked me straight in the eye and said, “Donald McCullin is my dad.”

The next afternoon we set off for our location — a 90-minute drive outside Prague, where we were going to be shooting all night. As the Czech countryside rolled by, we drove past the gates to the Theresienstadt concentration camp, a place which figured in a documentary that would take over my life for seven years.

A horrible thought came to me. There was no band, no drummer, no guitar player to cut away to in this video I was about to make. Apart from Motorcycle Boy, Celine was the only person in it. I had to make the story work, while ensuring that we filled every available second of the six-minute song. How had I not figured that out before? I pulled out my storyboards and frantically started adding shots of blowing curtains and lightning bolts.

Though the hours of darkness would be short, the location we'd found completely justified my decision to shoot in the Czech Republic. What had once been the summer palace of the Czech emperor now lay empty. Every time we asked if we could do something which might have raised eyebrows elsewhere, they said yes. Can we ride a motorcycle down the stairs? Sure, no problem. We set to work. The job Celine and I worked on in France had been rushed, with plenty of moving parts, so there hadn't been much time for chit-chatting between takes but here, with no extras, jugglers or clowns, we had plenty of time to talk. I was struck by her incredible (and rather raunchy) sense of humour.

At meal break I was stunned by the long line in front of the catering truck. Where had all these people come from? Tomas explained that we had more than a hundred people in the art department alone. As we got back to work and the sun set, I heard a huge groan from the garden and went to check it out. A large-screen TV had been set up behind the house, the soccer was on, and the crew's home team had just conceded a goal.

We set up a circular dolly track in the palace salon for the crucial moment when Celine is haunted by the ghost of her dead lover wherever she looks. We shot take after take. Celine did everything I asked of her, but I worried the scene would not capture the emotion suggested in the treatment. I hoped that we could make it work in post.

On the last day at the palace, we shot Celine running barefoot through the grounds. The local production company had delivered a crane which was nothing like the sophisticated units I was used to. It was ingenious but required the operator to walk in circles while operating it, and that required a bit of practice. In every take Celine was perfect, but a bump would somehow appear in the crane move and we'd have to do another one. Celine never said a word. It wasn't till we showed up on the stage in Prague the next day and Celine limped into her dressing room that she revealed the cuts and bruises on the soles of her feet from the stones she was running across. She'd given me take after take and never said a word about the pain she was in.

The set in Barrandov's studio was the largest I had ever had built. The bedroom was about 80 feet across, and the corridor off it was another hundred — and there was still plenty of room for craft service tables, the video village where the client would sit, etc. The bedroom had a massive four-poster bed and an enormous working fireplace, which worried the hell out of me as we were working in a building made entirely out of wood.

After two nights of work, we were setting up the one remaining shot on my storyboards. Celine would run down the long hallway. Time was running out, and I had promised Celine she could leave at 6:00 a.m. to catch a flight to the next stop on her busy schedule. As so often happens, one thing after another kept holding us up; I saw Celine quietly double-checking the time with her sister. With just seconds to spare, we were finally ready, when the gaffer — an English gent who was breaking down the lighting in that vast bedroom — appeared at the far end of the corridor, carrying two lights, making his way slowly towards us. I sighed, put my head in my hands and impatiently yelled at him, "C'mon, hurry up — Celine has to leave and I've two minutes to get this final shot." He slowed down, stopped right beside Celine, put one of his lights on the ground and replied, "I've got two speeds, guv. And if you don't like this one, you certainly won't like the other one!"

Celine looked at me and rolled her eyes. She had been patient and gracious throughout the whole shoot, and for our gaffer to respond to me like that while standing beside her appalled me. He slowly picked up his light and made a meal of carrying it out of shot. Five minutes later, the shot was in the can, Celine hugged us, thanked everyone on the crew and was gone.

The shoot for Celine's video had been ambitious, and the post-production process proved no less taxing. In 1996, sophisticated computerized techniques were still in the developmental stage, and that circular dolly shot where Celine sees Motorcycle Boy everywhere was proving to be a tough nut to crack. I was still worried that it didn't have the life and the emotion that the scene required. Seeing still frame mock-ups of parts of it wasn't giving me a sense of how it would work, so I asked the post-production team if they could render it for me before I signed off on the various elements. They looked nervously at each other and told me that the render would take almost two days! We scratched our heads, but I couldn't visualize how it would look, so I asked them to go ahead with the render. The computers crashed after a day and they had to start again. By the time I finally got to see the shot, we were running out of time, and I had little choice but to make some minor changes and ask the team to start the render for real. Nowadays you could probably create that shot on a laptop before lunchtime and try various tweaks to improve it. That scene has come to haunt me, and I still wish I could make it better.

To this day, I'm not entirely happy with this video. I think Steinman's idea was overblown and not entirely suited for Celine. While Steinman's material is perfect for Meat Loaf and his over-the-top persona, it doesn't sit so well with Celine's grace and that beautiful smile of hers. But even so, many people like the video. In fact, I was recently asked to pitch on a commercial that used "It's All Coming

Back to Me Now" as its reference and described the video in glowing terms. I didn't get the gig — they felt that some other guy could recreate the video better than the guy who shot it originally. Yeah — that makes sense!

I never played a single Celine song ever again but, if someone called this afternoon and said, "Can you get on the plane to fly to Timbuktu tonight to shoot something for Celine?" I'd say yes without a moment's hesitation.

Celine Dion does not perform my kind of music but, without doubt, Celine is my kind of people.

Not long after that, I was back on the French Riviera shooting a duet with Italian pop star Eros Ramazotti and Tina Turner. Once again, when the shoot was over, I had to go to do a job with Ozzy. Which is how I found myself back in Prague at the Barrandov studios prop house looking at a pickled baby in a bottle!

The song was "Back on Earth," and I'd got it into my head that the video should be loosely inspired by the work of the 15th century Dutch painter Hieronymus Bosch. My idea was to have Ozzy crucified on an enormous structure reminiscent of the one we'd built for Alice Cooper's "Poison" video, rise from the dead and break out of his coffin, yelling "Back on Earth!" as it is being carried through a medieval town. I was going to need 200 extras dressed in sackcloth and a location that resembled a 15th century European town, so Prague seemed like the obvious choice. There was a medieval film set outside the city, easy access to sackcloth and the prop house filled with extraordinary props, including that poor pickled baby who I christened Derek. We put the art department to work building a massive crucifixion machine.

Tomas, the local producer, was back on the job with us. I asked how we would find the 200 extras. "No problem," he said. "I've put out a call on the local radio station, and we'll do a casting session on Friday night." I was worried, as the shoot was on Saturday and Sunday. Planning a casting call like that in L.A. where rock fans were blasé and had long been abused by people like me was not a good idea, but Tomas assured me that in Prague there would be no problem.

On Friday morning, I checked the weather for the weekend. Thunderstorms were expected later in the day but Saturday and Sunday were expected to be chilly and rain-free. "How's the casting session looking?" I asked Tomas. "Good," he said. We climbed into a cab and traipsed across the city to meet Ozzy in the same hotel Celine had stayed in. We would go through details of the shoot with Ozzy and Sharon and then catch a cab to a nearby town square, where I was assured I would meet a huge crowd of potential sackcloth-wearing Ozzy fans.

Heavy rain pelted the windows while we talked in Ozzy's suite; the forecast was proving to be accurate. Then, as we waited for the cab to take us to the extras casting, Tomas's phone rang. I knew something was very, very wrong. He turned away to finish his conversation. "Change of plan," said Tomas. "We're going back to the office."

"Why?" I asked. Tomas tried to be vague but soon confessed that the huge crowd of extras he'd promised had failed to materialize. I knew it. I was angry — this was exactly what I had feared, and now we had 12 hours to solve the problem. "So, how many people showed up?" I asked.

"Some," said Tomas.

"How many?"

"Not enough."

"C'mon, Tomas. How many?"

"Nine!"

Nine? For Ozzy's video to work I had envisaged a crowd, a riot waiting to happen — a rabble, a mob in sackcloth — 200 of them, and I had nine. What the fuck? Back at the office, Tomas gathered his troops and instructed them to call a homeless shelter, the university, the clubs, some out-of-work bands, actors, friends, girlfriends, mums, dads, sisters, brothers. The crowd Tomas had envisaged getting from his radio ad would be frenzied Ozzy fans eager to work for free but now we were going to have to pay people. I was shaking with anger — this was a big, important job, and I had been let down. I settled in a corner, tried to cool my fury, put my headphones on and re-examined my shot list.

Ten minutes later, I heard a shout. Tomas came racing over to me and pulled off my headphones. “Come with me now! We’ve found them!”

Downstairs we climbed into a waiting car and raced across the city as Tomas, beaming with laughter, explained that his coordinator had found the nine sodden Ozzy fans standing in the square during the thundershower I’d witnessed through the window in Ozzy’s suite, hired them on the spot and sent them home. What he’d missed was the 600 — SIX HUNDRED! — other fans sensibly sheltering under a nearby bridge.

At the designated meeting spot, we were instantly surrounded by a mob — just the kind of mob I’d imagined, although dressed in ripped jeans, Ozzy sweatshirts and denim jackets. Most of them had long, unkempt hair and questionable dental work — perfect! Tomas gave me 200 coloured cards as he tried to hold the crowd back. “Give a card to every extra you want to hire, and we’ll send the rest home,” he yelled. As I handed out the first few cards, the crowd registered its frenzy by pushing forward harder and stronger. I imagined the small article that would appear at the bottom of page five of the next day’s paper: *Ozzy Osbourne director crushed to death on Prague side street.* I had the impression that I was not handing out tickets for a chance to hang with Ozzy in a windswept field for two days but a ticket to get on the last chopper out of Saigon. Mercifully, I was saved from a good trampling in the melee that ensued. I made my way back to the hotel, safe in the knowledge that somewhere in Prague there were 400 Ozzy fans with a grudge against me. I imagined them forming a rebel gang to track me down and lynch me because they didn’t get chosen to be in Ozzy’s video.

I arrived on set at 6:00 the next morning and found the 200 Ozzy extras all wearing sackcloth, going through hair and makeup. The lucky few who had good teeth had some of them blacked out. If their hair had been combed at some point since February, that was soon rectified.

As they made it out on set to join Ozzy, I didn't need to direct the desperation in the faces of the extras. I simply told the Czech AD that they should remember how they felt the evening before, when they were reaching out to me for their tickets to their own exclusive *Ozzfest*. At one point, while we were changing setups, I remembered that angry letter my mother had sent me: "If you spent as much time on your French reflexive verbs as you do listening to that Black Sabbath album..." I smiled happily to myself. Yes, I had taken a pass on becoming fluent in French, but sitting on a set with Ozzy, Derek the pickled baby and 200 of Ozzy's wildest Czech fans was so much more fun. I wasn't exactly sure what my dreams were as a young teenager, but this surely surpassed every one of them.

Back in L.A., Steve Einczig — who had commissioned the Celine and Ozzy videos — convinced me to make the footage grainier, more like a '20s horror movie, which was a great idea. I wasn't as happy when he insisted we also add some footage from *Nosferatu* that I found to be a bit of a distraction. To my everlasting regret, Derek the pickled baby didn't make the final cut. However, I was pleased with the final video and felt that I'd created something that was quite original and really suited Ozzy well.

Sharon Osbourne did not agree and, though she allowed it to have some airplay on MTV, it soon disappeared. It was resurrected with the advent of YouTube but then pulled again. It's back up on YouTube now. I'm really proud of that video and so glad I flunked those French lessons so I could spend more time listening to that first Black Sabbath album.

CHAPTER 35

I Got You Babe

ONE OF THE DELIGHTS OF MY JOB has been finding myself sitting in a chair across a table from an icon. With Cher, it wasn't like that at all — I was sitting cross-legged on a huge faux-leopard-skin carpet, laying out 40 magazine clippings for her to look at. Things weren't going too well, and I was feeling desperate.

When I was 12 and spent summer afternoons escaping from my parents' endless rows, I'd walk along the fragrant mountain road in Platres, Cyprus, on the way to the swimming pool, singing "I Got You Babe" to myself as I wondered how to escape the nightmare I was going through. The best part of the record was the runout, where Sonny would sing "I got you to hold my hand" and Cher would wail back, "I got you to understand!" I was mostly into male groups, but two female singers really delivered for me: Cilla Black, when she sang "It's the end of my world for me" at the end of "You're My World," and Cher during that "I Got You Babe" runout. I suppose that a psychoanalyst might conclude that "I got you to understand" was an easy crutch for me to grab hold of. But I don't think so — all that really mattered was that voice, that final harmonious "I got you babe" and then the wonderful oboe during the coda. What a great record it was.

One grey morning, I drove to Cher's house in Malibu, listening to her new single, "Believe." She was very polite but kept me at arm's length, as many celebs do to keep people from becoming too familiar too fast. The meeting went nicely, and I went home and wrote up a few ideas. None of them stuck. I pitched more ideas at a second meeting, but they fell on stony ground as well. The label person asked, "Are you sure you want to keep doing this? Just so you know, the single will never be released in the U.S. — it's a UK-only release, so it's not going to be anything big." I didn't care. It was Cher. I wanted to do this to pay her back for getting me through that summer from hell in Cyprus. Besides, I loved the record. These guys were nuts if they weren't going to release it in the States — it sounded like a hit to me.

I returned to Cher's house a third time; I knew this could be my last chance. Flailing about for ideas, I'd gone to my treasure trove of magazines and ripped out page after page of images that I felt might spark something, and now I was laying 40 of these images out on Cher's leopard-spotted carpet as she sat and watched. Finally, I said to her, "Look at all these images and tell me, is there anything that catches your eye that we could turn into a video?" Cher leaned forward and pointed: "This one."

The photo, which was slightly out of focus, showed three young women dancing together in a club, the sort of image you find in a fashion magazine where the models are having fun, with prices and information on where to buy the clothes under it, but, when you look back at the picture, you have absolutely no idea what they're wearing. It was not terribly well lit, but it had life. I put the picture at the top of the pile, said goodbye to Cher, went home and wrote an idea around it. Next thing I knew I was on a plane to London to shoot the video.

Old friend and UK producer Phil Barnes and I were in Cher's hotel room. The standoffish Cher was gone; the new, friendly one admitted that she was feeling a trifle melancholy. "This is the suite where

Sonny and I always used to stay when we visited London. This is the first time I've stayed here since he died, and it makes me feel sad." It was a wonderfully honest moment, and it made me want to give her a big hug. (Of course, I didn't.) We sat down to talk about wardrobe, casting and all the other important stuff like what kind of food she'd like on set.

The idea I'd come up with for "Believe" had three Chers in a club full of bright young things. One Cher ("Regular Cher") performed on a stage for the dancing audience. Another Cher ("Mechanical Cher") was in a glass booth that clubgoers could come up to and examine. The third Cher ("Guardian Angel Cher") would appear at the end of the video to save our heroine. The AutoTune vocal effect, which became so memorable, sounded almost robotic to me, so I imagined Mechanical Cher rather like an Elvis suit on display at the Hard Rock Café, only with an animatronic Cher inside the suit. Looking for her man in the crowd, the heroine pushes through the throng to watch Cher in the booth before continuing her search.

As I ran through the details, Cher said, "I think it might be fun if we put plastic straws in my hair, don't you?" It was the most ridiculous thing I'd ever heard, but being English and polite and not wanting to upset, I agreed it was a great idea. Sometimes being polite and English pays off, because in her glass case she has plastic straws in her hair and she looks fabulous.

Two days before the shoot, I got a message from Cher. She was making an appearance at a famous gay club in London that night; perhaps I'd like to come down and see the show. When Cher calls, you cancel your plans and climb into a cab and get across town pronto. I walked into her dressing room as she was doing her makeup in the mirror. "Hi Nigel, you know Ben, don't you?" I turned around, and it was Ben Kingsley. Holy crap, I was marooned in a dressing room with two Oscar-winners. What do you do? What do you say? I'm a bald man and so is Mr. Kingsley, so the first thing that came into my head to say was, "Pleasure to meet you. Great haircut!" He scowled and turned away. A while later, Cher was ready to go out and sing two songs, one of which was "Believe." The packed club went mental as Cher walked onstage. Between songs, she told her audience, "I just want to say how grateful I am to you, to my fans for being so faithful for so long. You've kept me in jewellery all these years!" They loved it.

We started off with the scene in the glass booth. As I stood in front of Cher, I was suddenly at a loss for words, stumbling. *Oh my God*, I thought. *I'm directing Cher. You know, the one who's turned back time. The "I Got You Babe" Cher. The one who won the Oscar*. Sensing my predicament, she gently put a hand on my arm. "Nigel, when you're in my house, I want you to be nice to me. When we're on set, just tell me what you need me to do." She'd instantly pricked the balloon of anxiety that had been building up all morning, and I felt free and able to tell her exactly what we needed to get the video done.

At the end of the video, after our heroine has seen her lover with another girl, she climbs onto the roof of the club. Sensing that she needs to see reason and not do anything stupid, Guardian Angel Cher appears on the roof and, because Cher is magic, makes her see sense. We were using an empty old warehouse with no elevator up to the roof, not even a staircase — just a rusty iron ladder bolted onto the side of the building. It was dark, windy and raining. How was I going to get my iconic Oscar-winner up there in the middle of the night in the pouring rain? I took Cher's advice and just told her to climb the ladder to the roof. Up she went without a word of complaint.

"Believe" became a hit, and I was asked to come up with an idea for Cher's next single, "Strong Enough." Once again, many ideas were rejected until eventually Cher suggested that she saw herself as a screensaver. The final treatment ("version 11a") had a young man sitting down at his computer to make a screensaver; while creating a robotic-looking woman on his desktop, a lightning bolt strikes his apartment block, and the robotic woman turns into Cher. As she sings, everyone in the building — the young man and his girlfriend, a lesbian couple, kids fighting over a video game controller, a string section,

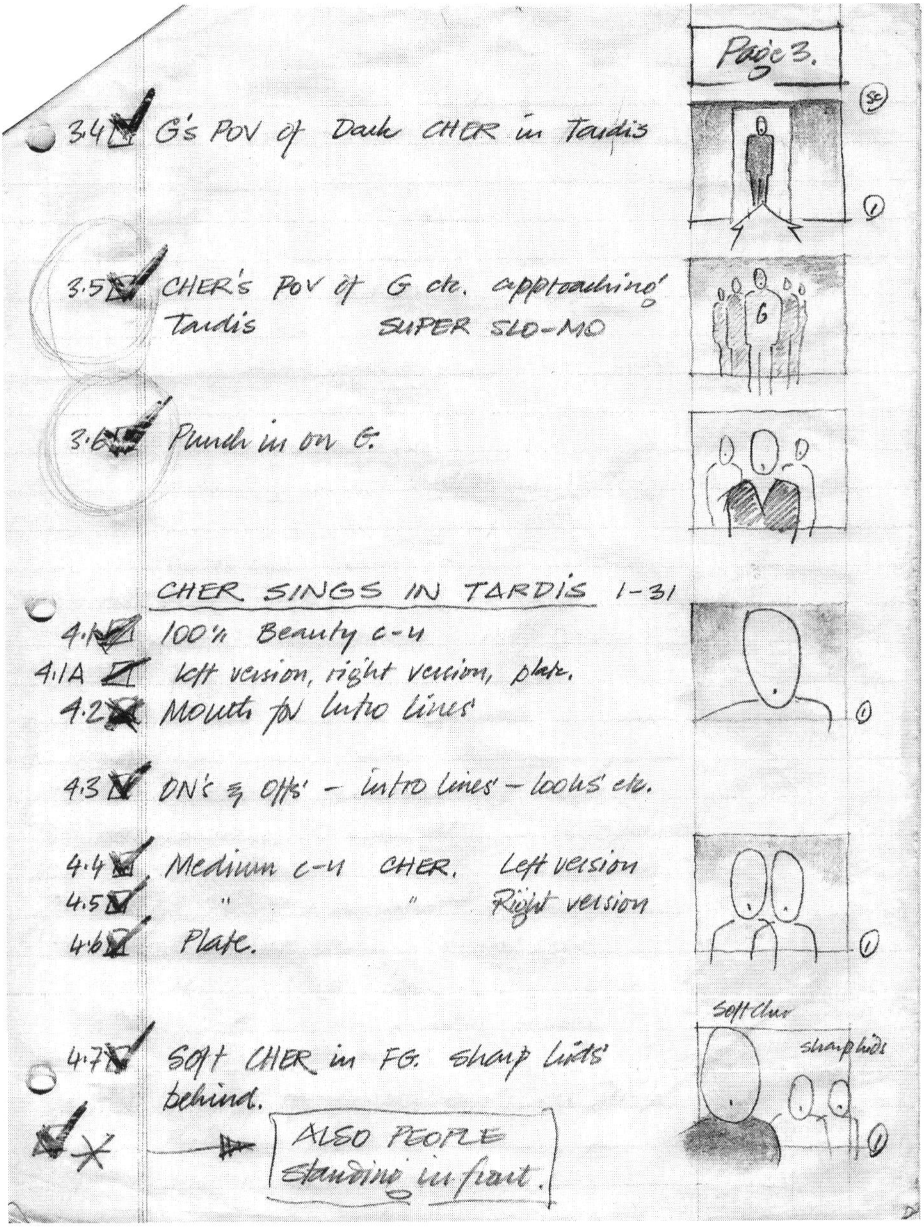

Page 3 of my storyboards for Cher's "Believe" video. *Dr. Who* fans will notice that I've nicknamed the glass box in which Cher performed the Tardis. I'm glad to report I got everything on this page. Having a storyboard means that when it's getting late, you, the crew and the client have a clear idea of what you must get before it's a wrap.

two burglars — resolve their differences or have their days changed thanks to Cher's performance in the computer screens or TVs in the various apartments.

We chose the abandoned Ambassador Hotel down the road from my house in L.A. and set to work. I'd shot in the hotel's faded glory before, making videos for both the Temptations and Guns n' Roses. The rooms gave us a host of options for the various apartments, one of which would be robbed by the burglars. Art Director Liz Kay prepared all the rooms, leaving 20 bucks worth of fake jewellery in the "Burglar" apartment ready for the shoot the next day. Overnight, the hotel was broken into, real burglars found our sets and, among other things, stole the fake jewellery. We laughed ourselves silly all day imagining the crooks paying a visit to a fence and being offered a few bucks for what they must have imagined was a fortune in diamonds!

Cher had insisted we fly her favourite hair guy in from New York at great expense. He was the costliest hair person I'd ever worked with; I was dying to see what he came up with. So, I couldn't hide my disappointment when he arrived with a Cheshire cat grin and showed off the platinum blonde wig he'd purchased for Cher at an Asian hair salon downtown. "It cost 12 dollars!" he said, giggling to himself as he walked to Cher's trailer and plonked it on her head.

A young makeup assistant who was a total Cher fan couldn't hide his delight that he'd be working on a video with her. He showed me a scrapbook filled with pictures of Cher over the years that he'd purchased at a thrift store in Las Vegas. It was certainly a thing of wonder. He asked if I could help him get her to autograph it, but I worried she might find it a bit creepy; it seemed to have been compiled by a stalker. Halfway through the afternoon, the generator ran out of gas; we had to wait half an hour while the electricians ran out to fill it up. As Cher sat calmly in her director's chair, desperate to keep her entertained, I told the assistant to pull out his scrapbook and show it to Cher. She was delighted and told him to pull up a chair. Together, they leafed through page after page, checking out her outrageous costumes over the years. There was much laughter, and more than once she said, "Oh my god! What was I thinking?" The makeup guy was in heaven. When they reached the last page, Cher closed the book with a big smile on her face. "How long before we're ready?" she asked. "We've been ready for 20 minutes," I told her. I hadn't had the heart to bust up the trip back through time as Cher and her number-one fan visited her back pages.

My final Cher video was for a song entitled "The Music's No Good Without You," and I wrote an idea inspired by Mervyn Peake's *Gormenghast* trilogy. To my surprise, Cher not only knew about *Gormenghast* but liked the idea. I'd hit the target on the first try.

The location I chose was a vast, modern office building that I imagined as a modern-day version of Gormenghast. We peopled it with maids-in-waiting, dancers, flunkies and courtiers, all buzzing around in the orbit of the lonely queen thinking about her distant lover so far away. Unfortunately, Cher's team did not love the video and had it recut in a way that I disliked.

In many ways I think becoming hugely famous and iconic, like Cher has, is a bit like living in Gormenghast, surrounded by courtiers and flunkies. This kind of fame so often manifests itself in unpleasant ways, but I saw none of that in the time I spent with Cher. It was a pleasure to be briefly in her orbit. And every time I look back at the work I did with Cher, I remember how her label told me "Believe" would never be released in the U.S. It went on to become a number-one hit in 23 countries, including the U.S. and the UK, and remains one of the best-selling singles of all time — it sold over 11 million copies. Cher is the oldest female artist to ever get a number-one in the U.S. I'm so happy I stuck with my gut and made that third trip out to Malibu — I knew that record was a hit.

CHAPTER 36

That Britney Guy

ON A WET NEW YORK AFTERNOON in July 1998, I jumped into a cab and made my way downtown with no idea of the ramifications the meeting I was headed towards would have on my career.

A few weeks previously, Jive Records had sent me a track by an unknown 16-year-old and a picture of her planned album cover, which I thought was awful. If they were trying to create something cheesy, unappealing and out of date, they'd nailed it. The track was a different story. As much as I adore anything with loud, crunching guitars and crashing drums, I also love a really well-produced pop song, and this girl was unquestionably the owner of what I sensed was going to be a big, fat pop hit. My producers told me not to waste my time with it, even suggested it could harm my career, but I persisted. After all, if you make a great video for a crap record, who will know? But if it's a hit, everyone will see it. Anyway, Jive was flying me to New York for a couple of days, so what the heck?

The cab dropped me off in the drizzle outside an unremarkable building and I walked up the stairs to a dance studio. I peered through the door and nervously looked around for the singer I was going to meet. I wanted to make the video for her song, and meeting this young woman was akin to going on a job interview. I wanted to make a good impression.

A small figure with blonde hair turned around and smiled. She held out her hand and said, "Hi. My name's Britney."

I have no memory of what we talked about on that first meeting, and I doubt if we chatted for longer than ten minutes. She seemed outgoing, bubbly and polite. I probably came across as very polite and quite dull. I'm sure we agreed that I would write a great idea for her video.

A week later, I still had no ideas. Sometimes it comes to you the first time you listen to a song, but there are inevitably days where not even a good idea, but any idea, is totally elusive.

I listened to "...Baby One More Time" over and over but still nothing was coming. And then I remembered what a friend had said months earlier: "I have a great idea for a video. It's a winner! Here's what happens..."

It wasn't a great idea, in fact it was corny, but it was no worse than that awful record sleeve and it wouldn't go away. I have probably written two or three thousand ideas for videos; I know that if an idea keeps popping up in your brain, one of the ways to get rid of it is to write it out. A bad idea can be like an impatient puppy that needs to go outside — you have to open the door and let the idea out to play. Once the idea has run around the garden for five minutes it becomes exhausted and settles down in a corner for a nap. Then you can focus on something better.

That ploy worked like a treat, and soon another idea popped into my head: Britney in a boxing ring. There would be moody lighting, and the mic would come down on a cable from the ceiling as if we were in Madison Square Garden. She would sing into it: "Hit me, baby, one more time." Get it? Looking back at it now, that idea was awfully, terribly wrong. I checked the treatment for spelling, sent it off to the label, went and made a cup of tea and relaxed. I knew I hadn't really delivered the goods, but I had been able to cross something off my to-do list, and there are times when that seems more important.*

If that sounds like an act of creative laziness, in many ways it was. But another thing I've learned is that, to get on with your life, you have to accept that sometimes you just have to submit something, even if it's crap. A few days later, the label confirmed that my boxing ring idea sucked but, to their credit, still wanted me to make Britney's first video. Perhaps I could talk to her on the phone? Britney had some ideas she wanted to share with me.

I took the call as I sat in my car on a Hollywood side street. Britney said, "I want the video to take place in school and there's lots of cute boys and dancing and I look out of the window and I don't want to be in class." She wasn't interested in a linear story but felt strongly that being in school, dancing and cute boys were ingredients that had to be in the video.

After the call ended, I sat in my car and fumed as I watched people go in and out of the health food store across the street. I was in my forties, and I was finding it very, very difficult to get my head around being told what to do by a girl 25 years my junior. But once I started to cool down, the details of what Britney was asking of me started to come into focus, and some truths started to make themselves known. I was no longer in my teens; Britney was. I'd never been in a school with girls after I was 11; Britney had. I'd never been to an American school; Britney had. Britney was a girl and thus, when it came to knowing what girls wanted, was surely something of an expert.

I took a deep breath. Perhaps the tables had been reversed? Perhaps, after all, Britney knew what needed to be in her video better than I did. After all, we had to make a video that would appeal to other 16-year-old girls across the American heartland. Who was I, a

* There are a number of articles on the web, backed up by former Jive label boss Barry Weiss, which suggest I pitched an idea for this first video with Britney traveling to Mars and dancing on the planet. Wrong — that never happened. I suspect that someone else submitted that idea and in the years that have passed Barry credits me with the Mars concept. These articles also suggest that this idea was again pitched by me for "Oops!...I Did It Again," where it finally gained traction. That is also not true.

British-born guitar-mad nearly middle-aged man, to say that Britney was wrong? Perhaps I should just swallow my pride, write the idea up, embellish it a touch and see if I could swing the job. If it was successful I could claim the credit, and no one would ever know. When I got home that night, I wrote out the idea in half an hour.

The concept was approved, and we started in earnest. The first thing we needed was a school — one with corridors that had lockers but was also wide enough to allow a dance sequence. As I stepped into the first of the locations we scouted, a terrible thought entered my head. I was about to spend $350,000 of someone else's money recreating an iconic scene I'd seen in dozens of movies and TV shows: schoolkids opening their locker doors at break and going to class, a scene of which I had no personal experience. In my life, I lived at school, so we didn't need lockers. The only reason I knew American kids did this is because I'd seen it on TV. In fact, the first school we visited might well have been the very first American school I'd ever stepped inside. Perhaps I was the director who arrives to film a scene at NASA and is confused at the absence of Vulcans in real spaceships because his only experience of interplanetary travel was *Star Trek*?

That first school wasn't going to work. It had no lockers at all. The second was more promising: it had one corridor with lockers, but they were all welded shut. When I asked why, the teacher showing us around told me it was so kids wouldn't bring guns to school. This is perhaps not the place for my thoughts on gun ownership, but suddenly my own school days seemed as fantastical as the ones I was trying to recreate for Britney.

We eventually walked into Venice High, which ticked all the boxes. When I found out they'd shot some of *Grease* there, that sealed the deal for me. Perhaps a little bit of Olivia Newton-John's stardust would rub off on us.

Britney arrived in L.A., dance rehearsals started and I went down to check out how things were going. I was instantly impressed. Stars were often underwhelming at dance rehearsals: they didn't have the chops, they weren't fit and, surrounded by full-time dancers, were nervous and self-conscious. Not Britney. She was the leader of her gang and could definitely dance. She was hardworking and ready to do another take and another take to get it right. She may have been young, but she was eager, enthusiastic and totally professional.

There are three or four versions of the treatment in my files. Some of them mention school uniforms and some of them don't. I lived just off Olympic Boulevard at the time, and I would often drive past a high school, where I could see kids crossing the road and waiting for the bus. Once I had the job, I made note of what the kids were wearing. None of them were wearing uniforms, so I told the stylist to select teen clothes like T-shirts and sneakers. But when Britney appeared from the changing room at a fitting in a T, sneakers and jeans, she turned up her nose. "Wouldn't I be wearing a school uniform?" she asked. I winced. I'd never been fascinated by young girls in school uniforms, but I knew of men who were, and I was instantly worried about sending the wrong message. I was already nervous about a song whose hook was "Hit me, baby, one more time." Adding school uniforms to the mix seemed like exceedingly dangerous territory. But my producer Nina Dluhy and my client Lynda Simmons convinced me Britney was right. If they approved of the look, then perhaps I should find other things to worry about.

The morning of the shoot was unremarkable. Britney and her dancing chums showed up and went through hair and makeup. No one knew who she was, the school was in summer session and everything ran smoothly. We started off with a close-up of Britney leaning on the car door. One big lesson I'd learned is, whenever possible, bang off a scene with a vocal performance at the beginning of the day. Whatever happens now, you have a major part of the video in the can, and everyone can breathe easily — especially the client. The first day finished off with the dance session in the commissary area; when we were nearly done, Britney asked if we'd like to see her do a body flip. I hadn't seen her do that in rehearsal and was a bit gun-shy — what if she landed on her head on the concrete? — but I threw caution to the wind, and the

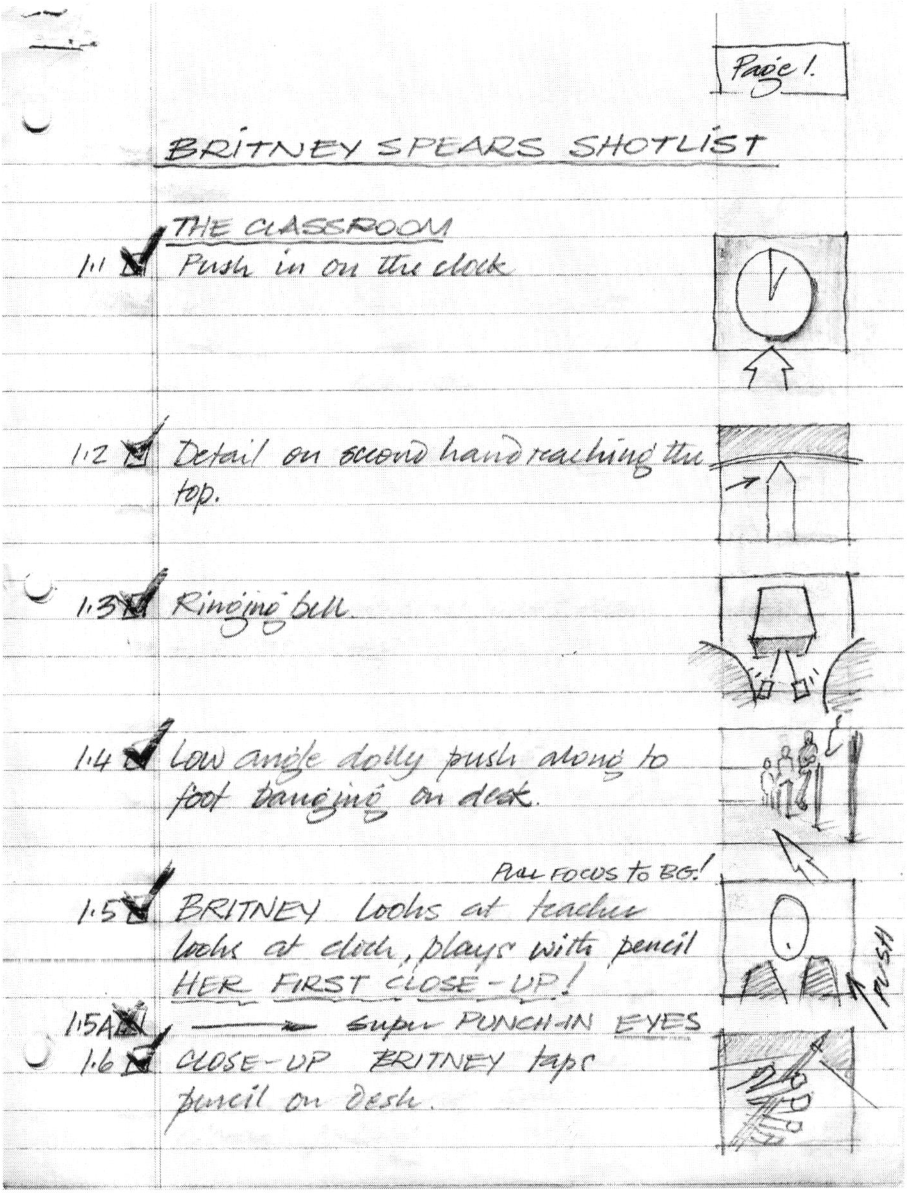
Page 1.

BRITNEY SPEARS SHOTLIST

THE CLASSROOM

1.1 Push in on the clock

1.2 Detail on second hand reaching the top.

1.3 Ringing bell.

1.4 Low angle dolly push along to foot banging on desk.

PULL FOCUS TO BG!

1.5 BRITNEY looks at teacher looks at clock, plays with pencil HER FIRST CLOSE-UP!

1.5A → super PUNCH-IN EYES

1.6 CLOSE-UP BRITNEY taps pencil on desk.

The opening of Britney's first video. It's all there: the clock, the bell, Britney's pencil, her banging foot, the camera movement. Not a single wasted shot...I hope it works in the edit! As Britney was a female, her head was drawn as an oval. Males were always drawn with oblong heads, which is as far as my artistic talents go.

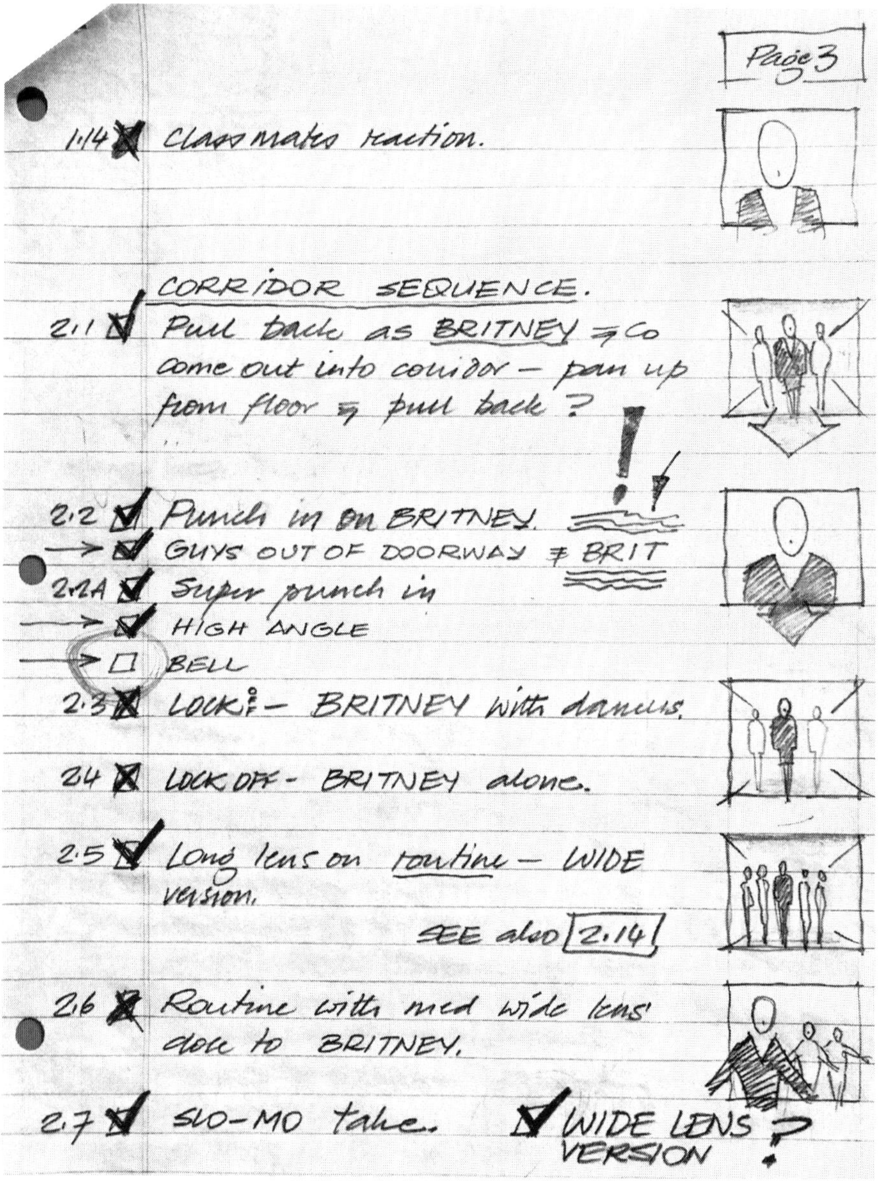

Here are my ‘boards for the first dance sequence in the hallway. We didn’t shoot frames 2.4 and 2.6. Not because of time but because, as we’d shot the other angles, I figured we didn’t need them: another useful result of doing boards in advance.

flip is in the video. I can't tell you how many people have asked who the stunt double was!

Day two found us in the gym. We'd developed a scene where Britney looks longingly at a handsome guy sitting in the bleachers. She asked me if her cousin could play the hunk. I said yes. He was right for the part, it made Britney comfortable to be looking at someone she knew, and it solved a casting problem without time or effort. Sadly, that sound logic eluded some people who, over the years, have made salacious comments about cousins flirting with each other.

As we were setting up the scene I sat down next to Britney in the bleachers and we chatted for a short while. I asked what her ambitions were and she said, "By 23 I'd like to be as big as Madonna, married and have a couple of kids." Then she giggled. I don't suppose in that moment that either of us suspected those dreams would all come true.

The other star of the video, who appears at the beginning and the end, was Felicia, Britney's on-set guardian and a friend of the family. Again, I think it was Britney's idea to have her in the video, and she was totally game to dress up and join in the fun.

We shot the opening scenes of the video on the third and final day, which was a Saturday. There were summer school classes being held on Thursday and Friday, so we had to wait until the weekend for empty classrooms and shoot, as we often do, out of order. Before dance rehearsals began, I made a point of telling the choreographer that this sequence would take place in a corridor that was 12 feet wide, so I was shocked to see the run-through spread across the rehearsal room. I pushed and whined and squeezed until the dance became longer and thinner. Britney arrived on set in her school uniform. I paid no attention to the bare midriff — what caught my attention were the pink furry bands around her pigtails. Even if I'd known the furore that outfit was going to cause I don't know if I would have changed anything. As usual, I was watching the clock, keen to get something in the can. "Everybody ready? Let's shoot!"

The next sequence was a series of close-ups of Britney standing against the lockers singing the first verse. Years later, a friend pointed me to a review of the video on IMDB. Someone had written their own version of what happened next: "Britney do this, Britney do that, Britney smile seductively! Britney look at the camera this way, Britney look at the camera that way!" While I was certainly guilty of telling Britney, "Look over there, now look back at the camera," I would never have dreamed of suggesting that she do it seductively. I get very nervous asking grown men and women to give seductive looks on camera (thank you, repressed English upbringing), so I most certainly wouldn't have asked a 16-year-old girl to do it. The fact is Britney just did it, and I was as shocked as that IMDB writer would be. It wasn't till months later that I learned about Britney's years with *The Mickey Mouse Club,* which, being a foreigner, I'd never seen. Of course, she was relaxed in front of the camera — she'd been doing it for years! The IMDB comment concluded, "Of course, Mr. Director had an astute idea of JUST EXACTLY WHAT WAS GOING TO SELL LIKE HOT CAKES!" I don't know if I would have put it in those words, but I knew Britney had something, and those close-up shots in the corridor were gold.

In many ways the shoot for "...Baby One More Time" was just another job. I don't think any of us went home that night thinking we'd been part of something out of the ordinary. We had a great cast and crew and we did good work. Once you start a production, it takes on a life of its own as if a mysterious animal made from invisible smoke is being born in front of you on the set. There are times when you get a sense that this newborn is completely out of control, and you have to wrestle with it every step of the way to keep it from growing up to be an ugly stepchild that no one wants to be responsible for. And there are other times when, with exactly the same amount of care and hard work, the production moves along smoothly and all you have to do is nudge it here and push it there to get it where you want it. I think the trick is paying attention, being really present and aware on set and knowing when you need to wrestle with the child you're creating and when to back off and let it grow and attain a life of its own.

A client or artist manager will often turn to me on set and ask hopefully, "Is this going to be an award-winner?" They really seem to believe that you woke up that day and decided that on this job, rather than the one you did last week, you're going to work your magic so that it will win some awards. All I want to do is slap them and say, "Don't you understand? I want every job to be an award-winner!" But it doesn't work like that. You do the work and then the world decides for you whether it's genius or a piece of crap. So much of the work we do is tied into a moment in time; once completed, we have no control over what happens next. I'm sure I went home that Saturday night and did what I always did after a shoot — feed the cat, order some pizza, crack open a beer and collapse in front of the TV.

Declan Whitebloom cut the video. After making some changes requested by the label, it was done. I liked the finished version and, a few days later, brought it with me to a meeting I was taking to see if I could get hired to work at A Band Apart, a new production company owned by Quentin Tarantino and Lawrence Bender. Producer Michael Bodnarchuck, who I'd known for a few years, asked if I had any new work he could see. I proudly handed him a copy of "...Baby One More Time." He slotted Britney's video into his machine, but halfway through hit the eject button. He was not impressed. The video was released to MTV the next day. By that Monday morning, everyone was talking about it and Britney's life changed forever.

People loved the school uniforms, but my concerns were not entirely unwarranted. One reviewer declared that Britney was "guided, one guesses, by oily menfolk who realise the marketable worth in kitting her out in school uniforms." After the video hit MTV, I was asked to make videos for other young women, including Mandy Moore and Jessica Simpson. Just as, once I'd shot Guns n' Roses, I was asked to shoot every hair metal band in town, now I was being sent tracks by every female teen artist. I was told the only reason I never made a Christina Aguilera clip was that she had specifically instructed her team *not* to hire the Britney Guy. It reached a nadir for me at a dinner when someone across the table looked me in the eye and calmly asked me if I was a paedophile. Once again, I had to explain carefully that even at the highest points of your career you don't go looking for people to shoot videos for, they come looking for you. And even then, you only get the job if you come up with the right idea. The irony was not lost on me — I was the one who'd questioned the wisdom of kitting out Britney in a school uniform and now I was the one getting stick for it. The funny footnote to the school uniform drama is that, at the end of the shoot, the wardrobe team told me that the entire cast had been clothed with uniforms from K-mart. Not a single item in the video had cost more than 17 bucks!

I recently interviewed Michael Omartian, who produced American number-one records in three separate decades. We were discussing what had changed in the business over the last 20 years. He sighed and said that, though it pained him to admit, the demise of the big label system was a big loss. For all their faults, labels developed artists and provided the funds to help them grow. Though A&R departments were notorious for not signing some great artists, they also worked as an effective filter for acts that did not have what it took to succeed in the long run. In Britney's case, Jive had developed Britney's career from scratch and ultimately decided, God bless them, that I should make her video. They'd flown me to New York to meet her and then insisted, when they read treatments they didn't like, on me going back to the well. They had the common sense to listen to the unknown girl who had a few ideas of her own, and we came up with something which nudged the pop Richter scale that year. I'm happy that I made a great video for Britney and launched her career, but I'm happier still that if you look back on that late-'90s period in some pop almanac, there's a good chance you'll see a shot of Britney and her pals dancing in that school corridor. As someone whose very lifeblood growing up was music and the culture of pop and rock and roll, this gives me great pride.

And then I was asked to do it all over again for Britney's next single, "Sometimes." The job got off to a bad start when Britney injured herself in dance rehearsals and we had to delay the shoot for a month.

This time, we were going to the beach; a key dance sequence would take place on the pier at Paradise Cove. During our scout I'd noticed that the pier was fabricated from rough hunks of timber with huge splinter-like chips sticking out everywhere — a fall on that would have nasty consequences. I told the choreographer to make sure there were no dance moves that required sliding along the ground, otherwise everyone would be on their way to hospital after the first take. Needless to say, at the first rehearsal I saw a move where everyone slid across the floor on their knees and had to excise it.

The dark side of the internet was starting to rear its ugly head for the first time, and a rumour was going round that Britney had had a boob job. The Cove was a public place, and we couldn't keep the journalists and paparazzi at bay. Even worse, we were just up the road from Malibu, which is pap central, so Pamela Anderson et al. had a day off while we were besieged by the worst elements of the press. Between takes they shouted questions at Britney about her "operation." She eventually ran for cover, sobbing.

All day long I kept asking the photographers to take a step back. In the afternoon, we shot a sequence on the beach. At one point, a pap — the worst example of a British Smudger overseas — started snapping away during a take. His cell phone was jammed between his chin and his shoulder as he talked to someone about another job while simultaneously taking picture after picture of Britney. With his motor-drive purring and his yelling getting louder and louder over the playback, he calmly wandered in front of our camera during a take as if he were in control of the set. I grabbed the collar of his shirt and dragged him out of my shot. His phone dropped to the sand, and he was about to knock me senseless when he suddenly realised what he'd done. "Sorry, guv," he muttered as he retreated up the beach trying to grab some more shots of Britney. It was all a terrible sign of things to come in the months ahead.

By the time "...Baby One More Time" and "Sometimes" were completed, Britney was an established young star and tongues had started wagging. People wanted to know what was going on between her and

Justin Timberlake. A British TV crew came to town and asked to interview me about the latest pop sensation. The lady interviewer did a passable job of hinting that, as she and I were both Brits and both worked behind the camera, we were mates and that I could share a few secrets with her that I perhaps wouldn't share with others. Her first few questions were softballs about what Britney was like on set, did she hang out with her dancing buddies, did she really do the flip in the middle of "...Baby One More Time," that sort of thing. Then she delivered the zinger: "We all know that Britney and Justin are an item, what we need to know is do you think she is a virgin?"

WHAT?

"She's a teenager, she must be having sex with Justin, don't you think?"

"I'm sorry, I'm not going to answer that question."

"Do you think it's OK for a girl who's 16 to be having sex?"

"I'm not answering that question, either."

"But surely you must know what's going on? You and Britney have been spending a lot of time together."

"No, we haven't. We've done two jobs together."

She was relentless. I kept stonewalling. She asked another inappropriate question and I lost it. "Whether Britney has sex or has ever had sex or not is none of my fucking business and it's none of your fucking business either and I wouldn't fucking tell you even if I fucking knew and I'm going to keep saying fuck over and over again so you can't use any of this. She's 16. Leave her the fuck alone. You should be fucking ashamed of yourselves!"

"Thank you," she said in a tone that meant we were no longer besties and turned to her camera guy. "OK. You can cut now." The sound guy came over, gave me a meek smile and spoke quietly to me as he removed my lav mic. "Nice work, boss. Well done."

Nine months after my third video with her, "(You Drive Me) Crazy," Britney had a new album out and some ideas for the first single's video, "Oops!...I Did It Again." She told me she wanted to be on Mars in a red jumpsuit with a handsome spaceman but that she did not want there to be any rockets in the video. Before our call, I listened to the track a few times and noticed a ridiculous section, which I presumed had something to do with the *Titanic* movie, in the middle. "What are we going to do about that part? Are we going to flash back to 1912?" "Oh, you'll think of something," she said.

Was it challenging to hear the outline of the video from Britney? No. In many ways there's nothing worse than being handed a new song by the label and being told, "Surprise us. Come up with any idea you like." As you sit down at your desk with a fresh pencil and a blank piece of paper the possibilities are endless. Should this be a domestic drama in a housing project? Maybe Britney is a race car driver? Perhaps she's the unlikely presidential candidate in a banana republic! As you start crossing out idea after idea that seems too unlikely or wrong, you fall into the trap of writing an idea because it's safe. You become crippled by doubt as you imagine another director at their desk not far away coming up with a much cooler idea. So, when your artist says they want to shoot something in space — albeit a fantastical version of it — you become instantly more focused. And when you are told that the chosen location is Mars, you don't even have to worry about choosing a planet. Saturn? Pluto? Uranus? Nope — it's going to be the red one.

In many ways, Britney's briefs for her videos were perfect in that they were descriptive — Mars, jumpsuit, spaceman — but contained no detail whatsoever. She'd handed me the skeleton, it was up to me to come up with the connective tissue and that, for me, has always been the fun part.

The budget was around the $750,000 mark, which, along with Celine's "It's All Coming Back to Me Now," was the largest budget I'd ever had for a video. It had to be good. I set to work.

Along with Britney's red planet sketch, the label insisted the album artwork be included somewhere in the video. I wrote down the markers — Mars, red suit, spaceman, album sleeve, Titanic sequence — and tried to stick it all together. And dancing, of course, there had

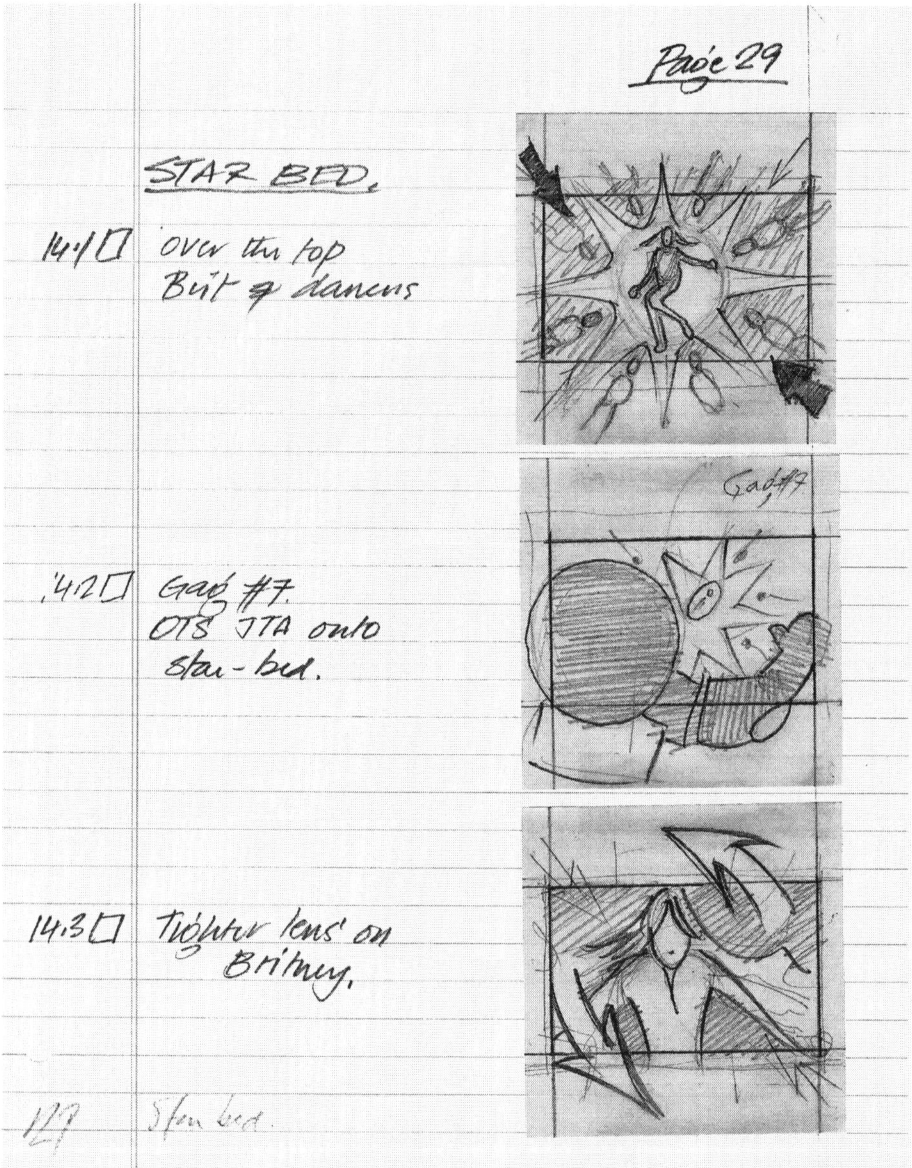

Page 29 of the storyboard for "Oops!...I Did It Again," which shows the fateful angles where the matte box fell on Britney. By this time I'd changed my approach and was drawing every shot onto post-it notes, which meant the drawings were bigger and more detailed — and also meant my storyboards grew to dozens of pages.

to be dancing. I decided there also needed to be a controller back on Earth talking with our spaceman.

The concept was approved, contracts were signed and we were into pre-production. Then I did something I will always regret. In a business where you're only as good as your last job, you are always looking for ways to improve and up your game. Making videos back then was a continuous arms race to do bigger, better things. It was a cutthroat business; though directors would sometimes meet to discuss an issue that affected us all, I actively kept them at a distance. I didn't want my work environment to be competitive, but I had to admit I found it useful — without it, I became lazy and complacent.

Around this time, another successful video director was quoted as saying, "You can't make a video for less than a million bucks." I thought this was ridiculous as I'd made hundreds of the things and never had a million bucks to spend. However, I now had three-quarters of a million bucks, and I intended this thing to look big. So, I fired my art director.

Liz Kay had art directed a slew of videos for me over the years. She was a compact, funny, tough lady who did great work, never complained and ran her team of set guys like a military action squad. Liz and her crew had become a part of my team. As a director traveling around the world, your producers, AD's, DP's and art directors form an emotional support unit as well as crucial ingredients to a successful job. After you've crisscrossed the country a few times, they also become good friends. Robbo, my old boss at Stiff, used to say, "You've got to boss to be the boss," and over the years I learned the wisdom in this crass statement. There were times where you had to be the stern dad, but, if you pick the right people, you never have to threaten or throw tantrums — they'll know when something isn't working and fix it before you have to say anything. Liz was one of those good people. She'd done sterling work for me on many jobs, but I'd never seen her build a big set for me, and I needed a big set for "Oops!" Tradition says that when a director rises through the ranks, he or she should take their team along, and I had done that for many years. But I wanted the upwards trajectory to continue, so I ditched Liz and hired someone else to design and build the set on Mars. Charles Infante did a grand job, but I still wonder what Liz Kay's Mars would have looked like.

It took more than a week to build the set on a stage on the Universal lot. The stage rental alone was more than the budget for many videos I've done. Casting was quick and easy, dancers were hired, fire-eaters were sourced and, by the end of the week, there was not a spare can of red paint to be found in Hollywood. Dance rehearsals went according to plan — there were no space restrictions, so I didn't have to caution Tina Landin, the choreographer, one jot. In fact, the set was larger than the dance rehearsal space, which was quite unusual for us.

Then there was the red suit.

If you're making a video that costs the price of a large house and the artist is wearing one outfit for most of it, that outfit needs to be special. After some searching, I was shown something that I loved. At the wardrobe fitting, Britney tried it on and it looked awesome. We'd found some red sneakers that Britney loved that matched the outfit perfectly. I asked if she could dance in them. "Yes, no problem," she replied. Everything was ready.

The day before the shoot, I was told the red suit had been rejected and that Britney had asked the guy who made costumes for Michael Jackson to create something overnight for her. The fitting would take place the morning of the shoot. I rolled my eyes — the set was costing a fortune and the cast was huge, but the focus of the video would be Britney. If her outfit sucked it would pull the rest of the video down with it. There was nothing I could do but cross my fingers. The next morning, the shiny red suit was revealed — and I didn't like it. The suit that stylist Estee Stanley had located was sophisticated and sexy; this one was form-fitting and shiny, but it wasn't special. I was disappointed, but I wanted Britney to be happy and the clock was ticking, so I caved.

Choosing wardrobe with the talent is always a prickly manoeuvre — a dicey tightrope walk of diplomacy, honesty and the creative needs for the job in hand. If you dig in your heels and get the outfit you think is best for the job you can pat yourself on the back for being hard-nosed, forceful and doing what is right, but you risk upsetting the talent and, if they choose to become petulant and resentful on set, you're going to have a long, hard day in front of you — and no amount of fabulous scenery and sexy camera moves is going to convince them this is fun anymore.

When Britney came to the stage, I was appalled. The poor girl was crowded by "making-of" camera crews, still photographers and helpers. I could only see her blond ponytail bouncing around amid a forest of lenses and microphones. As a director, you want your talent to feel safe, relaxed and protected — especially on the morning of a big shoot. You want them to feel at ease and ready to do their best work. Having a camera from MTV pushed right up your nose before the first take of the day does not create a relaxing atmosphere. As no one else was willing to do it, I rushed over and pushed everyone away — Britney and I had work to do. We did a level check for playback and shook hands — as I did with everyone before the first shot of a video. "I'll see you on MTV," I said.

I went back, sat in my chair and told AD Chris Medak we were ready. The first run-through went well, and the makeup and wardrobe team dashed in to touch up Britney, who was undoing the laces of her cute red Mars sneakers, "They're hurting me," Britney said. "I'll wear these instead," and put on the battered black sneakers she'd arrived in. No one else has ever commented, but when I watch the video now all I see is thousands of dollars of art direction, weeks of planning and rehearsal and a pair of battered black sneakers!

I was starting to relax when my executive producer Catherine Finkenstaedt leaned over and whispered in my ear, "Um, Nigel, are you seeing what I'm seeing?" I didn't know what she was talking about. "Two words: camel toe!" Holy crap — the form-fitting red suit was more form-fitting than we wanted it to be. It was a problem I'd never come across before. I was blushing. How do you solve this one? Whispered words were had with the wardrobe department. I have no idea what happened, but I just had to assume that as we'd done ten takes and I hadn't noticed anything, perhaps no one else would either.

I just hoped the problem would go away and, as no one has ever mentioned it again, I suppose it did.

On day two, a lighthearted party atmosphere had broken out on set. We were on schedule, the footage was looking great and the guys from *2gether* — the boy band film I'd directed for MTV — had shown up to meet Britney. I get nervous when everyone on set starts enjoying themselves, as concentration slips a notch or two. What we do needs to be fun, but we're here to work, and if I'm not watching for the little things I'll be kicking myself later in the cutting room. This was when Britney arrived on set for another scene, wearing an outfit I hadn't seen before. I was shocked. I felt it was tasteless and 12 degrees too revealing for a teen star releasing her second album. The picture session Britney had done with David LaChappelle for *Rolling Stone* the previous year had caused a furore, and this felt like similar territory. I turned to the label rep, Lynda Simmons, and Britney's manager, Johnny Wright. What did they think? Nobody liked it. But nobody wanted to suggest to Britney that she change it, either. I was concerned — if the people who ran her label and managed her career thought the clothes were not appropriate, shouldn't they intervene? But nobody moved, so I did.

Britney wasn't pleased that I wanted to see another outfit. She loved this one. I explained that, though I respected her wishes and her choices, I felt that this outfit was too much, that she was maybe five steps ahead of her key audience in that outfit and three steps would be better. We went back to her trailer and looked through everything on the racks, finally choosing the white angular mini-dress and crop-top turtleneck that you see in the video. I knew she wasn't happy about it, but I felt that, in the long run, I was making the right choice for her. I went back to the stage and waited for her to come back on set.

Ten minutes later, we were ready to shoot. Britney was lying on the plinth, looking up at the camera above her on the crane. I was checking the monitor when I heard a crash and a yelp — the matte box on the front of the camera, a black angled unit into which filters are inserted in front of the lens, had fallen off and hit Britney in the head.

This is exactly the kind of thing that should never ever happen on set. The matte box, which should have been properly secured, hadn't been. The camera assistant was very apologetic, but that wasn't going to change anything now — Britney was hurt.

The on-set medic was called over and we shooed everybody away. There was a cut on her head and some blood. The medic took Britney back to her trailer. I think, more than anything, Britney was in shock. After a chat with the medic and a visit to Britney, we agreed the best thing to do was wait an hour or so, let her rest in her trailer and then see how she felt. And, luckily, an hour or so later Britney was ready to work again. Once again, she impressed me with her incredibly professional approach.

By that evening, however, rumours were rife. Britney's mum announced that a camera had fallen on Britney and she'd been rushed to hospital, which was not remotely true. If a 35mm camera with all the fixings had fallen on her head from ten feet up, the result might well have been tragic; thank heavens it didn't. Other stories circulated: in one, the camera fell from the roof, and a respectable fashion magazine published a story that a red-hot light fell from the ceiling and hit Britney in the face. That is also a fiction: a matte box is heavy enough, and it should never have come loose. But it did not fall from the ceiling, and it was not a whole movie camera or a hot light.

I never worked with Britney again, and I accept that she probably wanted to move on and try working with somebody else. I think that asking her to change her outfit had a lot to do with that, and — though I had the best intentions — she probably felt I was holding her back and not allowing her to express herself. Maybe she was right. But if I had to make that decision again I would do the same thing. I also wonder if that tumbling matte box didn't seal the deal for her. It was not my job to make sure it was secured to the camera, but when you're the captain of the ship you must take responsibility for your crew.

Sometime after "Oops!" was completed and the *Making Of* video had been played and played on MTV, I went on another cycling holiday

— this time to Arizona. Driving back through the desert after a relaxing week in the middle of nowhere, I stopped at a lonely gas station to refuel my car. As I stood there in the late afternoon soaking in the warm air, I felt totally relaxed and free. A truck rumbled up to the next pump. A guy in cut-offs climbed out and started gassing his vehicle. He glanced over at me, looked away then turned back again, removing his shades for a good look. "Hey — you're that guy. You're that guy ... You're that Britney guy!"

Fame is an awful bedfellow. They say, given the choice of fame and wealth, you should choose wealth every time. I'll not deny there's something nourishing for the soul about standing in the middle of nowhere at a gas station and being recognised for your work, but it's also nice to be able to drive away from it. Britney had no such luck. I was appalled when things started going south for her. I was sitting at home watching the news one night and it showed helicopter footage of Britney in a Mini, driving her kids somewhere in the Hollywood Hills, trying to escape the cameras. The focus of the story was that she wasn't wearing a seat belt, but for me the story was that she could not go anywhere without a horde of paps and hacks following her. If I'd had a magic wand, she would have been instantly airlifted to somewhere safe and calm away from the storm.

I was once tasked with following Pam Anderson around with a camera for eight weeks. One afternoon, we wound up on the bluffs above Malibu, where she'd gone to watch her sons playing soccer. She'd wrapped herself in an enormous blanket that covered her head and hid most of her torso — she looked like a refugee from a *Star Wars* extras audition. I asked if she could remove the blanket so I could shoot this peaceful, motherly moment. She refused but politely explained why: "I don't want those photographers getting shots of me today." I looked around, couldn't see anyone and chuckled at her paranoia. "Come on, Pam. No one's here. No one's watching you!" She flashed me a look from the shadows under her blanket, "Look in the back seat of the Ford Explorer over there; check out the Jeep Cherokee in the parking lot and the Land Cruiser behind it." I turned around and, sure enough, in the shadowy back-seat area of each car was a photographer with a long lens, waiting for that blanket to fall down.

Cher told me a similar story when she woke up one Sunday morning and found there was no milk in the fridge. She drove to the store in her sweats. As she was about to leave the store, the paps had arrived and were waiting for her outside. She retreated into the shadows and called her son, who backed his SUV right up to the store so Cher could climb in the back and avoid the picture session. I once shot a commercial on David Copperfield's island in the Bahamas — a property that was a 45-minute boat ride from the nearest road. It was remote and peaceful ... and had a boatload of tourists, 40 yards offshore, leaning over the gunwales taking snaps and waving at us.

You and me, those of us with normal lives, have no idea what it's like to have this kind of attention. We are not prepared for this kind of intense, intrusive 24-hour scrutiny. How could Britney be prepared for this kind of attention when her life changed so suddenly overnight when that first video hit MTV? For anyone so young it must be incredibly challenging. And here's the other thing I've noticed about sudden and enormous success for anyone, whether they're a schoolgirl or a clerk. One day you have a bunch of friends and you all have similar problems like paying the rent, going on bad dates, getting your car fixed. A year later, your pals still have the same problems while you are deciding which mansion to buy, have hooked up with a movie star (or two) and can't decide whether to take a drive in the Bentley or the Ferrari. It takes someone with enormous strength of character not to be changed by this huge switch in circumstances.

I was shocked as Britney's story unfolded with the two-day marriage, her mum, her dad, the manager who came from nowhere, the head-shaving, the umbrella attack and the rest of it. I felt guilty that I had played a part in all of this. Celebrity is a frightening mantle to put on people unless they're really, really grounded, and it doesn't always end well. The young woman I knew and had worked with was a good soul, funny and a pleasure to be around. Life had changed irrevocably for her, and I felt for her. Being interviewed for a TV programme once, I was asked how things had changed for Britney. I recounted the moment she'd arrived on set for the "Oops!" video surrounded by cameras and mics and the look of fear I'd seen on her face. Suddenly, I felt ice running down my spine and I was reliving the moment when I'd been bundled onto that plane in Cyprus so many years ago and the tears started to form. I asked for a moment to compose myself. And, of course, they used that moment in their show. Fame is a vicious beast.

For a while, I swore I would never do another interview about her. I didn't want to become "That Britney Guy." But as time passes, things change and I've found talking about that work easier. One English interviewer asked me about "...Baby One More Time" and how I felt about creating something "so iconic." I replied that was his perception, not mine.

In his book *A Fabulous Creation,* David Hepworth looks back on the release of Pink Floyd's *Dark Side of the Moon* and notes, "Well over 40 years after its making, its ownership has long passed from the people who made it to the people who, one way or another, have lived with it." At this point, my relationship with the work I did for Britney feels very complicated. It's the first thing you see on my website, and I'm obviously proud of it, but on some level I feel it is part of the world now. Even though I was there on the day calling the shots, I somehow don't feel connected to it at all anymore, as it belongs to everyone.

But, as time has passed, I'm confident of one thing.

When I croak, my obituary — should I get one — will be short and sweet, possibly just one sentence, and will read something like this: The bloke who directed that Britney video is dead.

CHAPTER 37

Life's a Bitch

FILMMAKING REQUIRES tremendous luck. To be a successful director, I'd argue, that as well as talent, hard work, determination and world-class diplomatic skills, you need enormous amounts of luck. Sometimes, no matter how clever you are, no matter how hard you work, how good you are at keeping everyone happy, your luck deserts you and you're left with a mess that nobody can clean up.

At the end of a job, there's nothing more satisfying than a call from your producer to say it's been approved. You breathe a deep sigh of relief and try to figure out why the job went so well. Whatever that magic powder was, you want to know what it's made from so you can sprinkle some on the next one. The problem is that it's magic, and there's no formula. So, you start analysing the opposite of magic powder — disaster dust — because if you can't discover the formula for magic powder, you'd better figure out the essence of its opposite element fast. One smattering of that can cause untold havoc and turn a job to shit in a nanosecond.

I once got sick the night before a shoot. I felt awful and was blowing my nose all day on set, and the job turned to shit. On another job, it all went to shit at the end when the manager, who was a notorious cocaine fiend, rang me up after viewing the first edit, screamed abuse at me and made a solemn promise — over the bodies of his wife and children and over the grave of his dead mother — that I would never, ever, ever work in this town again. Then there was the time the client told me that I'd been awarded the job because my idea was the least worst one she'd received. Unsurprisingly, after a start like that, the job never left the runway. The client interfered incessantly; I vowed never to work with her again.

I shot a live show for a major artist who later re-recorded her vocals without looking at the cut and rejected the footage when it wouldn't synch up. As the job spiralled downwards into a vicious war of letters, the manager accused me and my team of being unprofessional and refused to make their final payment to us. But tears turned to laughter when the show finally made it to air and was nominated for three awards, one of which was *Best Direction in a Music Special or Series*.

And then there were the two jobs that took me to North Carolina. The first was a video for Hootie and the Blowfish. The shoot went well, but post-production turned into a nightmare when the well-known husband of someone tangentially involved with the job nixed the edit that had already been approved by the label.

Of all the jobs I've presided over, none has been such an unmitigated disaster from start to finish as the one that took me to North Carolina for the second time. Sometimes it doesn't matter how much effort you put into a job, it still gets fucked up. And no amount of determination, creativity, luck or resolve will unfuck it.

I'd received a track from an English band I'd never heard of called Shooter. Their song, "Life's a Bitch," was lively and catchy — a fairly typical message of teenage rebellion. My first reaction was to toss the track and the band, since they had chosen a band name which ignored one of the music business's basic rules of engagement: the curse of the "er" bands. The curse is quite simple — any band that has "er" at the end of its name is ultimately doomed to obscurity and the cutout bin: Strider, Runner, Stryper, Feeder, Sleeper. One band bucked the trend and became the exception that proved the rule: Foreigner.

"Life's a Bitch" was slated to be part of a soundtrack album for a TV show which was very popular at the time, and it seemed like a worthwhile venture. What the label wanted was quite specific — the video would not feature any of the stars from the TV show or any of its footage but instead show familiar locations from the show, which was shot in the Wilmington area of North Carolina, thereby creating a kind of subconscious link to it. I had never watched the show but set to work and quickly discovered that one of the frequently used locations was a local school.

I tossed around a couple of ideas and soon had a plan mapped out. The band, whose lead singer was a spunky young lady I'd spoken to briefly on the phone from England, would be found in a classroom in the school, which fans of the show would recognise. During class, the band would cause trouble and be sent to detention — much to their chagrin, as this was also graduation day.*

The band would be pissed off, break out of detention and storm the stage outside the school where graduation was taking place. The singer would grab the mic from the furious principal and start rocking out with her bandmates, causing their fellow students to run riot and leave the school in a shambles. At the end of the video, the band would escape, pursued by the authorities, as the chorus echoed around the school grounds: "Life's a bitch and then you die!"

I typed out my idea, sent it off to the label and in due course was told to book a flight for Wilmington. The evening before my flight, as I stuffed the last T-shirt in my bag, I turned on the news. And the news was horrible.

Earlier that day, two teenage boys had dressed up in long black coats, armed themselves with guns and bags of ammo and driven to their school. They walked through the doors and embarked on a horrific killing spree, murdering 13 schoolmates and one teacher. Like most people, I'd never heard of the suburb in which they lived and their

* I understand that this chain of events is quite unlikely to happen in any American school, but nobody ever questioned the logic of it.

school was located, but by the end of the day there was not a household in America unfamiliar with it. The place was called Columbine.

Somehow the news of the carnage in Columbine had eluded me all day. But now I was concerned. I rang Catherine Finkenstaedt, my executive producer.

"I'm leaving for North Carolina in the morning to shoot a video whose storyline centres on a band of pissed-off students who break out of detention to cause havoc on graduation day. The band is called Shooter, and the chorus goes like this: 'Life's a bitch and then you die.' Do you think we have a problem?" Catherine said she'd call the label and get their input. Ten minutes later, "They think it's going to be all right. Catch the plane in the morning and call me when you get to Wilmington."

By the time I'd crossed the country, the label had changed its mind. The shoot would go ahead, but the idea would have to be changed — any storyline involving the school was out, though it would still be OK to use the idea of the band storming the stage and causing mayhem. And I would still have to use a location that featured in the TV show.

Producer Dave Robertson and I met with one of the show's location guys and spent a day driving to its familiar locations, one of which was the dockside in Southport where I'd shot the Hootie video. We agreed that the impressive house down by the water where one of the show's characters lived would make an ideal location for the video, which I now decided would take place at a formal garden party of some sort where Shooter would cause mayhem before escaping in their van. I typed up my new idea and sent it off to the label who quickly approved the new direction.

Meanwhile, things in the mid-Atlantic weren't looking brilliant. A front was developing, and it looked increasingly likely that the Wilmington coastline was in for some weather. I crossed my fingers. Meanwhile, Shooter were making their way to London's Heathrow airport, looking forward to flying to America to make a music video for their first single.

The shoot was scheduled for Friday and Saturday. On Wednesday, I was told I needed to speak with an Executive Producer of the TV show.

EP guy: So, please explain to me. What are you doing?

I told him: Shooter, school, Columbine, house party, TV show soundtrack album, brilliant, exciting, fun, youthful, edgy, etc. EP Guy interrupted me, and our conversation went something like this:

EP guy: You can't use any of MY locations and you will NOT be intercutting your music video footage with any of the footage from MY show.

Me: But that's the brief — to use one of your locations, to promote the show and the soundtrack album.

EP guy: You're not listening to me. You will not be using ANY of the show's locations in your video. I expressly forbid you to use this to sell the soundtrack album.

Me: Then why am I in Wilmington? I was told I HAD to come here and use one of your locations precisely because we couldn't use footage from the show.

EP guy: I don't care. You will not use the school, you will not use the house, you will not use the club...

He listed every location we had looked at except one — the dock in Southport where I'd shot Hootie. Producer Dave scribbled on a piece of paper and passed it over to me. "We have to file a permit within two hours or we can't shoot on Friday."

EP guy: ...in fact I'd rather you not use any location in North Carolina at all.

Me: You've not mentioned the dock at Southport. Can I shoot there?

EP guy: It's not really a location from the show.

Me: Here's my problem. I'm contractually obligated to shoot in less than 48 hours. I have a band flying in from England and a DP flying in from L.A. right now. I have to write a new story, and I have to file a permit in the next two hours. Can I use the dock in Southport?

EP guy: I'd rather you didn't.

Me: I need to get off the phone right now. The location is a 40-minute drive away, and I need to go and scout it now to see if I can rework the story and still have time to file a shooting permit.

Dave and I jumped in our car. It was grey and dark outside — the front was virtually upon us.

As we skidded to a halt on the dockside in Southport, it was starting to drizzle. A stage would be set up here, some kind of event would be taking place involving TV cameras, Shooter would crash the event, the TV cameras would roll and Shooter would escape in the beat-up van we'd already rented. It didn't make a lot of sense, but it would have to do.

I told Dave to file the permit, and he got through to the permit office five minutes before they closed for the day. While Dave did his business I did mine, pitching the latest idea to the label. They had little choice but to approve my third version of the story.

The next morning, we — me, my DP, the AD, art director, production manager, grip and gaffer — were back on the dock for the tech scout. Whenever possible, you have a tech scout before the shoot to figure out where the stage will be built, where the crew trucks will park, how the location will be lit and how the director thinks he's going to shoot it. This normally involves walking around the location looking at sun charts that predict where the sun will rise and set. People who do my job become terminally bored while everyone else decides what size the generator needs to be and how much dolly track should be ordered. This normally involves getting out of the van that has driven us to the location.

But this wasn't a normally situation. The rain was falling in bucketloads, pounding on the roof of the van. None of us ventured outside. Complex decisions, usually arrived at after tape measures have been produced and much pacing up and down has been done, were completed through fogged-up windows with much pointing at the dock, where rain was bouncing three inches off the woodwork. We retired to a restaurant for the traditional tech scout meal and drew plenty of diagrams.

The band had arrived in Wilmington, their excitement somewhat dulled by the weather. We went out to eat, to try and get to know each other. Dave and I huddled at the end of the table with the label person newly arrived from L.A. Thousands of dollars were on the line, but the rain outside continued its torrential onslaught. The forecasters promised rain, rain and yet more rain through the weekend. Tomorrow's shoot would have to be delayed. The record label would have to foot the bill.

We peered out of our hotel windows for the next three days, watching the rain fall in increasingly large buckets. Wilmington got ten inches of rain. Quite by chance, a BBC documentary crew was staying at the same hotel. While you might imagine that, under these circumstances, the music video crew and the rock band would be leading the festivities and hosting the orgies, the only orgy we indulged in was watching every film in the hotel's extensive video library while the BBC crew — one of whom had brought a trumpet — got copiously and professionally drunk, leading riotous, drunken trumpet-laden singalongs from rainswept balconies late into the night as the storm continued.

The record label was haemorrhaging money every day we spent languishing in the hotel. Hoping to find a solution, Dave and I visited every hotel on the coast, looking for one with a ballroom big enough to shoot in. None were large enough; all we found on that dark and soggy weekend were some sad-looking wedding receptions. We gave up. On the way back, we stopped at a pawn shop; he bought a guitar and I bought a mandolin. There was nothing left to do but go to our rooms, tune up our instruments and ride out the storm.

By Monday morning the storm had exhausted itself and we were back to work. The art department had built a stage on the dock in Southport, bunting and lights were hung, extras were dressed and we went joyfully about our business. Even better, the sun came out. I was in high spirits — our luck had changed.

We shot the heck out of the dock at Southport for two days as the sun continued to shine, and we wrapped on time. The band flew back to London, and I flew back to Los Angeles, where I instantly set about doing the colour transfer of the film and overseeing the cut of the footage before I sent it off to the label.

But my troubles were far from over.

The label rejected the colour transfer. They had signed off on samples they had seen but, on second thoughts, wanted it redone — and we had to pay. The news was worse when we delivered our cut: the TV show's EP guy had seen the video, decided he could do better and rejected it. We were instructed to send him the footage — he had a great idea of how to save the job, and his editing guy was going to cut it his way. In short, I was fired.

That was fine by me. I was tired of this job, its ups and downs — mostly its downs — and I wanted to move on. There was no pleasing some people, least of all the gods who had not smiled on us at all. I saw the finished cut when MTV played it for a few days. I'd been told quite clearly that my footage would never be intercut with footage from the show, and yet that's exactly what they'd done. It was a standard band–TV show–band–TV show job — bland and uninteresting and, in my opinion, did nothing for Shooter or the TV show. But the most powerful man in the equation had spoken, and that was all that mattered.

I have never heard of Shooter since. A shame — they seemed like good people, and I liked their song and its catchy chorus: "Life's a bitch and then you die."

CHAPTER 38

As Long as You Love Me

I WAS PREPARING to fly back to London to make a video for British alt-rockers Mansun when Jive Records asked me to come up with an idea for an unknown band that had five members, none of whom, so far as I could tell, played an instrument. They weren't the first boy band in the history of pop, but the Backstreet Boys would become the leaders of the next chart craze. I was told that they were backed by a very rich businessman who ran an airline and a transportation company; they were already huge in Germany but needed a video to get their career off the ground in the U.S. The song was called "All That I Have to Give," and I initially had trouble coming up with an idea. Sometimes, when inspiration doesn't strike, I try to think of the obvious idea and then turn that on its head. Having spent hours, if not days and weeks, of my life in casting sessions picking young women to appear in videos with male bands, I wondered what would happen if the tables were turned — women were the execs behind the desk and, one by one, the Backstreet Boys were the talent in the casting session and had to introduce themselves. Like they did for screen tests for old Hollywood pictures, we'd have a small blackboard chalked with the name of each

Backstreet Boy so that people seeing them for the first time would know which one was Nick, which one was Brian and so on.

I sent the treatment to Jive and got on the plane to London. The label didn't like the idea at all — I got the clear impression they hated it — so could I come up with something else? The Mansun shoot was complicated and involved a lot of flowing water on the set — toilets and baths and people upside down on the ceiling. The prep for it had not allowed me much time to focus on a new idea for the Backstreet Boys. I got back from the studio late one night, ripped some pictures from magazines, banged out an idea and went to bed relieved that I'd managed to spit something out, even if it was not very inspired. I was fairly confident it would be rejected.

They loved it.

I flew home and set about prepping that first Backstreet Boys video, which would be shot in a spacious store on La Cienega that had previously been occupied by Esprit but was now empty. The shoot went well, and a few days later, Lynda Simmons from Jive rang again. "We need another video for the Backstreet Boys to be shot next week for a song called 'As Long as You Love Me.' Do you think you could adapt that idea you first wrote for 'All That I Have to Give' and make it work for this other song?"

And that's how the idea I first had for the band, the one they rejected, the one they really hated, was suddenly pulled out of the wastebasket, reheated, given a new coat of paint and a lube job and became the second video I shot for them inside two weeks. I now had to do a casting session for the young women who would run the casting session in the video. Lynda was there to watch the whole thing come together. When the last girl had walked out, we sat down and gradually whittled the list down to a bunch of favourites. Of course, the subtext of the video would be that there were five executives and five Backstreet Boys. The video wasn't going to show whether each Backstreet Boy would get a girl to call his own in the end, but it made sense to suggest it.

I felt we'd done a good job of avoiding the obvious — the girls were all beautiful, but each had something different. Then Lynda told me she wanted there to be six girls, not five. It seemed too obvious to her that the number of women running the casting session should equal the number of guys in the band. I respected her viewpoint, so Girl Number Six was selected.

We'd chosen a disused laundry building in Pasadena. On the morning of the shoot, we'd called the women first so they could go through makeup and wardrobe before the band arrived. We were all ready to go when the band arrived and were about to enter the building through the door you see in the video. Just by chance I happened to look up as they appeared and saw Girl Number Six checking them out. When she saw Brian Littrell, she homed in on him like a laser. They're married now. (I was delighted when Blink 182 chose to take the piss out of "All That I Have to Give," as well as Britney's "Sometimes" video, which I had also shot recently, in their clip for "All the Small Things.")

It was during this two-week period that I first met Lou Pearlman, a chubby-faced, doughy man who had a big smile and didn't say much. Before the Backstreet Boys vids, I'd been flown to Florida to meet the band for the first time in his compound outside Orlando. It was a huge space with a rehearsal area and offices located round the back of an industrial park — like nothing I'd ever seen before in my years in the industry. Instead of the widgets being produced by the company in the warehouse next door, Lou's building was turning out boy bands — *NSync and C-Note were just two of them, and I would work with both.

When Sears sponsored the Backstreet Boys on a tour, I was picked at the last minute to shoot a tie-in commercial. In it, the band were being chased through New York City by screaming female fans, so another casting session took place. We needed a dozen or so key extras who would be at the front of the phalanx of fans chasing after the guys. More than a hundred young women turned up; at first glance, I was completely underwhelmed. They seemed quiet and did not display any of the energy we would need. I worried that this wasn't going to work at all.

At one point in the spot, the Boys would escape from their chasers, race up to an elevator and press the button, only to be greeted by a dozen screaming fans bursting from the elevator. We asked the first dozen ladies to step forward, indicated a line of tape on the floor and told them they should stand behind the line and pretend they were in an elevator. I told them that when I yelled "Action!" they should scream and hyperventilate just the way they might if they came face-to-face with the Backstreet Boys. I was not optimistic that this was going to work out — the women seemed so quiet and laid back.

"Action!" There was a millisecond of silence and then the first dozen went completely ballistic. Hours later, my ears were still ringing from the high-pitched shrieks. Tears were shed and young bodies shook as if overwhelmed with emotion. I yelled "Cut!" They went perfectly silent as if nothing had happened and the next dozen stepped up. On my "Action," every one of those hundred-plus young ladies transformed themselves instantly into hysterical fans with wobbling knees and dribbling tear ducts and, just as quickly, turned it off again. I was stunned — it was a whole new view of the psychology of young women that I had no previous knowledge of. I wished that I could have cast every one of them.

I shot a fourth video, "Drowning," for the group in 2001. As we wrapped, AJ McLean said to me, "Nothing's changed — you're still calling me Howie!" In the meantime, I'd also shot a video for C-Note. I loved "Wait Till I Get Home," but the song and video went nowhere.

But Big Lou was not done with me yet. One day I found myself on a call with Hulk Hogan and his wife Linda. Their daughter Brooke had made a record, and they wanted me to shoot the video. Lou's company was involved, and the video would be shot in Florida. I cooked up a treatment involving Brooke sitting in the bleachers at her school practicing with her cheerleader friends while she watched her handsome beau working out with the football team on the field. The job was awarded, flights were booked and that's when things started getting weird.

I was told that, when producer Dave Robertson and I landed in Florida, someone from Lou's company would meet us and take us to the filming location — despite the fact that we had a location scout booked. This was the first and only time in my career when a shooting location was chosen and booked for me without any prior discussion or consultation. While Dave and I both thought this not only peculiar but somewhat offensive, we decided to play along to be diplomatic. At the airport we were met by a brace of smartly dressed young men who worked for Lou's company — they could have been junior agents from a talent agency but looked frighteningly like henchmen for some kind of organisation that dabbled in the black arts. I thought one of them might have been in the C-Note video I'd shot. It turned out the location was completely workable, but it was an hour's drive from our hotel. Surely there was something closer?

I met with Brooke, Hulk and Linda, who were all very nice. Before parting, I gave Brooke the same advice I give to every artist, young or old, male or female: "No partying the night before the shoot. Get to bed early and come to set rested — it's going to be a tough day!" The day before the shoot, I was told Lou needed to talk to me in his office, a half-hour drive from where we were staying.

Another director had famously issued a manifesto some years previous that listed all the things he would and would not do during a shoot. It was pages and pages long and became the focus of much ridicule in the business. My rules, over the years, had taken up one line: there must be hot tea on set and cakes and/or biscuits — preferably British ones. Of course, that rarely happened, so I'd have coffee instead and deal with it. However, I did have one unwritten rule for myself: get a full night's sleep before the shoot. If there needed to be any meetings the night before, I would insist, whine, beg — whatever it took — that they were over before my bedtime. Surely a client would understand that hiring this Dick person and flying him cross-country to shoot your cherished artist made no sense if he showed up on set bleary-eyed, yawning and wanting a nap.

So, when Dave told me Lou wanted to meet me at his offices I insisted the meeting be over by 7:00 p.m. We could grab dinner on the drive back and I would hopefully be in bed by 8:00. For the 5:00 a.m. call the next morning, we'd have to leave the hotel at 4:00. It was a one-day shoot and we had a lot to get done. I wanted to be on my toes and fresh. We were in Florida in the middle of the summer, shooting outside, so the day ahead would be hot and very humid.

Dave spoke to Lou's people and said the meeting would be at 8:00 p.m. and kept short. As we left for Lou's office, we heard it had been delayed even later. I toyed with refusing to go at all, but Dave convinced me that it was good business to make the meeting. At 11:00 p.m. I was still sitting outside Lou's office waiting for the meeting to happen. I was furious. I hadn't eaten, and I had to be up in five hours. Finally, the door opened and our presence was requested. Lou smiled and sat in a big comfy chair in his palatial office; it seemed he just wanted to chat. A while later, some of his minions walked in and started setting up video cameras — it wasn't clear if I was going to interview Lou or he was going to interview me. It didn't matter; I was in no mood for any of it. I told him I needed to go. "You can't leave yet," he told me. "We're waiting for Brooke!"

At midnight, Brooke, Linda and Hulk arrived. Pictures were taken; video footage was shot. Not only was Brooke not getting the beauty sleep she needed, it was very clear that this whole meeting was purely an exercise to stroke Lou's ego. When the camera was pointed at me, I was asked my opinion about how great Lou's organisation was and perhaps I'd care to comment on how he was such a remarkable guiding light to so much talent. I squirmed, uttered some horrible b.s. and eventually made it clear that Brooke needed to get some sleep and I had to leave. It was after 2:00 a.m. when I got back to my hotel room. I slammed my door and tried to sleep. Ninety minutes later, the alarm rang. I showered, dressed and made my way down to the lobby to meet the other crew members. I was still delirious with anger as we pulled out of the hotel and told everyone to shut the hell up. I pulled a jacket over my head and tried to grab an extra hour on the drive, but I was still raging and didn't get a wink.

I felt awful. This was worse than jet lag. A cold chill was running down my spine, and I was shaking — partly with anger and partly with nervous exhaustion. I pulled the AD and DP — my old pal Russ Swanson — to one side and explained how I felt. The heat was already rising, and I was concerned I might faint during the morning. A PA was assigned to watch me and make sure I didn't fall over. I asked to use a room in the school at lunchtime that would be quiet so I could sleep — I didn't want food; I needed rest. I made it through the morning somehow; when lunchtime came, I lay down on the floor of the room they'd set aside for me.

After lunch, feeling marginally better, I was back on set when a line of cars arrived. Big Lou climbed out of one and his minions flitted around him. One of them made his way over to me. "Mr. Pearlman is here and would like to be in the video!"

"I'm sorry," I told him. "We're already slipping behind schedule, I'm in a foul temper after his behaviour last night, there's no part for him in the video and we still have a lot of work to do." The minion didn't care and lowered his voice. "You don't understand. Mr. Pearlman is here and is going to be in the video. I'll let him know you'll be ready to shoot him in ten minutes." He wandered off in Lou's direction.

I was stunned. I'd never been threatened on a set like that before. I ripped a couple of scenes from my shot list and told Lou to get on the field with the training footballers and look like he was taking notes. With Lou's cameo in the can his entourage left the set.

In the following months rumours started to circulate that Lou's company was in trouble. It was already public knowledge that both Backstreet Boys and *NSync had successfully sued him and were no longer part of his organisation. But what was emerging was that the trouble with Lou's company was not just disaffected artists who wanted a decent royalty rate — there were serious financial irregularities about other businesses Lou had his fingers in.

The FBI showed up at Lou's office building and carried boxes of paperwork out of the building. Lou's airline, transportation and investment businesses started crumbling into so much sand. And Lou? He was nowhere to be found.

Over the next months, as the indictments piled up and the list of irregularities in Lou's businesses grew longer, it seemed there never had been an airline or a transportation company. Lou was still MIA. Eventually a couple on holiday in Bali spotted him on the beach. They contacted the FBI, and he was arrested and brought back to the States. Lou had been operating a Ponzi scheme and frittered away millions of other people's money — mostly money invested by retirees. One estimate suggested that he'd embezzled half a billion dollars. The irony of it all was that Lou's boy bands had earned him so much money that, with a bit of work, he could have paid back all his investors and just maybe he could have avoided the attention of the Feds.

Lou was sentenced to 25 years in jail, but the judge offered to reduce the sentence by one month for every million dollars Lou repaid to the investors he'd bilked. Lou died in jail before a single penny was repaid.

At the height of his reign, Lou was surrounded by acolytes, assistants, bandmembers and hangers-on asking for selfies and autographs. When he was buried, just five people were at the graveside.

CHAPTER 39

The Crazy Life

I USED TO THINK that working in film was like the Formula 1 race car series. You turn up every weekend to race; sometimes you win and sometimes one of the other guys wins. Rivalries develop and, whether you like it or not, you find yourself heading into the first corner trying to out-brake the same guy again and again.

For me, that guy was Wayne Isham. We're very different people and we go about our work differently, but interestingly we have worked with the same artists in different phases of their careers. I've never wasted time trying to figure out who's won the most rounds in our battle of ideas, but I suspect Wayne would come out with a comfortable lead, which is OK: he does great work. To be racing for the same corner against Wayne is an honour in itself.

Consequently, I was a bit startled when, after Wayne directed the hugely successful "Livin' la Vida Loca" for Ricky Martin, I got to make his next one, "She's All I Ever Had." If we'd been in racing cars, that first corner would have been coming towards me fast; I was looking around and checking my mirrors and Wayne was nowhere to be seen. Ricky was then the hottest thing around, so it was certainly a compliment to be shooting the follow-up to the summer's biggest record.

The brief was simple and straightforward. One of Ricky's managers explained to me that they wanted to push his all-American image and that, as people seemed to think that Ricky was gay (which was later revealed to be true), we needed to shoot in L.A. and show him with a beautiful all-American blonde — preferably a famous actress or model.

I'd been around the "famous actress has to be in the video" merry-go-round before and it never worked out. The actress would ask for a big chunk of change, her agents and managers would advise against her doing it and the negotiations would take so long that the label would give up and make the video without her. In most cases that I'd seen, the only reason top-line talent would agree to be in a video was either out of friendship with the artist or because the video and song was somehow tied in with a film or show the actress was in.

Despite my misgivings, we approached all the major agencies; soon, the pictures and résumés of all their blonde leading ladies were spread out across our desks. We picked two or three favourites and negotiations got slowly under way. Knowing we needed a backup, Jeff Tannebring, producer of the video, put together a just-in-case casting session for every gorgeous blonde model in Hollywood. That was quite some casting session; more than 200 8x10s were piled on my desk at the end of the day. You might think that this a heavenly task, but in reality it's a special kind of hell: you have five minutes to put her on tape, see if she has any acting experience, is available on the day of the shoot and make a note of her height to see whether or not she will tower over her leading man. Chances are she's been to four other casting sessions already today (and late for two more) and worried about whether her car is being towed because the street outside is chock-a-block with the vehicles of the other hopefuls in the waiting room. She impatiently spits out answers to your questions; you try to discern whether she's always like this or just having a bad day. As she leaves, you're not checking out her backside — you're scribbling notes so days later you can remember your first impressions. When you get home that night your head is not spinning from all the beauty paraded in front of you, you're simply empty and weary, craving pizza and a beer and a comfy chair to lounge on.

In the middle of all this, one of Ricky's managers rang. "We've found the girl!" The previous night in a bar somewhere, someone from Ricky's team had chatted up a young lady who was apparently ideal. But this perfect young lady was shooting a commercial in a different state a few time zones away, so I was asked to audition her over the phone. In a business in which, let's be honest, looks count for a great deal and acting ability is a prerequisite, this was frankly ludicrous, but I accepted the challenge. Charlotte Ayanna was a delight to talk to, funny and open — that was certainly a plus. I checked that she was blonde. She said no, brunette. I asked about her intriguing last name, and she told me that she'd given it to herself. She had been born in Puerto Rico like Ricky, had been fostered for many years and had written a book titled *Lost in the System*. Her given name was Charlotte Lopez. That was all fascinating and indeed heart-wrenching too, but I rolled my eyes. The brief called for, nay insisted, that we cast a blonde all-American girl from the heartland, and yet I was now instructed to hire a brunette from Ricky's island hometown. Well, if that's what they wanted.

Another issue was what Ricky would wear in the video. I was told that everyone was dissatisfied with the fit of Ricky's clothes in previous videos. This time there would be no excuses — the suit that Ricky wore had to look special. L'Wren Scott, onetime model, highly regarded designer and Mick Jagger paramour, was brought on as a stylist, and a suit was chosen for Ricky. In the month before the shoot, frantic requests were delivered to Ricky's people to arrange a fitting, but Ricky was everywhere. "He's just left for New York," we were told. "He's on his way to Miami but will be in L.A. next week." Next week, "He's got interviews all day, call tomorrow." We rang the next day, "We're just getting on a plane for New York..."

A fitting for Ricky was finally scheduled the evening before the shoot. It was late, but better than never. I hadn't spoken to or seen

Ricky in the flesh, so I was looking forward to talking through the idea in advance of the shoot. A car drew up outside. "At last!" I thought. A door opened and a good-looking man walked in — but it wasn't Ricky. "I'm here for Ricky's fitting," he said.

"Nice to meet you, when does Ricky get here?"

"Oh, Ricky's not coming. I'm the same size as Ricky, so I always go to his wardrobe fittings, and if it fits me, it will fit Ricky." Was this why Ricky's clothes never seemed to fit?

The next morning, I met Ricky on set. He was gracious, charming, and I liked him instantly. My abiding memory was finding him sitting in a corner between takes reading a travel book about India. "Are you going on a holiday there?" I asked. "No. I have a small house there. When I want to get away from all this I go and stay. The locals don't know who I am. They think I'm just an American guy who likes to sit on the beach at sunset."

There were dramas on set that broke my heart but, through it all, Ricky was solid as a rock, and I have pleasant memories of working with him. He eventually came out to the world, and I didn't think less of him that I'd been involved in an attempt to prove to the world that he was straight. I've often wondered if he had any idea of the waters that swirled around him. I like to think of him reading a book and watching the sun going down on his Indian beach. I hear he has four kids now, so I guess there's not so much time for relaxing — it sounds like he's happy. That makes me smile.

CHAPTER 40

Talking Old Soldiers

IF YOU'RE A FAN of the man known to his mum as Reg Dwight, then you may be upset by what follows.

Elton John was certainly a hero of mine; by the time I started working for record labels I owned more records by him than by any other artist. I wasn't the only one with a lot of his records — it's said that at one point he sold ten percent of all the record output in the entire world. So, when I came to work with Elton occasionally over a number of years, I was saddened to find my admiration for him gradually diminishing. Not for nothing, it seemed, was his documentary called *Tantrums and Tiaras*.

One drizzly morning I answered the phone in the press office at Stiff.

"Hello, it's Elton."

I was confused. Elton and I had both studied architecture at Bath and, as I recall, he was in a different year than me. It was years since I'd left university and, as we weren't more than acquaintances, there was no reason to keep in touch. So, why was he calling me and why did he sound so friendly? I mumbled something about it being a long time since we'd seen each other and how was he doing? Had he found a job as an architect or was he out of the game?

Now it was Elton's turn to sound confused.

"I'm calling about Wreckless Eric..."

It dawned on me that the Elton I was speaking with was not a onetime architecture student but the very successful piano player. I'd made myself look like a complete idiot.

Wreckless Eric, whose career — despite the best efforts of everyone at Stiff — was still notable only for his first single, "Whole Wide World," was about to release a double album called *Big Smash!* In a desperate lunge for credibility, label boss Robbo had come up with the idea to get as many famous people as we could think of to come up with quotes about Wreckless and use those quotes in full-page ads in the music press. The list of celebrities had been long and unremarkable; the most notable names we'd come up with were Prunella Scales (the actress who played Mrs. Fawlty on *Fawlty Towers*) and Elton John.

We knew about Elton John's encyclopaedic record collection, and it was rumoured he was a big fan of Wreckless Eric. I put out some feelers and found that a friend of a friend knew someone who would try to send Elton a request. Could he supply a few kind words about Wreckless's new release? I never expected to get a response but, as I gazed over the soggy roofs of West London, I realised that Elton hadn't bothered to send a cursory note back down the chain of command — he'd simply located my number and called me directly!

I recall trying to explain to the man who had written at least two of my favourite albums why I'd mistaken him for an architecture student, but it came out all wrong. The unmistakable voice on the line suggested I get a pencil and paper together quickly as he had a quote for me and more pressing matters to see to.

Two minutes later, the quote dictated, Elton hung up. I was visibly shaken. Fiona Grimshaw, my assistant, asked if I was OK.

"Bloody hell!" I said. "I've just spoken with Elton John."

Despite the heroic efforts of Elton, Prunella and others, *Big Smash!* did not live up to its title, though I still think it was Eric's best album. But for months I was able to share with my mates the time I'd mistaken the world's most famous gap-toothed pianist for someone I vaguely knew at university.

In early 1985, after I'd directed the "Do They Know It's Christmas?" video for Band Aid, I got to meet Elton in the flesh. For some reason, Elton had not been available to be at the shoot, but now the record and video had leapt to the top of the charts he was eager to help the cause. I was tasked with taking a camera to Elton's house in Windsor and record an interview with him.

His house was, on first view, unremarkable. I remember a winding corridor, off which every room seemed to be filled with thousands of albums, all neatly shelved as in a library. Ushered into a large living room filled with furniture and garish furnishings, we quickly set up and announced that we were ready for Elton.

Elton walked in, sat in a large chair and was ready for his interview. He was articulate and gave us everything we needed in one take. I decided not to apologize for that embarrassing phone call, and we beat a hasty retreat.

Years later, he headlined the AIDS Project Los Angeles (APLA) charity show that I assembled video footage for. Bernie Taupin, Elton's longtime writing partner, who produced and organised the event and turned out to be a wonderful man to spend time with and work for, ran interference for Elton. All decisions regarding Elton would run through him.

On the night of the show, I was particularly excited because Elton and his band were debuting his latest single, "Believe." I couldn't wait to hear the live version. I was not disappointed, and it remains one of my favourites. I still don't understand how it didn't make a bigger impression on the charts.

After singing, Elton approached the centre of the stage and addressed the audience. What he had to say took my breath away. He apologized for his years in the wastelands, his enormous drug intake and his legendary tantrums. Then he admitted his prodigious sexual appetite for one-night-stands with attractive men around the world and his confusion, wonder and relief that he'd somehow managed to live through the AIDS epidemic without contracting the disease. He didn't need to be so frank to get his point across, but his honesty captured the imagination, and the house was desperately quiet as he spoke. I wasn't the only one who was deeply impressed. I left the auditorium that night with a new measure of respect for the man.

The years rolled by and I was asked to write a video treatment for "The Heart of Every Girl," sung by Elton and featured in the Julia Roberts film *Mona Lisa Smile*, which was set in the early '50s at Wellesley College. My job was to find a way to mix clips of the film with footage of Elton performing the song — and convey the impression that they were somehow all part of the same production. It was a fool's errand: you either hit the target directly or you get into trouble trying to mix a small video crew shooting 16mm on a one-day shoot with footage from a massive Hollywood production and someone higher up the food chain looks down his nose at your attempts to mimic his work and tries to rubbish it.

The movie had a scene at a dance, so my idea was to insert Elton into the dance hall and intercut movie footage using the image of a spinning girl moving across the screen as a cutting technique. And, *voilà*, I had written the winning treatment and was picked to shoot the video. But we would only have Elton for five hours, and there was no wiggle room in his schedule.

Our chosen location was the Park Plaza Hotel, which is next to MacArthur Park in Los Angeles. I'd shot Guns n' Roses' "Welcome to the Jungle" and Anastacia's "I'm Outta Love" downstairs, but we were going to use the upstairs room where I'd shot Mandy Moore's "I Wanna Be With You." We dressed the room to be a '50s dance hall with bunting and streamers. All the women were wearing beautiful ball gowns; the backing band consisted of women playing period instruments. The piano that Elton would be playing was centre stage.

In deference to the style of the set and the honour of finally getting to direct Elton, I had elected to wear a suit. Elton was due on set at 9:00 a.m., and we made absolutely sure that we'd be ready when he arrived. Lennie Appelquist, my first AD, laughed at me as I nervously paced up and down. We'd been through many battles together and knew we could pull this off. But even so, there was always a chance that something somewhere could put a spanner in the works.

Lennie's walkie chirped five minutes before Elton's call time and the voice of Bob, his second AD, crackled out of the tiny speaker. "Elton on set." Lennie and I looked at each other. "Action stations!" Lennie smiled again. "Good luck!"

We had a motorhome for Elton parked downstairs, right outside the front door. I was about to go downstairs and greet him when Bob's voice chirped again, "Elton's on his way upstairs."

Ross Richardson, the DP, climbed behind the camera; the musicians picked up their instruments; the clients from the movie studio turned off their phones and sat behind the monitors in video village; the sparks and grips assumed their positions. We were totally ready.

Elton appeared, marched across the stage wearing a fabulous tuxedo and bow tie get-up and sat at the piano. I was walking over to say hello when he said, to no one in particular, "Where's the camera?"

I jumped back beside the camera: "Over here, Elton."

"What? Fucking hell!" he yelled at no one and everyone. "They're trying to shoot my profile. Can't you see? They want to shoot my profile!" He leapt from the piano stool, ran across the stage still shouting, his fury garnished with more expletives, and was gone. I hadn't had time to welcome him and explain what I was doing. Some worried-looking people in his entourage raced across the stage after him.

The piano had been placed pointing across the stage so that the audience, the dancers and the camera would have been to his right. As the movie was set in the '50s, I had placed an old Elvis-style mic at the side of the keyboard, the way Jerry Lee Lewis used to have it. I imagined that Elton would turn his head and sing to the audience — and thus the camera — to his right. The shot would not have been a profile at all. Elton had not given me the chance to explain the setup; he'd seen the camera, sensed it was looking at his profile, had lost his marbles completely and ran.

Lennie strolled over to me laughing and held his walkie up to my ear; all I could hear was banging and shouting. Lennie chuckled, "Bob's holding his walkie up to the door of Elton's trailer — he's having a fit and rearranging the furniture!"

A Scot from Elton's team came over and asked me what had happened. I explained and said we were moving the camera so that Elton would not be shot in profile and we would be ready when he had simmered down. It was a less interesting setup, but I'd already lost 30 minutes of my precious five-hour allotment; art sometimes has to be sacrificed to get the day in the can. Meanwhile, walkies were crackling — Elton was on his way back upstairs.

As Elton settled at the piano, I went over, introduced myself and apologized for the cock-up regarding the profile. Elton gave me half a smile and said, "Let's shoot!"

After the first setup was complete, I did something I've never done before or since. I handed my storyboard to Lennie and the DP and told them to carry on and make sure we got everything on my boards. On this day, my one job was to keep Elton happy and on the set. As the camera was moved for the next shot, I told Elton about my love for *Tumbleweed Connection* and how I'd learned to play piano simply so I could perform "Talking Old Soldiers." Over the next few hours, between takes, he played every track on the album and we sang along together. We discussed his recent work for Disney and how, at any point in time, there were at least three of his productions being performed somewhere in the world. We even got to talk about Wreckless Eric. I mentioned that while I was at Stiff I'd heard a rumour that the bosses wanted to sign Loudon Wainwright III, who I knew Elton admired. He confessed to having had a huge crush on Loudon, and the conversation moved on to recent albums by Loudon's son Rufus. Elton asked me if I'd heard Rufus's most recent album, and I said I had not. "You have to give it a listen."

While the cameras were moved again, Elton took a break and I went to check in with the clients at video village — an impressive collection of suits and executive producers from the film studio there to make sure things were going according to plan. Was everything OK for them? Yes, they were very happy. Would they like to be introduced to Elton? They all went white. Elton's early-morning tantrum had left a deep impression. No thanks! "Whatever it is that you're doing," they told me, "keep doing it!"

Elton was back on set. We had exhausted *Tumbleweed Connection* and *Madman Across the Water*, skipped past *Don't Shoot Me I'm Only the Piano Player* and were now running through my favourites from *Goodbye Yellow Brick Road* when a breathless member of Elton's entourage rushed onstage and handed Elton a yellow Tower Records bag. Elton handed it to me. "The new Rufus Wainwright album. I think you'll like it." Lennie yelled that we were ready for the next shot, and the day's work continued.

Soon Elton's shots were complete. We'd managed to get everything done with 30 minutes to spare. We shook hands, and he was gone. Word from video village was that the studio people were happy, but they wanted to know what Elton and I had been talking about for the last four hours. "All I can tell you is that I'm glad he wasn't here for longer. If we'd gone deeper into his catalogue and I'd had to talk intelligently about *Rock of the Westies* we would have been fucked." No one got the joke.

The video was a mild success, but the movie's producer was not impressed by my cut and insisted on a satellite link-up between L.A. and New York so that all the movie shots could be rearranged. As predicted, she was disappointed in the disparity between the gorgeous movie footage and the scenes we'd shot with Elton. Personally, I think she was wrong. When I look at the video now, I think we did a great job of matching the look.

This was not the end for me and Elton. In 2006, I was commissioned to shoot a commercial for a duets album recorded by the legendary

Tony Bennett to coincide with his eightieth birthday. Retail giant Target was doing a push for the record, which featured Mr. Bennett singing with Stevie Wonder, k.d. lang, John Legend, Michael Bublé, Diana Krall, Tim McGraw and, yes, Elton John. A TV special was being shot in the Los Angeles Theatre and, as each performer finished his or her piece with Tony, we would get ten minutes to shoot them singing "Happy Birthday" for him against a green screen. With the addition of red balloons, glitter and presents wrapped in ribbon, the footage would be assembled so that it appeared Tony and his guests were all gathered together in one moving dolly shot which ended with a birthday cake. Working with the ad agency, we chose a key and a tempo and set up in a small space in the bowels of the theatre as the line of stars rolled in upstairs and then down to us. Stevie was indeed wonderful and had a harmonica with him, so when I asked if he could play that as well as sing, he obliged. Diana Krall asked me if I'd worked with Elvis Costello, her husband, during my days at Stiff. k.d. lang told me that her mother was friends with the mother of the Nickelback brothers, Chad and Mike. And then it was time for Elton.

Once again, the walkies crackled, "Elton is on his way." I went to meet him and held out my hand. "Hi, Elton. Nice to see you again, Remember me? I'm the guy who directed you for the 'Heart of Every Girl' video." He harrumphed and pushed past me into the room, surrounded by his entourage. He was wearing another beautiful tux and trousers combination with a brightly coloured shirt. We'd decided that Elton should sit to sing his part and I directed him to a chair. As he sat down, his untucked shirt tails fell between his open legs. It was not flattering and looked ridiculous. "Er ... Elton, can we do something about your shirt?"

I'd lit the blue touch paper again and Elton exploded. "What's fucking wrong with my shirt? This is ridiculous. Who's this for anyway?"

"Target."

"Target? TARGET? Who gives a fuck about Target? Why am I doing something for Target?"

The entourage looked at each other, desperate for someone to take the blame. I'd had enough and stepped into the breach.

"Elton, don't give Target a hard time. I asked you to do this, don't blame them. I'm trying to make sure you look great. If you're going to blame anyone, blame me."

This was Elton's cue to stand up and drop his pants!

He stood there in front of the entire crew with his pants around his ankles, his hands on his hips and his hairy legs on full display. A wardrobe person rushed in with safety pins and started fumbling with the shirt tails that were now dangling precariously in front of his crotch. I sighed and poked my head around the black drape that separated the agency folk from Elton, who was barely ten feet away. "Would you chaps like to say hello to Elton?" A row of white faces all waved their hands in the universal sign language that said NO, NO, NO!

The shirt was fixed, I was happy, Elton sang and ten minutes later was on his way.

I've read and heard many times that Elton has a good heart, is incredibly generous and is a good friend. I've thought about that assessment given my own experience.

When we were making that video and he sent an assistant out to get me the Rufus Wainwright album, it had been barely half an hour since the subject had come up. In those 30 minutes, Elton's aide had dashed to Tower Records, bought the album and brought it back. Elton grabbed it from him and pushed it into my hands with a perfunctory, "Here, this is for you!" The manner with which Elton presented me this small gift was not terribly gracious, but I think now I understand better where he was coming from. Like me, he had a dad in the Air Force who was often away; I think he had enormous trouble connecting with people. Thrusting the package at me, rather than presenting it with grace, was so much easier and less embarrassing for him. His difficult childhood and upbringing, that stupid British pretence of not showing emotion, the implied insecurity of walking on set and throwing a tantrum, were all things I had experienced myself.

In that moment, I understood him. I wish now I'd had the balls to give him a hug.

Elton, if you should ever read this, I don't apologize for portraying you honestly ... but I'm so grateful that you played *Tumbleweed Connection* for me in its entirety and let me sing along with you on every song. And telling me about your experiences with Gus Dudgeon and Paul Buckmaster. That album has given me so much pleasure over the years and that morning at the piano was certainly a memory of a lifetime.

Thank you.

CHAPTER 41

Show Up

WHENEVER I GIVE A LECTURE, I'm often asked the same question. "What's the best advice you can give to someone starting in the film business?" My reply is always the same, "Show up." They think I'm joking, but I'm deadly serious. That's my answer. Show up.

I was sick with the flu — so sick that I'd taken the afternoon off and done something I never do — I went to bed. The phone rang as I was drifting off, but I ignored it and heard the message go to voice mail. I tried to go back to sleep but two competing voices bounced around inside my head.

"What if it's the Stones and they're about to go on tour and they need a video?"

"I'm sick. Leave me alone."

"It could be important."

"Bugger off!"

"This could be a career-changing moment. You never know."

"Oh, all right then."

I got out of bed, shuffled to my office and replayed the message. It wasn't the Stones. But a newish band were in town, playing their first hit on a late show at CBS on Beverly Boulevard. Could I meet them at 5:00 p.m. to talk about doing a video? I rang the office.

"I'm sick, can't you tell?"

"It'll only take half an hour."

"I feel like shit. Can't we do it over the phone or something?"

"Well ... if you don't want to do it..."

"I'll see how I feel in half an hour."

That bed looked so inviting and my throat felt like a section of desert road, but I turned on the shower and vibed myself up for a meeting. At CBS, I was ushered into a meeting room and made a big fuss about positioning a large box of Kleenex in front of me and trying to clear my throat.

Which is when Nickelback walked in.

I listened to the band tell me what they had in mind, staggered home, wrote up a treatment, ate soup and went to bed. Since then, I have done 18 jobs for Nickelback.

Perhaps it wasn't a career-changing moment, but it was certainly a life-changing one, and I've never heard a single word of criticism from my accountant. Yes, the moral of this story is: show up!

I'm often asked, "Why Nickelback?" and the easy answer is why not? But there are other truths here. I got into this business because I was a fan. Sometimes I have had to work with music I might not play at home, and that's OK. I can throw myself deeper into the project to make up for the lack of familiarity with the music, and the work improves. Distance from the music gives me the opportunity to be more analytical about whether this idea is right for the artist and what I can do to make this the best work it can be. The older I get, the more I realise that it is impossible to know everything about every new record that is released. As a young man I could tell you the name of every drummer and guitar player in every band on the planet; I could tell you who produced every record I had in my collection and who wrote every song. I wanted to be like Elton John and buy every record that was released every Friday: pop, glam, disco, metal, punk, prog or whatever. I now know that no new music will affect me or move me like Free's "Be My Friend" did when I was a teenager, quite simply because I'm not a teenager anymore.

The thing I love about my job now is the people. Whenever I see Nickelback, Mike Kroeger always makes a point of saying how happy he is to see me, and I make a point of telling him it is great to see him, too. It's nice to be working for them, but it's also wonderful to spend time with the band. They are good people. They are funny and decent. They have surrounded themselves with good people who have worked with them for many years. They are a family and, when you spend time with a strong family, you walk away with a glow. I can't recall the track listing of every Nickelback album, but I would walk through fire for them, and I take any work I do for them very seriously. My passion for music has ultimately been replaced by my passion for people, good people. My intense love of music as a young man was really a substitute for decent human connections with people I understood and liked in my real life. Perhaps "Be My Friend" wasn't the greatest song in the world, but its message was at the core of my yearning. My love for music hasn't waned, and my passion for spending time around good people will never leave me.

That first Nickelback video was for a song called "Too Bad." Chad and Mike told me that the song loosely reflected their own lives: their father had left the family, and the boys had grown up with their mom, though some kind of reunion had taken place years later. The treatment was detailed and took some time to write; I was very happy when the job was awarded and the finished video played extensively.

I later received an e-mail from someone in New York. She told me she'd come home from work and found her partner sitting alone in front of MTV with tears rolling down his face. When he recovered, he told her that the "Too Bad" video had struck a chord, as practically every scene in the clip mirrored a scene from his own life. His openness about this period in his life had brought them closer, and she

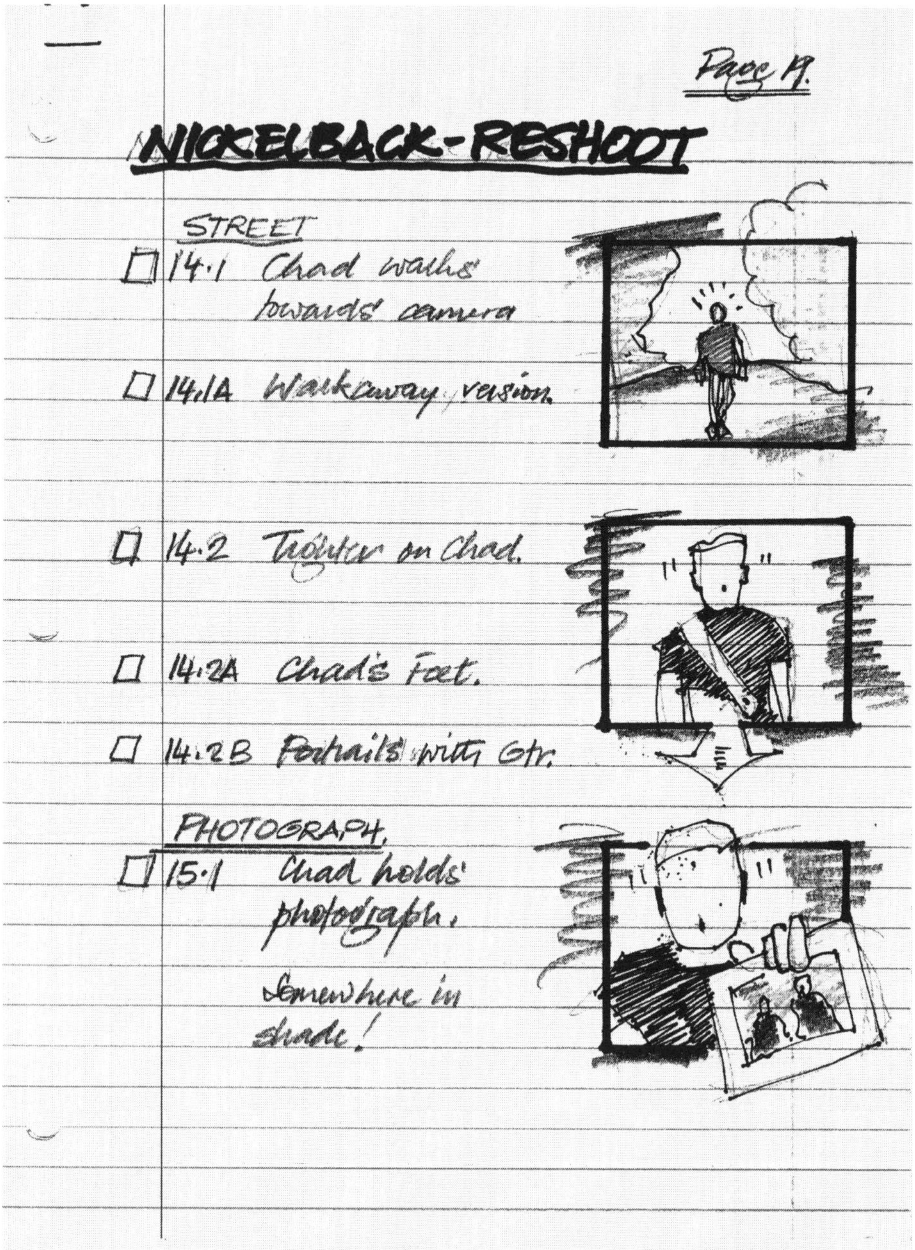

The first 18 pages of Nickelback's boards for "Photograph" covered the shoot in Canada. This page was part of the reshoot in California just for Chad and includes frame 15.1 that turned into a meme on the web of Chad holding the photograph.

wanted to reach out to give her thanks. I'm so grateful she shared her story. It was another useful reminder that videos can resonate deeply with viewers; as makers, we don't always know the far-reaching effects of our work.

I did a multi-camera concert video for Nickelback in Edmonton, *Live at Home*, followed by two other videos. Then they needed an idea for "Photograph." By this point, we had a routine: I'd submit an idea, they'd reject it, then we'd get on the phone a couple of times until an idea they liked was hashed out. This process was time-consuming but ultimately enjoyable. For "Photograph," they all liked my initial idea; it only required a little polishing. The plan was to shoot in Hanna, Alberta, the band's hometown.

Hanna is a two-hour drive from Calgary. The countryside gets flatter and flatter; when you finally peel off the main road and drive into town it feels like miles from anywhere. I won't repeat what Chad shared with me about the mischief he got up to in that town, but I got the impression the local police were relieved when the brothers Kroeger finally drove out of town to seek fortune and fame. The irony of this situation was capped by the huge road sign at the edge of town: "Hanna welcomes you. Proud to be the home of Nickelback."

We shot the band's performance in the local high school as indicated by the lyric, "This is where I went to school..." Chad had been expelled from the school, and the lyric acknowledges the reason why: "criminal record says I broke in twice." Between takes I noticed Chad having his photograph taken with a shorter, older gentleman who had a huge smile on his face. Chad was smiling and laughing, too, as he hugged the man. "Remember, I told you I was expelled from school? This is the principal!" Old sins had apparently been forgotten; everyone was happy to have the band home, albeit briefly. Whether it was the music, the weather, the scenery, the local people we cast or all of those elements together, the video really recaptures the nostalgic sense of carefree teen years growing up in a small town. In the end, the footage of Chad outside his house needed to be reshot in California, but no one has ever commented or complained about the hills that appear in

Chad's section, which are quite unlike the scenery in Hanna. (In case you're wondering, the kissing couple are still together. The last I heard they had kids.)

After shooting "Far Away" — a firefighting story shot in pouring rain — I had to pitch idea after idea for the final video from *All the Right Reasons* — a wonderful song called "Savin' Me." Guitarist Ryan Peake's wife Treana suggested an idea in which our hero, a young man, is about to step in front of a bus when a stranger pulls him back. The stranger had seen a rapidly descending series of numbers, invisible to other passers-by, over our hero's head. Now that our hero has been rescued, that magical vision has been transferred to him, and he sees numbers descending over the heads of every person on the street; we soon realise it's the amount of time they have left to live. Our hero then sees a young woman about to unlock and climb into her car; the numbers above her head suddenly descend precipitously, indicating that her death is imminent. The hero pulls her away as a huge statue dangling from a crane falls and crushes the car. Our hero can now walk away and get along with his life as it is now the young woman who can see numbers over everyone's heads.

The band's videos were becoming ever more complex and costly to make; their label was beginning to make noise about the spiralling costs, and I was under pressure to minimize the budgets. The concept for "Savin' Me" was simplicity itself in terms of locations — it could all be shot outside on the street — but it did call for lots of work in post (those descending numbers) and that stunt involving the falling statue and the wrecked car. The label asked why we needed two days. I had to explain about shooting in Vancouver in January: there isn't enough daylight for an exposure till 9:00 a.m. and it's effectively dark again by 4:00 p.m. We had barely seven hours of usable light every day.

I've always been very happy with the way "Savin' Me" turned out, and I was particularly pleased when a commercial producer rang me up and asked how we'd created the numbers over people's heads. They admired the video and were stealing the idea for a commercial they were making. I gladly gave the producer the number for my pal and onetime bandmate Mark Leiss, whose company had created the rolling numbers. But then they hired someone else to direct. Every time this happens, I can't help but feel annoyed — this thing you made turned out so great that we want to find out how you did it but, just so you know, we're going to use someone else to do it for us. Ah, showbiz!

No matter how hard we tried, budgets for Nickelback videos kept rising. For the "Far Away," video the band wanted a helicopter to land in the middle of the film. I agreed that was a great gag, but an hour's worth of helicopter time was roughly ten grand, an expense the label approved. Then Chad asked if there would be a second helicopter shooting the first helicopter. I had to be a complete party-pooper and tell him not to waste the money. Chad and the band always wanted to make the work better and more exciting; I once said an idea they had was perhaps over the top. Chad's response made me laugh and also think hard about what I did for a living, "It's supposed to be over the top — it's a music video!"

When you work regularly you have two choices — either spend as much of your client's money as humanly possible and get all the gadgets and explosions and flashing lights that you can, or you can spend your client's money wisely. After many years doing this, I think you have to find a reasonable middle ground, if such a thing exists. If your client wants five helicopters you can say yes and get a result that everybody's talking about, but you run a real risk of getting a reputation as a spendthrift. On the other hand, you can persuade everyone to be sensible and run the risk of having unremarkable work that lacks that *Apocalypse Now* moment.

That juggling act came to a head on the video we did for "I'd Come for You." We developed an idea where a father watches his daughter go on a date and then has to come to her rescue when the boy becomes too aggressive. The plan was to intercut the story with a performance by the band on a large stage. The band insisted the stage look massive, with a huge lighting rig. We budgeted out the job, and the label balked at the cost. We had to pull more than $100,000 out of the budget. The story section only involved three people, a small house, a baseball field at night and two aging vehicles so, even if we dropped that entire part of the video, we wouldn't save enough money. The only solution was to drastically cut the stage lighting. I told the label rep I would make it work but insisted that he get the band's approval to slash the budget before I flew up to Vancouver for the shoot. I was assured he would.

The reduced rig was built, the lights were focused in the enormous shed we'd chosen, and we waited for the band to show up. Chad stepped out of the van, took one look at the stage and his face dropped. "What the fuck is this?" It became immediately obvious that no one had told the band that a large chunk of change had been sliced from the budget and the impressive lighting rig they were expecting had been drastically reduced. Everyone turned in my direction — why had I let them down? I was now the fall guy, and the band were upset as I knew they would be if they hadn't been warned about the budget cut. The label rep had conveniently disappeared, and I was dragged into the band's motorhome to discuss a solution.

The discussion that ensued was sober, open and honest. One reason for making a video of this sort is to show your potential concert audience how awe-inspiring your stage set is. There comes a point in a band's career where a video isn't just a commercial for a new release but also a preview of what it will be doing onstage for the next year. Chad was very articulate and vocal about the ambition he felt the band needed to display at this stage of their career. "Don't we want to be competing with Coldplay, U2, the Stones?" He was right. You might argue that this discussion was really just about dick size (pun not intended), but it was more refined than that — it was about perception, stature and ambition. The band were furious that compromises had been made behind their back, and I repeated again and again that I'd been promised they would be informed in advance. The band decided to spend the money. A call was made, more lights were ordered, and the entire shoot was delayed for six hours.

I've always been impressed by Nickelback's professional behaviour, by the way they want to make things better, their no-b.s. attitude and their down-to-earth view of things. They've been hugely successful, and that evening I knew why. Certainly, the band has its detractors, but many bands I've worked with could learn a whole lot from them.

I decided to watch the video again and scan the comments on YouTube. As a director, you can waste a lot of time looking for any comment about the video you've made. Normally, the only reward you can expect is the number of views the video has had, which is fair enough because all you've been doing is making a commercial for the song. But tonight I was struck by how many of the comments were about families, dads and daughters and about romantic situations which had gone sour and the effects that those moments had had on the victims. As a maker of music videos, this is enormously rewarding — the viewers are not worrying about the craft, they are responding to the message. This is what I do for a living and I've been richly rewarded, but when you hear that you've moved someone emotionally, I can't tell you how powerful that is. When you get up at four in the morning to go to set, mostly what you're worried about is shooting great footage and finishing on time and on budget if you possibly can. If you try to create something that will resonate years later, you will almost certainly miss the target or overplay your hand. But then, if you hear that you've made one teardrop fall, or made one person chuckle, or brought music into someone's life and saved them, like music saved me, that is very powerful. It makes every missed flight, every rejected treatment and every shitty hotel room worthwhile.

"If Today Was Your Last Day" turned out to be another large production. There were three separate story lines that start out looking very menacing — two young men in dark clothing and hoodies in Philadelphia who look like terrorists, three twentysomethings in a pickup truck headed for a post-9/11 New York City and a man with a large black bag who walks into a bank in Miami and slips a note across the counter. It seems that none of these stories will have a happy ending, but the guys in Philly pour out hundreds of pieces of coloured paper over a busy pedestrian area that inspire people to change their lives.

The team in New York hands out free jackets in Times Square with uplifting slogans inspired by the lyrics printed on the back. The man in Miami is not a bank robber but a man who cashes out his bank account and then walks around town handing out $20 bills to people who need it. It was a massive production made even larger when the band decided it be shot not in a disused factory in Philadelphia as planned but in the Qwest Center in Omaha, Nebraska. Producer Lewis Weinstein and I had to fly around the country for more than two weeks scouting locations and casting actors, then retracing our steps to go and shoot the scenes. I can't remember making another video which required so much flying and so many hotel rooms.

More recently, I was asked to shoot two videos from the *No Fixed Address* album back-to-back. "Get 'Em Up," which details a bank robbery, and "Satellite" are quite different in tone, but we decided to make them two parts of the same story — the first being the build-up to the bank robbery and the second being the aftermath, when everything goes wrong. The band wouldn't appear in either of them and the combined budget was a fraction of any other video I had made for Nickelback. I was eager to show that we could pull it off, and it proved to be great fun.

One of the locations we needed was a bank. My producer for this job, Paul Bock, had a bank in mind in Los Angeles where we could shoot, but it fell through three days before the shoot; with time running out and permits to file, we had to find a location fast. A working bank was out of the question, and the small budget meant we couldn't create one, so we needed a location that we could just walk into, add some extras and shoot. Paul knew the perfect location, but it was in Taft, an oil town 120 miles from L.A. I was in location hell. With the clock ticking, I decided to roll the dice. We got in the car and headed north, driving as fast as we dared while trying in vain to get hold of the property owner. We still hadn't reached the owner by the time we arrived and had less than half an hour left to file a permit.

Paul and I climbed back in the car. Driving down Main Street, I saw a deserted store with a FOR LEASE sign posted in the window.

Would that work? We looked in the window. The store had been empty for some time — old papers lay on the floor; a partition wall was partially collapsed. I revised my aversion to trying to create a bank out of nothing and figured we could cheaply create one in that space. Paul rang the number on the For Lease sign. Within ten minutes, the owner had arrived and we were inside making plans to shoot there. We needed to do a tech scout with the art department and the DP the next day. Would the owner be able to meet us the next morning to let us in? "I can't make it," he told us. "Here's the key. Do what you need to do and let me have the key back after the shoot!" It wasn't the location I had in mind, but it would suit us just fine and the main street was perfect for the rest of the story. We were back in business and able to file our permit with minutes to spare.

So much of my filmmaking career has hung on moments like these, where perspiration is as much a part of the job as inspiration. It's extraordinary that this store owner put his trust in us and walked off, leaving us the key to his property barely ten minutes after we'd first met him. "Get 'Em Up" is one of my favourite Nickelback videos and was such fun to make. As I often do, I inserted a piece of my own life story into the video. I had one of the robbers ride a Honda 125, the bike I'd ridden to work when I'd been a cab driver so many years ago.

Working with Nickelback has been the most productive relationship I've ever had with an artist. I frequently wonder what would have happened if I'd decided not to pull myself out of bed that afternoon and go meet them. In case the moral of this story still hasn't sunk in...

Show up.

CHAPTER 42

Backword

WHILE I'VE HEARD TALES of directors and their rock and roll pals going on holiday and spending hours rampaging through the clubs together, that never happened to me.

So, if I spent so little time with them, what has given me the right to write about them in such detail? I spent many years going to a shrink who told me, "People tell you who they are within ten minutes of meeting them." I believe he's right. Of course, it can take months or years to really find out what makes a person tick, but you can learn a huge amount about them by just listening or observing during that short time you spend with them. The five-hour window I had with Rod Stewart — to shoot his entire album — was shortened considerably because he arrived on set with one of his toy trains: it was damaged and he urgently requested a PA be sent forth to find a replacement part for the injured engine.

As I sat and drank coffee with Jessica Simpson five minutes after we'd first shaken hands, I asked what she wanted to achieve with her video — she told me she wanted to out-Britney Britney.

That incredibly difficult day with Yes told me everything I needed to know about the tensions inside the band and the crew. When I shot a video for Tesla, Frank, the guitar player, held out his hand and told me, “There’s one in every band, and I’m that guy.” Ronnie James Dio gave me a variation on that theme as we met to make a Black Sabbath video: “I think you’ll find I’m a very easy guy to work with.” He wasn’t.

So, if none of these episodes offers an in-depth view of these incredible people I got to meet, every interaction told me something about who they were and what they were going through.

On the day I spent shooting Paul and Linda McCartney, Linda went off to go through hair and makeup. Paul turned to me and said with a smile, “The only time we’ve been apart since the day we met was when I was busted for drugs in Japan and I had to spend three days in jail!”

That was all I needed to know.

Glossary

Film terms and a beginner's guide to jobs on set

AC The First Assistant Camera (First AC) is in charge of mounting the camera magazine and lenses on the camera as well as checking or "pulling" focus (one of the hardest jobs in the business). When shooting film, the 2nd Assistant would load film into the mags and operate the slate; on a larger production, he/she would be known as the Clapper/Loader. On larger productions and movies there may be more many more assistants in the camera department. AC's fall into two types: those who want to become DP's and those who love their craft and intend to stay at the side of the camera forever.

AD The First Assistant Director (First AD, or just First) organizes the shooting schedule with the producer and director and runs the set during filming. On anything but a tiny shoot the First will have a 2nd AD, or Second, who will bring the talent to set and herd the extras/background as required.

ART The Art Director is responsible for the set decoration and props. On movies and larger productions, the Art Director will be likely called a Production Designer and have separate department people who just handle set decoration (Set Decorator) and others who handle props (Property Master). On music videos we'd just call this whole team the art department and they would handle all of it. They'd often be the first on set and the last to leave. It was not uncommon to see the "Art Dogs" fast asleep on the floor in a dark corner of the set as they'd been up all night building and painting the set.

BACKGROUND Also known as extras, they fill out a scene and walk through in the background and foreground. Once I'd been working in Hollywood for a while, I started noticing extras I'd worked with in other productions and on the big screen. One actor I worked with told me his dad worked as an extra in Hollywood's golden age his whole life and was the man who takes Gene Kelly's umbrella at the end of "Singin' in the Rain"!

CASTING The Casting Director is responsible for providing a shortlist of on-set talent for a casting session, whether it is the love interest of your key artist or other onscreen talent. They often have a history of working in theatre or film as actors themselves. Ideally they have a good relationship with a number of agents and actors and will weed out the chaff for you and provide you with a number of good choices for every role, who you then meet in a casting session.

CATERING Catering (not to be confused with Craft Service — see below) will arrive approximately five hours into the shoot and set up in an area away from filming and have heated trays full of choices of food laid out ready for the crew to eat when the crew breaks for lunch. Depending on the job or the catering company they might operate out of a catering truck. If the job requires it, the catering truck might also handle Craft Service. On a tiny job you'll go to McDonald's!

COLOUR TRANSFER A costly process in which film is fed into a sophisticated telecine machine to make the image warmer or cooler, lighter or darker, more or less contrasty, etc.

CRAFT SERVICE Craft service, also known as "Crafty," has a most important job: making sure the Craft Service table is filled with a constant supply of water, hot coffee, nibbles, fruit, etc. for the crew to snack on during the day's work. If working at night or in colder climes, the Crafty who walks on set eight hours into the shoot with a tray of cups of hot soup is the most welcome sight imaginable.

CYC or Cyclorama is a backdrop used in photographers' studios and on film sets. Walls and floors are painted white; there is a curved section where the back wall joins the floor so that light does not form a shadow.

DAILIES The term dailies (or rushes) describes every bit of footage you have shot on your recent project before any editing or colour work has been done. When you're making a movie, you try and watch yesterday's dailies after today's shoot so you can see what you've missed, what's working and what isn't and how good your focus puller is! On a video you'll probably watch the dailies after you've finished shooting.

DIRECTOR The Director is the person in charge and creates, describes and approves everything that winds up in the camera from the story, action, design and energy to makeup and wardrobe. If the director doesn't know what he/she is doing, no-one else can do their job properly.

DOCO That would be my abbreviation for a documentary film. My guess is that serious doco-makers are squirming in their seats if they're reading this!

DP The Director of Photography is responsible for lighting the set, choosing lenses, suggesting camera moves, etc. Apart from onscreen talent, the DP (also known in the UK as the Lighting Cameraman) is the person the Director works most closely with on set, as the DP's work defines the finished look of the film being made.

DT The Digital Technician is probably the most recent job on set now that most filmwork is shot digitally and not on film; the DT is responsible for downloading the digital footage at the end of a day's shoot and making sure it is accurately logged and duplicated before the camera cards are wiped. The DT's job has replaced some of the work done by AC's in the camera department.

GAFFER The Gaffer is the head of the electrical department, responsible for adjusting the lights on set. The Gaffer and his crew (known in the U.S. as the Electrical Department and in the UK as the Sparks) works closely with the DP to get the correct exposure on set and, especially if working with film, carries a light meter to ensure the film is correctly exposed.

GAG As well as being something that a comic works on, I use it as shorthand for describing what we're planning to do. For example: The gag in Britney's video is that she's a schoolgirl dancing with a bunch of cute boys.

GRIP The Grips are responsible for moving the camera, rigging, setting up and moving large scrims and reflectors, etc. The senior Grip is the Key Grip; the one who pushes the dolly is the Dolly Grip. Confusingly in the UK, Grips only move the camera; all work requiring scrims, etc. is taken care of by the Gaffer and his electrical department. Also in the UK, any hanging of lights from on high is taken care of by Riggers.

HAIR & MAKE-UP Hair and Make-Up (also known as "The Vanities") is pretty self-explanatory. On a small video production one person might take care of both jobs. Ideally, on a larger job, especially one with a female artist, you would have at least one, if not more, of each. Your Vanities team will probably spend up to three hours with a female artist in the morning before they come on set, so it's important they have a good demeanour, too. If there's a bad atmosphere in the makeup trailer you'll notice it when your artist walks on set!

LINE-CUT If you're in a truck directing a live concert with a wall of video monitors — each one showing you the feed from a different camera — you might have an editor at your side cutting the show together as you go. This means that after the show is finished you already have an edit of the show to watch. This is the line-cut. Even though the editor in the truck is probably very good, you'll now want to tweak that cut and make sure the guitar player is onscreen during his big solo and not the bass player! (N.B. My understanding of this term may be different from what "real" filmmakers think it means.)

LOCATION SCOUT The Location Scout (a.k.a. Locations) will scour the locale for the required places that are mentioned in the script/treatment for the job. The scout will return with pictures which will then be shared with the director who will select his/her favourite options. Then the director and producer will go and visit the locations and make their choices, leaving the Scout to secure permits, etc. Finally a Tech-scout will take place a day or two before the shoot with the Director, Producer, Production Manager, 1st AD, Transpo, Grip and Gaffer to plan where the camera will be, the trucks will be parked, lights will be staged, talent will be housed, etc.

MAG TRACK This term is now out of date but means Magnetic Track. When I started out, the record label would supply a quarter-inch tape of the song (the mag track), which would be played back through a hugely expensive and rather wonderful Swiss tape machine made by Nagra. The artist would then mime to the mag track. Nowadays playback is probably through a laptop or phone.

MOHO Short for motor home. The Moho would probably be quite large and have an area at one end for production with a printer and internet connection while at the other end there would be a space for Hair & Make-up to do their work.

OPERATOR A cameraman who operates the camera. On a music video this job will usually be taken care of by the DP.

PA A Production Assistant (also known as Runners in the UK) will have any one of a number of jobs on the day of a shoot — from collecting talent from their hotel to keeping the public out of a shot to shielding talent with an umbrella to keep them out of the rain or sun. If you're good in this entry level position, you will quickly find yourself moving up into production, camera department or somewhere else in the crew.

POST-PRODUCTION This varies on size from job to job. The Editor cuts the film together; the Colorist works on the colour and contrast of every shot in the finished film. Where required, Special Effects will work on various aspects of altering work. Nowadays, post-production may be one person with a laptop or dozens of people spread around the world working like slaves to deliver the final images. Post-production is often the team that delivers the final look of the film.

PRODUCER The Producer deals with the client, communicates with the director and oversees the budget. The producer is the first person hired after the director (if they're not already a team) and hires everyone else on set.

PRODUCTION MANAGER The Production Manager works under the producer and makes the calls, handles the paperwork and call sheets and is possibly the hardest working person behind the camera.

SOUND Ninety percent of music videos have no audio apart from the music which is supplied by the label in advance of the shoot, so the Sound Department is usually one person who sets up a powerful playback system so the artist can mime to the pre-recorded track. The Sound Department will also run the "Smart Slate," which has a rolling timecode to make synching up the footage with the master audio in post easy. The Smart Slate will be handed to the Camera Department at the start of the shoot. If there's a moment that requires recorded audio on set, the Sound Department may consist of two people, one of whom will operate the boom mic.

STORYBOARD ARTIST Before production begins, the Storyboard Artist draws pictures and sketches which show everyone from the client to the DP what each shot is supposed to look like. For most of my career I have also been my own storyboard artist.

STUNTS Stunts are overseen by a Stunt Coordinator, who hires Stunt people as required who are experienced in car work, motorcycles, falls, fights, etc.

TALENT The Talent is the singer, the band, the artist or anyone else in front of the camera.

TRANSPO Properly known as the Transportation Department. On a big job, Transpo will be responsible for any picture cars (vehicles used in shot), parking arrangements and shuttling artists and clients to set from hotels. Unless a music video has a big budget there's not usually a Transpo team.

VIDEO ASSIST On the modern-day set, the client, director and producer will have a screen which is fed directly from the camera so that you can see in real time what the camera is shooting. The Video Assist person will also be able to play back previous takes as required. While the director often has his or her own monitor, the clients and producer have their own screen and an area which is known as Video Village.

VIDEO VILLAGE see VIDEO ASSIST

WARDROBE Also part of "The Vanities," the wardrobe department takes care of all clothes and costumes worn on set in front of camera. In some cases the Wardrobe team will shop for days and have a huge collection of clothes available for the artist to choose from. In other cases where the artist has arrived in their own clothes the wardrobe department will simply appear on set before every take with a lint brush and make sure the artist(s) look(s) smart!

Acknowledgements

My thanks to editor Ira Robbins, who sagely navigated me through cutting out the flab ... or what people in Hollywood call "killing your children!"

Many thanks to Dan Beck for the recommendation to Ira — you need to read his memoir *"You've Got Michael"* — also on Trouser Press Books.

Special thanks to my long-time Stiff All-Star pal Andy Murray and onetime cycling buddy John Tomko for reading an early version of the book from end to end (at least once) and offering advice (John) and important corrections (Andy).

Forever thanks to Paul Conroy and Alan Cowderoy, who hired me for that first showbiz job at Stiff and to Cynthia Lole who took the call that day.

I have been blessed with an extraordinary collection of friends who have stuck with me through the years. I would love to mention you all by name but must limit specific mentions to my mostly Norfolk crew, without whom I might never have made it this far: Ed Howard, Eddie (Miles) & Sheila Firth, Patrick & Tish Peal, John &

Elly Peal, Nick & Tricia Timms ... you were all the sisters and brothers I never had.

And finally, all my love to Kastle, who has patiently and lovingly dealt with my crazy lifestyle and who would only go on a date with me if I could correctly answer a Clash trivia question. I'm so glad I aced that gig!

Before the first shot of any video I would shake hands with the band and say, "See you on MTV!" That doesn't work anymore, so nowadays I say this...

"I'll see you in the charts!"

P.S. You can find my filmography at nigeldick.com — click on the "films" icon on the menu bar.